AUGUST HOME'S

Cuisine®

VOLUME 4

AUGUST HOME
S PECIAL
P UBLICATIONS
2200 Grand Avenue
Des Moines IA 50312
www.augusthome.com

WELCOME OLD FRIENDS AND NEW

It's hard to believe that we have four complete volumes under our collective belt. What's unique about this latest volume is that you can follow *Cuisine's* transformation over the past year—especially starting with Issue 21—the one with grilled skirt steak and baked french fries.

You have to change with the times and that's just the point—time. There is never enough. While most of us cooking enthusiasts still consider cooking a hobby, we've developed other interests that fragment our time. We can no longer afford to spend all day in the kitchen like we used to. With that in mind, *Cuisine* made a few adjustments. The recipes and cooking times are shortened, utensils and cookware is minimized, and most recipes are divided up so you can prepare the dishes in stages or well ahead of time.

But the one constant is that *Cuisine* is still loyal to step-by-step instructions and techniques. No matter if you're a rookie embarking on your first dinner, or a seasoned veteran looking for a new twist, you won't fail with our easy-to-follow steps. Now, with bigger photos and easier recipes, *Cuisine* is just that much more fun to cook with. Hope you enjoy Volume Four.

VOLUME 4

Cuisine

THE YEAR AT A GLANCE

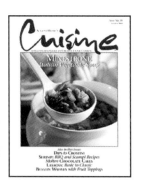

Please contact us to find out about other *Cuisine* products and services:
By Phone: 1-800-311-3995
By Mail: 2200 Grand Avenue, Des Moines IA 50312
By Email: Cuisine@CuisineMagazine.com
Or Visit Our Web-Site: www.CuisineMagazine.com

ISSUE NO. 19
JAN/FEB 2000

AUGUST HOME'S

Cuisine

AN ILLUSTRATED GUIDE TO CREATIVE HOME COOKING

MINESTRONE
Italian Vegetable Soup

Also in this Issue:
DIPS *to* CROSTINI
SHRIMP: *BBQ and Scampi Recipes*
Molten CHOCOLATE CAKES
LASAGNA: *Basic to Classic*
BELGIAN WAFFLES *with Fruit Toppings*

Cuisine

Editor
John F. Meyer

Art Director
Cinda Shambaugh

Associate Editor
Susan Hoss

Assistant Editors
Kelly Volden
Ellen Boeke
Sara Ostransky

Senior Graphic Designer
Holly Wiederin

Graphic Designer
Stephanie Hunter

Test Kitchen Director
Kim Samuelson

Contributing Photographer
Dean Tanner
Primary Image

Pre-press Image Specialist
Troy Clark

Publisher
Donald B. Peschke

Corporate
Creative Director: **Ted Kralicek**
August Home Books: **Douglas L. Hicks**
Senior Photographer: **Crayola England**
New Media Manager: **Gordon C. Gaippe**
New Media Art Director: **Eugene Pedersen**
E-Commerce Analyst: **Carol Schoeppler**
Web Site Product Specialist: **Adam Best**
Controller: **Robin K. Hutchinson**
Senior Accountant: **Laura J. Thomas**
Accounts Payable Clerk: **Mary J. Schultz**
Accounts Receivable Clerk: **Margo Petrus**
Human Resource Assistant: **Kirsten Koele**
Production Director: **George Chmielarz**
Elec. Publishing Director: **Douglas Lidster**
Network Administrator: **Cris Schwanebeck**
Production Assistant: **Susan Rueve**
Pre-press Image Specialist: **Minniette Johnson**
Admin. Assistants: **Julia Fish, Sherry Ribbey**
Receptionist: **Jeanne Johnson**
Mail Room/Delivery: **Lou Webber**

Circulation
Subscriber Services Director: **Sandy Baum**
New Business Director: **Glenda K. Battles**
New Business Manager: **Todd Bierle**
Promotion Manager: **Rick Junkins**
Renewal Manager: **Paige Rogers**
Billing Manager: **Rebecca Cunningham**
Asst. Subscription Manager: **Joy Krause**
Marketing Analyst: **Kris Schlemmer**
Creative Manager: **Melinda Jo Haffner**
Senior Graphic Designer: **Mark A. Hayes, Jr.**

Customer Service and Fulfillment
Operations Director: **Bob Baker**
Merchandise Buyer: **Linda Jones**
Administrative Assistant: **Nancy Downey**
Customer Service Manager: **Jennie Enos**
Technical Representative: **John Audette**
Customer Service Reps: **Anna Cox**
April Revell · Tammy Truckenbrod
Deborah Rich · David Gaumer

Cuisine® (ISSN 1089-6546) is published bi-monthly
(Jan., Mar., May, July, Sept., Nov.) by August Home
Publishing Co., 2200 Grand Ave., Des Moines, IA
50312. Cuisine® is a trademark of August Home
Publishing Co. ©Copyright 1999 August Home
Publishing. All rights reserved.
Subscriptions: Single copy: $4.99. One-year
subscription (6 issues), $21.94. (Canada/Foreign add
$10 per year, U.S. funds.) Periodicals postage paid at
Des Moines, IA and at additional mailing offices.
"USPS/Heartland Press Automatable Poly"
Postmaster: Send change of address to Cuisine,
PO Box 37100 Boone, IA 50037-2100.
Subscription questions? Call 800-311-3995,
8 a.m. to 5 p.m., Central Standard Time, weekdays.
On-line Subscriber Services: www.cuisinemag.com
Cuisine® does not accept and is not responsible
for unsolicited manuscripts. PRINTED IN U.S.A.

From the Editor:

Every issue brings the same dilemma and discussion among members of the *Cuisine* staff. Since there's no advertising, our page count never fluctuates. Space is at a premium—pages can only be divvied up so many ways. The challenge is finding a way to balance what's important in a *good* cooking magazine. So we constantly ask ourselves if information about food and cooking techniques is as big of a deal as the recipe.

In the shrimp article on Page 28, I wrestled with what I thought was the right balance of information and recipes. My thought was that you have to know your ingredients before you begin working with them. So that's why I used four pages to talk with you about shrimp "how-to": How to understand what you're buying and how to pick the best shrimp. That way, if I told you the best shrimp for a particular entree are "16–20 green headless," you know what I'm talking about. Like anything, understanding your tools, equipment, and subject are critical—definitely the first step to a successful recipe.

And by the way, we have some exciting stuff going on around here. Last month we started building our new test kitchens. Next issue, the kitchens will be finished, and I'll show you photos of our new digs. I'll also put the pictures on our Web site as soon as we move in. Write to me and let me know what you think. I always like hearing from you.

John

BBQ Shrimp is not what you might think. No grilling and no sweet, tomato-based sauce. This is done in the oven and the sauce is Creole hot! Cooked in their shells, the shrimp are peeled while still hot (warm) and then dipped back into the sauce. Serve with French bread and you've got a whole meal.

AUGUST HOME'S Cuisine®

AN ILLUSTRATED GUIDE TO CREATIVE HOME COOKING

A CHEAPER, KINDER BENCH KNIFE

Working with dough, I've found that a $13 bench knife can scratch and gouge wooden cutting boards and hard-surfaced countertops. So I bought a 6" plastic joint knife at the hardware store. It has a nice bevel, great handle, and works perfectly. The best part—it only set me back 88¢.

This plastic joint knife was enclosed in the tip letter sent by Mr. Waters.

H. Waters
St. Cloud, FL

NOOK AND CRANNY CLEANER

It's difficult to get those tight spaces clean in my waffle iron and bread machine. But I've come up with a simple, inexpensive solution. Cut a cheap, "throw away," white bristle paint brush down to about $^1/_2$". It can be made as stiff as necessary by cutting the bristles shorter, and comes in a variety of widths. Choose the size that best suits your appliance.

R. Sapirstein
Cupertino, CA

DOUGH TAMPER

I use a small ball of pastry dough to tamp or press dough into tart pans. That way I don't push my fingers through to the pan, but the dough is pressed firmly into the fluted grooves.

S. Sanders
Marietta, GA

TEA BALL SPRINKLER

When I want a sprinkling of powdered sugar on things like brownies or cake, I fill a tea ball with the sugar and "thump" it over the food. Works like a charm.

L. Norcross
Clarksburg, MA

SLICK PIZZA CUTTER

When I cut pizza with a pizza cutter, the cheese always sticks to it and lifts off the crust. So now I spray the cutter first with non-stick cooking spray. It slides right through the crust and the cheese doesn't stick.

R. Schentes
Thousand Oaks, CA

Editor's Note: This timely tip can also be applied to a knife blade when cutting lasagna.

FREEZING PARSLEY

As an 84-year-young gardener on a fixed income, I'm always looking for ways to stretch a dollar. Here's a tip to preserve parsley so it's as flaky and green as the day I picked it.

Rinse and dry parsley. Pull leaves from stems and spread on double layer of paper towels. Microwave on high $1^1/_2$ minutes. Toss and redistribute parsley. Microwave another 2–3 minutes, tossing at 30 second intervals, until parsley is completely dry.

Then line a small glass jar with a plastic bag. Crush dried parsley and add to jar. Screw on lid, trim excess liner to 2" from top, freeze.

J. Baker
East Chicago, IN

ODOR-FREE EGGS

I used to transfer my eggs from their cardboard box to the plastic storage tray in my refrigerator. But I found that the thin egg shells are permeable and can absorb refrigerator odors. So now, I keep them in the carton they come in. The box acts as an odor barrier and saves me the step of having to unload them.

S. Buck
Seattle, WA

STORING GREEN ONIONS

Here is a tip for storing green onions. Cut the roots and trim the green tops to fit a jar. Rinse and dry completely. Cover and store in jar in the refrigerator. The onions will keep for weeks and won't get all soft.

J. McClintock
Calgary, Alberta, Canada
Editor's Note: You can also store them in a sealable plastic bag. Blow a little air into bag and seal.

LINING CAKE PANS

For heavy, sticky cakes that are hard to remove, I make parchment paper liners.

For an 8" round pan, cut a 12" square of parchment paper. Fold into square quarters. Round off open sides of square to a 6" radius. Next, make 2" cuts along the rounded edge— for smooth cake sides and easy lifting.

Spray pan with nonstick cooking spray. Open paper, press into pan, and spray. The paper peels off easily.

B. Mason
Pawleys Island, SC

QUICK CITRUS STRAIN

When I need a squeeze of lemon juice but don't want to fish seeds out of my food, I hold a strainer directly over the pan or bowl, and squeeze. It catches unwanted seeds and pulp.

J. Harte
Strawberry Hill, TN

Tips

FROM THE TEST KITCHEN

STORING SPINACH

A couple of bad spinach leaves can ruin the whole bag. So here's how we store it in the test kitchen, especially when we need crisp leaves for a photo shoot. First, stem, wash, and dry the spinach (yank out any bad leaves). Place in plastic container or sealable bag. Dampen doubled paper towels, wring out, and lay over spinach. Seal and refrigerate up to two weeks.

CUTTING A PINEAPPLE

Here's a way to peel pineapple with as little waste as possible and get the added bonus of decorative slices.

First, cut off the top and bottom of the pineapple. Now trim the skin, slicing off thin strips from top to bottom. Angle your cut to the curve of the pineapple.

Next, remove the "eyes." See how they conveniently spiral the pineapple? Follow the spiral, and cut an angled line along both sides of a strip of eyes, leaving a trough when the strip is removed. Continue cutting the trough around pineapple until all the eyes are removed. Cut into slices and core with a small round cutter.

DIPS *to* CROSTINI

Photograph: Scott Little, Food Styling: Janet Pittman

You've got to believe in evolution. No, I'm not talking monkey-trial stuff. I'm talking food evolution—how you can take something as simple as a dip, then watch

it grow into a more developed member of the appetizer family—crostini.

First, here are four great dips made in the best Italian tradition—simple and with quality ingredients. Now, you could stop right here and not even explore the next step. Simply serve them with the dippers to the right, or grissini (those are the breadsticks on Page 20), and you've got an elegant, but simple appetizer.

Or, you can take these dips to the next level and serve them with crostini. On Pages 8 and 9 you'll see how to make crostini, then finish them with toppings and garnishes. These are easy, eye-popping appetizers.

For something different, here's what I want you to do. Don't assemble the crostini yourself, but set out the little toasts and all the dips, toppers, and garnishes in individual bowls to create a crostini bar!

This way each person can build their own crostini using combinations they like. The chart on Page 8 shows you what you could end up with.

This crostini bar works for two reasons. It's easy because you don't have to make individual appetizers. And second, it's a great ice breaker to get conversations going. Food is common ground, and everybody will be quick to share their favorite combination.

DIPPERS OR CRUDITÉS
Crudités [kroo-dee-TAY] are raw seasonal vegetables used with a dip or sauce. You've seen the typical cut-up broccoli and carrot sticks, so why not try something just a bit different?
Vegetables:
• Belgian endive leaves
• Blanched asparagus or green beans
• Steamed artichoke leaves
• Radicchio wedges
• Slices of daikon or bok choy
• Roasted sweet potato sticks
• Bundles of bell pepper strips and pea pods tied with chives
Other Suggestions:
• Assorted crackers
• Grissini, *Page 20*
• Pita bread or other flat bread

Quick Dips

Dips are not rocket science, nor should they be. With a name like that, you expect something easy. So that's what you get. You either stir everything together or blend them in a food processor.

These dips are true to the Italian tradition. They use classic flavors and minimal ingredients. Because of that, buy high-quality foods and let their good taste do the talking.

These dips have the best flavor at room temperature. All can, and should, be made ahead and refrigerated. (Time lets the flavors meld.) But let them warm up for at least 30 minutes before you plan to serve them.

Olive Tapenade

Arugula Dip

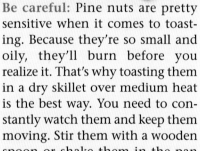
White Bean Dip

Sundried Tomato Dip

OLIVE TAPENADE

(MAKES 1 CUP)
WORK TIME: 20 MINUTES
TOAST:
3 T. pine nuts
PROCESS NUTS IN FOOD PROCESSOR UNTIL SMOOTH WITH:
1 cup kalamata olives, pitted
2 T. olive oil
1 t. garlic, chopped
STIR IN:
1½ T. capers, drained and chopped
2 t. lemon zest, minced
Salt to taste
Freshly ground pepper to taste

Be careful: Pine nuts are pretty sensitive when it comes to toasting. Because they're so small and oily, they'll burn before you realize it. That's why toasting them in a dry skillet over medium heat is the best way. You need to constantly watch them and keep them moving. Stir them with a wooden spoon or shake them in the pan for even browning.

SUNDRIED TOMATO DIP

(MAKES 1½ CUPS)
WORK TIME: 10 MINUTES
COMBINE; MIX WELL WITH FORK:
1 cup (6 oz.) soft goat cheese
½ cup chopped sundried tomatoes packed in oil
3 T. chopped fresh oregano leaves
2 T. roasted garlic, *see below*
Dash of cayenne pepper

ROASTING GARLIC

To roast garlic, preheat the oven to 375°. Cut off the tops of whole heads of garlic to expose cloves. You can peel a layer or two of paper off to expose more cloves.

Place the heads, cut side up, in an ovenproof dish or pan. Drizzle 2 T. olive oil over each head, cover pan with foil, and bake for 45 minutes, or until garlic is soft when pierced with a knife. Squeeze from root end of garlic head to pop out cloves.

ARUGULA DIP

(MAKES 1 CUP)
WORK TIME: 15 MINUTES
COMBINE:
2½ cups Italian bread, cut into chunks, crust removed
2 T. white wine vinegar
PLACE BREAD IN PROCESSOR WITH:
2 cups fresh arugula, trimmed
2 T. capers, drained
1 t. anchovy paste
1 t. Dijon mustard
1 clove garlic, crushed
WITH PROCESSOR RUNNING, DRIZZLE IN:
2 T. olive oil
SEASON WITH:
Salt to taste

WHITE BEAN DIP

(MAKES 1 CUP)
WORK TIME: 10 MINUTES
PROCESS UNTIL SMOOTH:
1 can (15 oz.) cannellini beans, drained and rinsed
1 T. roasted garlic, *see right*
1 T. white balsamic vinegar
1 T. olive oil
STIR IN:
1 T. chopped fresh thyme leaves
SEASON WITH:
Salt and freshly ground pepper to taste

Beyond Dips

As Emeril would say, "Bring it up a notch!" The dips are good on their own but making crostini "all the way" creates a finished appetizer that looks great and tastes even better.

Here's how it works. Check out the chart to the right. It shows you a progression of steps to build crostini.

First, make a bunch of the "little toasts." (Crostini can also refer to just the bread, *see below*.) Then, choose one of the four dips you just made on the previous page. Spread it on the toast. Not too thick, though! These dips have powerful flavors.

Next, pick one of the four toppings from Page 9. Spoon some of it on top of the dip layer. The toppings not only add great flavor, they also add color and height (just as important).

And finally, like any good dish, garnish it. Garnishes not only add more flavor but complete the look.

This ends up pretty cool. With just these few ingredients, you can make 64 different combinations for crostini. Something for everyone.

Dips
▲ *Spread a little dip on the crostini.*

- Olive Tapenade
- Arugula Dip
- White Bean Dip
- Sundried Tomato Dip

Toppings
▲ *Add a topping. Let it spill over the dip.*

- White Bean Salad
- Mushroom Saute
- Tomatoes with Basil
- Sauteed Red Peppers

Garnishes
▲ *Finish with a garnish.*

- Toasted pine nuts
- Shaved Parmesan
- Crumbled Gorgonzola
- Fennel strips

Crostini

You may be a little unsure about the name crostini. Is crostini the toasted bread or the actual appetizer? Well, crostini translates to "little toasts." Technically, the appetizer is named after the toast that makes up its base.

Crostini are small slices of bread, usually brushed with olive oil or butter, then toasted. The toasts may be rubbed with garlic, then are topped with a variety of savory toppings.

Crostini are often confused with bruschetta, which is a rougher country cousin. Bruschetta is the original garlic bread, made with thick slices of country bread, rubbed with garlic, then drizzled with olive oil.

On the other hand, crostini are made with long, narrow loaves, like baguettes. The slices are fairly thin, about 1/2". Because of this, the bread needs a firm texture and chewy crust. If the bread's too light and airy, the thin slices won't be able to stand up

to a juicy topping. And you need thin slices of bread, so you won't have problems biting a stacked crostini.

Toasting the bread also helps give it the strength it needs to hold toppings. Toast isn't flimsy like bread, and it's dry enough to absorb lots of liquid. Rubbing a little garlic on it adds a nice flavor punch.

The spreads and toppings are what make crostini a real appetizer. That's why you're taking the dips from Page 7 to the next level of appetizer evolution. On crostini, the dips act as spreads, forming the base for toppings. The toppings and garnishes help make each one an interesting finished appetizer that tastes great.

MAKING CROSTINI TOASTS

1 Use a narrow baguette-type loaf of bread for crostini. Cut slices a little less than 1/2" thick. Spread out on a baking sheet. If you want, you can brush both sides of slices with olive oil.

2 Toast the bread under a broiler for 2–3 minutes per side, *or* bake at 400° for 12–15 minutes, turning slices over once. Rub toasted slices lightly with cut garlic cloves. Serve warm or at room temperature.

Toppings

Toppings are the second tier of building crostini. They give added texture and color to the finished crostini, not to mention great flavor!

The following four toppings can be used alone as a crostini topper, but are intended to be layered over a dip on the toasted bread.

White Bean Salad is an Italian classic. Made with creamy cannellini beans and scattered with red bell peppers for crunch and color.

The *Mushroom Saute* is terrific warm or at room temperature. Its earthy flavors help to balance assertive dips.

Tomatoes with Basil is another traditional topper. This combination tastes fresh all year 'round. The key to the taste is using fresh basil.

WHITE BEAN SALAD

(MAKES 2 CUPS)
WORK TIME: 10 MINUTES
COMBINE; LET SIT AT LEAST ½ HOUR:
1   can (15 oz.) cannellini beans, drained and rinsed
¼   cup red bell pepper, seeded and diced
2   T. chopped fresh Italian parsley
2   T. olive oil
1   T. chopped fresh oregano
1   T. shallots, minced
1   T. fresh lemon juice
    Salt and freshly ground pepper to taste

MUSHROOM SAUTE

(MAKES 1½ CUPS)
WORK TIME: 10 MINUTES
COOK TIME: 7 MINUTES
HEAT OVER MEDIUM-HIGH HEAT:
¼   cup olive oil
SAUTE IN BATCHES UNTIL GOLDEN:
2   cups crimini mushrooms, sliced
2   cups shiitake mushrooms, sliced
ADD AND SAUTE 1 MINUTE:
1   T. minced garlic
REMOVE FROM HEAT; STIR IN:
3   T. fresh thyme leaves
    Salt and freshly ground pepper to taste

Sauteed Red Peppers are really unique. They have an unexpected and opposing tangy-sweet combination. The long simmer really intensifies the peppers' natural sweetness. And as the balsamic vinegar reduces, its flavor concentrates on the peppers. Serve them warm or at room temperature.

SAUTEED RED PEPPERS

(MAKES 2 CUPS)
WORK TIME: 10 MINUTES
COOK TIME: 1 HOUR
SAUTE SLOWLY OVER MEDIUM HEAT:
3   red bell peppers, seeded and cut into strips (about 4 cups)
5–6 T. balsamic vinegar
¼   cup olive oil

▲ *Combine peppers, 4 tablespoons vinegar, and the olive oil in a large saute pan. Simmer over medium heat, stirring occasionally. Add a little more vinegar as it reduces and bubbles away. After an hour, the peppers are glazed with an intense, rich sauce.*

▲ *Use medium-high heat to saute mushrooms, and don't pile too many in the pan. You want them to have nice golden edges, not steam.*

TOMATOES WITH BASIL

(MAKES 2 CUPS)
WORK TIME: 10 MINUTES
COMBINE ALL; LET SIT FOR AT LEAST ½ HOUR:
2   cups Roma tomatoes, seeded and chopped
½   cup fresh basil chiffonade
3   T. olive oil
2   T. shallots, minced
2   T. red wine vinegar
    Salt and pepper to taste

▲ *To chiffonade basil, layer several large leaves together. Then roll them up lengthwise into a "cigar." Cut across the cigar to make thin strips or shreds.*

Garnishes

Garnishes are to an appetizer what a top hat is to Fred Astaire—they finish things with style. Below are just a few suggestions, but you can use a variety of cheeses (fontina, goat cheese, fresh mozzarella, ricotta), fresh herbs, or chopped nuts.

Toasted Pine Nuts: A sprinkling of toasted pine nuts, whole or chopped, look nice. They have a delicate crunch and flavor, too.

Shaved Parmesan: Parmesan is the most traditional garnish. Get a good one, like Parmigiano-Reggiano, since you don't use much. Use a vegetable peeler to make thin shavings.

Gorgonzola: This Italian blue cheese can be identified by its bluish-green veins and creamy, slightly pungent flavor. Like Parmesan, it too has a strong flavor.

Fennel Strips: Fresh fennel adds crisp crunch and delicate flavor. First, slice or shave the fennel very thinly, *see Page 25.* Cut slices into strips, and pile on a few for garnish.

Photograph: Scott Little; Food Styling: Janet Pittman

LASAGNA
with Marinara Sauce

No one's crazy about change. But when it comes to lasagna, something has to be done. The problem isn't the taste. Pasta, tomatoes, cheese—what's not to like?

It's the execution that needs help: thick, rubbery noodles, layers that slide around from excessive sauce and fillings, pools of sauce in the bottom of the pan, and cheese so thick you can't get a knife through it. But we accept those flaws because lasagna just tastes too good to change.

Well, these three lasagnas solve the problems without giving up flavor. They're like *real* Italian lasagna—made with thinner pasta, traditional sauces (but less of them), and a lot of layers.

Pasta: Italian cooks claim the best lasagna pasta is so thin you can read a newspaper through it. But typical store-bought dried pasta is usually thicker to survive shipping. And that makes lasagna heavy and gummy.

You *could* make your own pasta, but making lasagna would be a bigger production than it already is. It'd taste great, but you'd be too tired to eat.

Have no fear. I found some pasta that works perfectly—it might surprise you. Read about it on Page 12.

Fillings: Americans like "stuff" on things—pepperoni on pizza, sauce on spaghetti, cheese and meat in lasagna.

But Italians are more controlled. They go much lighter on sauce, ricotta, and mozzarella. Which is why you can eat a whole piece of these lasagnas and still get up from the table.

Since these are Italian lasagnas you're making, traditional sauces (Marinara and Bolognese) and cheeses (ricotta, mozzarella, and Parmesan) make sense. Okay, the Red Pepper and Goat Cheese lasagna on Page 16 isn't really Italian—but it still tastes great.

Assembly: The trick to assembling lasagna isn't as much about *what* you put between the layers as *how much* you put between them. Again, a controlled hand is key—the layers won't slide because there's not as much stuff to slip on. Plus, eight layers of pasta create structure, preventing tumbling.

Assembling a lasagna isn't hard, just be sure to have all the ingredients ready beforehand. Then follow the steps and illustration on Page 13.

THE DAY BEFORE: FILLING AND SAUCE

Making lasagna takes a while, so give yourself a break by doing some things the day before assembling.

Make the Filling: First, prepare the ricotta filling—it only takes a few minutes in a food processor. Then chill it until you assemble the lasagna.

If you grew up eating cottage cheese in lasagna, *stop right now*. Ricotta tastes so much better and doesn't have that chunky consistency. Plus, cottage cheese releases water when baked, making lasagna soggy.

But ricotta isn't perfect, either. Its grainy texture is almost as bad as chunks of cottage cheese. To solve that, you're going to blend the ricotta in a food processor first, until it's smooth and fluffy, almost like frosting. Blending also makes the ricotta easier to spread over the pasta.

Use whole-milk ricotta for lasagna. Lower fat versions lack flavor and texture because the fat is replaced with chemicals and additives.

Ricotta Filling

(MAKES 3½–4 CUPS)
WORK TIME: 10 MINUTES
IN A FOOD PROCESSOR,
BLEND UNTIL SMOOTH:
2   15-oz. containers whole-
      milk ricotta cheese
ADD AND BLEND WELL:
2   eggs
2   t. sugar
1   t. salt
½   t. black pepper

▲In a processor fitted with steel blade, blend ricotta until very smooth, about 2 minutes. Scrape down sides, add remaining ingredients, and blend another minute.

Make the Sauce: Making Marinara sauce doesn't take long, but do it the day before so the sauce can chill and thicken. The same thing goes for the Bolognese on Page 15, and the Red Pepper sauce on Page 17.

The last time you made Marinara (Issue 1), you seeded the tomatoes. Don't do it for this sauce. Here's why.

Those gel-like sacs that surround the seeds are full of flavor, and when you use winter tomatoes, you want to keep as much flavor in the sauce as you can. A food mill will strain a lot of them when you process the sauce, but don't worry if a few fall through the holes—they don't hurt a thing.

Marinara Sauce

(MAKES 8 CUPS)
WORK TIME: 20 MINUTES
COOK TIME: 40–55 MINUTES
CHILL TIME: OVERNIGHT
SAUTE IN ¼ CUP OLIVE OIL:
1   cup yellow onion, diced
ADD AND SAUTE:
1   T. garlic, minced
ADD AND SIMMER:
4   pounds Roma tomatoes,
      quartered (about 12 cups)
2   T. tomato paste
1   T. balsamic vinegar
PROCESS, THEN STIR IN:
¼   cup fresh basil chiffonade
2   t. salt
½   t. black pepper
COVER AND CHILL MARINARA
SAUCE OVERNIGHT TO THICKEN.

2 Stir in tomatoes, paste, and vinegar. Simmer until tomatoes break down and the sauce turns orange, 30–45 min. (until most liquid is gone).

LASAGNA WITH MARINARA SAUCE

(MAKES ONE 13" X 10" X 2½" PAN)
WORK TIME: 1 HOUR
COOK TIME: 40–45 MINUTES
REST TIME: 15 MINUTES
PREPARE, THEN ASSEMBLE:
24   oven-ready lasagna sheets,
      blanched (about two 8-oz. pkgs.)
1   recipe Ricotta Filling
1   recipe Marinara Sauce (reserve
      3 cups to serve with lasagna)
2½   cups mozzarella cheese,
      shredded
2½   cups Parmesan cheese, grated

NUTRITIONAL INFORMATION PER (1/12)
SERVING: CALORIES 542; TOTAL FAT 26(G); CALORIES FROM FAT 43%; SODIUM 1184(MG); CARB. 46(G)

WINTER TOMATOES
When buying tomatoes in the dead of winter, go for Romas. They're small, but the flavor is mighty—and you want all the taste you can get.

In a large skillet, heat olive oil over medium heat. Add onion and saute until translucent, about 10 min. Then add garlic and saute another minute.

3 A food mill is great for processing the sauce—use the big holes for a fairly chunky texture. No mill? Just pulse in batches in a food processor.

PASTA AND PANS

The pasta and the pan are what hold the lasagna together. Here's what you need to know about both of them.

Choosing Pasta: Buying pasta for lasagna can be overwhelming. There are so many types—fresh and dried sheets; long, narrow noodles with frilly edges; and accordion-folded rectangles. And then, do you boil it first or not? All of it's about enough to just make you go buy a frozen lasagna.

Well, here's the story: Fresh pasta sheets are, hands down, the best. Now, you could make your own (check out our Web site, www.cuisinemag.com for the step-by-steps). Or buy them at specialty stores or Italian markets. Believe me, they're worth looking for.

But the next best thing is dried pasta labeled "oven-ready" or "no-boil." It's thinner than other lasagna pasta, and like Uncle Ben's rice, it's precooked so it cooks faster.

The whole point of oven-ready pasta is to save on preparation time— just assemble the lasagna and bake. But working with dry pasta is a pain. You can't trim it if the sheets don't fit the pan, and they curl up like paper when you lay them on the wet sauce.

That's why you're going to blanch the pasta first—just enough so it's pliable. It's easier to handle, and you're *still* not in the kitchen long.

But not all oven-ready pasta is the same. The accordion-folded variety is thinnest and fits the pan better.

Picking Pans: You also need to consider a proper lasagna pan. Think big—this is a meal for a crowd.

The pan I use is 13" x 10" x 2½" deep. A 13" x 9" pan works too, but it's not as deep, so you won't get the height (just five or six layers). To see if your pan will work, arrange three dry pasta sheets on the bottom, like the photo, *right*.

If a big lasagna is more than you need for one meal, just divide it into three loaf pans (9½" x 5½" x 3") instead. I'll show you how on Page 17.

Use glass, stainless steel, or glazed ceramic pans. They're nonreactive and won't discolor or change the flavor of acidic foods, like tomatoes.

PASTA

Dried pasta sheets (left) are great for lasagna, but can be hard to find. And "traditional" lasagna pasta (center) is too thick and makes the lasagna heavy.

The accordion-folded "oven-ready" type (American Beauty, Ronzoni, or San Giorgio, all made by Hershey) is the way to go. You can build more layers for dramatic height and better structure. Plus, the dish isn't nearly as heavy. Look for them in most grocery stores.

Selecting and Preparing Pans

▲ Before making lasagna, see if the pan is the right size—three dry noodles should fit across the bottom without overlapping (they will expand when cooked).

▲Before assembling, spray the baking dish with nonstick spray. Even though there's not much cheese in the lasagna to really stick, extra insurance never hurts.

Cooking and Holding Pasta

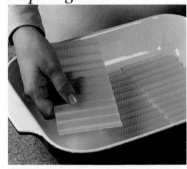

▲ In a large saucepan of boiling, salted water, blanch pasta in batches (5–6 sheets at a time) for 1 minute. They should be *just* pliable, not cooked through.

▲ Stack cooked pasta in single layers between foil. Use a slotted spatula or strainer (tongs or fork can tear). And don't rinse—the fillings stick better if starchy.

1 Preheat oven to 400°. Set aside 3 cups Marinara for serving, then spread ¼ cup on bottom of pan—this way, the lasagna won't be runny.

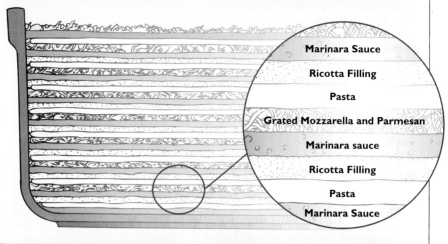

Marinara Sauce
Ricotta Filling
Pasta
Grated Mozzarella and Parmesan
Marinara sauce
Ricotta Filling
Pasta
Marinara Sauce

2 Now, lay 3 blanched pasta sheets side by side on the sauce. They should not overlap—they'll expand a little bit when the lasagna is baked.

3 Top each one with a large spoonful (about 3 T. on each) of Ricotta Filling. Carefully spread it over the sheets with the back of the spoon.

4 Spoon a 3 T.-stripe of sauce down the middle of each sheet. Don't worry if the marinara separates a little and gets watery around the edges.

5 Next, sprinkle about 2 T. grated mozzarella over each stripe of sauce. There's not much cheese on each layer—but lots of layers!

6 Finally, sprinkle the entire layer with about ¼ cup of grated Parmesan cheese. Lay 3 more sheets on top to make the next layer.

7 Gently press the pasta down on top of the last layer—this helps spread the fillings out underneath. Repeat the layering as in Steps 3–6.

8 Layer until all the pasta is used (you'll have 8 pasta layers). Spread 1 cup sauce over the last layer, then sprinkle with ½ cup Parmesan.

9 Bake the lasagna uncovered, for 40–45 minutes, until filling is bubbly and cheese melts. Rest 15 minutes; cut, using the tip of a sharp, thin knife.

10 A flexible spatula is great for removing the pieces from the pan. Serve with some of the reserved Marinara and more Parmesan cheese.

LASAGNA
with Bolognese Sauce

Let's get one thing straight. Bolognese Sauce is not everyday spaghetti sauce. It's easy to make that mistake since they're based on similar ingredients—

meat and tomatoes. But to say it's "just" spaghetti sauce is like saying *Cuisine* is just another magazine!

Bolognese [boh-loh-N'YEH-zeh] is prepared like a stew. Ingredients are sauteed and then simmered in liquid. Original recipes call for four hours of simmering because the meat (usually skirt steak) needed time to tenderize.

The ground meat in this recipe doesn't need time to tenderize. But it still needs time—liquids reduce, intensifying the flavor and thickening. Perfect for layering in lasagna.

One of the unique things about Bolognese is how the flavors are "layered" on top of each other. You'll start with one flavor layer (vegetables), then build on top of it, adding all other flavors (meat, milk, wine, and tomatoes) separately. That way, each flavor can blend with the ones before it, rather than simmering in a huge mass. This takes longer, but the sauce has a deeper flavor in the end.

And, yes, I said milk. It adds an unusual sweetness and richness to the sauce, but doesn't make it creamy.

A *true* Bolognese lasagna is made with spinach pasta, Bolognese sauce, and béchamel. Here's where you're going to deviate from the norm.

Spinach lasagna sheets can be hard to find, and béchamel is really rich. So instead, use the same dry pasta and ricotta filling as the Marinara lasagna, *Pages 10–13*. Then, you're going to add a layer of Swiss chard leaves for great color contrast and flavor.

LASAGNA WITH BOLOGNESE SAUCE
(MAKES ONE 13" X 10" X 2½" PAN)
WORK TIME: 1 HOUR
COOK TIME: 40–45 MINUTES
REST TIME: 15 MINUTES
PREPARE, THEN ASSEMBLE:

24   oven-ready lasagna sheets (about two 8-oz. pkgs.)
1   recipe Ricotta Filling, *see Page 11*
1   recipe Bolognese Sauce
2   bunches Swiss chard, stemmed, blanched, and dried
2½   cups mozzarella cheese, shredded
2½   cups Parmesan cheese, grated

Bolognese Sauce

(MAKES 6–7 CUPS)
WORK TIME: 40 MINUTES
COOK TIME: 4¼–5½ HOURS

SAUTE IN ¼ CUP OLIVE OIL:
1   cup yellow onion, diced
1   cup carrots, diced
1   cup celery, diced
½   cup fennel, diced

ADD:
2   T. garlic, minced

STIR IN AND SAUTE:
¾   lb. ground chuck
½   lb. ground pork
3   T. Italian Seasoning, *Page 22*
1   T. salt
1   t. black pepper

ADD AND REDUCE:
1½ cups whole milk

ADD AND REDUCE:
1   cup dry red wine

STIR IN AND SIMMER:
4   lbs. tomatoes, quartered
2   T. tomato paste
2   T. salt
¾   t. black pepper
3   bay leaves

For the Bolognese Sauce, heat the oil in a large skillet over medium heat. Add the vegetables and saute until soft, about 15 min. Stir in the garlic and saute another minute. Add the ground meats, breaking them up with a spoon. Season, then cook until meat is no longer pink, 8–10 minutes. ▶

Now, add the milk and simmer gently until the liquid is almost evaporated. This will take a long time (25 or 30 minutes), so be patient and don't increase the heat! You need to reduce the milk slowly, otherwise the sugars in the milk will scorch and make the sauce taste burnt. Stir frequently to prevent scorching. ▶

Add the wine and reduce until evaporated, about 20 minutes. Then add tomatoes, paste, and seasonings, and simmer gently over medium-low heat until very thick, 3–4 hours. Stir often to keep the sauce from sticking or burning. Remove bay leaves, cool, and chill. Bring sauce to room temperature before assembling lasagna. ▶

ASSEMBLING LASAGNA WITH BOLOGNESE SAUCE

1 Blanch cleaned Swiss chard leaves in boiling, salted water until wilted, about 3 seconds. Transfer to paper towel-lined baking sheets to dry.

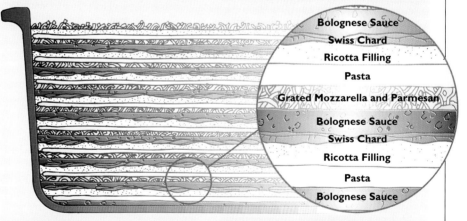

Bolognese Sauce
Swiss Chard
Ricotta Filling
Pasta
Grated Mozzarella and Parmesan
Bolognese Sauce
Swiss Chard
Ricotta Filling
Pasta
Bolognese Sauce

2 Following steps 1–3 on Page 13, spread ½ cup Bolognese on bottom of pan, then layers of pasta and ricotta filling. Top with a layer of chard.

3 Now spread ¾ cup Bolognese on the chard—it won't totally cover. Sprinkle with ¼ cup of *each* cheese; repeat layering, beginning with pasta.

4 Spread remaining ricotta over the last layer of pasta and sprinkle with ½ cup Parmesan cheese. Bake, rest, and cut as in Steps 9–10 on Page 13.

LASAGNA
with Roasted Red Pepper Sauce

Here's a vegetarian lasagna even hard-core meat lovers can like. That's because it's got flavors and textures similar to meat—a smoky, grilled taste from roasted

Photograph: Scott Little; Food Styling: Janet Pittman

red pepper sauce, and a chewy, meaty texture (and flavor) from mushrooms. Meat? Who needs it? Okay, I'm exaggerating, but this is really good stuff.

Like the other two lasagnas, make some components ahead so you don't spend a ton of time in the kitchen. First, make the sauce the day before and chill it. Like the Marinara, chilling thickens it and intensifies flavor and color. Never roasted peppers? See Issue 12 (Nov/Dec 1998), Page 7. They're on the Antipasto Platter.

Second, make the Ricotta Filling the day before, but don't stir in the herbs until just before assembling. And third, saute the mushrooms and refrigerate them overnight.

Loaf Pan Lasagna: If you want to make lasagna in three loaf pans rather than one big pan, take a look at the steps on Page 17. It isn't hard—just think of each loaf pan as one-third of a big pan. Put the pans side-by-side and assemble them just like you would a big pan. Then, bake one loaf pan for dinner and freeze the rest (see below for baking instructions).

LASAGNA WITH ROASTED RED PEPPER SAUCE
(MAKES THREE 9½" X 5½" X 3" LASAGNAS, OR ONE 13" X 10" X 2½")
WORK TIME: 1 HOUR
COOK TIME: 35–40 MINUTES
REST TIME: 15 MINUTES
PREPARE, THEN ASSEMBLE:

- 24 oven-ready lasagna sheets, blanched (about two 8-oz. pkgs.)
- 1 recipe Roasted Red Pepper Sauce
- 1 recipe Herbed Ricotta Filling
- 1 recipe Mushroom Filling
- 2½ cups mozzarella cheese, shredded
- 12 oz. mild goat cheese

FREEZING LASAGNA
Lasagna is great to have on hand in the freezer—perfect for an easy weeknight dinner. Just tightly wrap *unbaked* lasagna in two layers of foil, then freeze. Bake straight from the freezer (unthawed, uncovered) at 375° for 1–1½ hours. Check the temperature with an instant-read thermometer (180–200°).

Roasted Red Pepper Sauce

(MAKES 4 CUPS)
WORK TIME: 10 MINUTES
COOK TIME: 30 MINUTES
PUREE:
10 red bell peppers, roasted,
    peeled, seeded, and torn
BLEND IN:
1   T. Italian Seasoning, *Page 22*
1   T. sugar
1   T. red wine vinegar
1   T. salt
½   t. black pepper
⅛   t. cayenne pepper

▲ Puree peppers in food processor until smooth, then blend in the remaining ingredients. Chill the sauce overnight to thicken.

Mushroom Filling

(MAKES 4–5 CUPS)
WORK TIME: 20 MINUTES
COOK TIME: 30 MINUTES
SAUTE IN TWO BATCHES:
½   cup olive oil
¼   cup shallots, minced
3   lbs. mushrooms, cleaned,
    sliced (mixture of button,
    shiitake, and criminis)
ADD AND REDUCE:
1   cup dry white wine
    Salt and black pepper

▲ In a large skillet over medium-high heat, saute half the shallots and mushrooms in ¼ cup oil. Deglaze with ½ cup wine and reduce. Season, remove from skillet, and repeat with second batch.

Herbed Ricotta Filling

(MAKES 3½–4 CUPS)
WORK TIME: 10 MINUTES
*FOLD INTO 1 RECIPE RICOTTA
FILLING, PAGE 11:*
2   T. chopped fresh thyme
2   T. chopped fresh parsley
2   T. chopped fresh rosemary
2   T. chopped fresh basil

▲ Make ricotta filling as on Page 11 and chill. Then fold in chopped herbs before assembling lasagna.

ASSEMBLING LOAF PAN LASAGNAS

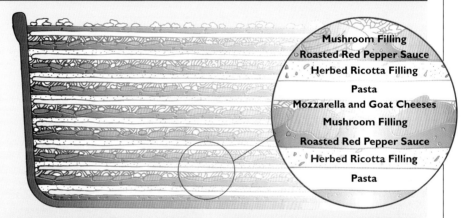

Mushroom Filling
Roasted Red Pepper Sauce
Herbed Ricotta Filling
Pasta
Mozzarella and Goat Cheeses
Mushroom Filling
Roasted Red Pepper Sauce
Herbed Ricotta Filling
Pasta

1 Begin assembling the lasagna by spreading 2–3 T. pepper sauce on the bottom of 3 prepared loaf pans. Place pasta on top of sauce.

2 Spread a large spoonful (3 T.) of herbed ricotta over the pasta, then a stripe of pepper sauce (3 T.). Top with ¼ cup Mushroom Filling.

3 Sprinkle 2–3 T. mozzarella, then dot 2–3 T. goat cheese on top. Add another pasta sheet and continue, making 7 more pasta layers.

4 Spread ½ cup sauce on top of the last sheet and dot with remaining goat cheese. Bake at 400° for 35–40 min., or wrap and freeze.

Minestrone means "big soup" in Italian. And this one is big in two ways— flavor and body. Just like that TV ad says, "You could eat it with a fork,

but you'll want to use a spoon." So, what makes this soup big? It's a combination of ingredients that both flavor and thicken.

Flavor: The full-bodied flavor of this minestrone comes from an Italian bacon called pancetta, 11 different vegetables, and a powerful Parmesan.

Pancetta: Pancetta adds a mild salty flavor but doesn't overpower the soup like its American cousin, bacon. That's because it's cured with only salt and spices—not by smoking.

Vegetables: Minestrone contains lots of vegetables. Sauteing them before adding the broth brings out their natural sugars and juices—a must for a full–flavored soup.

Parmesan rind: This is a great way to use a Parmesan rind that might otherwise be tossed out. As it breaks down, it adds tons of flavor.

Thickeners: This minestrone has two thickeners—beans and starch.

Beans: Cranberry beans are the classic beans used in minestrone, *see right.* But don't fret if you can't find these little burgundy beans—any medium–sized bean will do. It's the protein in beans that thickens the soup and makes it supper-worthy.

Starch: Minestrone should contain some kind of starch like pasta or rice. It's best to cook the starch right in the soup. This way the pasta or rice absorbs the broth while, at the same time, the starch thickens the soup. *AH*

MINESTRONE
ITALIAN VEGETABLE SOUP

MINESTRONE *(MAKES 8 CUPS)*

WORK TIME: 45 MINUTES
COOK TIME: 1–1½ HOURS

SAUTE IN 2 T. OLIVE OIL:

2   oz. pancetta, diced small

STIR IN:

1   cup yellow onion, chopped
1   T. garlic, minced

ADD EACH SEPARATELY AND STIR:

3   cups cabbage, chopped
2   cups green beans, trimmed
1   cup celery, diced
1   cup carrots, sliced
1   cup fennel, diced
1   cup zucchini, diced
1   cup russet potatoes,
    peeled and diced

STIR IN AND SIMMER:

4–5 cups beef broth
1   can (14½ oz.) diced tomatoes
¼   cup dry red wine
1   cup cranberry beans, *see below*
¼   cup orzo
1   2 oz. Parmesan rind
2   T. Italian Seasoning, *Page 22*

ADD:

2   cups red Swiss chard, chopped

NUTRITIONAL INFORMATION PER CUP:
CALORIES 234; TOTAL FAT 10(G);
CALORIES FROM FAT 36%; SODIUM
967(MG); CARB. 26(G)

CRANBERRY BEANS

Cranberry beans are also called borlottis, Romans, or shell beans. This pinto-shaped, tan to burgundy colored bean has a creamy texture, and a mildly nutty flavor.

To precook the cranberry beans for the minestrone, place one cup in a small pot. Add water (to 2" above beans) and 1 teaspoon salt. Cover pot and bring to a boil. Turn off heat. Allow beans to sit 30 minutes. They finish cooking in the soup. Can't find cranberry beans? Use kidney, cannellini, pinto, or any medium-sized bean.

1 Before you begin, go to your garden. Oops—wrong season. Go to your grocery store and buy the best vegetables available. Chop the vegetables beforehand, except for the potato and the fennel (they start discoloring immediately), and refrigerate. This helps take the pressure off mealtime.

2 In a large pot, saute the pancetta over medium-high heat in 2 tablespoons of olive oil until crisp. This should take about 10 minutes. Pancetta isn't as greasy as bacon and will stick to your pot without a little oil. Stirring will also keep it from sticking. Add the onion and garlic, and cook 2 minutes.

3 Add each vegetable separately, stirring and allowing the vegetable to saute a little before adding the next. They will become crowded and begin steaming. That's okay. You want those juices to begin flowing. Once all the vegetables have been added, let them steam about 10 minutes.

4 Add the liquids—4 cups of broth, the diced tomatoes, and red wine. Stir well, then add the cranberry beans, orzo, Parmesan rind, and Italian Seasoning. Simmer over medium heat for 1–1½ hours, stirring occasionally, until the vegetables and beans are soft. Add one more cup of broth if necessary.

5 Prepare the Swiss chard by removing the stalk. Chop enough for 2 cups. When the cranberry beans are soft, add the Swiss chard. Stir until wilted. The soup has reduced considerably at this point. Remove any visible chunks of Parmesan cheese rind and discard. This is great with Grissini, *see Page 22.*

GRISSINI
(breadsticks)

After waiting 45 minutes to get into a restaurant, I couldn't care less if the breadsticks are rock-hard and tasteless, or fat and bready. I'm hungry! At

that moment it just doesn't matter. They do *exactly* what they're supposed to do—pass the time until the food arrives. Unfortunately, that's *all* they do. But good grissini (Italian for breadsticks) isn't just a time-killer or filler. What makes them good? Balance.

Stick Balance: You want a stick that'll crack when you break it, but has a tunnel of tender, chewy bread on the inside. That coveted balance is within reach—by rolling and baking just the right amount of dough.

Rolling: Rolling the dough strips long and thin gives them a good proportion of crispy crust to chewy bread inside. The technique for dividing the dough measures the right amount for each strip, *see Steps 6 and 7.*

Baking: A high oven temperature bakes the grissini quickly. Ovens vary, so keep an eye on your sticks. You're looking for a light tan color—*too* dark and the inside won't be soft. If the first pan is too crisp or soft, adjust the baking time for the next pan.

Toppings: Toppings are the major flavor carriers for breadsticks. Sort of like pizza. No matter how great your crust, it's what you load on top that determines the flavor and personality. One recipe splits into quarters, allowing four different personalities.

Versatility: There are advantages to breadstick schizophrenia—there's a personality to go with almost anything. Choose your favorite toppings and serve with soup, like Minestrone on Pages 18–19. Or use them to dig into dips from Dips to Crostini on Pages 6–9. Italian Seasoning creates a light alternative to heavy garlic bread with Lasagna on Pages 10–17. While they go with anything, I eat them hot out of the oven, with nothing at all.

In a large bowl, sprinkle yeast over warm water, whisking until dissolved. Let stand 5–10 minutes until foam appears in the center. Now stir in the olive oil, but don't expect it to incorporate into the yeast and water mixture—it just can't, and that's okay.

◄ *Here's what you're looking for when the yeast activates and foams in the center.*

2 Add the flours, sugar, and salt. Stir until dry flour is no longer visible. The dough looks blotchy and chunky at this point. Don't worry, it'll all incorporate as you knead the dough.

Up close and personal, you can see spots of oil throughout the very rough dough.►

GRISSINI

(MAKES 24)

RISE TIME: 1 HOUR
WORK TIME: 45 MINUTES
BAKE TIME: 10–12 MINUTES

DISSOLVE:
1 cup warm water (105–115°)
1 package (2¼ t.) active dry yeast

STIR IN:
¼ cup olive oil

STIR IN; KNEAD:
2½ cups all-purpose flour
½ cup semolina
2 t. sugar
2 t. salt

SPRINKLE WITH:
   Flavor Toppings, *Page 22*

NUTRITIONAL INFORMATION PER GRISSINI (NO TOPPING): CALORIES 82; TOTAL FAT 2(G); CALORIES FROM FAT 27%; SODIUM 195(MG); CARB. 13(G)

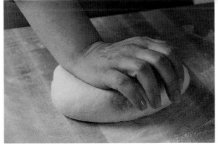

3 Turn the dough out onto a lightly floured work surface. Use an additional 2 T. flour to dust surface as you knead. At first, dough is soft and lumpy, but it stiffens and smooths as you knead.

To knead, fold dough in half toward you. With heel of hand, push dough firmly down and away. Give dough a quarter turn. Now fold and push again. Continue kneading for 10 minutes.

WHAT IS SEMOLINA?

Semolina is durum wheat (the hardest wheat grown) ground to the consistency of fine sand. Ground even finer, it's called durum flour, and feels like flour. Use the semolina-grind for making these breadsticks.

Manufacturers have labeled the same semolina product with a lot of different names—just make sure the word "semolina" is on the package. Find it at a grocery store or Italian market. Or order it from **King Arthur Flour** at (800) 827-6836, Item #3545, in 2- or 5-lb. bags for $1.95 or $3.95, plus shipping.

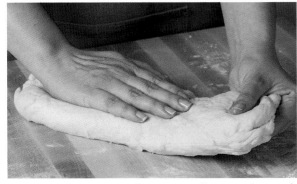

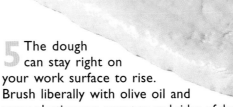

4 Let the dough rest 5 minutes. Shape and stretch the dough into a 14" x 4" rectangle by pressing dough down and forward with one hand, while gently pulling the end outward. Press in sides of dough to keep even 4" width. Now press and stretch from other end. Repeat process until you reach 14" length.

5 The dough can stay right on your work surface to rise. Brush liberally with olive oil and press plastic wrap over top and sides of dough. Let the dough rise (proof) for 1 hour at room temperature. The dough will become puffy and your finger will leave an imprint when you press into it.

6 Preheat oven to 450°. Remove plastic wrap from dough; brush with olive oil again. Cut dough into 4 equal parts. Work with one quarter of dough at a time, covering remaining dough with plastic wrap. Choose a topping from column at right; sprinkle onto dough quarter. Make sure topping covers completely to edges. *Lightly* press topping into dough.

7 Now you're going to cut the quarter into 6 strips. Start by cutting the dough quarter in half horizontally. Then cut each half (*again* horizontally) into 3 equal strips.

8 This dough is soft and very pliable—perfect for stretching. Hold the strip at both ends and *gently* pull outward until length is doubled (about 8"). Lay on surface rubbed with a dab of olive oil—it will roll easier.

9 With hands resting on the center of the strip, roll hands simultaneously, forward then back, moving outward in a zig-zag. Lighten your touch as your hands reach the ends. Repeat until strip reaches 14–16".

10 Give the strip a slight twist using a push/pull motion. Place the palms of your hands (lightly) on each end of the strip. Simultaneously roll one hand forward and one hand back.

11 Lift and place strips on a large baking sheet lined with parchment paper. Bake 10–12 min. until light brown (for even browning, turn sticks at 6 min.). Cut and roll next quarter of dough while these bake.

12 To achieve the perfect balance of crisp and chewy, bake these breadsticks the old-fashioned way—one pan at a time. I tried cheating by baking two pans at a time. They still looked great, but lost their crunch. Eat them soon—they'll be hard tomorrow.

FLAVOR TOPPINGS

For each quarter of dough choose one:

Salt and Pepper
$1/2$ t. kosher salt
$1/2$ t. coarse black pepper

Sesame Seed
$1 1/2$ t. sesame seeds

Parmesan Cheese
$1 1/2$ T. Parmesan cheese, grated

Poppy Seed
1 t. poppy seeds

Italian Seasoning
Use 2 t. of this mix per dough quarter:
1   T. dried oregano
1   T. dried basil
1   T. dried parsley
1   T. red pepper flakes
1   T. granulated garlic
$1 1/2$ t. dried rosemary
1   t. fennel seeds
1   t. kosher salt

Sundried Tomato
1   T. sundried tomatoes (packed in oil), minced

Fennel Seed and Salt
1   t. fennel seeds, coarsely ground
$1/4$ t. kosher salt

WHAT'S HAPPENING IN FOOD?

◄ SLICK NEW CAN OPENER

KUHN RIKON has produced my new favorite kitchen gadget. Their **Safety LidLifter** does more than open a can—it completely removes the lid, leaving no sharp edges. You don't even have to touch the lid. Just use the beak-like Lid Gripper to grab it and pull it off. Left- and right-handers can use this baby equally well, too.

The LidLifter is available in two styles. The basic model ($16) is made of white plastic. The Deluxe model ($25), *above*, is made of stainless steel with a soft-grip turning knob. Call **Tavolo**, KUHN RIKON's recommended resource, at **(800) 700-7336** to order, or visit **www.kuhnrikon.com**.

ALL-CLAD BAKEWARE ►

All-Clad's Gold Standard Bakeware features three layers of aluminum sandwiched between two outer layers of stainless steel. The result is heavy, high-quality pans destined to last for years.

You'd think that was enough, but the gold surface is its crowning glory. It's stick-resistant and shouldn't chip, flake, or stain. It *is* tough—I cut through brownies with a sharp knife, and it didn't leave a mark. The down side? Well, looking at the price you'd think they were gold-*plated*. An 8" square pan retails for $70 and a jelly roll pan goes for $110. If you want to make an investment, call **(800) 255-2523** for a retailer near you.

FRESH ORGANIC PRODUCE ▼

Now you can get fresh organic produce on your doorstep the day after it was picked. The owners of **Diamond Organics**, Jasch and Kathleen Hamilton, work with organic farmers on the central California coast to provide all the produce that appears in their catalog. Their Original Sampler ($46, including shipping) is shown here. It features 10–12 fruits, five vegetables, greens, and an info sheet with recipes and cooking tips. You can get everything from herbs and mushrooms, to breads and pastries. Call them at **(888) 674-2642** to get a catalog, or check out their Web site at **www. diamondorganics.com**.

◄ LAMSONSHARP KITCHEN TOOLS

The maker of my favorite knives now has a complete line of kitchen tools. **Lamson & Goodnow** just added eight new items to their kitchen-tool line, bringing the full line to 16 items. These babies are great, too. They're heavy and sturdy. Just picking one up shouts quality.

LamsonSharp kitchen tools are made of hardened, tempered stainless steel that runs through the handle. The handles are triple-riveted with nickel. That means style and durability. And they're dishwasher safe!

Shown are the 3" x 8" perforated turner ($18), a pancake turner ($16), and a 6" offset spatula ($15) for frosting large cakes. Other items include a 2¹/₂" square server/turner ($14), and a 12" pizza rocker ($20) that can be resharpened. (A rocker is a curved blade that "rocks" from side to side when cutting.)

Call **(800) 872-6564** to find out how you can get these tools.

FENNEL

Fronds or leaves

Stalk or rib

Bulb

Core

Root base

Italians love to eat—think of those ancient Roman banquets. Even back then, overindulgence had its pitfalls, like bad breath and indigestion. But the

Romans didn't have breath mints or Tums. They had fennel.

History: Fennel might be new to your produce section, but this is one vegetable with a long history. In Roman times it did triple duty as digestive aid, breath freshener, and palate cleanser after meals. It's still prized for its medicinal qualities (nursing mothers sip fennel seed "tea" to help colicky babies), as well as its licorice flavor (anisette liqueur is made from fennel seeds). Yes, fennel tastes *a little* like a black jelly bean, but don't turn your nose up—the licorice flavor is subtle.

What Is Fennel?: There are two types of fennel. The one you've seen in your store is called Florence, or bulb fennel, *shown left.* It has a large bulb base, long celery-like stalks, and feathery leaves (fronds) that look like dill.

The pale green-white bulb is made of overlapping broad stems that surround a thick core. It's the bulb that's usually eaten—raw or cooked. Raw fennel is crisp and sweet. Cooking makes it tender and mellows the flavor.

The second type of fennel is called common, or wild fennel. Unlike Florence fennel, it doesn't produce a bulb, but the bright green, feathery fronds look like the bulb variety's. Wild fennel resembles a tall dill plant (it can grow nearly five feet!) and produces the familiar ribbed fennel seeds.

Because bulb fennel is new to many grocery stores, and unfamiliar to both consumers and produce managers, it's often mislabeled "sweet anise" [AN-ihs]. But anise is a stronger-tasting relative generally used as an herb in Europe.

Uses: Bulb fennel is versatile. Italians like to dip strips of raw bulb into olive oil then coarse salt, and eat it as an appetizer. It's also great shaved raw into salads, like in the citrus salad on Page 26. Roasted, breaded, and fried, or braised, as in the salad on Page 27, are a few ways to cook it.

The bulb isn't the only part you can use—the stalks and fronds are also edible. Use the stalks as a "rack" for roasting fish. Or chop them up and add them to chicken or fish stock in place of celery. Fennel leaves are perfect to flavor fish—remember the bouillabaisse in Issue 5? And they can even be chopped and stirred into tomato soup just before serving (long cooking will diminish the flavor).

As if that wasn't enough, the seeds are a great flavoring for soup, tomato sauce, and breads. Italian cooks like to flavor cookies and pastries with fennel seeds. And maybe you've had them on pizza—fennel seeds are a common ingredient in sausage.

It's important to toast the seeds before crushing them. Toasting brings out the oils and intensifies the flavor.

THE THREE "S'S"

Like most vegetables, you want to follow the three "S's" (season, selecting, and storing) for the best flavor.

Season: Fennel is a winter vegetable—its main season is October through April, but it's available year 'round. If your store doesn't have any, ask the produce manager to order it.

Selecting: Choose fennel with a heavy, firm bulb about the size of a tennis ball. Larger ones tend to be tough, stringy, and lack flavor. Bulbs can be round or flattened—both are good but round ones tend to be sweeter and more mellow in flavor.

Look for white bulbs with no bruises or cuts. The fronds should be bright green and fresh—avoid fennel with the tops cut off. The leaves indicate freshness and are the first to go.

Storing: You'll want to use fennel within a few days of purchase—it dries out and the flavor fades fast.

First, cut the stalks and fronds off. They go bad quickly and will cause the bulb to deteriorate faster, too. Stand the stalks and fronds in a glass of cold water (like the photo below), and refrigerate until you're ready to use them. The stalks and fronds are good for two to three days.

Second, wrap the whole bulb in plastic and refrigerate. It lasts up to a week, but gets tough and loses flavor over time. If the bulb happens to get limp, crisp it by soaking it in ice water for 30 minutes to an hour.

If you need to, use a vegetable peeler to remove any discolorations on the outer layer of the bulb. **AH**

FENNEL SEEDS

Fennel seeds come from common fennel, not the bulb variety. But the greenish-brown seeds have the same subtle licorice flavor as the bulb. You'll find them in the spice aisle of your grocery store.

Toasting then crushing the seeds will give you the most flavor. Toast them in a dry skillet over medium heat, shaking the pan frequently so they don't burn. When they smell "toasty," they're done (about 2 minutes).

A mortar and pestle is best for crushing, but if Santa didn't bring you one, place the seeds in a sealable plastic bag. Seal it, then gently crush the seeds using a rolling pin.

HOW TO CUT FENNEL

▲ **Bulb:** Trim a ½" piece from the root end. Cut off the stalks 1" above the bulb, reserving the ribs. Peel away any blemished outer pieces with a vegetable peeler.

▲ **Stalks:** Stand stalks in cold water to keep fresh. The thin ones can be used in salads or pasta dishes. Use the stalks as you would celery in sauces, soups, or as a roasting rack.

▲ **Fronds:** Leave fronds on stalks when storing. Use whole sprigs of fronds as a garnish for seafood and fish, or chop them and stir into cooked dishes, dips, and salads.

▲ **Slices:** A trimmed, whole bulb can be cut into flat slices then julienned for salads or braising. Stand the bulb on the root end, then cut vertically into thin (⅛–¼" thick) slices.

▲ **Wedges:** Cut the trimmed bulb into quarters, and trim out the centermost piece of core (not the entire core!). Leaving a little bit will keep wedges from falling apart.

▲ **Strips:** Wedges of quartered fennel can be cut crosswise into small pieces for salads, stir-fries, and soups. The wedges can also be cut lengthwise into longer strips.

CITRUS-FENNEL SALAD

(MAKES 4 SERVINGS)

WORK TIME: 30 MINUTES

PREPARE:

1   cup oranges, peeled and
    sliced into rounds (2 oranges)
1   cup fennel bulb, thinly sliced
¼   cup radishes, thinly sliced
¼   cup oil-cured black olives,
    pitted and slivered
¼   cup Parmesan cheese, shaved

COMBINE FOR VINAIGRETTE:

2   T. fresh orange juice
2   T. white wine vinegar
1   T. shallot, minced
1   T. olive oil
1   t. sugar
1   t. fennel seed, toasted and crushed
½   t. salt
¼   t. freshly ground black pepper

GENTLY TOSS WITH:

4   cups arugula, cleaned and
    torn into bite-sized pieces

NUTRITIONAL INFORMATION PER SERVING:
CALORIES 150; TOTAL FAT 9(G); CALORIES
FROM FAT 51%; SODIUM 648(MG);
CARBOHYDRATES 12(G)

Photograph: Scott Little, Food Styling: Janet Pittman

MAKING CITRUS-FENNEL SALAD

1 To peel oranges, cut off top and bottom, just to the pulp. Cut away peel and pith, following curve of the fruit. Cut orange into thin rounds.

2 Thinly slice the fennel using a knife or a mandoline, *see Page 25*. Trim the stems and roots from radishes, and thinly slice. Set aside.

3 Use an olive pitter to pit olives, or "crush" them with the side of a chef's knife and remove the pit. Slice olives into very small slivers.

4 Toast fennel seeds. Then, with mortar and pestle, crush seeds until fragrant. Whisk them into remaining vinaigrette ingredients.

5 In a large bowl, toss the fennel, radishes, and vinaigrette with arugula. Use your hands—it's gentler on the greens and coats them evenly.

6 To assemble the salad, first lay down 3–4 orange rounds. Mound some salad mixture on top. Garnish with olives and shaved Parmesan.

LEMON-BRAISED FENNEL

(MAKES 4 SERVINGS)
WORK TIME: 15 MINUTES
COOK TIME: 40 MINUTES

FRY UNTIL CRISP; REMOVE:
4   oz. thick-cut bacon, cut into
      1" pieces (4–6 slices)

BROWN IN 1 T. BACON DRIPPINGS:
2   fennel bulbs, cut into
      1" wedges

ADD AND SIMMER:
1   cup chicken broth
¼   cup fresh lemon juice
2   T. sugar

ADD ALONG WITH COOKED BACON:
2   T. chopped fresh parsley
½   t. salt
¼   t. black pepper

TOP WITH FENNEL MIXTURE:
4   cups curly endive, cleaned,
      dried, torn into pieces

GARNISH WITH:
      Parmesan cheese, grated
      Fennel fronds

NUTRITIONAL INFO. PER SERVING: CALORIES 140; TOTAL FAT 7(G); CALORIES FROM FAT 40%; SODIUM 709(MG); CARB. 18(G)

PREPARING LEMON-BRAISED FENNEL

1 In a large saute pan, fry bacon over medium-high heat until crisp. Transfer to a paper towel-lined plate and pour off all but 1 T. drippings.

2 Reduce heat to medium. Place fennel wedges, *see Page 25,* cut-side down in pan. Saute wedges on both sides until brown, 10–15 min.

3 Combine broth, juice, and sugar, then add to fennel. Simmer until liquid reduces to about ¹/₂ cup and fennel is very tender, about 30 min.

4 Curly endive tends to hide a lot of grit and sand, so be sure to thoroughly rinse and dry it. Now tear the endive into bite-sized pieces.

5 Remove pan from heat and add the bacon. Stir in parsley, salt, and pepper. Be gentle—the cooked fennel wedges are very fragile.

6 Divide endive on four serving plates. Top with braised fennel and garnish with grated Parmesan (a new job for your zester!) and fronds.

SHRIMP

A GUIDE TO BUYING & PREPARING

So, I'm at the fish market the other day, checking out the catch that had just been shipped in. Next to me was a guy trying to order shrimp, but he was obviously frustrated with all the

Head · Body

Swimming legs

Walking legs · Tail

different piles of shrimp labeled with terms, numbers, and names. He just wasn't getting it. And with good reason—shrimp are not controlled by the USDA like beef and other meats, so labeling can be very confusing.

Here are some names and terms you might see on those signs in front of each pile of shrimp at your market: Jumbo, Large, Prawns, 10–15, 16–20, Previously Frozen, Green, Whites, Pinks, Tiger, Rock, P&D. No wonder the guy standing next to me was frustrated. All he wanted was some shrimp! Maybe this will help.

Figuring out the mystery of shrimp doesn't have to be hard. You just need to know three things.

First, you need to learn the different names given to these crustaceans. Second, you need to understand how shrimp are sized (this *should* be done by count, not by market terms like large or medium). Finally, you should know how to select quality shrimp. And, by the way, most of what I'm telling you refers to the United States. There are hundreds of varieties of shrimp in the world. This article is all about what we can get here.

Accurate Names: There seems to be confusion when referring to shrimp. Many times the term "prawn" is substituted for shrimp. This is not accurate. Generally, shrimp are found

in saltwater and prawns in freshwater. While we do have real prawns here in the U.S., they aren't marketed commercially. Occasionally, you might run across a true freshwater prawn that's caught and sold locally. What you see most of the time in markets and restaurants are shrimp. And just when you think you've got a handle on it, the wrong names get thrown around.

Wrong Names: Let's just cut to the chase. Here in the States, we cook shrimp. They're not called scampi and only rarely are they accurately called prawns. Here's the difference.

Prawns: Prawns are freshwater crustaceans that are similar to shrimp but with a more slender body and longer legs. They're raised and harvested in warmer climates like India, southern Asia, Africa, and Central and South America. The problem is you'll often hear the term prawn used to refer to large shrimp. This is inaccurate. Big shrimp are just that—big shrimp.

Scampi: Another term often incorrectly applied to shrimp is scampi. Scampi accurately describes a lobster-like crustacean called a Dublin Bay prawn. Here in the States, when you hear the name scampi, it refers to a recipe with shrimp, garlic, white wine and lemon, *see Page 34.*

Types of Shrimp: Here are three of the most common types of shrimp sold in the U.S.

Gulf of Mexico: Most of the shrimp we eat are Gulf shrimp (from the Atlantic coast too). Although they're named by color, the colors aren't distinctive.

White shrimp are firm and sweet. They're considered the best.

Pink shrimp are very similar to whites in flavor and texture and are also considered a premium shrimp.

Browns are considered inferior to whites and pinks. They aren't as firm and can have a slight iodine taste.

Green: Fooled you! This is a term referring to raw, shell-on shrimp that are either fresh or frozen. So all types of shrimp can be green. Get it?

Black Tiger: This farm-raised, Indo-Pacific shrimp is easy to recognize—it has a nearly all-black shell with brown stripes. Personally, I think it's inferior to domestic Gulf shrimp.

Rock: These shrimp have firm, sweet lobster-like meat. Because of their hard shells, this Atlantic-coast shrimp usually comes peeled.

QUALITY VARIATIONS

Three things can affect shrimp quality before you ever see them.

Wild vs. Farmed-Raised: There can be a slight difference in flavor between wild and farm-raised shrimp. It has to do with diet and feed.

We get out of our bodies what we put in. Shrimp are no different. Wild shrimp eat plankton (miniature animals and plants), which is readily available, but it varies in its nutrients.

Shrimp from reputable farms eat high-quality feed for firm, sweet meat. But low-quality feed can produce mushy and bitter meat.

Chemical Usage: There are two chemicals used to treat shrimp.

One is *sodium bisulfite*, a bleaching agent, which prevents black spots, called melanosis. Used incorrectly, it can cause meat to yellow and make the shell gritty like sandpaper.

The other chemical is *sodium tripolyphosphate* (STP), which makes the shrimp retain water to prevent weight loss. But too much can leave a soapy taste and slimy feel.

In moderation, they're okay. If you're concerned, check their packaging to see if they've been treated.

Fresh vs. Frozen: Unless you live on a coast where fresh shrimp is harvested, most of what you buy will be "previously frozen" then thawed.

Fortunately, shrimp freezes well. The problem isn't freezing but how how long it has been thawed at the market. This is why you have to read Quality Checklist on the next page.

But I'll tell you right now, if you ever have the opportunity to eat fresh shrimp, do it. The texture is firmer and the meat is sweeter than any shrimp you'll ever eat—as long as you eat them within two days of purchase.

SIZES OF SHRIMP

You need to know right off the bat that shrimp are usually labeled inaccurately at the market. Those little white signs with red lettering list ambiguous words like jumbo, large, or medium. They're called market terms, and they're vague and undependable because there are no set standards. So what do you do?

Count: In order to get an accurate size of shrimp, always go by the count. This is the number of shrimp it takes to make one pound. So, "16–20" means it takes between 16 and 20 shrimp to make a pound. Why the range? Obviously, we're dealing with nature. Some shrimp are a tad larger or slightly smaller than the others. So a range is best to determine size. When trying to figure out how many shrimp I need for a recipe, I always use the number smack dab in the middle of the count—like 18 for the 16–20 count shrimp.

So what do you do if you're stuck with just the market terms? First, understand that they're not going to tell you much of anything. Second, ask the person behind the counter what count they are. He should know. Third, if he doesn't, take a look at the chart to the upper right. It gives you an approximation of a count compared to market terms.

Market Term Mix-up: Here's an example of how you can run into trouble with market terms.

I had a two-serving recipe that called for 12 extra large shrimp (six per person). I went to three different markets—each listed a different count for extra large. Here's how each serving broke down: Market A sold 16–20s, for 6 oz. per person. Market B sold 21–25s, for 4 oz. per person. Finally, Market C sold 26–30s, for 2½ oz. per person. That would leave me hungry!

MARKET TERM*	TO MAKE 1 POUND
Colossal	10 or less
Jumbo	11–15
Extra Large	16–20
Large	21–30
Medium	31–35
Small	36–45
Miniature	about 100

* Keep this in mind: Market terms are variable, ambiguous, and won't tell you anything except the general size of the shrimp. Buy by the count.

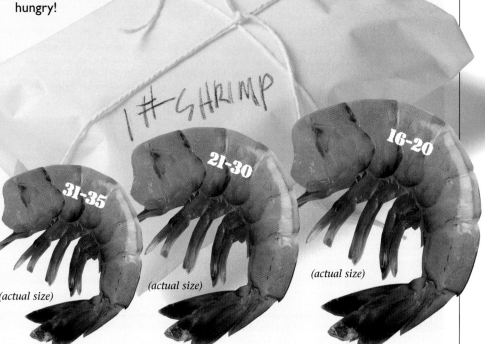

1# SHRIMP

31-35 *(actual size)*

21-30 *(actual size)*

16-20 *(actual size)*

QUALITY CHECKLIST

When you walk into a fish market to buy shrimp, you're already armed with some heavy artillery—your senses. Here are some clues to look for and some bombs to dodge.

✔ **Smell:** First and foremost, rely on your nose. The smell of shrimp will tell you more about its quality than anything else. Shrimp should smell sweet, mild, and like salt water. Don't buy any that smell like ammonia or those that smell bad—they've been thawed for too long and they're beginning to spoil.

✔ **Texture:** Next, count on your sense of touch. The whole shrimp (if not frozen) should feel firm, not mushy. If the shells are soft, it's okay—the shrimp could have molted just before harvesting. But if soft shells are covered in a slimy film, steer clear—they've been out too long. Also refuse those that feel rough, like sandpaper—they've been exposed to too much sodium bisulfite, see *Page 29*.

✔ **Color:** Finally, use your eyes. The natural color of shrimp isn't a good indicator of quality. But certain colors are bad. Black spots or rings on the shell or meat (except with tiger shrimp) means the shrimp are starting to deteriorate. Yellow-colored meat or shells indicate overexposure to sodium bisulfite.

UNCOOKED SHRIMP

Unless shrimp are cooked immediately, thaw and store them as follows.

Thawing Frozen Shrimp: Buy frozen shrimp if you're not planning on using them right away. They can last up to three months.

The key to thawing shrimp is doing it slowly—the slower the better. When shrimp are thawed too quickly, they can experience *drip loss*. During the thawing process, the cells of the shrimp break down, releasing moisture. And with the moisture goes a loss of flavor and texture. That's bad.

Frozen shrimp is sold two ways. It can be sold in bags in which the shrimp are separate and not all stuck together. This is called IQF (individually quick frozen). Or they are sold in blocks—usually five pounds.

If they're in an IQF bag, take out what you need, and put them in a colander inside a bowl. Cover and thaw overnight in the refrigerator. If you're in a hurry, put them in a colander under *cold*, running water—hot water can start to cook them.

If the shrimp are in a block, lay it in a colander, and run cold water over a small section. Then break off the shrimp you need, and put the rest of the block back in the freezer.

Storing Thawed Shrimp: If the shrimp will be cooked right away, go ahead and buy previously frozen, thawed shrimp. Just be sure to check their freshness. You can do this by asking how long they've been thawed. If it's been more than 48 hours, you don't want them. And also be sure to refer to the Quality Checklist, *left*. Remember, thawed shrimp has a maximum shelf life of only two days.

And don't refreeze thawed shrimp. Thawing and refreezing breaks down the meat and makes it mushy, watery, and flavorless.

To store thawed shrimp, first place them in a sealable, plastic bag. What you don't want is the shrimp sitting in standing water. This causes them to break down. Place the bag in a colander filled with ice, and then lay more ice over the top of the bag. Place a bowl under the colander to catch any melting ice. They'll keep for two days—as long as they haven't been sitting out for that long in the market.

SHRIMP MARKET FORMS

These are some of the forms of shrimp you may see in the market. In general, you're better off staying away from those that have been commercially processed—like cooked shrimp. Everything that's done to them before you buy them (shelling, deveining, etc.), can decrease their shelf life.

Head Removed, Shell On, Raw: This is how shrimp are most often sold. Wholesalers refer to these as "green headless." The beauty is that you get shells to make stock, *see right*. And if the shrimp are large enough (say 16–20 count), shelling is less of a chore.

Raw with Heads: Shrimp with heads are usually fresh—they've never been frozen. This is great, but there are pitfalls. Acids from the head cause the shrimp to deteriorate faster. That's why they're often removed. Also, when the head is removed, the shrimp loses half its body weight. So, one pound of shrimp yields roughly a ¹/₂ pound of raw tail meat.

Cooked: These are peeled, shelled, deveined, cooked, and frozen. They're the form I talked about earlier—commercially processed to death. They won't be half as good as the other forms.

Peeled and/or Deveined Raw: Peeled, undeveined shrimp are called PUD, and peeled and deveined shrimp are called P&D. They're mostly sold for commercial use in restaurants, but you may see them in your market. Know that you'll be paying for the peeling and deveining. And you won't get shells for stock.

Live: Without a doubt, live shrimp offer the most in flavor and firm texture. They're fresh from the water and usually not chemically treated. Unfortunately, unless you live near the coast, you aren't likely to find them.

PREPARING SHRIMP

Shelling: It's a good idea to remove the shells if the shrimp will be in a soup or lots of sauce—it's too difficult to fish them out and then peel them. But I'm keeping the shells on in the BBQ Shrimp on Page 32 for added protection against high heat.

To shell the shrimp, start on the underside of the large end. Grasp the swimming legs, and peel the first few sections of the shell to one side and around back to the other. Then pull off the tail, and remove any stray legs or pieces of shell.

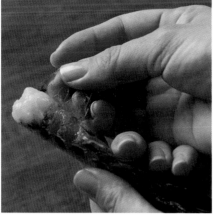

Leaving or Removing Tail Shell: The tail shell can be left on or it can be removed to get to the small piece of meat inside it.

When the shrimp are going to be served as finger food, keep the tails on. Remove the shell, but stop just before the last segment above the tail—it'll help keep it attached.

But to get to the tail meat, flatten and fan the tail out. Gently pull and wiggle the shell back and forth until it separates from the rest of the body.

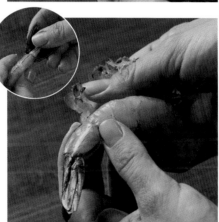

Deveining: A shrimp's vein is really its intestinal tract, and removing it is a matter of choice. Eating it won't hurt you, but some people don't like the gritty texture of larger veins. So, I always devein—especially with 16–20s or larger. To, devein the shrimp, grasp it on both sides of its body, and gently squeeze (it tightens the meat, making it easier to cut). Make a shallow cut down the length of its back, then lift out the vein with the tip of a knife.

Butterflying: I always butterfly my shrimp (no matter what size) when I'm going to saute them, like in the Scampi on Page 34. This does two things. First, it lets the shrimp cook evenly and quickly—that means less time on the heat and less chance to overcook. And second, it looks nice—fanned white meat against pink skin. To butterfly shrimp, after deveining, make a deeper cut down the center of the shrimp being careful not to cut it in half. **AH**

MAKING STOCK

One of the best parts about buying shrimp with shells is that you have a great base to make a stock. If the shells are left on, as with the BBQ Shrimp on page 32, you can still make a shrimp-like stock. Just use half the water (4 cups) and 4 cups of bottled clam juice in place of shells. When making any stock, the trick is to *quickly* bring it to a boil, and then immediately reduce the heat. You're looking for a gentle simmer. *Constant* boiling (along with pressing the ingredients when straining) can make the stock cloudy.

SHRIMP STOCK

(MAKES 8 CUPS)
WORK TIME: 20 MINUTES
COOK TIME: 20 MINUTES
SAUTE IN 2 T. OLIVE OIL:

1	onion, roughly chopped
2	ribs celery, roughly chopped
2	carrots, roughly chopped
3	cloves garlic, smashed

ADD:

8	cups water and shells from 2 lbs. 16–20 count shrimp (or 4 cups water and 4 cups clam juice, if no shells)
1	lemon, halved
3	sprigs fresh thyme
3	sprigs fresh parsley
1	sprig rosemary
2	t. salt
1	t. black peppercorns
3	bay leaves

▲ *Heat olive oil over medium-high heat. Add the onion, celery, carrot, and garlic. Saute until onion is translucent (5–8 min.). Add the remaining ingredients, and bring to a boil. Reduce heat and simmer for 20 minutes. Strain and cool.*

BBQ SHRIMP

This BBQ Shrimp is not what you may think. First of all, it's a New Orleans dish. Second, there's no grilling involved. And finally, the sauce isn't a typical BBQ

sauce like you'd put on ribs. The only thing this has in common with familiar barbecue dishes is that you're going to get messy—BBQ Shrimp should be eaten hot, with your fingers and plenty of long-neck beers.

The Cooking Method: Unlike most barbecue, this New Orleans dish is baked. It's a great cooking method for shrimp since baking is more gentle than direct-heat grilling—the

shrimp still cook quickly, but without drying out. And leaving the shells on helps keep the shrimp moist.

The Sauce: Don't let the "BBQ" in this recipe throw you. This sauce isn't the sweet, ketchup-based one you know (and love!). It's *spicy*, with some honey to take the edge off. The base is made with butter, a Creole-seasoned stock, then thickened with a dark roux—another New Orleans tradition.

One more thing: You can make the sauce ahead of time, then chill it until you're ready to bake the shrimp. But bring it to room temperature first so it heats through in the oven.

The Eating: The way BBQ Shrimp is made and presented is typical of its roots—designed to be eaten slowly, with plenty of time between peeling and eating to laugh and talk.

And when you sit down to eat, be sure there are napkins and crusty French bread to sop up that sauce!

BBQ SHRIMP

(MAKES 4–5 APPETIZER SERVINGS)
WORK TIME: 30 MINUTES
COOK TIME: 50 MINUTES
FOR THE ROUX—
MELT:
½   cup unsalted butter (1 stick)
WHISK IN AND BAKE:
½   cup all-purpose flour
FOR THE CREOLE SEASONING—
COMBINE:
1   T. paprika
2   t. dried rosemary
2   t. salt
1   t. *each* black, white, and
     cayenne pepper
½   t. *each* dried thyme and oregano
½   t. dry mustard
¼   t. celery seed
3   bay leaves, very finely crumbled
FOR THE SAUCE—
SAUTE:
½   cup unsalted butter, melted
3   T. Creole Seasoning, *above*
2   T. garlic, minced
ADD; BRING TO A BOIL:
2   cups Shrimp Stock, *see Page 31*,
     or 2 cups bottled clam juice
¼   cup honey
1   T. Worcestershire sauce
1   T. tomato paste
1   t. Old Bay seasoning
ADD BY TABLESPOONS:
     Prepared roux, *above*
FOR THE BBQ SHRIMP—
POUR SAUCE OVER AND BAKE:
1   lb. (16–20 count) shrimp,
     deveined, shells on, *see Page 33*
GARNISH WITH:
2   T. green onion, bias-sliced

NUTRITIONAL INFORMATION PER APPETIZER SERVING: CALORIES 660; TOTAL FAT 49(G); CALORIES FROM FAT 66%; SODIUM 1579(MG); CARBOHYDRATES 37(G)

THE SECRET TO THE SAUCE

New Orleans cuisine wouldn't be the same without using a dark roux.

Roux: A roux [ROO] is made of equal parts of flour and fat that are cooked together. And the longer it's cooked, the darker the roux becomes. Light rouxs thicken sauces and soups (but don't add much flavor). But dark rouxs add flavor *and* color.

And since it's a New Orleans tradition, you're going to cook this roux like they do—in the oven. This gives you better control (for even cooking), and it won't need constant stirring.

When using any roux, be sure to add the *roux to the stock*, not the other way around. This way, you can adjust amounts to get the best thickness.

COOKING SHRIMP WITH SHELLS

There are two advantages to cooking shrimp in their shells. First, you get a tastier shrimp—the shells hold in the natural flavor of the shrimp, and they impart a flavor of their own.

Second, you have a larger margin for error when you cook them (shrimp can overcook faster than you can blink). In effect, the shell becomes a barrier against the extreme heat of grilling, sauteing, or boiling. But that protection doesn't mean they take longer to cook—the shell traps steam, heating the shrimp from the inside. All of this means shell-on shrimp are less likely to get dry and rubbery.

▲ *You can devein a shrimp in its shell using manicure scissors. Place the tip of the scissors under the shell at the head end of the shrimp. Then cut the shell down to the last tail segment. Use the scissors' tip to pull out the vein—just like with the tip of a knife.*

MAKING BBQ SHRIMP

1 Preheat oven to 350°. Melt butter in an ovenproof saute pan over medium heat. Add flour, and whisk to combine. Then place the pan on the middle rack of the oven.

2 Cook roux for 30 minutes, whisking it every 10 minutes. When it's the color of peanut butter, remove it from the oven and set aside. Increase the oven temperature to 425°.

3 While roux cooks, mix together the Creole Seasoning, then melt remaining butter in a large saucepan over medium heat. Add Creole Seasoning and garlic; stir to combine.

4 Stir in the shrimp stock, honey, Worcestershire, tomato paste, and Old Bay. Return sauce to a boil over medium-high heat, then whisk in prepared roux, 1 T. at a time.

5 You'll probably only need about 3 T. of roux (freeze extra to use another time). The sauce should be the consistency of maple syrup. Use sauce now, or chill for later.

6 Place shrimp in a single layer in shallow baking dish. Ladle sauce over shrimp and bake 6–8 min., or until *just* firm. Garnish with green onions and serve.

SCAMPI

Photograph: Scott Little, Food Styling: Janet Pittman

1 Lightly dust both sides of shrimp with flour. Melt the butter in a large saute pan over medium-high heat. Then add the shrimp and saute for 1 minute.

2 Turn the shrimp over and cook for 1 more minute, then *immediately* remove them from the pan. They'll be light pink and slightly firm—underdone is okay.

3 For the sauce, stir garlic into butter. When you can smell it (about 1 min.), deglaze with wine and lemon juice, scraping up brown bits. Season with salt.

4 "Mount" sauce with remaining 3 T. butter. When butter melts, return shrimp to pan, tossing *quickly* to coat. Remove pan from heat. Add parsley and serve.

As I said before, scampi usually refers to a recipe, not a type of shrimp. And while scampi is simple to cook, you can mess it up as quickly as it takes to make it—in minutes. But this recipe minimizes the danger of overcooking the shrimp.

Dusting with Flour: Dusting the shrimp with flour does one important thing—it turns a traditionally thin butter sauce into one that clings. But only *dust* them! Anything more and the sauce will be too thick.

The cooked, pink color of the shrimp still shows through after that light dusting. And don't worry—the flour doesn't change their texture.

Sauteing with Speed: You can overcook shrimp in a heartbeat. The best way to guard against it is to only saute them for *one minute* per side. Take them out of the pan, finish the sauce, then return the shrimp to the pan. Leave them in just long enough to coat—about 15 seconds.

SCAMPI

(MAKES 4–5 APPETIZER SERVINGS)
WORK TIME: 20 MINUTES
COOK TIME: 5 MINUTES
DUST IN ALL-PURPOSE FLOUR:
1   lb. (16–20 count) shrimp, shelled with tails intact, and butterflied, *see Page 31*
MELT, THEN SAUTE SHRIMP IN:
½   cup unsalted butter (1 stick)
REMOVE SHRIMP; ADD:
2   T. garlic, minced
DEGLAZE WITH:
½   cup dry white wine
2   T. fresh lemon juice
SEASON WITH:
    Salt to taste
"MOUNT" WITH:
3   T. unsalted butter
RETURN SHRIMP AND ADD:
¼   cup chopped fresh parsley

NUTRITIONAL INFORMATION PER APPETIZER SERVING: CALORIES 398; TOTAL FAT 33(G); CALORIES FROM FAT 73%; SODIUM 339(MG); CARBOHYDRATES 4(G)

Photograph: Scott Little, Food Styling: Janet Pittman

Belgian WAFFLES

Come on, 'fess up—you're a closet eater. You eat unusual combinations of food at unorthodox times: pizza at breakfast, pie after midnight, or saltines spread with butter and dipped in cold chili—anytime.

You do this secretly because you think you're a nut and no one else would ever do this sort of thing. Well, I'm here to tell you that most of us do.

That's the beauty of Belgian waffles. They're anything you want them to be—from a special breakfast to a classy late-night finale. And these waffles can be eaten anytime, as an unusual main course or unique dessert (check out the Back Cover). At last, here's an open invitation to eat breakfast at night and dessert for breakfast!

What Are They?: There's more to Belgian waffles than their characteristic deep holes and height. Here's what sets them apart from Bisquick.

Yeast: A little yeast in the batter gives these waffles lightness and a slightly tangy flavor. Without the yeast to lighten them, you'd be hard pressed to eat a whole waffle—it'd kill your appetite for the day. And since the batter needs to rise overnight, the waffles are prepared in stages. Perfect for a relatively hassle-free meal.

Waffle Iron: The goal of an iron is to make a waffle that's crisp outside, and light and airy inside. Not all irons are up to that task, so read Wares, Pages 38–39, before hitting the stores.

Believe me, you really do need a Belgian waffle iron for these waffles, not a regular one. The deep holes and extra height create more surface area for the best crispy-to-airy ratio (and for holding maximum maple syrup!).

Baking: A good iron is useless if the waffles aren't baked long enough—for three full minutes. Just ignore the "ready" light, don't peek, then serve them straight from the iron. They don't hold well, but can be revived in a toaster, if necessary, *see Page 36.*

Toppings: Check out the fruit toppings on Page 37. They're so good you don't even miss the whipped cream.

I The night before you plan to serve the waffles, prepare the batter by first combining the dry ingredients in a *large* bowl (the batter needs growing room because the yeast will cause it to rise and bubble).

Then, melt the butter, combine it with the milk, and whisk it into the dry ingredients. Cover with plastic wrap, and let it sit on your kitchen counter overnight.

BELGIAN WAFFLES

(MAKES 10–12 WAFFLES)
REST TIME: OVERNIGHT
WORK TIME: 10 MINUTES
COOK TIME: 30 MINUTES
COMBINE IN LARGE BOWL:

2   cups all-purpose flour
2   T. sugar
¾   t. salt
½   t. active dry yeast

WHISK INTO DRY INGREDIENTS:

½   cup unsalted butter, melted
2   cups whole milk

COVER AND LET SIT OVERNIGHT.
THE NEXT MORNING, ADD:

3   eggs, separated

NUTRITIONAL INFORMATION PER WAFFLE: CALORIES 236; TOTAL FAT 13(G); CALORIES FROM FAT 48%; SODIUM 219(MG); CARB. 24(G)

2 In the morning, heat up the waffle iron. Then separate the eggs, whisking yolks into the batter and whipping whites to soft peaks with a hand mixer.

3 Using a rubber scraper, gently fold the whites into the batter. Be careful not to overmix it—a few white streaks or lumps are just fine.

4 When the iron is hot, pour ½ cup batter into each square section (measurements may vary). Spread it so all the grids are covered with batter.

5 Cook waffles for 3 minutes. When done, the tops may be blotchy (right). The bottoms should be more evenly browned. Serve bottom side up.

REHEATING WAFFLES

Belgian waffles are kind of like soufflés—they suffer if they wait around too long. But does that mean you need an army of irons just to feed the family? Not necessarily. Here are two ways to extend the "life" of waffles.

One way is to preheat the oven to 275° at the same time you plug in the waffle iron. Then place the waffles on a rack on a baking sheet and keep warm in the oven. Serve within 15 minutes or they'll get soggy.

But the best way I found is to toast the waffle in a toaster (use a low setting) for about one minute. This recrisps the outside while keeping the center soft. Be sure to keep an eye on them so they don't burn.

And if you have leftovers, wrap them in plastic, freeze, then toast for a quick breakfast.

6 Take a look at this waffle—fluffy on the inside (almost like a soufflé), golden brown, and lightly crisp on the outside. They shouldn't be heavy at all.

7 Serve waffles *immediately* with plenty of warm toppings, or butter and pure maple syrup. If needed, recrisp waffles in the toaster on a low setting.

TOPPING IT OFF

There's a reason why Belgian waffles have those big holes—to trap big chunks of fruit and nuts. And these toppings take full advantage of them!

Get a head start on the toppings by making the Maple-Rum Sauce the night before, along with the waffle batter. It's important to use *pure* maple syrup here—sure, it costs more, but the flavor is worth every cent.

Then, before you start baking the waffles in the morning, reheat the sauce and add the fruit. But be careful—you just want to heat everything enough to *slightly* soften the fruit (especially the apples) and warm the ingredients through. If the fruit cooks too long or boils in the liquid, it will turn mushy and break down.

(MAKES 1½ CUPS)
WORK TIME: 5 MINUTES
COOK TIME: 8–10 MINUTES
BOIL, REDUCE, AND STRAIN:
1 cup pure maple syrup
1 cup apple juice
3 strips lemon peel
1 T. fresh lemon juice
1 vanilla bean, split, scraped
1 cinnamon stick
RETURN TO SAUCEPAN. WHISK IN:
1 T. dark rum
½ t. salt
COMBINE AND ADD:
4 t. cornstarch
1 T. apple juice

NOTE: Make the Maple-Rum Sauce the night before and chill. In the morning, reheat the sauce, add the fruit, and simmer until warm.

▲ *Boil, reducing first 6 ingredients to 1½ cups, 5–7 min. Strain and return to pan.*

▲ *Add rum and salt; return to a boil. Combine cornstarch and juice in small bowl, then whisk into syrup to thicken.*

BANANA-PECAN TOPPING *(MAKES 3½–4 CUPS)*
WORK TIME: 5 MINUTES
COOK TIME: 10 MINUTES
TOAST IN 2 t. UNSALTED BUTTER:
1 cup whole pecans
REHEAT 1 RECIPE MAPLE-RUM SAUCE. ADD, HEAT THROUGH:
  Toasted pecans
3 cups bananas, sliced
  (about 3 bananas)
1 t. minced orange zest

▲ *Melt butter in small skillet over medium heat. Add pecans and toast, tossing constantly until golden.*

APPLE-SAUSAGE TOPPING *(MAKES 3½–4 CUPS)*
WORK TIME: 5 MINUTES
COOK TIME: 10 MINUTES
REHEAT 1 RECIPE MAPLE-RUM SAUCE. ADD, HEAT THROUGH:
8 pork breakfast sausage links, fried, cut into chunks
3 cups apple slices, unpeeled (about 3 apples)
¼ cup dark raisins (optional)

▲ *Jonathan apples (or other firm, tart apples) are great in this topping. To slice them, first cut four sides from the apple, top to bottom. Then slice each side into ¼" thick half-moons.*

MIXED BERRY TOPPING
(MAKES 3½–4 CUPS)
WORK TIME: 5 MINUTES
COOK TIME: 10 MINUTES
REHEAT 1 RECIPE MAPLE-RUM SAUCE. ADD, HEAT THROUGH:
1 cup frozen red raspberries
1 cup frozen blueberries
1 cup frozen blackberries
1 cup frozen dark cherries
1 t. minced lemon zest
OFF HEAT, ADD:
¼ t. almond extract

▲ *Simmer the berries in the syrup just long enough to thaw and warm them, but not until they break down.*

BELGIAN WAFFLE IRONS

When I was experimenting with the Belgian Waffle recipe on Page 35, I knew the key to a good waffle, besides the recipe of course, was a good waffle iron.

So, I dusted off the only one I had in our test kitchen, plugged it in, and sat there and stared at it. The instruction manual was long gone and so was my memory of how to actually work the thing. Being a guy, I didn't need directions, so I fell back on the one thing we all have—instinct.

What I Was Looking For: Since I'd had *good* Belgian waffles in the past, I reminded myself of what they were like:

1) An evenly browned exterior.
2) A crispy, toast-like exterior.
3) A thoroughly cooked interior.

Now that I knew *what* I was looking for, I had to figure out *how* to get there—without directions.

Testing: Going on instinct, I let the waffle iron heat up for 10 minutes (or when beads of water danced on the plates). Then I cooked the waffles for three minutes (when the steam stopped).

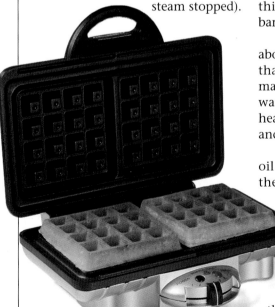

I was pleasantly surprised during my testing—and all I was doing was winging it. My waffles turned out consistently brown, crispy, and thoroughly cooked. But to be fair, I ran out and got six different waffle irons, just to see how technology had changed. I also wanted to follow the instructions in the manufacturers' manuals. Here's what I found.

Performance: As you can see on the next page, four irons tested above average. Those four had no problem with even browning and a cooked interior. And only one had a small problem with a crispy exterior.

The thing that seemed to really make the difference was the heat-up time. Everybody has made pancakes, and everybody knows the hotter the griddle, the better the result—it's the same with waffle irons. A surface that's not hot enough gives you one thing: a soggy, pale waffle that's barely fit for your dog's snack.

So letting the irons heat up for about 10 minutes (compared to half that time listed in the instruction manuals, if a time was given at all) was perfect. It generated the high heat waffles need for even browning and a crispy outside.

The manuals also said to lightly oil or spray a nonstick spray onto the plates to avoid sticking. But I got better results if they were left uncoated. Why? Think about pan-searing a steak. Great browning comes from two things: really high heat and a *dry* pan. It's the same thing with these waffle irons. 🔳

The signs of a good waffle are even browning, a crispy exterior, and cooked throughout. Take a look at the photos below. This is what you want to see in your waffles. Just know that each iron was tested using my Belgian Waffle recipe. Results may vary based on different waffle recipes.

▲ *Even Browning: Your waffle should look like the one on the left. The one on the right didn't have enough heat.*

▲ *Crispy Exterior: Your waffle should feel sturdy and "crumb" when scraped with a knife—like toast.*

▲ *Thoroughly Cooked: The inside of a good waffle isn't doughy, but light and airy throughout, like this one.*

BRAND	WHAT WE PAID	SUGGESTED WARM-UP TIMES	EVENLY BROWNED (BOTTOM)	CRISPY EXTERIOR (BOTTOM)	COOKED INTERIOR	OVERALL RATING	COMMENTS
 **Salton** #WM8 BEL	$14.99	About 5 minutes or until green cook light comes on.	Poor	Fair	Poor	C	Browning was uneven and the exterior slightly crispy. Batter was still gummy. Green cook light, which tells you when waffles are done, was way off.
 **Farberware** #FWM800P	$29.99	About 5 minutes or until ready light goes off.	Poor	Poor	Poor	D	Browning was very uneven and hardly noticeable. Was not crispy at all. Batter was still raw. Created flatter waffles than other irons.
 **Cuisinart** #WMB-2	$59.95	Until green indicator light comes on.	Good	Excellent	Excellent	A-	My second choice. It made a near-perfect waffle: fairly even browning, crispy exterior, and completely cooked. It beats the VillaWare on price.
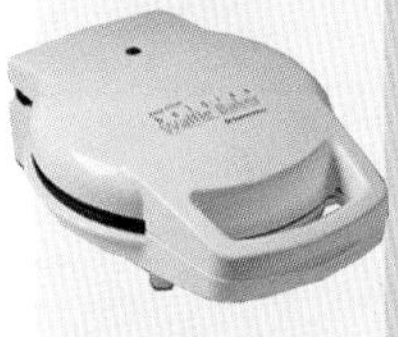 **Toastmaster** #233	$30	When indicator light goes off.	Good	Fair	Good	B-	Made a darn good waffle for the price. It was pretty evenly browned, crispy, and completely cooked. Gave too small a batter amount in manual.
 **Krups** #654	$49.99	When ready light goes off.	Good	Good	Good	B	The only one of the irons that almost burned the waffles after the warm-up time. Did pretty well for a four-waffle iron. Inched by Toastmaster for crispiness.
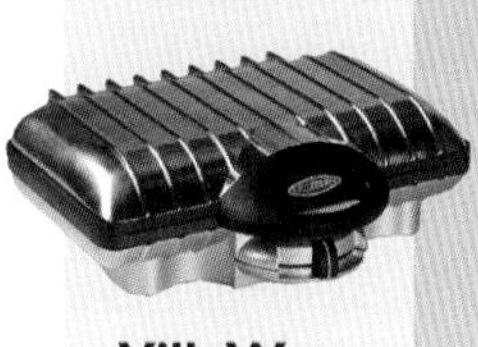 **VillaWare** #2000	$80	When green light comes on and "chime" sounds.	Excellent	Excellent	Excellent	A+	The clear winner. It made a perfect waffle every time—except for the tops. Its only two downfalls: the chime (kind of sounds like a sick bird) and the price.

AND ANOTHER THING...

There are a couple of side notes about these irons.

First of all, every one of the irons, even the top performer (the VillaWare), turned out waffles with tops that looked pretty bad. Just look at the photos here (bottom side, *left*; top side, *right*). The biggest reason for this glitch is gravity. The waffle batter naturally settles into the bottom plate and is pressed down by the weight of the top. But the heat generated from the top just isn't enough for even browning. The easy solution: Flip the waffles over and serve top side down—nobody will know the difference.

Secondly, if your iron isn't performing up to these standards, try this: Ignore the manufacturers' manuals (and all the bells and whistles) and do your own testing. The majority of them tell you that the instructions are only *suggestions*, and that you can make adjustments. Don't be afraid to try it.

Q *What's the deal about cooking with wines? Which ones should I use, red or white? What about dry and sweet?*

A Cooking with wine can be as intimidating as tasting it with a wine buff. Here are four basic rules.

First, never use anything called "cooking wine" or "cooking sherry." They're bad wines with added salt.

Second, as a *general* rule, red wines go with red meat and game, white with fish and poultry. But taste is most important—a pinot noir sauce over a piece of grilled salmon is fantastic.

Third, it's okay to buy a lower-priced wine for cooking—as long as it's good quality. It doesn't make sense to add expensive stuff to beef stew with all those other flavors going on.

And, finally, for cooking, look for "dry" wines (not sweet). All of the wines listed below are on the dry side.

RED WINE	WHITE WINE
Cabernet Sauvignon	Chardonnay
Merlot	Sauvignon Blanc
Chianti	Dry Vermouth, *as a*
Pinot Noir	*white wine alternative*

Q *Some cake recipes call for beating eggs (or just egg yolks) and sugar to the "ribbon stage." What is that?*

A The ribbon stage happens when the beaten egg mixture leaves "ribbons" as the beaters are lifted out, like in the photo above. At this point, the mixture will be a pale yellow and look like lightly whipped cream.

It pays to be patient—it can take up to 10 minutes of beating to reach the right consistency (20 if you're crazy enough to beat by hand!). But your cake will be lighter for the effort.

Q *Is there a difference in the way that cornstarch, flour, and arrowroot thicken? When would I use each one?*

A First you need to know all three are starches (cornstarch and flour are *grain* starches, arrowroot is a *root* starch). And a starch's thickening power comes from its ability to absorb water. As it does, starch granules swell and burst, thickening the liquid.

But even though they're all starches, they each have different thickening properties. The one you use depends on what you're cooking.

Grain starches thicken better than root starches (and cornstarch better than flour). Flour forms an opaque gel—perfect for coconut cream pie,

Q *What is a nonreactive pan, and when would I need one? Will it really make a difference?*

A Nonreactive describes cooking vessels or utensils that do not chemically react with foods. Nonreactive materials include glazed ceramic, glass, plastic, and stainless steel.

But certain metals are reactive—aluminum, copper, and iron top the list. And that means you have to look out for what types of food you put in them.

Problematic foods are highly acidic, like tomatoes, rhubarb, vinegar, and lemon juice. Put a reactive cooking vessel and an acidic food together, and you could end up with gray-colored rhubarb or a metallic-tasting tomato sauce.

So, yes, it does make a difference. Didn't know you had a science experiment going on in your pots and pans, did you?

where the cream needs to be thick enough to hold its shape when cut, but it doesn't matter if it's cloudy.

Cornstarch gels clear, making it good for fruit pies because you can see the fruit through it. Just don't freeze it—freezing ruins the "set." And if cornstarch is heated too long or whisked too much, it thins out.

Arrowroot also creates a clear, glossy sauce, but you need to use more to get the same consistency as cornstarch. So, while it's perfect for cherry pie, you need to use more of it. And that will make your pie worth its weight in gold!

Bottom line—use the thickener a recipe calls for. For the majority of them, that'll be flour or cornstarch.

Q *I've seen containers of Fines Herbes, Herbes de Provence, and Beau Monde in stores. What are they?*

A Fines Herbes and Herbes de Provence are classic French herb blends. Beau Monde is ground, dried onion and celery seed, an all-purpose seasoning.

Fines Herbes [FEEN erb] is typically tarragon, chervil, parsley, and chives. "Fines" refers to the fact that they're finely chopped. You can get it dried (like the photo above), but the mixture tastes best when fresh. The flavor is subtle, so it's best to add it at the end of cooking, or use as a garnish (especially if you're using fresh herbs).

Herbes de Provence [EHRB duh proh-VAWNS] is a dried blend of some of southern France's most common herbs: oregano, savory, thyme, rosemary, marjoram, basil, fennel seed, lavender, and sage. Traditionally, it's packed in small clay crocks, and sprinkled into stews or over chicken before roasting.

Q *Why is it that so many recipes call for vanilla extract, but tell you to add it at the end of the cooking process? Why does it matter when it's added?*

A In the Nov/Dec 1999 Q & A, I told you that an extract is made from organic material that's soaked in water and ethanol. When that organic material is strained out, you're left with an alcohol-based solution—or extract.

Now, when you cook with alcohol (like wine), you want to add it early enough in the cooking process so the alcohol properties burn off. The flavor of wine stays, but the alcohol "burn" doesn't.

But if you heat extracts for too long, you burn them off completely and evaporate all flavor. It will taste as if you never used them. Just like with the almond extract in the Mixed Berry Topping, *Page 37*, hold out, and add it at the end.

Q *I have my grandmother's old measuring spoons and I just got a new set for Christmas. My baking recipes aren't turning out the same now. Is it the spoons?*

A Probably. We faced a similar problem in the test kitchen working on Gooey Butter Cake in the last issue.

The recipe was originally given in weights (standard for professional bakeries, since accurate measurements are critical in baking). While converting the weights to "cups and spoons," I found two of the tablespoons in the kitchen were different. So I filled them with salt, then weighed the salt.

Then I bought and checked some other spoons. Look below—there's *big* difference in how much they hold.

According to the Office of Weights and Measures at the Department of Commerce, a true tablespoon should hold one-half liquid ounce, or about 19 grams of salt. *None* of these spoons measured up.

Don't despair. Even if you have an "accurate" tablespoon, most recipes were likely developed with inaccurate ones. These differences shouldn't affect your day-to-day cooking. If baked goods vary, adjust the ingredients that used measuring spoons.

GLOSSARY

Arugula: [ah-ROO-guh-lah] Also called rocket, arugula is a green related to mustard. It has a strong peppery tang and looks like radish leaves. Choose only green leaves—the yellow ones are old.

Béchamel: [BEH shah mehl] One of the "mother sauces," béchamel is a simple white sauce made with milk and thickened with a blond roux (flour cooked with butter).

Braise: [BRAYZ] A method of cooking where food is first browned in fat, then slowly cooked in a small amount of liquid. Braising develops flavors, and tenderizes tough foods.

Caper: [KAY-per] The flower bud of a Mediterranean bush. The tulip-shaped buds are picked, sun-dried, and pickled in a vinegar brine or packed in salt. They range in size from a small peppercorn to as large as the tip of a little finger.

Curly Endive: Related to and often called chicory, curly endive grows in loose heads of lacy greens with curly tips. The crispy leaves have a slightly bitter taste.

Mount: A cooking technique where small chunks of cold butter are whisked into a sauce right before serving. This adds flavor and a glossy look, and slightly thickens the sauce.

Pith: The soft white membrane found on citrus fruit between the rind (zest) and the flesh of the fruit. It has a bitter taste.

Tapenade: [TA-puh-nahd] A thick paste typically made from capers, ripe olives, anchovies, olive oil, lemon juice, and seasonings. It's used as a condiment and served with crudités.

ABBREVIATIONS

t. = teaspoon
T., Tbsp. = tablespoon
oz. = ounce
lb. = pound
Dash = scant $1/8$ of a teaspoon
Pinch = $1/16$ of a teaspoon

8.5g 12g 17g 11.3g 14.2g 17g 14.2g 14.2g

MOLTEN CHOCOLATE CAKES

Photograph: Scott Little, Food Styling: Janet Pittman

Moist chocolate cake—there's a contradiction in terms. These days, the only sure bet for moist chocolate cake are those cupcakes with fluff inside.

And as a kid, that fluff was the one thing that kept them from being traded in for *really* good stuff—Rice Krispy treats and barbecued potato chips. Even then you had discerning taste.

But these Molten Chocolate Cakes are another story. This time the "fluff" is a pocket of chocolate that oozes out of a warm cake. And since it's obvious your tastes have *really* evolved, they're served with warm Black Cherry Sauce.

The recipe is simple, but you need to keep a couple things in mind as you make the cakes—two kinds of chocolate and the "B's" of technique.

Chocolate: These cakes use two kinds of chocolate: bittersweet and semisweet. Why both? Because they balance each other out. All bittersweet and the cakes are too chocolatey. But they're too sweet with all semisweet.

There's espresso powder in the cakes, too. Don't worry, you won't even taste it—the coffee flavor intensifies the chocolate. Instant espresso powder is best, but if you can't find it, instant coffee granules work fine.

The Two B's: Beating and baking are important techniques with these cakes. Here's what you need to know.

Beating: Be patient—the batter needs *a lot* of beating. This incorporates air, lightening the cake's texture.

Baking: It's critical to bake these cakes for the right amount of time. Otherwise, they'll either be way too "molten," or end up as brownies.

Oven temperatures vary, so check the cakes after 15 minutes. If they're really moist on top, bake one minute and check again. Make sure they rest after baking—they'll unmold better.

MOLTEN CHOCOLATE CAKES

(MAKES SIX 6-OZ. CAKES)
WORK TIME: 20 MINUTES
COOK TIME: 15 MINUTES

MELT TOGETHER; COOL:
4   oz. bittersweet chocolate, chopped into small pieces
4   oz. semisweet chocolate, chopped into small pieces
¾   cup unsalted butter, cut into pieces (1½ sticks)

IN A LARGE BOWL, BEAT:
4   eggs
½   cup sugar

BEAT INTO EGG MIXTURE:
¼   cup all-purpose flour
1   T. unsweetened cocoa powder
2   t. vanilla extract
1   t. instant espresso powder (or 2 t. instant coffee granules)
½   t. salt

ADD AND BEAT IN:
     Melted chocolate mixture

SERVE WITH:
     Black Cherry Sauce, *see right*
     Sweetened whipped cream
     Shaved milk chocolate

1 Preheat oven to 375°. *Liberally* spray six 6-oz. ramekins with nonstick spray. Chop chocolate into pieces about the size of chocolate chips, then melt them with the butter in a small saucepan over low heat. Stir often to prevent burning. Cool.

2 In large mixing bowl, beat eggs and sugar with electric hand mixer until "ribbon" stage, 7 min., see Q & A, Page 40. At that stage, it will be pale yellow and look like lightly whipped cream.

3 Add the flour, cocoa powder, vanilla extract, espresso powder, and salt. Beat the batter 2 more minutes, then add the melted chocolate mixture and beat another 5 minutes.

4 Use an ice cream scoop for spooning the batter into the ramekins—use 2 level scoops, or ¾ cup, in each. (At this point, the cakes can be chilled, then baked later. Great for parties!)

5 Place the ramekins on a baking sheet and bake 15–17 min., until puffed and mostly dry on top around edges. Remove cakes from oven and rest 3 min. It's okay if they sink a little.

SHAVING CHOCOLATE

Chocolate shavings are an easy, elegant way to garnish desserts. And there's no need for fancy gourmet chocolate—the milk chocolate bars from the check-out lines at the store (like Hershey's) make the best curls.

Warm the wrapped bar in your hand for a minute. Then unwrap and use a peeler to slowly "peel" curls off. Don't worry if they crumble—they still taste great!

6 To unmold, place serving plate on top of ramekin and invert. Carefully remove ramekin, tapping lightly on the plate to loosen cake. Serve with sauce, whipped cream, and shaved chocolate.

BLACK CHERRY SAUCE
(MAKES ABOUT 2 CUPS)
WORK TIME: 5 MINUTES
COOK TIME: 15 MINUTES
COMBINE, BOIL, AND REDUCE:

1	cup dry red wine
⅓	cup sugar
1	t. balsamic vinegar
2	pieces lemon *and* orange peel
½	t. black peppercorns
¼	t. whole cloves
1	cinnamon stick

STRAIN; COMBINE THEN WHISK IN:

2	t. cornstarch
1	T. cold water

ADD:

1½	cups frozen black cherries

OFF HEAT, ADD:

¼	t. almond extract

FOR THE GARNISH—
WHIP TO SOFT PEAKS:

1	cup whipping cream
2	T. sugar
2–3	drops almond extract

▲ *Combine wine, sugar, vinegar, citrus peel, and spices in a small saucepan (use a peeler to shave off pieces of citrus peel). Bring to a boil and reduce to ¾ cup, about 5 min. Strain; return liquid to pan.*

▲ *In a small bowl, mix cornstarch with water. Bring wine back to a boil, whisk in cornstarch mixture, and simmer until thickened, about 2 min. Add cherries and simmer to heat through. Then, off heat, add almond extract. Serve warm.*

GRAND FINALE

CHOCOLATE WAFFLES WITH BLACK CHERRY SAUCE

Waffles for dessert?
Absolutely! It's fashionable
to be acceptably different.

CHOCOLATE WAFFLES

8 HOURS BEFORE, COMBINE:

1½ cups all-purpose flour
¼ cup unsweetened cocoa
¼ cup sugar
¾ t. salt
½ t. ground cinnamon
½ t. active dry yeast

MELT:

½ cup unsalted butter
4 oz. bittersweet
chocolate, chopped

ADD MELTED CHOCOLATE AND:

2 cups whole milk

BEFORE BAKING, ADD:

3 eggs, separated

SERVE WITH:

Vanilla ice cream
Black Cherry Sauce

▲ **Use the same technique** for Chocolate Waffles as for Belgian Waffles on Pages 35–37. First, combine dry ingredients. Then melt butter and chocolate over low heat, stirring often. Add the milk to the chocolate, then stir into flour mixture. Rest batter before adding eggs.

▲ **Bake waffles in heated** waffle iron, *Page 36*. To serve, cut diagonally into 2 triangles. Place one triangle on a plate, then a scoop of vanilla ice cream in the center of the plate. Lean the other triangle against the ice cream, and serve with Black Cherry Sauce, *Page 43*.

ISSUE NO. 20
MAR/APR 2000

AUGUST HOME'S
Cuisine

AN ILLUSTRATED GUIDE TO CREATIVE HOME COOKING ®

COCONUT CAKE
with Lime Filling

Also in this Issue:
The Basics of **EGGS**
MUSHROOMS: *Roasted, Sauteed, and Grilled*
Three **POTATO GRATINS**
INDIAN-STYLE CURRY *and Condiments*
BONELESS LEG OF LAMB *with Mustard Sauce*

Cuisine

Editor
John F. Meyer

Art Director
Cinda Shambaugh

Associate Editor
Susan Hoss

Assistant Editors
Kelly Volden
Ellen Boeke
Sara Ostransky

Senior Graphic Designer
Holly Wiederin

Graphic Designer
Stephanie Hunter

Test Kitchen Director
Kim Samuelson

Contributing Photographer
Dean Tanner
Primary Image

Pre-press Image Specialist
Troy Clark

Publisher
Donald B. Peschke

Corporate
Creative Director: **Ted Kralicek**
August Home Books: **Douglas L. Hicks**
Senior Photographer: **Crayola England**
New Media Manager: **Gordon C. Gaippe**
New Media Art Director: **Eugene Pedersen**
E-Commerce Analyst: **Carol Schoeppler**
Web Site Product Specialist: **Adam Best**
Controller: **Robin K. Hutchinson**
Senior Accountant: **Laura J. Thomas**
Accounts Payable Clerk: **Mary J. Schultz**
Accounts Receivable Clerk: **Margo Petrus**
Human Resource Assistant: **Kirsten Koele**
Production Director: **George Chmielarz**
Elec. Publishing Director: **Douglas Lidster**
Network Administrator: **Cris Schwanebeck**
Production Assistant: **Susan Rueve**
Pre-press Image Specialist: **Minniette Johnson**
Facilities Manager: **Julia Fish**
Admin. Assistant: **Sherri Ribbey**
Receptionist: **Jeanne Johnson**
Mail Room/Delivery: **Lou Webber**

Circulation
Subscriber Services Director: **Sandy Baum**
New Business Director: **Glenda K. Battles**
New Business Manager: **Todd Bierle**
Promotion Manager: **Rick Junkins**
Renewal Manager: **Paige Rogers**
Billing Manager: **Rebecca Cunningham**
Asst. Subscription Manager: **Joy Krause**
Marketing Analyst: **Kris Schlemmer**
Creative Manager: **Melinda Jo Haffner**
Senior Graphic Designer: **Mark A. Hayes, Jr.**

Customer Service and Fulfillment
Operations Director: **Bob Baker**
Merchandise Buyer: **Linda Jones**
Administrative Assistant: **Nancy Downey**
Customer Service Manager: **Jennie Enos**
Technical Representative: **John Audette**
Customer Service Reps: **Anna Cox**
April Revell • Tammy Truckenbrod
Deborah Rich • David Gaumer

Cuisine® (ISSN 1089-6546) is published bi-monthly (Jan., Mar., May, July, Sept., Nov.) by August Home Publishing Co., 2200 Grand Ave., Des Moines, IA 50312. Cuisine® is a trademark of August Home Publishing Co. ©Copyright 2000 August Home Publishing. All rights reserved.
Subscriptions: Single copy: $4.99. One-year subscription (6 issues), $21.94. (Canada/Foreign add $10 per year, U.S. funds.) Periodicals postage paid at Des Moines, IA and at additional mailing offices.
"USPS/Heartland Press Automatable Poly"
Postmaster: Send change of address to Cuisine, PO Box 37100 Boone, IA 50037-2100.
Subscription questions? Call 800-311-3995, 8 a.m. to 5 p.m., Central Standard Time, weekdays.
On-line Subscriber Services: www.cuisinemag.com
Cuisine® does not accept and is not responsible for unsolicited manuscripts. PRINTED IN U.S.A.

From the Editor:

Final details. They're always so small but carry so much weight—especially in cooking. It's like a good-looking tie with a suit, lit candles on the dinner table, or dark chocolate with champagne. None of them are necessary, but it's the little finishing touches that can make a moment memorable. We always try to do that with our recipes.

Take a look at the Parmesan basket on the back cover. What a nice way to present a salad—especially if you're going to put it on a plate with an entree. It not only acts as a container, but also as a kind of garnish. It's easy to do and is a final detail with impact.

Then turn to the curry article. Of course you'll find out how to make a great-tasting curry, but if you flip to Pages 28 and 29, you'll find out how to make three chutneys and a raita—the perfect final detail to Indian curry. Without these little bowls of complementary flavors, curry would just be another table without candles.

We always try to provide some type of interesting garnish, sauce, or presentation that will turn the recipe into something special. People eat with their eyes, and when you can put that special final detail into your presentation, it just makes the food taste better!

And that reminds me. We're about to move into our new test kitchens, and I've got to attend to those final details! Look for pictures in our next issue and on our Web site.

A roasted, boneless leg of lamb makes a perfect spring dinner. Unlike the unwieldy and sometimes gamey legs of lamb of yesteryear, this roast is mild and tender. It's delicately seasoned with mild aromatics. But the best part is that it's easy to carve (boneless) and it can all be prepared a day ahead.

August Home's Cuisine®

AN ILLUSTRATED GUIDE TO CREATIVE HOME COOKING

TIPS AND TECHNIQUES

NEUTRALIZING PAINT FUMES

When I paint a room in my house, the paint fumes linger and can be overwhelming. So I cut an onion in half, set it cut side up on a plate (it will sweat a little), and leave it in the newly painted room overnight. In the morning, the strong paint smell is gone!

M. Fink
Federalsburg, MD

QUICK CLEAN-UP

Want a better way to get stuck-on or burned food off your pans and dishes? Try a little Spray 'n Wash. Just squirt some on the surface of the pan or dish and wait five minutes—the grime will wipe off easily. No more dishes soaking overnight.

K. Neaves
Houston, TX

EASY FAT TRAP

I have a quick way to open canned broth that will trap the solid fats inside.

Use a can opener to make a 2" slit on one side of the can and a 1" slit on the other. Broth will pour easily from the 2" slit, but fat will be trapped in the can.

Leftover broth can be stored in the refrigerator as is. And the lid can be safely recycled with the can—just rinse with hot water.

J. Klise
Perry, IA

FLAWLESS THAW

I'm a retired Marine Corps Master Sergeant with a flawless way to defrost/thaw a turkey (or any other type of meat). And it doesn't take up refrigerator or sink space.

Put your turkey in a cooler filled halfway with cold water. Set the cooler out of the way in a hall, garage, or even the bathtub. Leave it overnight—the turkey will be thawed in the morning.

COOKING LARGE PASTA

Here's a method for cooking large pasta (like shells or manicotti) so they won't rip or tear. Boil water; place pasta in water and return to boil for 30–40 seconds. Cover; remove from heat. Let sit 12 minutes; drain.

J. Flanery
Burnsville, MN

PASTRY ROLLOUT

You can roll out pie crust that won't stick, without using flour. Roll it between two sheets of waxed paper or plastic wrap. Peel off top sheet, turn over into pan, and peel off second sheet.

C. Moss
Plymouth, MN

There's no worry about bacteria growing because the water stays at a constant cold temperature.

G. Carey
Vista, CA

PAPER TOWEL SPONGE

Use a plain white paper towel (I prefer Bounty—it's more absorbent) to brush over the surface of soup, stock, or gravy. Floating fat will immediately adhere to the towel. Just throw it away and repeat with a fresh towel until free of fat.

M. Chynoweth
Sauquoit, NY

USING O.J. CONCENTRATE

Frozen orange juice concentrate can be used to flavor a multitude of foods. I add a small amount to salad dressing, pie dough (especially for apple pie), stuffing for chicken or pork, cake batter, cookie dough, etc. It doesn't take much and won't thin batters like regular orange juice would.

P. Coulter
Bel Air, MD

SLICING FRESH BREAD

I make bread nearly every day, by hand, not with a bread machine.

For nice, even slices, I remove the loaf from the pan right after baking, lay it on its side on a cooling rack, and cover with a dish towel for 10–20 minutes. When I'm ready to slice, there are lines "drawn" on the side of the bread. A cooling rack with wider slats makes thicker slices.

E. Pero
Roy, WA

STEAMED SPUDS

For mashed potatoes with more potato flavor and no sogginess, I prefer to steam instead of boil. After steaming, I just transfer potatoes to a large bowl and mash.

M. Scalise
Claremont, CA

PLASTIC BAG FAT SEPARATOR

Here's a way to separate fat from drippings or gravy. First, put a large resealable bag in a large bowl. Pour in the drippings or gravy; seal the bag and let it stand for several minutes, until the fat rises to the top.

Then carefully lift the bag over a cup or bowl. Cut a small hole in the corner and let the drippings or gravy pour out into the cup. Stop pouring before the fat reaches the opening. Now the fat and bag can be disposed of together.

P. Gros
Mandeville, LA

Tips

FROM THE TEST KITCHEN

PEARL ONION SAUTE

For a garnish that's edible (Leg of Lamb, *Page 11*), prepare equal parts pearl onions and mushrooms.

To peel onions, drop in boiling water for 1 minute. Drain. Trim root ends, then gently squeeze onions to remove skins. Cook in olive oil over medium heat, covered, for 7–8 minutes, shaking pan occasionally. Add mushrooms (any variety). Saute, uncovered, 2–3 minutes over high heat. Finish with garlic, wine, salt, and pepper.

HARD-COOKED, EGG YOLK CENTERING

In this issue, you'll read about the parts of an egg, including the chalazae—it holds the yolk in the center of the egg, *see The Basics of Eggs, Page 6*. To help the chalazae do its job of centering the yolk, try this. Twenty-four hours before hard cooking, wrap two rubber bands around the carton to hold it shut. Then lay it on its side in the refrigerator. When you hard cook the eggs, voilá—perfectly centered yolks!

the Basics of EGGS

Chalazae: [kuh-LAY-zee]: This is the white "string" at the top and bottom of the yolk that holds it in the center of the egg. The fresher the egg, the more distinct it is.

Yolk and Yolk Membrane: The yolk is the yellow part of the egg. It contains all of the egg's fat and about half of its protein. The yolk membrane is the clear, strong layer covering the yolk that protects it from breaking.

Albumen: This is the white of the egg, and is both thin (closest to shell) and thick. In higher-grade eggs when they're cracked on a plate, the two types are distinctly different—one is much thicker than the other. But in lower-grade or older eggs, they'll both look the same, *see Egg Grades, right.*

Air Cell: This is a small pocket of air at the large end of the egg. It's formed when the egg contents contract after laying. The older the egg, the larger the air cell.

Shell and Shell Membranes: The shell is the outer egg covering, and it's color doesn't have anything to do with quality or flavor. The shell membranes (inner and outer) surround the albumen. The air cell forms between them when the egg cools after it's laid.

Eggs really are a natural wonder— nutrition-packed, economical, and readily available. But they've still developed a bad rep over time. It's a wonder chickens all over the world aren't out of a job. So, to keep the hen employment rate up, some mysteries need to be solved. Like, what's that white thing hanging from the yolk? What do the different sizes and grades mean? And how do you hard cook eggs without a green ring? But first, on to an egg's origins.

An Egg is Born: The egg starts its life inside a five-month-old laying hen. That may seem young, but she only spends 20–24 months producing eggs—one every 24–26 hours. And her eggs are never fertilized by a rooster, so they won't produce chicks.

Eggs are most commonly available in shades of brown or white. Despite old wives' tales, there isn't any difference in quality between them— they're just from different breeds.

But no matter the egg's exterior, they're all the same on the inside. Take a look at the photo above. It shows an egg with all its standard parts. But sometimes you'll come across some strange things.

Yolk color is a result of what the hen's eaten. Deep yellow yolks come from marigold petals added to feed. And lighter-colored yolks come from yellow corn and alfalfa meal.

Blood spots are caused by a blood vessel rupturing on the yolk's surface during formation. They're *not* undeveloped chicks and won't hurt you.

Double yolks are the equivalent of twins—two yolks that are created at the same time. They're about the same size as a regular yolk split in half.

To crack open an egg, tap the shell on a flat surface. If it's tapped on the rim of a bowl or edge of a countertop, it can shatter, pushing shell pieces into the egg. You just need to break apart the inner and outer shell membranes.

To separate an egg, first have two bowls handy. Crack the egg like you did at left, then pour the egg into your hand. Let the white slip through your fingers and into one bowl, then drop the yolk into the other.

SELECTION AND STORAGE

Selecting and storing eggs is a snap—it's just a matter of looking at the carton and at the eggs themselves.

A Good Egg: The hard work of selecting good-quality eggs is done for you through grading by the USDA, *see Egg Grades, right.* But before you put those eggs in your shopping cart, look for the following:

1) Grade A or AA eggs—they're the highest quality, and most restaurants use them. Grade B eggs are rarely sold in grocery stores and are more often used in food service institutions.

2) Eggs that are clean and free of cracks or imperfections, *see below.*

3) Eggs that are kept in refrigerated cases (between 35–45°). Eggs will "age" more in one day when they're at room temperature than in one week when properly refrigerated.

4) Eggs that are not past their Sell-By date and those with a Sell-By date as close to the Julian date as possible, *see Dates, above.* They're the freshest.

5) Large eggs—they're the most common size called for in recipes and the easiest to find.

Storage: Eggs can keep for up to 4–5 weeks past their Julian date when they're stored properly—refrigerated in their carton.

Egg shells have thousands of pores in them—like our skin. These pores allow odors from other foods in the refrigerator to permeate the shell and taint the flavor of the egg. They also can cause the egg to dehydrate.

So, store the eggs in their carton. It will protect them from odors and keep them from drying out.

DATES

There are two dates on egg cartons. One is the Julian date—the day of the year the eggs were packed. As an example, look at the last three digits (060) of the series of numbers below. They stand for March 1—the 60th day of the year. The other date is the Sell-By date, and it shouldn't be any later than 30 days after the Julian date and as close to it as possible.

00000000060
SELL BY 3/15/00

EGG GRADES

There are 3 grades of eggs: AA, A, and B. You are most likely to find AA and A in your store.

Grade AA Eggs *are compact when broken out. Yolk stands high, and there's a difference between thick and thin white.*

Grade A Eggs *spread out a little, but the yolk is still pretty perky. It's harder to tell the difference between the thick and thin white.*

Grade B Eggs *spread out a lot. The yolk is almost flat, and the thick and thin white are almost the same consistency—runny.*

EGG SIZES

Eggs come in six sizes—peewee, small, medium, large, extra large, and jumbo. You'll most often find medium, large, and extra large in the grocery store because these are what hens lay most often. So why are there different sizes?

First, the hen's age affects egg size. As she ages, her eggs naturally get larger. So a jumbo egg is most likely from a hen who's older and at the end of her laying cycle.

Breed is another factor affecting size. The White Leghorn (the most common laying hen) has been bred to lay eggs that are about the same size (usually large) every time.

Finally, even certain environmental conditions, like poor nutrition, heat, stress, and overcrowding, can produce a smaller egg.

Don't just *look* for cracks—move the eggs back and forth before buying. If any stick, they're probably broken. Secondly, the eggs should be in the carton narrow-end down—it keeps the air cell in place and from rupturing.

NUTRITION AND SAFETY

Eggs are not as bad for you as they're cracked up to be. Granted, eggs *are* high in cholesterol, but one egg has only about the same amount of saturated fat as a cup of 1% milk! They also contain every vitamin except C and are a great source of protein.

But what about salmonella? First, only about 1 in 20,000 eggs is infected. So, it's usually only a problem when egg *pooling* occurs—breaking large quantities of eggs and mixing whites and yolks. If one white or yolk is infected, it'll infect all the others. If you're concerned, cook eggs to the American Egg Board's recommended temperature of 160°.

EGGS AND HEAT

Understanding how eggs and heat work together (and against each other) is the best protection against rubbery whites and chalky yolks.

Turn it Up: Eggs are full of protein and water. When they're heated, coagulation occurs. Simply put, the egg becomes a solid mass. For whites, that usually happens around 145°; for yolks, it's about 155°.

As the egg heats, its tightly wound protein molecules (like tiny straight jackets) start to loosen and straighten out. The "arms" of the protein jackets become free. Once unhooked, they grab other protein jackets and hold on tight. That's why the egg's white turns opaque—the protein molecules are so scrunched together no light can get through them.

Up to a certain point (about 160°), this unwinding and binding is good for the egg—it creates little pockets within the protein that trap water. And that means tender, firm whites

and moist, set yolks. But if all this closeness is taken to the extreme (when there's too much heat or the eggs spend too much time in the heat), the pockets shrink and squeeze out all the water. And that means dry yolks and rubbery whites.

Turn it Down: The hardest part of cooking eggs is avoiding the temptation to turn up the heat and speed things along. Don't do it. The best way to avoid overcooked eggs is to cook them slowly, over fairly low heat.

In addition to turning down the heat and taking your time, try diluting the eggs with liquid—water, milk, cream, etc. The added liquid cools down the eggs and slows the coagulation process. For instance, add a little half-and-half to scrambled eggs just before serving—like my *Cuisine* eggs on Page 9. Or just cover the pan when frying sunny-side-up eggs—covering creates steam, which is gentler on the eggs than frying alone.

GREEN YOLKS AND RUBBERY WHITES

First things first—eggs cooked in their shell in hot water are not hard boiled, they're hard cooked. And it's *how* you cook them that keeps them from developing rubbery whites and that green ring around the yolks.

The two chemicals in an egg that affect yolk color are sulfur and iron. When the egg is cooked, heat draws those chemicals together, creating iron sulfide—and those ugly green rings. The longer the egg is heated, the stronger the chemical attraction. That means a darker ring and more rubbery whites. So for tender whites, creamy yolks, and no green ring, hard cook—don't boil, see *below*.

HARD COOKING EGGS

1 This is one time when older is better. Older eggs are easier to peel when cooked because their inner membrane has separated from the shell.

2 Place 4 eggs in saucepan—any more and they might bump and crack. Fill pan with cold water to cover eggs by 1". Put lid on pan and bring water to boil.

3 When the water comes to a full boil, remove the saucepan from the heat and keep covered for 11 minutes. Then, immediately drain the water.

4 Cover eggs with cold water (or put in ice water bath) for 5 min. Cold water immediately cools the eggs down, keeping sulfur and iron from bonding.

5 To peel, first crack the large end—where air cell is. Then crack all over on a flat surface. Start peeling at air cell. Peel under cold water if peeling is tough.

6 A perfectly hard-cooked egg! The whites are tender, the yolks are moist and creamy (not chalky), and there is absolutely no green ring.

FRANCO-AMERICAN EGGS

Short of burnt coffee in the morning, there's nothing worse than bad scrambled eggs—heavy, dry, and overcooked. But *good* scrambled eggs, those fluffy, bright yellow pillows, can make anyone's day. Well, there's no big secret. It's all about heat and pulling (not stirring).

Heat: Heat is no friend to scrambled eggs. So keep it at medium. It's hot enough to get them done fairly quickly, but low enough to keep them from turning into foam rubber.

Next, make scrambled eggs the *Cuisine* way, *see below*. The American technique of under-stirring is combined with the French technique of adding half-and-half at the end. It lowers the heat and stops the cooking.

Finally, remove the eggs from the pan before they're cooked all the way through—when they're still a little wet-looking. Residual heat will continue to cook them even as they're carried to the table.

Photograph: Scott Little, Food Styling: Janet Pittman

Pull, Don't Stir: Another key to large, fluffy curds is *pulling* the eggs, not stirring them.

Stirring scrambled eggs breaks up the curds into smaller pieces (like French scrambled, *see right*). Instead, pull the eggs away from the edges of the pan toward the center. And turn them over every once in a while so they're cooked evenly on all sides.

AMERICAN VS. FRENCH SCRAMBLED EGGS

Both these spoons show scrambled eggs—American on the top and French on the bottom. The difference between the two is a result of technique. American scrambled eggs are cooked over medium heat and are *pulled*, not stirred, see Step 4. This creates large, fluffy curds. French scrambled eggs, on the other hand, are cooked at a low temperature, and sometimes over a double boiler. They're stirred constantly to make the curds small—like the ones on the bottom spoon. Then liquid is added at the end—cream, half-and-half, or sometimes more liquid egg. All these steps create eggs that are almost like a custard—very creamy and moist.

CUISINE SCRAMBLED EGGS

1 Beat four large eggs back and forth with a fork until whites and yolks are well-combined. Then there won't be flecks of egg white once they're cooked.

2 In a 10" nonstick frying pan, melt 2 T. of unsalted butter over med. heat until foamy. Add eggs. A nonstick pan is a must—eggs stick without it.

3 Let eggs set for 30 seconds. Then, using a heat-proof spatula, pull the eggs away from the edge of the pan. Don't stir—it will break up the curds.

4 Let eggs set again, then pull from another side. Continue pulling toward center of pan until almost all the liquid has formed into large curds.

5 While the eggs are still glistening, turn off the heat, and fold in about 1 T. of half & half. This stops the cooking and adds a creamy texture.

FRIED EGGS

Fried eggs are low-maintenance—slide them into a well-oiled pan, let them cook for a while, and they're done. But there still are certain things to be aware of so those fried eggs don't turn out like Frisbees.

Heat: This is another time heat can rear its ugly head. So, keep it on medium and take it slow. The higher the heat, the more likely the eggs will end up overbrowned and tough—or with those small craters or holes on the surface of the whites.

Fresh Eggs: Older eggs are fine for hard cooking and scrambling. But for frying, fresh eggs are a must.

Fresh eggs have a more compact white. That means the thick and thin albumen will spread and separate less when the eggs are added to the pan.

And, the yolk membrane (a yolk's "armor") is stronger in a fresh egg, so it's less likely to break when flipped.

Photograph: Scott Little, Food Styling: Janet Pittman

Pan Size and Egg Number: Think small for both the size of the pan and the number of eggs when frying. Use a smaller pan (about 8"), and fry only two eggs at a time. A smaller pan keeps the whites contained for compact-shaped eggs. And it's easier to turn over two eggs at a time rather than four—whether you're flipping them or using a spatula. **Ati**

FRYING EGGS

Coat pan with nonstick cooking spray. Melt 2 T. unsalted butter over medium heat until foamy. Crack egg into small bowl (in case shell pieces get in it), then add to pan. Tip pan to join whites (about 30 seconds), making "one," solid egg.

Sunny Side Up: Once the whites are almost completely opaque (about 3 minutes), cover pan with a lid. The lid traps steam and finishes cooking the eggs. After 3 more minutes, the whites are completely cooked but yolks are still soft.

Over Easy: Place eggs in pan, *see above.* When whites are almost opaque (about 3 minutes), they're ready to turn.

Don't be afraid of the flip—practice with dried beans (off the heat). Jerk the pan forward, tilting the front edge slightly upward, and flip the eggs with one quick motion. Let them cook for about 10 seconds, then flip them back over.

SPATULA OPTION
The eggs can also be flipped with a spatula. The trick is to coat it liberally with a nonstick spray so it will slide easily under the eggs.

Boneless LEG of LAMB

Quick! What's the first food that comes to mind when you think spring? No, not those goofy coconut lamb cakes made with the molds that never worked. It has

to be real lamb—more specifically, leg of lamb. Unfortunately, leg of lamb carries a little baggage. It *used* to have a reputation for having a gamey taste and smell. And it's also hard to carve out nice slices because the grain runs three different directions, making the slices ugly and sometimes tough.

Well, there's no more baggage. If you buy the right leg of lamb and prepare it correctly, it can approach the flavor of a pricey rack of lamb. Which brings up another reason to try leg of lamb. Besides good flavor, a leg costs about $3 a pound while a rack hits around $10—yikes!

Domestic or Imported Lamb: Just the word "imported" conjures up high quality. But the fact is, imported lamb (usually from New Zealand) has a stronger, gamier flavor than our milder domestic lamb. That's because imported lamb mostly eat grass while our domestic lamb diet is heavily supplemented with grain. When you have the choice, buy domestic.

Age: The best lamb is usually less than a year old. You'll see it referred to as "spring," "genuine," or just "lamb." Anything older than two years is classified as mutton and leans toward the tough, gamey side of lamb.

BONELESS LEG OF LAMB
(MAKES TWO 3-LB. LAMB ROASTS)
WORK TIME: 30–45 MINUTES
COOK TIME: 1¼ HOURS
BONE AND POUND:
1   8–9 lb. whole bone-in leg of lamb

FOR THE RUB—
CRUSH TOGETHER:
1   T. whole mustard seed
1   T. Herbes de Provence
      Salt and pepper to taste
1   T. garlic, minced
1   T. lemon zest, minced

ROLL AND TIE ROASTS, THEN
BROWN IN:
1   T. olive oil

NUTRITIONAL INFORMATION PER 2 SLICES WITH 3 T. MUSTARD SAUCE: CALORIES 507; TOTAL FAT 23(G); CALORIES FROM FAT 41%; SODIUM 219(MG); CARBOHYDRATES 6(G)

BONING A LEG OF LAMB

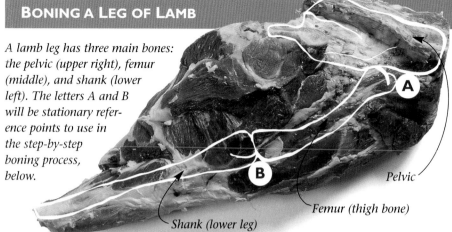

A lamb leg has three main bones: the pelvic (upper right), femur (middle), and shank (lower left). The letters A and B will be stationary reference points to use in the step-by-step boning process, below.

Shank (lower leg)

Femur (thigh bone)

Pelvic

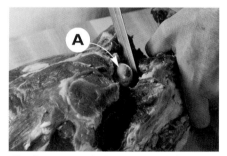

1 Remove most of the fat. Even in domestic lamb, the fat can carry a strong smell and flavor. Then remove the fell. (It's like the silverskin on beef.)

WHAT TO BUY

Boning any type of meat is more time-consuming than it is hard. Leg of lamb is no exception. But before you can bone it, you have to buy it.

Fresh or Frozen: Fresh lamb used to be a speciality item that made a much-ballyhooed appearance in the spring. Oh sure, you could always find it frozen, but now, it's available fresh year round. And that's good.

Fresh is always better than frozen because freezing creates ice crystals in the muscle structure. This causes the meat to weaken, leaving a muscle that's not as firm as it was originally. It's kind of like a street in winter. When it freezes, the street tends to heave in places and is never as structurally sound as before.

The ice crystals also leave water in the muscle when they melt, which can dilute the flavor a bit. I always recommend buying fresh lamb.

Bone-in or BRT: Legs of lamb either have the bones in or removed. Usually, when the bones are removed, the leg is rolled and tied. This is called BRT (boned, rolled, and tied).

BRT is a convenient way to buy lamb, but there's one problem—it's probably been overprocessed. In other words, it's been handled more times than a dollar bill at a state fair.

If you want the best from a leg of lamb, bone it yourself like I'm doing in Steps 1–7. Or better yet, have your butcher bone it for you (he'll do it for free). This way, you'll get a fresh piece of meat and still only pay leg prices.

2 Cut around the pelvic bone to remove it. Even if you are going to cook a whole bone-in leg of lamb, the pelvic bone needs to come off.

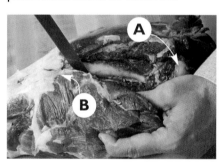

4 Begin cutting along one side of the femur. Use small, shallow strokes to cleanly expose the large bone. Don't cut through the other side.

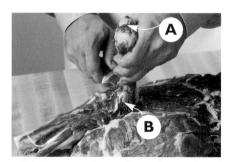

6 Now cut along the other side of the bones. Use small strokes to cut underneath both bones to free them. Lift the bones up as you go.

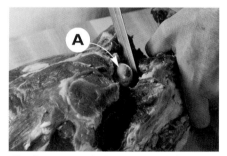

3 Cut around the socket (A) of the femur (thigh bone). The socket can't be popped out by hand, so use a knife to cut around the joint.

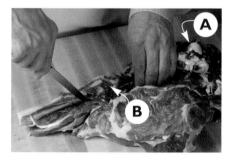

5 At the knee joint (B), cut along the shank (lower leg). Since the meat from this area will be used for stew or stock, you don't have to be as careful.

7 Remove the large hunk of fat found between top and bottom rounds, *see Page 13*. The fat contains a gland that can turn bitter when cooked.

CUTS OF MEAT

❶ TOP SIRLOIN: Considered to be the most flavorful. It has the most amount of fat on the leg and is the most tender.

❷ KNUCKLE: Sits under the top sirloin. Called the knuckle because it rests on the knee joint.

❸ BOTTOM ROUND: Center section of the butterflied leg. The bottom round is made up of two sections—the eye of round and the flat. Both are very lean and on the tough side.

❹ TOP ROUND: Easiest part to identify. It's the largest muscle and fairly lean. Despite its lack of marbling, this is still a tender cut in younger lamb.

❺ SHANK: Found on the lower part of the leg. The shank meat is very flavorful, but it's a tough cut because of all of the connective tissue. Use it as stew meat.

DEALING WITH A BONELESS LEG

If you take a look at the boned-out leg of lamb above, you can see the inherent problems of cooking and carving a whole leg.

To begin with, there are five cuts of meat within one leg: top sirloin, knuckle, bottom round, top round, and shank. You might recall cooking some of these different cuts in beef and remember that some were more tender than others. That's because some cuts have more marbling (fat within the muscle) and are used less than more muscular cuts.

Just for fun, feel your own leg. The top and outside of your thigh is much tougher and firmer than the inside of your thigh. A leg of lamb has the same differences in texture and muscle.

To overcome these differences, it's best to make two roasts from one leg, grouping the same textures together. Both are prepared the same way and are easier to cook and carve than one big roast. Refer to the diagram above.

To cut the leg in half, first remove the shank (section 5). Then, cut the leg in half through the bottom round (section 3). Now, follow Steps 2 and 3 for leveling and pounding.

LEVELING THE BONELESS ROASTS

1 Cut the leg into three pieces.
First, cut off the tough shank meat (section 5). Then cut the remaining leg in half to make two roasts. I think one large roast made from the entire leg is just too big and hard to carve. The first roast will be made with the fatter (more tender) top sirloin and the other from the leaner (tougher) top round.

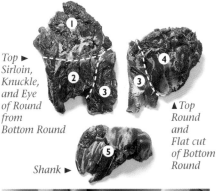

Top ► Sirloin, Knuckle, and Eye of Round from Bottom Round

▲ Top Round and Flat cut of Bottom Round

Shank ►

2 Trimming out the roasts.
Before rolling each roast, thick portions must be trimmed so it can be pounded to a consistent thickness. Cut the thick section of each roast to form a flap, but don't cut the flap off. You want it connected. Notice the absence of fat in the photo. This is the top round.

3 Level the roast by pounding.
Pounding the leg meat helps level the roast for even cooking, and it also breaks down some of the tougher pieces. Put a piece of plastic wrap over the meat to prevent splattering. Then with the flat side of a mallet, pound meat until it's one inch thick all over.

GETTING A GOOD ROLL

Now that each roast has been leveled, it's time to season the meat, roll it up, and then tie it to get it ready for roasting. I'll only talk about one roast here, but you'll do the same with both.

Seasoning: This roast is seasoned in stages. With the roast spread out (pounded side up), season the meat. First, season the side of the meat that will be rolled inside. Then, after browning, season the outside of the roast. This keeps the delicate herbs, garlic, and zest from burning.

Rolling and Tying: Once the inside of the meat is seasoned, roll it up like a jelly roll. Don't fret if the cylinder isn't perfect. Tying helps, but cooking really improves the shape by tightening up the muscle tissue.

Now, tie the rolled lamb. Use thick cotton string. Cotton doesn't burn in the oven, and if it's thick, it won't cut through the meat. Most grocery stores carry cotton string, but if you have trouble finding it, ask your butcher. He'll either give you some or know where to find it.

Start by tying the roast around its middle with individual strings spaced about an inch apart, as in Step 6. Then, tie a long string around twice from end to end. Notice in Step 7 that the long string loops around each short string. This makes the roast very secure for browning and roasting.

Browning: Brown the meat before roasting for a nice color—it's not in the oven long enough to develop deep color. Use just a little oil because any fat left on the lamb will render (melt).

Try to brown the roast on all sides. Browning won't seal in the juices—it's just for color and flavor. It's also a great start for the sauce on Page 15.

ROLLING, TYING, AND ROASTING LEG OF LAMB

4 With the pounded side facing up, sprinkle with half the herb mixture, garlic, and zest. After roast is browned in Step 8, season the exterior. This prevents the herbs from burning.

5 Roll the lamb up tightly—like a jelly roll. Since the meat isn't shaped like a perfect rectangle, pieces may stick out from the sides. Just tuck them in as you go and keep rolling.

6 To tie roast, first secure it around the middle with short individual strings. Space them about an inch apart. Use thick cotton string so it won't burn in the oven or cut into the meat.

7 Tie the roast securely by running a long string lengthwise (from end to end) around it. The long string will go around the roast twice and loop around each of the short individual strings.

8 Brown roast in oil over medium-high heat. Be sure all sides are brown—even the ends. Then coat the exterior with remaining seasonings. Roast lamb at 400° (rack is optional) until internal temperature reads 130° for rare (50–55 minutes). For medium doneness, internal temperature should hit 145°. Remove from oven and tent with foil 10 minutes before slicing.

MAKING A LAMB STOCK

To make lamb stock, cut the lamb bones (to expose marrow). Your butcher can do this. Then brown them in a 450° oven. This gives stock color and flavor. Put bones in a stockpot with cold water, celery, and onions. *Simmer* for 3–8 hours, skimming every hour to remove impurities. The longer the stock simmers, the more gelatin is extracted, making a thick, rich, flavorful stock.

LAMB STOCK

(MAKES 4 CUPS)
COOK TIME: 3–8 HOURS
ROAST LAMB BONES UNTIL DARK BROWN; ADD:

- 8 cups cold water
- 3 celery stalks, chopped
- 2 yellow onions, quartered
  Salt and pepper

SIMMER FOR 3–8 HOURS; STRAIN.

MUSTARD SAUCE

(MAKES 1½ CUPS)
WORK TIME: 10 MINUTES
COOK TIME: 10 MINUTES
SAUTE IN PAN DRIPPINGS:
½ cup shallots, finely chopped
ADD:
1 T. garlic, minced
1 t. tomato paste
ADD AND REDUCE:
1 cup dry red wine
ADD AND SIMMER:
1½ cups lamb or beef stock
¼ cup Dijon mustard
1 sprig fresh thyme
STRAIN; WHISK IN:
1 T. unsalted butter
SEASON WITH:
 Salt and pepper to taste

REDUCTION SAUCE

A reduction, in cooking, means a liquid (usually a stock or wine) is boiled until the volume is reduced through evaporation. This process intensifies the flavor and thickens. A reduction is the type of sauce made here.

Actually, this is a fairly quick sauce to make and can be completed while the lamb rests for 10 minutes. It may not look like a lot when you're finished but don't worry—you're making an intensely flavored sauce, not a big bowl of gravy. A little goes a long way.

For a reduction sauce, there are three main components: drippings, wine, and stock. That's not to say there aren't other ingredients, but these make up the body of the sauce.

To make the sauce, saute shallots in the pan that the lamb roasted in. This pan holds the very flavorful (and dark) drippings from the meat. Then, add wine to deglaze the pan (loosen all those browned bits of food stuck to the bottom). Be sure to scrape the pan to get all the flavor.

Reduce this wine until it's almost totally evaporated. Now, add the lamb stock and seasonings. Cook over a fairly high heat until the liquid is *reduced* by half. You can see how the sauce is beginning to thicken a bit.

Finally, strain it to remove shallots and herbs. Warm the sauce slightly before serving, and stir in butter to help thicken and flavor the sauce. **Ai**

9 For the Mustard Sauce, saute the shallots in the same pan the lamb was roasted in. Cook until translucent. Add the garlic and tomato paste. The paste needs to cook for a few minutes to add color and flavor. Make sure to stir the paste constantly.

10 Once the paste has cooked and starts to turn a deep maroon, add the red wine. Boil this until almost all the wine has evaporated (reduced). Notice in the photo how deep red the reduction is. Also take a look at how much liquid is left—hardly any.

11 Add the stock, mustard, and fresh thyme. Reduce this mixture by half over medium heat. Strain sauce and return it to the pan. Whisk in the butter. This adds flavor as well as body and gives the sauce a little sheen. The sauce will also naturally thicken as it sits and cools. Season to taste with salt and pepper.

▲*To serve the leg of lamb roast, remove all the strings. Then slice using a sharp knife. It's not necessary to use a carving knife because the roast is so small—long strokes aren't needed. Slice only what you need. Leave the remaining roast whole so it stays warm and doesn't dry out.*

▲*For presentation, arrange a row of slices with the remaining whole portion of the roast. You can add sauteed mushrooms and pearl onions along side for a garnish that can also be eaten, see Tips Page 5. Now, drizzle the Mustard Sauce over the lamb to make the meat glisten.*

Photograph: Scott Little, Food Styling: Janet Pittman

MAIL-ORDER SPIRAL-SLICED HAMS

There are hams—and then there are hams. The difference between the two lies in the process used to make them. And what you end up with is either a run-of-the-mill ham or one of these flavor-packed, mail-order, spiral-sliced hams.

Ham 101: Hams start out from a pig's hind legs, and come either whole or in halves. The bottom half is called the shank end, and the top half is called the butt end. The hams are then trimmed of all but a small layer of fat, and most are brined and smoked. It's brining and smoking that give hams their flavor: smoky, sweet, or salty.

Brining is the first step in flavoring a ham and is also what gives the ham its pink color. It's typically done with a salt cure—a combination of salt, water, spices, and often a sweetener (usually honey or brown sugar). The ham is either injected with the brine or it takes a bath in it.

The second step in flavoring the ham is smoking, but not all hams are smoked. That's too bad, because smoking is what separates "okay" hams from the ones listed here—it adds an additional flavor dimension.

The hams are smoked over burning embers. The type of wood used creates different flavors (hickory and applewood are common). Some hams are only smoked for a couple of hours, but others are smoked for up to 30 hours. Bottom line: The longer a ham's smoked, the more flavor it has.

Smoking also cooks the hams to an internal temperature of 150–160°. That means they just need to be heated through before serving.

The Price: The fact is, a lot of these hams aren't cheap, especially when shipping and handling are factored in. So how can ordering one be justified? Hands down, these mail-order hams offered a more complex flavor (smoky, sweet, *and* salty) than grocery store hams. They just couldn't compare—except one, *see Mail-Order Alternative, below.*

The Picks: Here are some of the stand-out hams based on their overall flavors. For a sweet-tasting ham, check out the HoneyBaked. For an applewood-smoked flavor, try Nueske's. And for a traditional ham flavor (smoky, sweet, and salty), Burger's Smokehouse is a great choice. **A**H

MAIL-ORDER ALTERNATIVE: A Great Grocery Store Ham

Spiral-sliced grocery store hams can be underwhelming, to say the least. But then there's Cook's. Just take a look at this one, *right*. It has a nice uniform shape, a beautiful color, and a really pleasant ham flavor. It was right up there in quality and flavor with the mail-order hams. And at about $14–$20 for an 8–10 pound ham, it's a great ham for the price.

Cook's
Available at A&P, Cub Foods, Dominicks, Kroger, and more.

Mail-Order Company	Comments	Price

Smoky

Nueske's
Rural Route 2, P.O. Box D
Wittenberg, WI 54499-0904
(800) 392-2266
Item #521R

By far the smokiest ham, and a real favorite because of that. But it also had a mild sweetness—like apples. It had a uniform shape and a beautiful amber-colored exterior. Moist and tender.

Ham (7–8 lb.):
$59.50
S&H: $10.95
(2nd-day
FedEx)

Harry & David
P.O. Box 712
Medford, OR 97501
(800) 547-3033
Item # 346J

This ham had a mild, traditional ham taste—mostly smoke and salt. It was moist, but wasn't the most attractive ham tested. The price was a little high—the second-most expensive ham ordered.

Ham
(7¹/₂–8¹/₂ lb.):
$59.95
S&H: $17.95
(7-day USPS)

Smithfield Princess Anne
P.O. Box 487
Smithfield, VA 23431-0487
(800) 628-2242
Item #1006

The Princess Anne was moist, and its flavor had a good combo of smoke and salt. The spiral slices were even and held together off the bone. Second-day air shipping is required west of the Mississippi River.

Ham (7–8 lb.):
$48
S&H: $13
(2nd-day
air required)

Sweet

**Basse's Choice
Virginia Ham**
P.O. Box 1
Smithfield, VA 23431
(800) 292-2773
Item #212

Basse's Choice was a fairly sweet ham, but it also had a slightly smoky flavor, with subtle cinnamon tones. It had a beautiful overall color. Second-day air shipping is required west of the Mississippi River.

Ham (5–7 lb.):
$34
S&H: $20.75
(2nd-day
air required)

Omaha Steaks
4400 S. 96th Street
Omaha, NE 68127
(800) 228-9872
Item #714

Omaha Steaks offers a really good-looking ham for a moderate price. Its evenly browned exterior, rosy interior, and uniform shape set you up for the great flavor balance of sweetness and salt.

Ham (7–8 lb.):
$50.40
S&H: $12.99
(UPS ground)

HoneyBaked Ham Co.
P.O. Box 965
Holland, OH 43528
(800) 892-4267
Item #09

HoneyBaked was a favorite sweet ham. But it also had a definite smoky flavor. It was very moist and tender, and the slices were thin and uniform. This ham was, however, the most expensive.

Ham (7–9 lb.):
$65
S&H: $18
(UPS ground)

Salty

Burger's Smokehouse
32819 Highway 87
California, MO 65018
(800) 624-5426
Item #H256

Burger's offered the best overall ham taste. This ham had a well-rounded flavor—the perfect balance of sweet and smoky, and all the saltiness you'd expect from a ham. Plus, it's a bargain to boot!

Ham (5–7 lb.):
$47.95
S&H: Included
(2nd-day UPS)

Hickory Farms
1505 Holland Road
Maumee, OH 43537
(800) 442-5671
Item #011070

The Hickory Farms ham tasted mostly of salt, with a bit of smoke. The interior was fairly moist (despite its slightly dry appearance). The meat was a pretty firm. The spiral slices were thick and apparent.

Ham (7–9 lb.):
$39.99
S&H: $15.95
(2nd-day UPS)

WHAT'S HAPPENING IN FOOD?

▲ TRIED-AND-TRUE SLOTTED SPATULA

Sometimes it's good to give a nod to an old standby. This slotted fish spatula isn't new, but its thin, long, flexible, and strong blade make it worthy of mention.

The spatula's design makes it perfect for lifting a delicate piece of fish out of a saute pan. It's thin enough to easily slide under the fish, but still has enough heft to transfer it to a plate, barely disturbing a flake.

It's also great for scooping fragile poached eggs out of a saucepan of simmering water.

These spatulas are sold in most kitchen stores. Or call **Bridge Kitchenware** at **800-274-3435**, **#APLX** ($18.95), to order.

IN THE KITCHEN WITH JACQUES AND JULIA ►

The new cookbook by Julia Child and Jacques Pepin, *Julia and Jacques Cooking at Home* (Alfred A. Knopf Inc., 1999, $40), pulls together the considerable knowledge of two old friends.

The book (a companion to the pair's PBS cooking series) follows an entertaining tit-for-tat type format—Julia gives her suggestions for a recipe and Jacques counters with his own. You can almost hear them bantering back and forth!

But the book's not just fun—it's practical, too. Julia and Jacques walk you through great classic French recipes with beautiful color step-by-step photos.

TASTY TREATS ►

There are cookies, and then there are **Carr's Chococcines**. On their own, these cookies are delicious—they nearly melt in your mouth. That's no surprise. They're mostly sweet meringue, with a creamy praline nougat center and a chocolate coating. For an easy dessert that's over the top, try them as part of an ice cream sundae (like the photo at right).

Look for Carr's Chococcines in select grocery stores nationwide. Or check out **www.keebler.com**.

◄ CHOCOLATE-DIPPED STRAWBERRIES BY MAIL

Forget about chocolate bunnies, marshmallow eggs, and green cellophane grass in Easter baskets. How about chocolate-dipped strawberries in a gold, velvet-lined box instead? **Shari's Berries**, out of Sacramento, CA, can deliver—literally.

For example, one gold box cradles a dozen juicy, surprisingly fresh, chocolate-covered strawberries—all for about $38. And there's no need to worry about the strawberries not being in great shape when you receive them. They're shipped overnight, anywhere in the nation, so they're at their best. Call **877-237-7437** (toll free) to order.

POTATO GRATINS

Photograph: Scott Little, Food Styling: Janet Pittman

You've read Cuisine *cover to cover and have decided that both the spiral-sliced ham and roast lamb are too good to pass up. But what would you serve with them?*

I've made it easy for you—potato gratin is perfect with both! A gratin is any dish topped with cheese or bread crumbs, then baked until brown and crisp on top. It's the same here, but with twists. Here's what is unique.

Cooking Method: Traditionally, potatoes for gratins are sliced paper-thin, layered in a casserole dish with cream, and baked. The problem is the outside cooks faster than the interior.

But the cooking method used here is different. These gratins start by simmering thicker slices of potatoes on top of the stove before baking. This way, they cook evenly *and* are infused with flavor from the milk, *Page 20.*

Flourless: There's no flour in these gratins to thicken the sauce. That's because flour tends to clump and get pasty, especially if you use too much.

Instead, take full advantage of the natural starch in the potatoes. That initial simmering helps release some of the starch into the sauce.

Cheeses: Cheese probably makes the biggest flavor impact on gratins. By simply using different ones, you totally change the way a gratin tastes.

Certain cheeses work better than others. A soft or semisoft cheese with a high fat and moisture content, like Swiss, is good because it melts and browns well—a must for gratins.

Gruyere [gree-YAIR] is a mild Swiss cheese that's a natural in a gratin. But if you can't find it, Emmental or Jarlsberg work well too.

Now, don't limit yourself to Swiss cheeses. Softer cheeses like blue and goat are also good—they're both used in the two gratin variations on Page 21. And don't forget about cheddar.

Dry cheeses, like Parmesan, tend to melt poorly because they're lower in fat and moisture. You'll want to avoid using a dry cheese on its own. But that doesn't mean you should rule it out. Just combine it with a softer one so it melts into the sauce better.

Bread Crumbs: Little things make a big difference—like using fresh bread crumbs for the topping instead of dry ones from the store. Fresh crumbs create a lighter, crispier crust that won't leave a "sandy" texture in your mouth. That's what we'll use in these recipes.

MAKING INFUSED MILK

Good cooks are always on the lookout for ways to kick up the flavor of a dish. One way to do this is to make an infusion. In cooking, this is when you extract a flavor from an ingredient, like an herb, by steeping it in a liquid that's usually hot. If you've made tea, you've made an infusion. And infusing the cream and milk for these gratins is an effective way to enhance flavor without a lot of hassle.

The process is easy. Herbs and spices go into a "tea bag," or sachet, which is then put into the liquid. This way, you don't have to strain them—just remove the sachet.

To make the sachet, fill a square of cheesecloth with herbs and spices, then tie it with kitchen twine, as in the photo below. If you don't have cheesecloth, don't despair. A paper coffee filter works just as well.

When simmering the milk, don't let it boil over. As soon as bubbles start forming along the edge, turn off the heat and let it steep at least ten minutes, up to 30 for the most flavor.

INFUSED MILK *(MAKES 3 CUPS)*
COOK/STEEP TIME: 20 MINUTES
PREPARE SACHET:
10 whole black peppercorns
2   cloves garlic, smashed
2   bay leaves
1   sprig fresh rosemary
SIMMER SACHET IN:
1½ cups heavy cream
1½ cups whole milk
1   t. salt
⅛   t. cayenne pepper

▲*Prepare sachet. Then, in a large, heavy saucepan, combine cream, milk, salt, and cayenne. Add sachet and bring to a simmer. Turn off heat and steep 10 minutes. Remove sachet before using infused milk.*

POTATO-GRUYERE GRATIN

(MAKES ABOUT 6 CUPS)
WORK TIME: 20 MINUTES
BAKE TIME: 40–50 MINUTES
SIMMER IN INFUSED MILK, BELOW:
6   cups russet potatoes, peeled, sliced (2 lbs; 6–7 potatoes)
LAYER POTATOES WITH:
1   cup Gruyere cheese, shredded
POUR MILK OVER POTATOES;
SPRINKLE WITH:
    Bread crumb mixture, *see right*

BREAD CRUMBS
(MAKES ABOUT 1 CUP)
COMBINE IN
FOOD PROCESSOR:
3   slices fresh white bread, torn in large pieces
3   T. unsalted butter, melted
¼   t. salt

▲*Combine all ingredients in a food processor. Blend until bread is ground and butter is incorporated.*

1 Preheat oven to 375°. Butter a 2" deep, 1½-quart baking dish. Infuse milk, *see left*. As milk steeps, peel and slice potatoes ¼" thick.

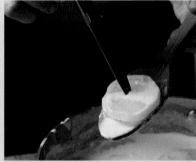

2 Remove sachet from milk; add potatoes. Simmer over med. heat until just soft, 15 min. They should resist slightly when pierced.

3 Use a slotted spoon to layer half the potatoes into the prepared dish. Sprinkle potatoes with half the cheese, then top with remaining potatoes and cheese.

4 Pour milk over potatoes and sprinkle with bread crumbs, see *above*. Place dish on a baking sheet (to catch any overflow) and bake 40–50 min., until brown and bubbly.

THE STORY BEHIND SIMPLE

One of the best things about potato gratins is how simple they are, especially in terms of ingredients. But if you look closely, you'll see there's more going on than you might think.

The two big players in all of these gratins are the potatoes and the sauce. And there are important points to know about each of them.

Potatoes: It really matters what variety of potato you use. But flavor isn't the issue. This is about structure.

All potatoes are made of starch and water. The more starch a potato has, the more liquid it can absorb. And a low water content means it doesn't release much moisture when cooked.

That's critical to a gratin because of the sauce. Starchy potatoes (like russets) are great in gratins because they're able to absorb more of the flavorful infused sauce. And since russets are dry, they don't release much water into the sauce and thin it out.

Waxy potatoes, like reds, are not a good choice for a gratin. They're great for things like salads because they hold their shape well during cooking. But because they're low in starch, they just can't soak up the sauce. And then the sauce is too runny.

Sauce: The sauce for these gratins is made of heavy cream and milk. So why not just use all half-and-half? Here is a very simplified explanation.

Milk products have varying levels of fat (cream, half-and-half, whole, 2%, skim). And a higher fat content means the product will be less likely to curdle when it's cooked.

Curdling occurs when milk proteins join together, either by adding an acid (like lemon juice) or heat. It's like scrambled eggs—the proteins start to solidify as they're heated.

But fat molecules tend to block proteins and prevent them from joining. Heavy cream has a fat content of up to 40%; half-and-half about 12%. But when you combine heavy cream with whole milk (at 4% milkfat), the fat content is still higher than it is if you used straight half-and-half. So, the milk and cream ratio is less likely to curdle. This is a round-about way of saying "don't take a short cut here." *An*

ROOT VEGETABLE GRATIN

(MAKES ABOUT 5 CUPS)
WORK TIME: 20 MINUTES
BAKE TIME: 40–50 MINUTES
SIMMER IN INFUSED MILK, SEE LEFT:
2   cups russet potatoes, peeled, sliced (about ½ lb., 3–4 potatoes)
1   cup sweet potato, peeled, sliced
1   cup turnip, peeled, sliced
1   cup parsnip, peeled, sliced
LAYER VEGETABLES WITH:
½   cup mild goat cheese (4 oz.)
TOP WITH:
    Bread crumb mixture, *see left*

▲ *The root vegetables cook slightly faster than the potatoes so slice them a little thicker, about ½". This ensures that they won't get mushy before the potatoes are done. Simmer potatoes and vegetables in milk, then assemble and bake the gratin as on Page 20.*

BACON AND BLUE CHEESE GRATIN

1 In a large saucepan, saute bacon over medium heat until crisp, 8–10 minutes. Drain bacon on a paper towel-lined plate; set aside. Pour off all but 1 T. fat and saute shallots until soft, 8–10 minutes.

(MAKES ABOUT 6 CUPS)
WORK TIME: 30 MINUTES
BAKE TIME: 40–50 MINUTES
SAUTE IN LARGE SAUCEPAN:
3   strips thick-sliced bacon, chopped
SAUTE IN 1 T. BACON FAT:
¼   cup minced shallots
ADD, SIMMER, AND STEEP:
    Infused Milk ingredients, *see left*
REMOVE SACHET, THEN ADD:
6   cups russet potatoes, peeled, sliced (2 lbs., 6–7 potatoes)
    Reserved bacon pieces
LAYER POTATOES IN DISH WITH:
⅓   cup blue cheese, crumbled (3 oz.)
TOP WITH:
    Bread crumb mixture, *see left*

2 Add all ingredients for Infused Milk; simmer and steep as on Page 20. Remove sachet; add potatoes and reserved bacon pieces, then simmer for 15 minutes.

3 Arrange a layer of potatoes in a prepared dish. Dot with half the blue cheese; top with remaining potatoes and cheese. Sprinkle with crumbs and bake as on Page 20.

Indian-Style CURRY

Most of us have had Indian curry one of two ways—really good or really bad. If you've had one in the bad category, that's a bummer. Good curry is a great dish,

both to prepare and to eat. So what makes curry *good*? It's all in the spices.

Indian curry centers around a mix of interesting spices. When used properly, they produce a dish with bright, fresh flavor—no thick, yellow sauce with so much spice you break a sweat.

But the true test to good curry is in the leftovers. If you get up early to eat last night's curry for breakfast, you know it's a winner. And you can with this one. *If* there are leftovers.

What's the secret? No commercial curry powder—you make your own blend. Then serve it with flavorful condiments for a great Indian meal.

What is Curry? Good question. Some people think curry is a dish. Others think it's a flavor. So which one is it? As it turns out, both.

The word curry comes from the Indian word *kari*, meaning sauce. That's because they're prepared like a stew (braised in liquid). A curry can be made with almost any meat, fish, or vegetables, but there's *always* sauce.

That "curry" flavor comes from a blend of spices most people associate with commercial curry powder—a little spicy, sort of sweet, always yellow. And if you've had some bad curry, you know what I'm talking about.

Curry Powder: You can thank the British for curry powder. Colonists to India developed it so they could make Indian-flavored dishes in England. With all the spices in one jar, it was convenient to transport and use.

But Indian cooks wouldn't use purchased curry powder any more than Italian cooks would use a jar of spaghetti sauce. It goes against the very spirit of their cuisine. Instead, Indian cooks grind spices to make their own blends, called *masalas*.

Masalas: The difference between masalas and purchased powder isn't about ingredients. It's freshness.

The minute any spice is ground, the flavor starts to fade. Who knows how long curry powder has been on the grocery store shelf? Making the masalas is the best way to be sure the curry will have the freshest flavor.

INDIAN MEAL PRIMER

The scope of an Indian meal can be overwhelming. Here's a rundown of foods you may see.

Rice: Indian cuisine relies heavily on rice. Meat and fish are expensive, so rice is used to bulk up almost every meal—like potatoes or pasta.

The most common variety of rice in India is basmati [bahs-MAH-tee]. It means "queen of fragrance" and got its name because it smells *really* great while it cooks—like popcorn.

Bread: It's common in India to serve rice and bread at the same meal. It sounds like carbo-loading, but it's not. Indians eat with their hands and use breads to scoop up foods, which is especially helpful when the dishes have a lot of sauce.

Naan [NAHN] is a popular Indian bread similar to pizza crust. It makes a great scoop because it's thin and flexible. Pita bread is similar to naan and makes a good substitute.

Condiments: Like ketchup and pickle relish, condiments (called chutneys) are served with Indian meals for added flavor, texture, and spice. They fall into three general categories.

Fruits/Vegetables: These are simple salads of raw fruits or vegetables tossed with citrus juice or plain yogurt, and seasonings. They're often eaten to cool down a spicy curry dish.

Herbs: These chutneys are similar to Italian pestos and are made from flavorful herbs, like cilantro or mint. Garlic, ginger, and chiles are added for kick.

Preserves: These are mixtures of dried or fresh fruits or vegetables cooked with sugar, vinegar, and spices. They're usually thick and spreadable, like jam, and can be spicy or mild.

Major Grey's is probably the most well-known brand and is okay to use in a pinch. But you might try making your own sometime, see *Page 29*. The procedure is simple and it tastes a heck of a lot better.

Making Masalas: This curry uses two types of masalas—dry (a powder) and wet (a puree). Don't worry. They don't require much work, and you'll be rewarded with a great-tasting dish.

Dry: The best place to buy whole spices for the dry masala is at a natural food store. They often sell spices in bulk and that generally means they're fresher. Plus, they'll be less expensive because you can buy only the amount you need.

If making a dry masala seems a little intimidating, take a look at Pages 24–25. Some of the common spices used in Indian cooking are right there. And nothing is very exotic or strange.

Wet: This curry gets its "heat" from the chiles in the wet masala. It's not scorching hot, so if you don't like super-spicy food, don't worry. The garlic and ginger help keep the chiles balanced and add flavor of their own.

Serranos are similar to the chiles used in India, but if you can't find them, jalapenos will work. They're larger, so you won't need as many.

Other Ingredients: If you're new to Indian curry, this is a great recipe to get you started. Except for some spices, you don't need unusual ingredients. Everything is accessible and available—a bonus when you eat *and* cook something for the first time.

You can use any meat you'd like, but my favorite for this curry is boneless, skinless chicken thighs. They're flavorful and have more fat than breast meat so they won't dry out during long simmering.

The Big Picture: But don't stop with the curry. Take a look at the photo above. The rice and condiments are important elements to an Indian meal—you'd be selling yourself short if you left them out. And besides adding flavor and texture contrasts, they make the whole meal fun to eat and share.

Not sure how to serve all this new food? No problem. I'll show you what to do on Page 29.

Spices are such a big deal in India that they're traded as a commodity, like gold. And these cooks know how to take full advantage of their flavor.

The most important thing Indians do is toast the spices before grinding. This draws out the essential oils and gets rid of "raw," bitter flavors. So if commercial curry powders taste harsh, the spices probably weren't toasted.

But Indian cooks also know that the bright flavors of spices don't last forever. So store whole and ground spices in a cool, dark place—not the spice rack above the stove. And no longer than six to nine months.

CARDAMOM PODS

I'll be up front with you—cardamom is not a user-friendly spice. Getting those tiny, black seeds out of their pods takes a little time, *see photo inset, right*. But it's worth working harder for the good stuff. You won't believe how much better they taste compared to what's already ground.

Don't worry, it doesn't take long. Each pod holds 8–12 seeds, and it only takes about 20 pods to make a teaspoon.

▲ *Split whole pods by pressing them with the side of a chef's knife (as with pitting olives). Tear the pod open and remove the seeds. Discard the pods.*

FENUGREEK SEEDS

These small, brownish-yellow seeds are actually a type of bean. But because of their strong flavor and scent, they're used like a spice. But sparingly. Fenugreek [FEHN-yoo-greek] is quite bitter in its raw state, but gets sweeter after it's been toasted. In fact, smell the spices as you're toasting them for the dry masala—does it remind you of caramel or maple syrup? It's the fenugreek you smell. And that's why fenugreek is often used to make artificial maple flavorings. It's also what gives commercial curry powders their distinctive curry scent.

CUMIN SEEDS

Cumin [KOO-mihn] is probably the most important and frequently used spice in Indian cooking, but it's also very common to Mexican, Southwestern, and Middle Eastern cuisines.

Cumin has a long history outside the kitchen too. Ancient Egyptians used it to mummify their pharaohs. And some Middle Eastern cultures make a paste of cumin, pepper, and honey to use as an aphrodisiac.

The spice has a distinctive aroma that can take some getting used to. But don't let that turn you off. Its flavor is a key element to every curry. Toasting brings out a nutty quality in the seeds, mellowing them out.

DRIED CHILE PEPPERS

As with Mexican cooking, dried chiles are an important part of Indian cuisine. They're used both for spicy heat and to bring out other flavors (just like salt).

The trick with chile peppers is knowing when to say when. This curry recipe calls for two chiles, but if you want more heat, go ahead and add another one. And if you want a milder curry, just cut back on one. Any small, red variety of chile pepper will work in this recipe. Mexican markets carry them, as do most grocery stores. But you can also substitute ¹/₂ teaspoon crushed red pepper flakes for each chile.

CINNAMON STICKS

Cinnamon sticks are the dried bark of a tropical evergreen tree. It's harvested during the rainy season when it's more pliable. Then, as it dries, the bark curls into tubes which are cut into sticks or ground.

Although we tend to think of cinnamon primarily as a dessert flavoring, Indian cooks never use it in sweet preparations. Instead, the sticks are fried in oil to infuse it with flavor. Ground cinnamon is also used in some spice blends.

FENNEL SEEDS

If you go to Indian restaurants, you'll often see a small dish of fennel seeds near the door. Take some to nibble on the way home—they're a great breath freshener and aid in digestion.

Fennel seeds are greenish-brown and look a little bit like cumin seeds. They have the same mild licorice flavor as fennel bulb, but come from common fennel, not the bulb vegetable, *see Issue 19, Jan/Feb 2000*. You've probably seen them used to season Italian foods and sausage.

DRY MASALA

(MAKES ABOUT ¼ CUP)
COOK/WORK TIME: 10 MINUTES
TOAST IN DRY SAUTE PAN:

2 T. cumin seeds
1 T. coriander seeds
2 t. fenugreek seeds
1 t. fennel seeds
1 t. cardamom seeds, *see box at left*

GRIND TOASTED SPICES, THEN ADD:

1 T. ground turmeric

Editor's Note: The finer you grind the spices, the more flavor you'll get from them. A mortar and pestle work, but a coffee grinder really pulverizes. Grinders aren't expensive, so buy one just for spices to avoid off flavors—in curry and coffee!

▲ *Place all the seeds in a dry saute pan and toast over medium-high heat, stirring frequently to prevent burning. When they begin to smell fragrant and turn brown, they're done.*

▲ *Transfer spices to a clean coffee grinder and process to a powder. Remove from grinder and mix in the turmeric. Covered, ground spices will keep for one month in a cool, dry place (just not over the stove!).*

GROUND TURMERIC

Turmeric is related to ginger, and used extensively in Indian cooking for its pungent flavor and coloring properties. Just a little gives curry (and prepared mustard) its distinctive hue. But beware—turmeric will stain everything it touches. Your wooden spoons will never be the same.

Turmeric is the only spice you'll use that's ground, not whole. Whole turmeric is hard to find because it must go through an extensive drying process before it can be used.

WHOLE CLOVES

Cloves are the nail-shaped dried buds of a tropical evergreen tree. These same buds you stud hams with are also important to Indian cooking. They're commonly fried whole (with cinnamon sticks), or toasted and ground.

Don't remember when you bought that jar of whole cloves in your cupboard? Try this test to see if their flavor is still strong. Drop a clove in a glass of water. If it floats vertically, it's still good. But if it sinks or lays on its side and floats horizontally, buy yourself a new jar.

BAY LEAVES

Indian cooks usually add leaves from the cassia tree to their curry dishes. But common bay leaves (sometimes called laurel) are readily available and make a fine substitute.

This is another herb from your cupboard that may need an overhaul. Take a whiff—if there's no scent, you need to buy another jar. Dried bay leaves can last up to a year if stored in a cool, dark place.

But you may be able to find fresh bay leaves with other fresh herbs in the produce section of the grocery store. Give them a try. They're stronger than dried so only use half as many.

CORIANDER SEEDS

Coriander [KOR-ee-an-der] is the seed of the cilantro plant, but it doesn't resemble the flavor of cilantro leaves at all. The seeds taste more like a combination of lemon and sage, and you'll really notice those characteristics when you toast them.

The tan-colored, round, ridged seeds are about the size of peppercorns. They're included in almost every Indian spice blend because they're less expensive than several other spices. But besides adding an important flavor element to Indian food, ground coriander is also used to thicken sauces (like filé powder in Cajun gumbo).

CARDAMOM PODS

After saffron and vanilla, cardamom is the third most expensive seasoning in the world. That's because the pods are hand-harvested from small shrubs (similar to saffron threads from crocus flowers). But don't worry—you don't need much to add a lot of flavor.

Buy cardamom in pods rather than ground. Even though the pods are a chore to work with, *see Page 24, opposite,* the seeds inside will give you the most bang for your buck in terms of flavor. Look for pods that are green, not white. White pods were green once, but have been chemically bleached, diminishing flavor along with the color.

Some Unique Techniques

Making Indian curry doesn't require learning any new cooking techniques. But there are some interesting things that deserve a little explanation.

Wet Masala: Remember the "trinity" in Cajun cooking—green pepper, celery, and onion? Well, think of the wet masala (a paste made from garlic, fresh ginger, and green chiles) as an Indian version of a trinity.

Most curry dishes contain at least two of those three elements, but there's no set formula. Each cook varies it to suit their taste—no garlic, more chiles, or add fresh coconut.

It's best to make the masala in a food processor. The blades can mince finer than you could if you cut everything by hand. Plus, like the dry masala, you release more oils (more flavor) if the masala is finely chopped.

Frying Spices: This is probably the most unique technique in Indian cooking. Frying spices might seem odd at first, but it's key to great flavor.

Actually, it's similar to sauteing garlic in oil. As the garlic sautes, it releases flavor into the oil. Then, whatever is cooked in the oil (like tomatoes) takes on the garlic flavor.

When you fry the spices, be sure to get the oil hot first (but not smoking). It should shimmer slightly on the surface of the pan.

Now, tilt the pan on the burner so a "pool" of oil forms at the edge, and fry the cinnamon and cloves in the pool of oil. Bubbles will form on the surface of the spices, then the stick of cinnamon will uncurl a little and the cloves will swell up.

Many Indian cooks will fry *all* the spices instead of dry toasting, as on Page 25. But some can burn—it's safer to toast delicate spices, like cumin.

CHICKEN CURRY WITH COCONUT RICE *(MAKES 6–8 CUPS)*

WORK TIME: 45 MINUTES
COOK TIME: 1 HOUR

BLEND FOR THE WET MASALA:

12 cloves garlic
1½" piece fresh ginger, peeled, sliced
2   fresh serrano chiles, stemmed and seeded

FRY IN ½ C. VEGETABLE OIL; REMOVE:

1   cinnamon stick
7–8 whole cloves

ADD AND SAUTE:

4   cups yellow onions, chopped
2   bay leaves
2   dried red chile peppers

ADD AND FRY:

2   T. dry masala, *see Page 25*
    Wet masala, *see above*

STIR IN; COVER AND COOK:

2   lb. boneless, skinless chicken thighs, cut into 2" pieces
2   cups Roma tomatoes, chopped
2   t. salt

FOR COCONUT RICE, SIMMER:

1½ cups basmati rice, rinsed
1½ cups water
1   can (14 oz.) unsweetened coconut milk
1   T. sugar
½   t. salt

OFF HEAT, STIR INTO CURRY:

3   cups spinach, cleaned and torn
1   T. dry masala, *see Page 25*

SERVE CURRY WITH COCONUT RICE AND CONDIMENTS (PAGES 28–29)

NUTRITIONAL INFORMATION PER 1 CUP CURRY WITH ½ CUP RICE: CALORIES 748; TOTAL FAT 40(G); CALORIES FROM FAT 48%; SODIUM 1136(MG); CARBOHYDRATES 61(G)

PREPARING WET MASALA AND FRYING SPICES

1 | All the ingredients for the curry can be prepared a few hours ahead of time, then refrigerated until you're ready to cook. To make the wet masala, process the garlic, ginger, and fresh chiles until finely minced. Then cut the onions, chicken, and tomatoes into fairly large pieces, as in the photo above. Larger pieces will hold up better during the long simmering time.

2 To fry spices, heat oil in large non-stick skillet over medium-high heat. Tilt pan to pool the oil at the edge; add cinnamon and cloves. Fry until cloves pop and cinnamon opens, about 5 min.

3 Remove spices with slotted spoon and discard. Add onions to oil and saute over medium heat until lightly browned, 10 minutes. Add bay leaves and dried chiles; continue cooking.

MAKING THE CURRY

Once you've fried the cinnamon and cloves, finishing the curry is pretty easy. But keep a few things in mind.

Sauteing Onions: The onions take a *long* time to cook—don't be surprised if 20 minutes go by before you add the masalas to the pan. But be patient. They need to get to a certain point before you proceed. Here's why.

The onions play a few different roles in curry. First, they are essential for flavoring. Second, as they fry, they caramelize and turn brown, which adds color (and more flavor) to the sauce. Just be careful not to get them too dark, or the curry will taste burnt.

Finally, as the onions cook, they break down and soften so much they almost melt into the sauce. In fact, Indian cooks use them to thicken sauces, similar to the way we use roux.

Adding the Masalas: Once the onions are browned, stir in both masalas and cook briefly, just until you can smell them. Don't forget, the spices in the dry masala have already been toasted. And the garlic in the wet masala can burn quickly. One or two minutes is all they need.

Cooking and Finishing: All that's left now is to add the chicken and tomatoes, then let the curry simmer.

Cover the pan during simmering. This helps draw the juices out of the chicken and tomatoes, which creates that sauce curries are known for. If the sauce seems watery after 30 minutes, remove the lid to reduce it more.

Finish the curry by adding the fresh spinach off heat. Then sprinkle in another tablespoon of the dry masala for one last hit of flavor!

Making Coconut Rice: Since there's so much flavor in this curry, plain rice is a fine accompaniment to the meal. But this Coconut Rice adds just the right amount of sweetness that goes perfectly with the spices.

Make an effort to find basmati rice for this—the flavor and texture are amazing. Jasmine is another aromatic rice that works well, but any other long-grain white rice is fine (*except* quick-cooking and converted styles).

Rinse the rice before cooking to remove excess starch and keep the grains separate. Then when it comes to a boil, stir it to loosen any rice stuck on the bottom, cover, then simmer. If the liquid isn't absorbed after 18–20 minutes, simmer 3–4 minutes more. Then let it stand off heat to evaporate excess moisture before fluffing.

FINISHING THE CURRY AND MAKING COCONUT RICE

4 Fry onions 10 more minutes until golden, but not burnt. Add both masalas and fry until fragrant, 1–2 min. Stir to prevent sticking and burning.

5 Add chicken, tomatoes, and salt; stir to coat. It may seem dry, but the tomatoes will release liquid. Reduce heat and cover; simmer 30–40 minutes.

6 While curry simmers, make Coconut Rice by combining rice, water, milk, sugar, and salt in large saucepan. Bring to a boil, stirring occasionally.

7 Cover pan, reduce heat to low and simmer 18–20 minutes, or until liquid is absorbed. Remove from heat and steam 5 more minutes. Fluff with a fork.

8 The curry is done when the liquid has reduced and the sauce has thickened. If it's too thin, simmer the curry, uncovered, for a few minutes to reduce.

9 Finish the curry by stirring in the torn spinach and 1 T. dry masala, off heat. Serve with the Coconut Rice, condiments, and warmed pita bread.

CONDIMENTS FOR CURRY

Sure, the curry tastes good on its own, but for over-the-top flavor, you'll want to serve these condiments with it.

The reason behind it is contrast. They're all meant to oppose the curry in some way—crunchy cucumbers and cool yogurt in the raita [RI-tah] tone down the spicy heat. And the tart Mango-Onion Chutney is dynamite with mild, sweet Coconut Rice.

By itself, the curry is fairly mild. But for those who like their food a little spicier, the Cilantro-Mint Chutney is for them. That's because you use a *whole* serrano in it—seeds and all. The seeds and membrane are where the chile's punch is. But if you want to tone it down, just remove them. The chutney will still taste great. **AH**

MANGO-ONION CHUTNEY

(MAKES ABOUT 2 CUPS)
WORK TIME: 15 MINUTES
COMBINE:

2   cups underripe mango, peeled, diced (2 mangoes)
¼   cup red onion, minced
½   serrano chile, seeded, minced
1   T. honey
1   T. fresh lime juice
     Pinch cayenne pepper
     Salt to taste

BEFORE SERVING, STIR IN:

¼   cup fresh cilantro leaves, roughly chopped

▲ *Use firm, underripe mangoes for this—they hold up better and add a tart twist to the meal. Remove skin with a peeler, then slice down each side of the pit to obtain lobes. Slice, then dice each lobe.*

Toss all ingredients, except cilantro, in a bowl and marinate at room temperature for at least ½ hour. Add cilantro just before serving to retain color and flavor.

CUCUMBER-TOMATO RAITA

(MAKES ABOUT 3 CUPS)
WORK TIME: 15 MINUTES
COMBINE:

2   cups cucumber, peeled, seeded, diced (1 cucumber)
1   cup Roma tomatoes, seeded and diced (3–4 tomatoes)
¼   cup green onion, minced (white and green part)
2   t. fresh lime juice
1   t. dry masala, *see Page 25*
½   t. sugar
½   t. salt
¼   t. black pepper

ADD TO COAT:

2–3 T. plain yogurt

▲ *Combine vegetables, juice, and seasonings in a bowl. Add just enough yogurt to coat everything lightly, but not drown it. Serve at room temperature within 2 hours, or the vegetables will deteriorate.*

CILANTRO-MINT CHUTNEY *(MAKES 1 CUP)*

WORK TIME: 15 MINUTES
COMBINE IN FOOD PROCESSOR:

2   cups fresh cilantro leaves
½   cup unsweetened coconut flakes
¼   cup fresh mint leaves
1   serrano chile, stemmed
1   clove garlic
1   t. sugar
¼   t. salt

ADD AND PROCESS TO MAKE A PASTE:

1   T. plain yogurt
2   t. fresh lime juice

▲ *Combine cilantro, coconut, mint, chile, garlic, sugar, and salt in a food processor. Process until finely minced, scraping the sides often.*

Add the yogurt and lime juice; process until a paste forms. Serve the chutney within 2 hours for the best color and flavor.

Photograph: Scott Little, Food Styling: Janet Pittman

APRICOT-DRIED CHERRY CHUTNEY (MAKES ABOUT 2 CUPS)

WORK TIME: 15 MINUTES
COOK TIME: 20–30 MINUTES

HEAT 3 T. VEGETABLE OIL; ADD:
- ½   cinnamon stick
- 3   whole cloves

ADD AND SAUTE:
- ¼   cup yellow onion, minced
- ½   serrano chile, seeded, minced
- 1   T. ginger, peeled, minced

ADD AND SIMMER:
- 2   cups dried apricots,
      cut into ½" pieces
- 1½ cups water
- ¾   cup white wine vinegar
- 2–3 T. sugar
- ½   t. salt
- 1   bay leaf

ADD AND SIMMER:
- 1   cup dried tart cherries

▲ *In a large saucepan, heat oil over medium–high until it shimmers. Add cinnamon and cloves, and fry until cinnamon opens and cloves pop, about 2 minutes. Remove spices and discard.*

Add onion, chile, and ginger to oil; saute until onion softens, 4–5 minutes. Stir in remaining ingredients, except cherries; reduce heat to low, and simmer about 15 minutes. Watch carefully so apricots don't burn.

▲ *Once most of the liquid has been absorbed, add the cherries and simmer 5 more minutes, until they soften slightly. (You can substitute dried cranberries for the cherries.) Cool chutney and chill. Remove bay leaf and bring to room temperature before serving.*

It's a good idea to make this chutney a couple of days before serving so the flavors mellow. It will keep for up to one week in the refrigerator.

SERVING THE CURRY

If you were served this meal in India, each person at the table would get a silver tray filled with small dishes of the curry, rice, condiments, and bread. That way, the meal can be eaten without the interruption of different courses being introduced (and dishes cleared). Plus, everybody has the chance to try their own combinations of the curry and condiments.

But if you don't have that kind of elaborate silver service, you can still have a great meal. Just serve the curry "family style," passing each component separately. This setup still gives your guests a chance to sample a little bit of everything and come up with their favorite combinations.

We had a really good time with this in the test kitchen. My favorite is to spread Cilantro-Mint Chutney on pita bread, add Apricot-Cherry Chutney, then top it with some of the curry. It's not bad for breakfast, either.

MUSHROOMS

Mushrooms—you either love them or hate them. Those feelings probably started when you were a

kid and the only mushrooms you had were those rubbery little jarred numbers or slimy, overcooked stuffers that appeared on every appetizer tray.

Don't let previous experiences taint your opinion of mushrooms anymore. Good ones—*fresh* ones—are up there with onions when it comes to adding character to a dish.

Describing their flavor is tricky. Like wine, you'll see mushrooms described as earthy or woodsy. No surprise. They grow in dark, damp places. Think of the good smell of freshly turned soil and you'll understand.

Read on about the top eight fresh mushrooms. Then on Pages 33–35, learn how to roast, saute, and grill mushrooms—most can be prepared using one of these techniques.

WHITE

Also called button or common mushrooms, whites are the most popular variety in the United States—sort of the vanilla ice cream of mushrooms. Fresh whites have a mild, nutty flavor when raw. This flavor gets richer as they mature or are cooked.

Young whites have a creamy color, and the bottom of the cap is tight to the stem. As they mature, the caps darken and they start to open. While this shows they are older, it also means more flavor.

Whites don't deserve the bad rep they get. Sure, they're the ones in the jars, but they are also very versatile and easy to find fresh. Sometimes familiar is best.

CRIMINI

Crimini, or Italian browns, could pass as over-the-hill whites. Actually, they're in the same family, but beneath that brown surface is a firmer texture and deeper, earthier flavor than white mushrooms.

Criminis are a good stepping stone if you've never ventured beyond white mushrooms. They are fairly easy to find and you can substitute them for whites in recipes. While they have a stronger flavor than whites, they're not overwhelming. On the other hand, they'll prepare you for gutsier mushrooms like portabellas or shiitakes.

SELECTION AND STORAGE

Selection: You'll see mushrooms one of two ways at the supermarket—in bulk, or plastic-wrapped in trays or boxes. Either way, they should look smooth with no visible moisture on their surface.

With bulk mushrooms, you can do more than just look at them. Make sure they feel firm and heavy for their size. Fresh mushrooms should also smell like clean dirt. Those that are getting too old often lose their fresh scent and become odorless.

Packaged mushrooms are trickier. That plastic just traps moisture. Look for browning and slime on the surface of mushrooms caused by that moisture. You just have to take your chances on the ones you can't see at the bottom of the box. Often, the package is dated, so be sure to check and pick the box with the latest date.

While it's hard to check odor, some plastic has holes in it. Slimy mushrooms take on a distinctly fishy smell that no plastic can contain.

Storage: Two things that spoil mushrooms are warm air and moisture. So, keeping them fresh is a bit of a balancing act—not too dry, not too wet.

First, keep them cold by refrigerating unwashed mushrooms. Second, don't store mushrooms in plastic bags or airtight containers, which just seal in moisture.

Put bulk mushrooms in a paper sack. You can transfer packaged mushrooms to a paper sack, too, or just loosen the plastic around around them. If you loosen it, leave it draped over the top to slow drying.

Stored properly, fresh mushrooms keep 5–10 days. It's best to eat them as soon as possible, though.

▲ *The best way to store fresh, unwashed mushrooms is in your basic, brown paper bag.*

PORTABELLA

If you think a portabella looks like a really big crimini, you're right. They are criminis that have grown up to six inches across. These big beauties are second to whites in popularity, probably due to their increased appearance in restaurants.

Because they're allowed to mature, portabellas develop a flavor and texture that's described as beefy. That makes them ideal candidates for grilling or broiling. They can absorb marinades without getting soggy, and like beef, you don't have to cook them until they are well-done.

Slice cooked portabellas and top salads or pasta with them. Or leave them whole for "burgers" or as an entree.

SHIITAKE

The third most popular mushroom in the U.S., shiitakes [shee-TAH-kays] are dark brown, umbrella-shaped mushrooms with a slightly smoky flavor and firm texture. They are a unique mushroom because their flavor won't get lost in a highly seasoned dish. In fact, they'll take on strong flavors and make them their own.

The stems of shiitakes are pretty tough. Trim them off but don't throw them away. Keep them in the freezer. Then when you make stock, add the stems for flavor.

For more on shiitakes, see Issue 11 (Sept/Oct 1998).

MOREL

These prized mushrooms are usually hunted wild, but sometimes appear in stores or farmers' markets in the spring. Morels have pointed, honeycombed caps and hollow stems. Once you try them, you'll never forget their distinct nutty flavor.

Clean morels quickly in salted water to flush out any bugs or grit. Drain well.

Since they are a wild mushroom, they need to be cooked. (Wild mushrooms contain some elements that are hard to digest.) See Issue 2 (Mar/Apr 1997) for more on morels and how to cook them.

CLEANING

I've always heard that you should *never* wash mushrooms under water. "They'll soak it up like a sponge!" Conventional wisdom says to clean mushrooms with a soft brush or wipe them off with a damp paper towel. That's fine if the mushrooms aren't too dirty to begin with. I like to use a brush, because it's a little easier and tidier than paper towels.

Washing really isn't necessary for sanitary reasons. Commercial mushrooms are grown in a sterile medium, such as peat moss, so they are safe to eat if they only get a light brushing.

But cleaning a bunch of really dirty mushrooms one at a time is downright tedious. And if you use paper towels, you'll go through a bunch of them. To save time, I've been known to defy the critics and wash mushrooms under the faucet. Turns out, I'm in good company.

Harold McGee took on this bit of kitchen lore in his book *The Curious Cook* (Macmillan Publishing). He reasoned, "Mushrooms are already 90% water, so what difference could a few drops more make?" Harold weighed 23 fresh mushrooms, soaked them in

water for five minutes, and weighed them again. Guess what? They barely soaked up any water—only 6 grams, or less than half a tablespoon, among all those mushrooms.

If a five-minute soak makes no significant difference, what could a quick rinse under the tap hurt? So, go ahead and rinse your mushrooms. Just remember two things. Pat them dry with a towel after their bath. And don't rinse them until just before you're going to use them. If washed mushrooms sit, they *will* get brown and slimy over time.

To clean mush- ▶ rooms with just a little dirt on them, use a soft-bristled brush to gently remove any grit. You can also use damp paper towels to wipe dirt from mushrooms.

◀ Rinsing isn't as bad as you think. Run dirty mushrooms briefly under cold water to clean them. Rinse them one at a time, or you can dunk a bunch in a sink full of cold water.

OYSTER

Named for their looks, oyster mushrooms come in soft colors from tan to light grey. They are delicate in both flavor and texture, though the stem is fairly firm. Oyster mushrooms are a pretty addition to recipes.

But you have to be careful. The heat from cooking really kills the flavor of oyster mushrooms. Add them at the end of cooking, or saute them lightly in butter and add to a finished dish. Strong flavors can really overwhelm oyster mushrooms, so only use them in lightly seasoned recipes.

ENOKI

Enoki [en-oh-kee] mushrooms are unlike any other mushroom. These fragile Japanese mushrooms have four-inch stems with tiny caps. They look a little like noodles with hats.

Enokis have a delicate, somewhat fruity flavor and are just a little crunchy. Cooking destroys both of these characteristics. Since enokis don't have to be cooked, use them raw in salads or sandwiches. Or add them to soups or Asian dishes right before serving as you would fresh herbs.

Enokis usually come sealed in plastic, so it's hard to tell if they're fresh. Make sure they're pearly white, not yellowish, in color. There shouldn't be excess moisture in the package either.

CHANTERELLE

There is a large number of chanterelle varieties, in colors ranging from white, yellow, grey, to black. The most familiar of these funnel-shaped mushrooms are golden chanterelles, which have a distinct apricot flavor and orange color.

Golden chanterelles can be easily paired with acids, like lemon juice or vinegar, without losing any of their flavor. They can also hold their own when paired with fresh herbs.

Golden chanterelles are at their best when they are the star of a dish. Serve them in sautes or with a light sauce.

Roasted STUFFED MUSHROOMS

I've had too many soggy, overcooked stuffed mushrooms dribble down my chin at parties. Then I learned a secret—roasting the caps before stuffing. Roasting not only cooks the caps, it draws out excess liquid. Sprinkling the mushrooms with coarse salt before roasting helps extract maximum moisture without overcooking and helps flavor the mushrooms.

You need large white mushrooms ("stuffers") for this recipe. The stems will get chopped and used in the stuffing, but sausage is the key player. Its quality will make or break this recipe, so pick a good one—mild or spicy is up to you. Asiago cheese has a big flavor that can stand up to the sausage. Grate it fresh—it'll melt better and hold the filling together.

Photograph: Scott Little, Food Styling: Janet Pittman

STUFFED MUSHROOMS

(MAKES 24 APPETIZERS)
WORK TIME: 20 MINUTES
COOK TIME: 20 MINUTES

TOSS WITH ½ CUP OLIVE OIL; ROAST:
24 large white mushrooms
    Kosher salt

BROWN:
6 oz. bulk Italian sausage

ADD AND SAUTE:
⅓ cup yellow onion, finely chopped
4 cups fresh spinach, chopped

STIR IN:
1 cup Asiago or Parmesan
    cheese, grated
¼ t. cayenne pepper

TOP WITH:
¼ cup dried bread crumbs

ROASTING AND STUFFING MUSHROOMS

1 Preheat oven to 425°. Remove stems from mushrooms. Finely chop stems; set aside. Toss caps with ½ cup olive oil until evenly coated. Arrange caps stem side up on baking sheet.

2 Sprinkle insides of caps lightly with salt. (This adds flavor and draws out moisture.) Roast 10 minutes. Turn caps over. Roast 6 minutes longer. Drain caps stem side down on paper towels.

3 While mushrooms roast, brown sausage in large skillet. Add chopped mushroom stems and onion. Saute until onion is tender, about 5 minutes.

4 Add spinach to pan. Saute until wilted. Remove from heat. Stir in cheese and cayenne. Stuff mushrooms with heaping tablespoon of sausage mixture.

5 Sprinkle tops of stuffed mushrooms with bread crumbs (½ t. each). Place mushrooms under broiler for 1–2 minutes, or until crumbs are browned.

Sauteed MUSHROOM VINAIGRETTE

SAUTEED MUSHROOM VINAIGRETTE

(MAKES 2 CUPS)
WORK TIME: 10 MINUTES
COOK TIME: 15 MINUTES

SAUTE IN BATCHES, USING 2 T. OLIVE OIL PER BATCH:

4   cups shiitake mushrooms, sliced

ADD:

½   cup shallots, minced
2   T. garlic, minced

DEGLAZE WITH:

1   cup white wine vinegar
¼   cup dry sherry

ADD:

2   T. sugar
     Salt to taste

ADD:

2   T. Dijon mustard
½   cup vegetable oil
½   cup olive oil
2   t. fresh thyme leaves
     Black pepper to taste

Photograph: Scott Little, Food Styling: Janet Pittman

Sauteing is probably the most popular way to cook mushrooms. It's easy and shows off the best a mushroom has to offer in flavor and texture. The trick is doing it right.

Here's the deal. Mushrooms are nearly 90% water. When they cook, all that water comes out. Now, the water carries a lot of flavor, which you don't want to lose. Sauteing evaporates just the water, letting the flavor concentrate on the mushrooms.

How do you make that happen? First, don't pack too many mushrooms in the skillet—cook them in batches if you have a lot. If the pan's crowded, the water can't evaporate, and you end up braising instead of sauteing. Braising results in a grey color and soft texture. You want golden, firm-yet-tender mushrooms.

Second, cook mushrooms over a relatively high heat. That helps the water evaporate quickly. If it takes too long, the mushrooms will get rubbery.

Sauteed mushrooms put a twist on a typical vinaigrette, *right*. They give it body and flavor. Use this vinaigrette as a sauce or a dressing in one of the ways suggested at right.

MAKING MUSHROOM VINAIGRETTE

1 Trim tough stems from shiitakes and slice caps. Divide mushrooms in half. Saute in two batches with oil over medium-high heat. Cook until lightly browned and most liquid evaporates.

2 Combine all sauteed mushrooms in skillet. Add shallots and garlic to mushrooms. Saute for 1–2 minutes, until shallots are tender and you can just smell the garlic.

3 Deglaze pan with white wine vinegar and sherry, scraping bottom of pan to loosen any browned bits. Add sugar and salt to taste, stirring to dissolve sugar. Reduce liquid by half.

4 Gradually stir in mustard, then oils, thyme, and pepper to taste. (Mustard helps bind the liquids together.) Warm briefly; remove from heat. Serve vinaigrette as suggested below.

Serving Suggestions: This hearty vinaigrette is delicious over roasted vegetables, such as asparagus or root vegetables. Try it with grilled chicken breast, pork, or tuna steaks. Or toss cooled vinaigrette with greens and serve it in the Parmesan Baskets from the back cover.

Grilled PORTABELLA PITA PIZZAS

PORTABELLA PITA PIZZAS
(MAKES 4 MAIN-DISH SERVINGS)
WORK TIME: 20 MINUTES
COOK TIME: 10 MINUTES

COMBINE:

4   portabella mushroom caps
    (4–5" diameter)
1   cup bottled vinaigrette dressing*

BRUSH WITH ¼ CUP OLIVE OIL:

4   soft pitas (6" diameter)

COMBINE FOR CHILI AIOLI:

½   cup mayonnaise
1   t. chili powder
1   t. garlic, minced
1   t. lemon juice

TOSS TO COAT:

4   cups mesclun salad mix
¼   cup bottled vinaigrette dressing*

TOP PIZZAS EVENLY WITH:

½   cup soft goat cheese, crumbled

*Just use a basic vinaigrette. You don't want it to be a dominant flavor.

Photograph: Scott Little, Food Styling: Janet Pittman

Grilling is a great way to cook portabellas. They hold up like a piece of steak. Brushing them with a vinaigrette adds flavor two ways—it soaks in a little and the extra drips onto the coals to create some smoking action.

Assemble and eat these pizzas as soon as you pull the pitas and portabellas off the grill. That way they'll be hot enough to soften the cheese, but the mesclun (a mixture of young greens) won't have a chance to wilt.

GRILLING PORTABELLAS AND PITAS

1 Prepare grill for medium direct heat. Brush both sides of mushrooms with 1 cup vinaigrette. Let sit for 15 minutes to let vinaigrette soak in a little.

2 Brush both sides of pitas with oil. For the Chili Aioli, combine mayonnaise, chili powder, garlic, and lemon juice. Add salt to taste. Set aside.

3 Combine mesclun and ¼ cup vinaigrette in a bowl. Toss to coat, using your hands—they're gentler on greens and ensure even coating.

4 Grill portabellas 3–5 min. per side, just until tender. Grill pitas 2–3 min. per side, until lightly browned. Grill tops of pitas and mushrooms first.

5 Spread the aioli evenly on hot pitas (2 tablespoons each). Mound about 1 cup mesclun on top of each pita. Slice mushrooms on a slight bias.

6 Fan the mushroom slices around mesclun mound in a circular fashion. Sprinkle crumbled goat cheese evenly over pizzas. Serve immediately.

Q *It seems like every time I make whipped cream, it gets weepy, especially if I don't use it right away. Is there any way I can prevent this?*

A I know what you're talking about—that little puddle of liquid that settles under whipped cream. There are a couple of things you can do to prevent this from happening.

If you won't be using it right away, underwhip it a bit, cover, and refrigerate. Once you're ready, whip the cream to the right consistency.

Or, add a stabilizer—like dissolved, cooled gelatin or *Whip it* (a commercial stabilizer). It contains starches that absorb excess liquid.

If the cream is already weepy, just rewhip. This won't work, though, if it's whipped to stiff peaks—any more whipping and it'll turn into butter.

Q *I usually use bittersweet chocolate when I bake German chocolate cake, but I recently came across a recipe that called for German's chocolate. What is it, and will it affect the taste if I substitute?*

A First, all chocolate comes from cacao beans, which are roasted then ground. What you end up with is a thick paste called chocolate liquor that contains cocoa solids and a yellowish fat called cocoa butter.

From there an emulsifier (lecithin), vanilla, and sugar are added. The amount of

Q *What is the difference between types of milk—skim, 1%, 2%, and whole? And how will it affect a recipe if I use one over another?*

A One big difference between types of milk is fat content, which is expressed in grams. Whole milk has 8 grams of fat per cup; 2% (reduced fat) has 5 grams; 1% (low fat) has 2.5 grams; and skim milk is considered fat free.

So, can you use one in place of another? Well, fat equals flavor and creaminess. So, if a recipe calls for whole milk and low-fat or skim is substituted, you could lose flavor and body.

Take homemade ice cream. Low-fat milk has more water than whole. If low-fat is substituted for whole, the ice cream could develop ice crystals.

Unless the amount of milk is small (a tablespoon or so) stick to the recipe. But if a recipe doesn't specify what type of milk to use, 1% or 2% will likely give you good results.

sugar added determines whether the chocolate is bittersweet or semisweet.

German's (named for the man who invented it) is a bittersweet chocolate, but it typically contains more sugar than most bittersweets.

Substituting is fine—the German's just might make your cake slightly sweeter tasting.

Q *A recipe I'm making calls for ground red pepper. What is that exactly? Is it the same thing as cayenne pepper? If not, is it okay to use cayenne instead?*

A Ground red pepper is a generic name for cayenne pepper, which is the dried, ground cayenne chile. But it can be made from any variety of red chile pepper that has been dried and then ground.

One can "fill in" for the other. It's just with ground red pepper, you can't be absolutely sure of the type of pepper used—or the heat level.

Q *What's the deal with commercials that say pure cane sugar is the best—better than beet sugar. Is it true?*

A Not really. In fact, the two are chemically identical. The only *real* difference between the two comes down to their sources and how each is refined.

Cane sugar comes from the 20-foot stems of sugar cane. The roots are left in the ground for the next crop of sugar to grow.

Beet sugar, which accounts for almost half the world's sugar supply, is from a type of white beet that looks like a fat, white carrot. It doesn't come from the red beets you're probably most familiar with.

Both types of sugar are produced the same way. The juice is extracted, boiled, then evaporated to form crystals. But during the final refining stage, some manufactures make the crystals smaller. That makes them dissolve faster and seem sweeter in the final product.

Q *I was watching a cooking show the other night, and the pastry chef was using sheet gelatin. What is it, and how is it different from regular powdered gelatin?*

A Sheet gelatin is an unflavored gelatin (like powdered gelatin) that's formed into a translucent sheet. A typical sheet measures about 2¹⁄₂ x 8¹⁄₂". And four sheets equal one packet of powdered.

Both powdered and sheet gelatin are softened, then melted, and used for stability and thickening in foods like molded desserts or Bavarian creams. Sheets are more popular in Europe, while the powdered variety seems to be an American favorite. You can order them from **The Baker's Catalogue** at **(800) 827-6836** ($1.95 for a packet of four sheets).

Q *I can't find crème fraîche in my grocery store. Can I use sour cream instead? And if I can't, how do I make crème fraîche at home?*

A Crème fraîche [krehm FRESH] is cream to which a "safe" bacteria has been added. This bacteria makes the cream thicker, richer-tasting, and more stable than sour cream. In most recipes, you can substitute sour cream. But when it's blended with hot foods, you're better off using crème fraîche—it won't break or curdle when it comes in contact with the heat.

You can buy expensive American-made versions, but it's easier and tastier to make your own. Combine 1 cup heavy cream, 2 T. buttermilk, and 2 t. lemon juice in a glass bowl. Cover, and let it stand at room temperature for up to 24 hours, or until it's thickened. It will keep up to one week, covered, in the refrigerator.

Q *I'm setting up a new home and am interested in cooking. What basic pieces of cookware should I buy?*

A There isn't an *all-purpose* piece of cookware, but a 3-quart saute pan is pretty close. It's like a frying pan with 2–3" straight sides. A saute pan is great because you can saute, fry, make sauces, and braise, all in the same pan.

Next, invest in a 2- or 3-quart saucier—it's like a saucepan, but with high, *rounded* sides. It's typically used for making sauces, but if you get a larger one, you can also make stocks and soups in it.

Finally, buy a fairly large (6- or 8-quart) stockpot and a large (10 or 12") frying pan. Also, consider buying a nonstick frying pan for eggs and foods that don't use a lot of fat. Just don't spend a lot—the coating can wear out quickly.

Look for the following in your cookware: multi-ply construction (more than one type of metal); ovenproof, metal handles; and a tight-fitting lid.

All-Clad is an example of good, quality cookware and what we use in our test kitchen. For more on choosing cookware, take a look at "Wares" in Issue 1 (Jan/Feb 1997).

GLOSSARY

Cheesecloth: Natural cotton cloth that is still used in cheese making. It's also used as a fine strainer or as a sachet for herbs and spices to be placed in soups or stocks.

Crumb coat: The initial thin layer of frosting applied to a cake. This layer helps seal in the crumbs and is then covered by a thicker second coating.

Deglaze: Removing browned bits of food or fat from the bottom of a pan by heating a small amount of liquid (usually wine or stock) in the pan, then stirring to loosen the bits. This makes a great base for a sauce.

Dehydrate: To remove a food's natural moisture by drying slowly over time. Used to preserve food so spoilage such as mold or fermentation can't happen.

Fell: Thin, connective-tissue membrane that covers animals' legs. It's similar to silverskin on pork or beef and should be removed before cooking.

Fold: To combine one mixture with another through repeated, gentle over-under motions—not beating or stirring.

Infuse: To extract flavor from a food in a hot liquid until the liquid absorbs the flavor. Usually refers to teas and coffees, but it can also apply to food.

Marbling: Veins of fat that run within the muscle tissue of meat, including beef and lamb. Marbling adds both flavor and a tender texture to the meat.

Pita: A round, Middle Eastern flat bread. It's split in half to form pockets that can be stuffed to make a sandwich. Or it can be cut into wedges to scoop up dips.

ABBREVIATIONS

t. = teaspoon
T., Tbsp. = tablespoon
oz. = ounce
lb. = pound
Dash = scant ¹⁄₈ of a teaspoon
Pinch = ¹⁄₁₆ of a teaspoon

Using Fresh COCONUT

Fresh coconut is worth the work. Its firm texture and mild flavor are miles away from what's in bags. But the biggest difference is that it's not super-sweet.

Coconuts grow in a shell, like walnuts. The large nut in the photo above is what comes off the tree. Open it up—the coconuts you buy are inside.

Buying: First, find a coconut that feels heavy for its size with no cracks in the shell. Now shake it—you want to hear and feel liquid inside. If you don't, it's leaked out (through a crack) or evaporated (the coconut is old).

Next, find the three "eyes" at one end of the coconut (like holes on a bowling ball). They should be firm and dry—if they're soft or moldy, that also means liquid may've leaked out.

Cracking: Cracking a coconut is a little messy, but not hard—just follow the steps on this page. Once you get to the meat, you can use it as is or make coconut milk, *see Page 39.*

Since coconut is high in fat, there's a chance the meat could be rancid, even if it looks okay. But the only way to tell is by cracking it—a rancid coconut will smell and taste bad.

GETTING TO THE MEAT

▲*Pierce* the "eyes" by tapping a screwdriver through each one with a hammer. Hold the coconut steady in a vice grip. Or line the drain of the kitchen sink with a towel and set the coconut in the drain.

▲*Pour* out the liquid inside and discard (or use it to make coconut milk). Place the whole coconut on a baking sheet and bake at 350° for 30 min. This will make it easier to pull the meat from the shell.

▲*Pry* away the outer shell when the coconut is cool enough to handle. You may need to gently crack the outer shell with the hammer first. Be careful—the coconut meat is hot.

▲*Peel* off the papery skin that's attached to the meat with a vegetable peeler. Rinse the meat and pat dry. Use the coconut in Cilantro-Mint Chutney, see Page 28, or make the coconut milk on the next page.

So you've gone to the trouble of cracking open a coconut—now what?

The first thing you should do is taste it. See how different it is from sweetened, shredded coconut? It's not what you want to use in a coconut cream pie, but tastes great with fresh fruit. Try it sprinkled on slices of ripe mangoes or fresh pineapple.

Making Milk: Making coconut milk is another way to use fresh coconut. The procedure is simple—just follow the four steps to the right.

Incidentally, coconut milk is not the milky liquid inside the coconut. That's coconut *water* and is a popular drink in some Asian countries. Some people cook rice in it. But don't use it in place of coconut milk in recipes.

Storing: An uncracked coconut will keep at room temperature for 2–4 months. But once it's cracked, chill the meat for up to one week or freeze it for up to nine months.

Coconut milk (fresh or canned) should also be stored no longer than one week. It spoils quickly and should be thrown away if it smells sour. And anything made with coconut milk, like the Coconut Rice on Page 27, will sour after three to four days. **AH**

▲ *Chop* small chunks of fresh, peeled coconut meat in a food processor fitted with a steel blade until finely chopped. One coconut will yield 2–2½ cups.

▲ *Steep* the chopped coconut in boiling water (or coconut water), using 1 cup liquid for each packed cup of coconut (2–2½ cups). Let stand for 30 minutes.

▲ *Puree* the coconut and water in a blender until smooth. Then pour the coconut mixture into a bowl lined with two layers of cheesecloth.

▲ *Strain* the liquid by gathering the cheesecloth and squeezing it into the bowl. You should have 2–2½ cups milk. Discard coconut.

COCONUT PRODUCTS

Fresh coconut is great, but there's no denying it's more convenient to have someone else do the work. Here's what you may run into.

Shredded: You already know about the sweet kind in bags. *Unsweetened flakes* are large, dried chips. Since there's no added sugar, it's much drier than the sweetened type—it should be mixed with moist ingredients (like cake batter) so it can soften. Buy unsweetened flakes at natural foods stores and some grocery stores.

Canned: Before there was sweetened, shredded coconut in bags, it usually came packaged in cans, like tomato soup. Every once in a while you can still find it. Baker's is one brand. Give it a try—it's not as sweet or moist as the kind in the bag. But it works great in the Coconut Cake on Page 40.

Coconut Milk: Coconut milk is a common ingredient in Thai and Indian dishes, like Coconut Rice on Page 23. You can make your own using fresh coconut, *see photos above*. Or buy it in cans at Asian markets and in the ethnic food aisle at grocery stores.

Pay close attention to the label when buying milk. "Lite" is okay for many recipes (like the Coconut Rice). But don't buy "cream of coconut" by mistake—it's used to flavor tropical drinks and desserts and has a lot of added sugar.

When you open the can, the milk may look strange, like it has spoiled. Don't be alarmed. The fat solids have just floated to the top and created that thick "cap" of white cream. All you need to do is blend it with a fork.

Once the can has been opened, coconut milk won't last long. Chill it no longer than a week.

COCONUT CAKE

Photograph: Scott Little, Food Styling: Janet Pittman

COCONUT CAKE
(MAKES THREE 8" LAYERS)
WORK TIME: 25 MINUTES
BAKE TIME: 25–30 MINUTES

SIFT:
1½ cups all-purpose flour
1½ cups cake flour
4   t. baking powder
½   t. salt

CHOP:
½   cup sweetened coconut flakes*

CREAM TOGETHER:
½   cup shortening
¼   cup unsalted butter, room temp.

ADD:
1½ cups sugar
3   egg yolks

COMBINE:
2   cups whole milk
½   t. imitation coconut flavor

BEAT TO SOFT PEAKS; FOLD IN:
3   egg whites

TO ASSEMBLE AND FINISH:
2½ cups sweetened coconut flakes*

Editor's Note: The coconut in the batter is chopped, but for the outside and between the layers, it's not. Fluff coconut on a plate before measuring it.

Think back years ago. Remember having a fresh home-made cake or pie sitting on the kitchen counter every week? It was just part of the landscape. Well, obviously times have changed. Oh sure, sweets are still in, but most of them come wrapped in plastic. Homemade cake now means a boxed mix. And it's pretty reliable—the cake always rises. It may not taste or look particularly impressive, but it gets the job done.

But why settle for mediocrity? It's time to produce a made-from-scratch cake with professional results—even if you're a beginner. Wet your feet on this big, beautiful coconut cake. The techniques are, well, a piece of cake.

On the next three pages you'll find specific but simple techniques for the cake, filling, frosting, and assembly.

The Cake: This cake is more than just white layers with some coconut sprinkled on top. It's a towering, moist, and tender cake with coconut in it, on it, and between the layers.

The key to creating these moist layers is in the mixing process. For this cake, you need to make sure the ingredients are fully incorporated, but *don't overbeat*. Long creaming and beating times at a high speed would make the cake heavy and compacted.

Be aware—sweetened coconut (in a bag) can be wet and sticky. It's easier to work with if you first fluff it on a plate and let it dry for a few minutes.

The Filling and Frosting: Coconut cake with citrus filling is a tradition borrowed from the South. In this cake, lime filling paves the frosted layers with just enough tartness to add a little punch and cut the sweetness. But it doesn't overpower the coconut. And like Key lime pie, the lime filling is yellow, not green. (You'll have left-over filling—try it on biscuits or English muffins, like jam.)

Frosting the outside of the cake couldn't be easier. You don't need to make any fancy swirls or strokes. Just spread the frosting smoothly over the entire cake—any imperfections will be hidden by the coconut.

The Assembly: Since you freeze the layers (1–48 hours) and thoroughly chill the filling, you can make both up to two days ahead. Assemble and frost on the day you serve it.

ALL CAKE PANS ARE *NOT* CREATED EQUAL

Here's the pan problem. If your pans can nest inside each other, you know the sides slope down slightly. This creates sloped cake edges. That means when you put the layers together, the sides will be uneven. You can't possibly make a cake with straight sides. The pans are "stacked" against you!

But straight-sided pans produce straight-sided cakes. You can spot these pans easily because they *won't* nest inside each other. They'll just stack.

And they're made of heavy aluminum. The pans coated with Teflon cause cakes to shrink, and dark pans will overbrown.

Sources: The brand name isn't important—it's the shape of the pan that counts. Look for straight-sided pans at your local kitchen supply store, or try a craft store—I found straight-sided Wilton pans in the cake decorating department. Or order pans from **Kitchen Krafts** at (800) 776-0575, Item #BP2408 (8" diameter, 2" deep), for $6.00 each plus shipping and handling. Order on-line at www.kitchenkrafts.com.

▲ *Dark interior pans will overbrown.*

◄ *Sloping sides on these pans produce an uneven cake.*

Straight sides ► *are what you want for an even, straight-sided cake.*

1 Start with prep work. Preheat oven to 350°. Grease *bottoms only* of three 8" round cake pans. Top with parchment circles. Measure then sift dry ingredients. Chop coconut; add to dry mix.

2 In a large bowl, beat shortening and butter at medium speed just until creamy. Add the sugar and egg yolks all at once and beat, only until incorporated. Scrape the bowl as needed.

3 Combine milk and flavoring. Add ³/₄ cup flour mixture and ¹/₂ cup milk mixture alternately to creamed mixture. Beat (low speed) after each addition to incorporate. Begin and end with flour.

4 Use a clean bowl and beaters to beat egg whites until stiff peaks form—they should be glossy and firm. Gently, but thoroughly, fold the whites into batter with a wire whisk.

5 Divide batter among prepared pans. Spread evenly to edges, making a *slight* "well" in the center so cake won't dome as it rises. Bake all 3 pans on center rack of oven for 25–30 minutes.

6 Insert a toothpick in cake center. If it comes out clean, it's done. Cool in pans 10 min. Run a knife around edge; invert onto rack. Remove parchment; cool. Wrap layers in plastic; freeze 1 hr.

LIME FILLING

(MAKES 1¾ CUPS)
WORK TIME: 20 MINUTES
COOK TIME: 15–20 MINUTES

COMBINE AND HEAT:
¾   cup fresh lime juice, strained
¼   cup unsalted butter, cubed

COMBINE:
1   cup sugar
¼   cup cornstarch
   Pinch of salt

COMBINE AND ADD:
2   whole eggs
2   egg yolks

OFF HEAT, ADD:
1   t. vanilla extract

7 Start the Lime Filling by combining the juice and butter in a medium saucepan. Cook over medium heat until the butter melts.

8 Meanwhile, combine sugar, cornstarch, and salt in small bowl. Combine eggs in another bowl. Whisk sugar mixture into eggs until smooth.

9 Slowly drizzle the lime juice mixture into egg mixture, whisking constantly. You need to pour slowly or the eggs will "scramble."

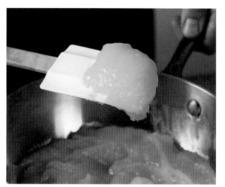

10 Return mixture to saucepan and cook over medium heat, stirring frequently. Cook until thick, 8–10 minutes. Off heat, stir in the vanilla.

11 Place filling in bowl; press plastic wrap on surface to prevent a skin from forming. Chill completely. It *must* be cold when you assemble the cake.

COCONUT-CREAM CHEESE FROSTING

(MAKES 3½ CUPS)
WORK TIME: 10 MINUTES

BEAT TOGETHER:
8   oz. cream cheese, softened
3   T. whole milk
1   t. imitation coconut flavor

BEAT IN:
6½–7 cups powdered sugar

Editor's Note: This frosting will start to set up as it sits. That's not a problem. Just keep your beater handy, and rebeat as many times as necessary during the frosting process—it'll cream perfectly over and over. Rebeating helps it spread easily, and the coconut will stick better.

12 In a large bowl, beat cream cheese on high for 1 minute, until very creamy. Add milk and coconut flavor, beating on low to incorporate.

Add powdered sugar 2 cups at a time, beating well after each addition. Add final ½–1 cup; beat 2 minutes on high. Frosting should be stiff, but spreadable.

PIECE-OF-CAKE ASSEMBLY

Freezing the Layers: Freezing the layers makes handling, brushing off crumbs, and assembly easier. When the layers have cooled, wrap them separately in plastic wrap and freeze for 1–48 hours. Remove the layers from the freezer as you need them.

Paper Guards: Build, frost, and serve this cake on the same plate. Lay four 5"-wide strips of waxed or parchment paper in a square around plate. Brush crumbs off all sides of cake layer and place in center of plate. Adjust strips so none of the plate is exposed. When finished frosting, carefully pull the strips and mess away.

Creating Stability: Three-layer cakes have a tendency to slide or lean—especially with a slick filling. Here are some stabilizers:

Frosting Dam: The frosting dam in Step 13 does double duty. It holds the filling so it doesn't squish into the outer frosting and discolor it. And the frosting rim adheres to the next layer.

Coconut: Sprinkling coconut on top of the filling provides traction so the next cake layer won't slide.

Freezing the Cake: Once the layers are assembled, freeze the cake for 1–2 hours before the final frosting. This makes it sturdy enough to stand up to the frosting process without leaning.

Finishing: Because the assembled cake has been chilled, the final frosting sets up quickly. Press the coconut onto the cake *right* after you frost so it will stick. Store in the refrigerator, covered with plastic. Serve chilled or at room temperature. **AH**

LEVELING CAKE LAYERS

Despite the best efforts, cakes will still sometimes dome in the middle or come out of the oven noticeably uneven, *as below.* For either problem, leveling is the simple solution.

Freeze the layer. Place in a pan with 1" sides. If necessary, place cardboard rounds under cake to raise it until the lowest part of the cake top is even with edge of the pan. Use a serrated knife to trim the top, using edge of the pan as a guide.

ASSEMBLY AND FROSTING

frozen cake layer

paper guards

cake stand

offset spatulas

▲ *Here's the equipment you'll need: cake stand or flat plate, waxed or parchment paper, and large and small offset spatulas for frosting (a table knife works too).*

13 With small spatula, spread ½ cup frosting ¼" from edge of layer. Make a dam by spreading more frosting toward edge to hold the Lime Filling.

14 Spread ⅓ cup Lime Filling inside dam. Sprinkle with ¼ cup coconut. Place second layer; repeat process. Place top layer and freeze 1–2 hours.

15 Rebeat the frosting. Remove cake from freezer. Use large spatula to spread a thin, smooth coat of frosting (crumb coat) over entire cake.

16 Rebeat remaining frosting and spread on top and sides of cake. Smooth frosting evenly, but don't fuss— the coconut covers a multitude of flaws.

17 Use 2 cups coconut to sprinkle top and press onto sides of cake. Gather excess coconut; keep pressing until covered. Remove paper guards.

Photograph: Scott Little; Food Styling: Janet Pittman

GRAND FINALE

Remember when it was the rage to put chili or chowder in a bread bowl and

then eat the whole thing? Well, this Parmesan Basket is in the same family—only a bit more classy. As you can see in the photograph, the edges are delicate and lacy. Plus, the sides are very thin so it doesn't look heavy.

Use an inexpensive *shredded* parmesan—I used the pre-shredded bag stuff.

And of course, the basket is made to eat. It goes great with the soft textures of mesclun lettuces and acidic vinaigrettes.

PARMESAN BASKETS

▲ Heat 10" nonstick pan over medium-high heat. Sprinkle Parmesan cheese into a disk shape. Keep the cheese light around the edges so it looks lacy. When slightly golden on underside, lift the disk out of the pan using a spatula and your fingers.

▲ Quickly drape cheese disk over a heavy glass with the golden side facing up. Press sides around glass to form bowl. Let cool and harden about 5 minutes. When cool, the baskets can sit out for several hours. Just don't put anything hot in them or they'll melt.

Issue No. 21 May/June 2000
www.cuisinemagazine.com

Cuisine®

an illustrated guide to creative home cooking

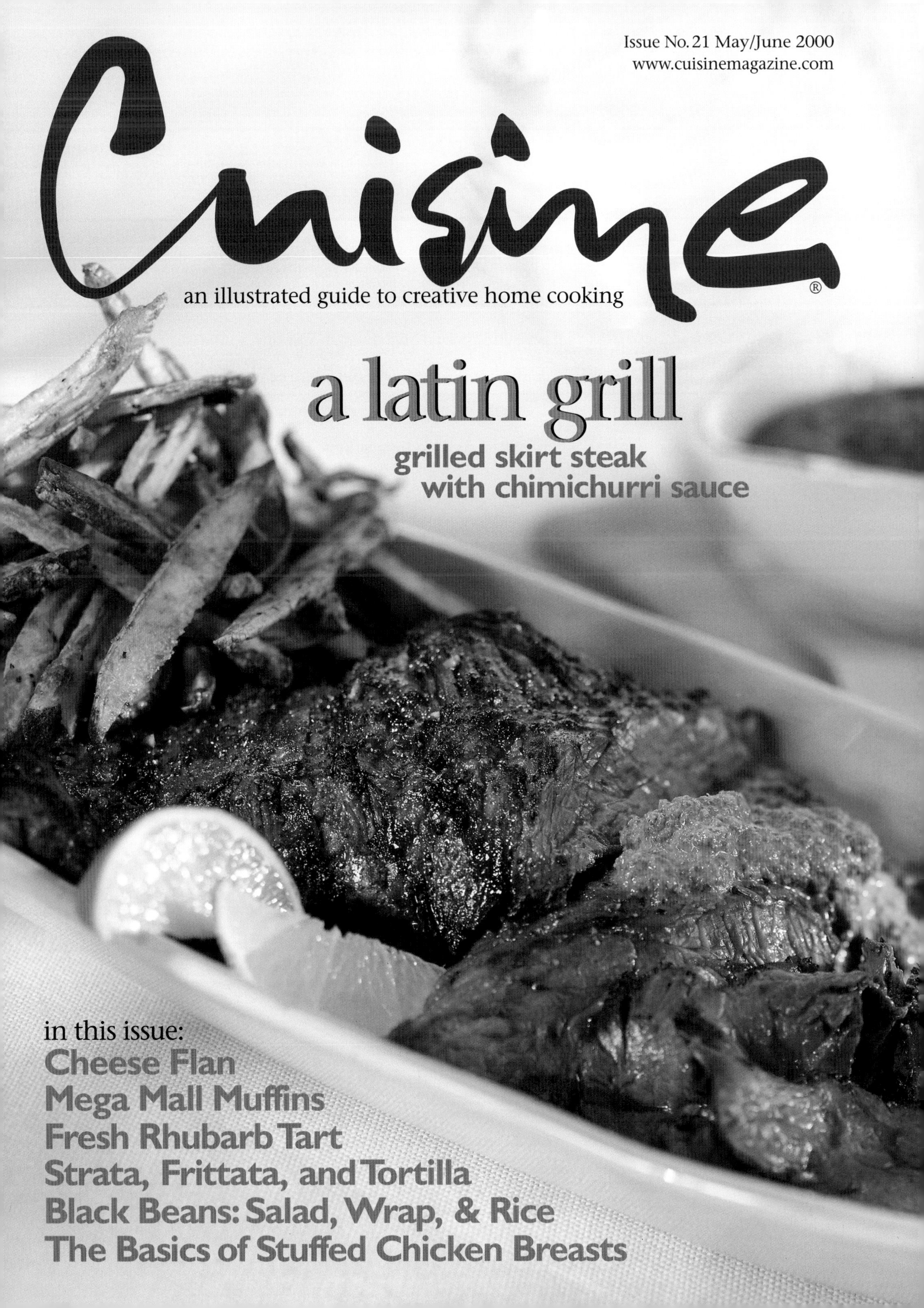

a latin grill

grilled skirt steak
with chimichurri sauce

in this issue:

Cheese Flan
Mega Mall Muffins
Fresh Rhubarb Tart
Strata, Frittata, and Tortilla
Black Beans: Salad, Wrap, & Rice
The Basics of Stuffed Chicken Breasts

Editor
John F. Meyer

Art Director
Cinda Shambaugh

Associate Editor
Susan Hoss

Assistant Editors
Juliana Hale
Sara Ostransky
Kelly Volden

Senior Graphic Designer
Holly Wiederin

Graphic Designer
Stephanie Hunter

Test Kitchen Director
Kim Samuelson

Contributing Photographers
Scott Little, Dean Tanner

Food Stylist
Janet Pittman

Prepress Image Specialist
Troy Clark

Publisher
Donald B. Peschke

CORPORATE:

Creative Director: Ted Kralicek • *New Media Manager:* Gordon C. Gaippe • *Special Publications:* Douglas L. Hicks • *Senior Photographer:* Crayola England • *Multi Media Art Director:* Eugene Pedersen • *E-Commerce Analyst:* Carol Schoeppler • *Web Site Product Specialist:* Adam Best • *Web Site Content Managers:* Terry Walker, David Briggs • *Controller:* Robin K. Hutchinson • *Senior Accountant:* Laura J. Thomas • *Accounts Payable Clerk:* Mary J. Schultz • *Accounts Receivable Clerk:* Margo Petrus • *Production Director:* George Chmielarz • *Elec. Pub. Director:* Doug M. Lidster • *Network Administrator:* Cris Schwanebeck • *Prepress Image Specialist:* Minniette Johnson • *H.R. Assistant:* Kirsten Koele • *Facilities Manager:* Julia Fish • *Receptionist:* Jeanne Johnson • *Administrative Assistant:* Sherri Ribbey • *Mailroom Clerk:* Lou Webber

CUSTOMER SERVICE & FULFILLMENT:

Operations Director: Bob Baker • *Customer Service Manager:* Jennie Enos • *Customer Service Reps.:* Anna Cox, Jeanette G. Rankin, April Revell, Deborah Rich, Tammy Truckenbrod • *Technical Representative:* Johnny Audette • *Merchandise Buyer:* Linda Jones • *Administrative Assistant:* Nancy Downey • *Warehouse Supervisor:* Nancy Johnson • *Fulfillment:* Sylvia Carey, Sheryl Knox, Dan Spidle

CIRCULATION:

Subscriber Services Director: Sandy Baum • *New Business Director:* Glenda Battles • *New Business Manager:* Todd L. Bierle • *Promotion Manager:* Rick Junkins • *Billing Manager:* Rebecca Cunningham • *Renewal Manager:* Paige Rogers • *Assistant Subscription Manager:* Joy Krause • *Marketing Analyst:* Kris Schlemmer • *Creative Manager:* Melinda Haffner • *Senior Graphic Designers:* Robin Dowdell, Mark A. Hayes, Jr.

www.cuisinemagazine.com

from the editor:

Most people tend to resist change, but I hope you're going to like what you see in this issue. We've been working overtime to make *Cuisine* easier to read with easier to follow recipes. In general, just a little more exciting to look at. But don't worry—the informational side of *Cuisine* is still there.

So what am I talking about? If you turn to the Black Bean article beginning on Page 14, you can see there are several recipes to each dish. To make things easy, each recipe has its own box along with specific step-by-step cooking instructions. This makes cooking almost foolproof.

Now, take a look at the chicken articles starting on Page 28. They employ the familiar *Cuisine* approach of showing a basic technique, followed by three easy-to-prepare recipe articles. Each article has larger photographs and fewer steps than before so you immediately see that stuffing a breast isn't hard or time-consuming—even during a hectic week!

These are just a few of the changes we've been making. What do you think? I'd like to hear your opinions. Just go to our specially created web site **http://survey.CuisineMagazine.com** (it's only for our readers). With your magazine in hand, answer a few questions about some of the changes. The questions are simple and there's even room for comments—the good *and* the bad!

And one more thing. Head to our web site and check out *Cuisine*Cam. Catch us working (most of the time!) in the test kitchen. It's pretty cool.

John

28

contents

Issue 21 May/June 2000

feature articles

in every issue

TIPS AND TECHNIQUES

ROASTING VEGETABLES

For a nice, caramelized crust on roasted vegetables, preheat a skillet or heavy duty baking sheet in a hot oven for 15 minutes. Meanwhile, toss vegetables with olive oil, salt, and pepper. Add the vegetables to the preheated skillet—they'll sizzle when they hit the hot pan, creating a beautiful caramelized crust.

B. Race
Strongsville, OH

MAKING THE MOST OF STOCK (AND LEFTOVERS)

I'm a firm believer in homemade stock as the basis for all good cooking. To give flavor and depth to stock, I add leftover vegetables and herbs that I've saved and frozen.

I use cleaned mushroom stems, clean onion and garlic peels, sliced or chopped onions, limp celery (along

with the leaves) and carrots, and stems from fresh thyme, parsley, or other herbs. It's a great way to use leftovers or discards, and the stock adds incredible flavor to soups, gravies, etc.

D. Wetzel
St. Charles, MO

MULTIPLE MOLDS

I like to make individual side dishes, quiches, and desserts. But I don't enjoy unmolding each ramekin separately or dealing with little dishes scooting around the baking pan.

Both problems are solved when I use a muffin tin for the mold. Spray tin with nonstick spray. When ready to unmold, lay a baking sheet over top and invert.

P. Neaves
Kansas City, MO

SLICK SHORTENING

If you don't like the messy job of measuring shortening, try this tip. Swirl a raw egg around in the measuring cup. Remove the egg (you can use it in your recipe). After measuring, the shortening will slide right out of the cup with no waste and easy clean up.

R. Watson
Reedley, CA

WATER GLUE

After rolled parchment paper is cut and placed on a baking sheet, it can slide around or curl at the edges. So wet the baking sheet first, then press the paper in place. It will adhere very well, making piping on it or any other task a cinch.

B. Strenkert
Naples, FL

MEET OUR TIPSTERS

Editor's Note: I get a wide variety of letters with tips. Often the people and their stories are just as interesting as their tips. Meet Mr. Marcelli—he had great ideas, and sent along beautiful photos to illustrate. —John

RE: FREE-FORM PEACH TART (Issue 16)

On my first try, I had trouble keeping the slippery peaches from spreading out during baking. So then I tried an 8" pizza pan to contain the fruit. It retained its shape, plus gave the tart nice height. A springform pan might make removal even easier. Next time!

You're right, baking the tart was relatively easy—and very tasty. Neither of the tarts lasted very long!

M. Marcelli
Villanova, PA

FROM THE TEST KITCHEN

BAKING TART SHELLS

I often need prebaked tart shells, but find the process of filling the shell with foil or parchment paper and pie weights to be excruciating.

Instead, I turn the pan upside down and press pastry over the *outside*. Then I trim, prick extensively, and bake. This prevents the bottom from puffing up, or the sides from slumping down as the fat melts in the pastry.

S. Pfefferkorn
Annapolis, MD

CHEESECAKE GIFTS

I like giving cheesecakes as gifts, but can't use my spring-form pan while the base is on loan. So I make disposable bases out of heavy aluminum oven liners.

Place tightened spring-form pan (without bottom)

on liner. Trace *inside* pan. Draw 1 x 4" tab on side. Cut out, place in pan (tab folds over rim), bake cheesecake as usual. Use tab to slide onto a disposable plate. Cut tab flush with circle.

S. Martin
Corbin, KY

CLEAN *CUISINE*

In order to keep my copy of *Cuisine* clean as I use it in the kitchen, I place it in a gallon-size resealable bag and seal. I can pick it up with sticky hands and don't have to worry about spills.

K. McDonough
Carmel, NY

FREEZING RICE

Freeze cooked brown and long grain rice to use later for stir-fries or a quick meal. (Short grain and wild rice get sticky.) Cook and cool rice, package in large resealable bags, and freeze flat.

P. Neaves
Kansas City, MO

TRIMMING GREENS

Many popular dishes now use peppery greens like collards, turnips, mustard, and chard. But trimming them can be a pain. To get rid of the tough

large stem and vein easily: Fold the leaf in half and slice down along the inside edge of the vein. One stroke eliminates both the stem and vein.

SAFER WATER BATH

Getting a water bath in and out of the oven can be hazardous. Here's a method to avoid sloshing the steaming water.

Place roasting pan on oven rack. Set filled baking dish in center of the pan. Pour near-boiling water into pan (halfway up side of dish), being careful not to splash on the food. Be sure to push oven rack in slowly.

After baking, use a baster to extract enough water to remove the dish safely. Leave the pan of hot water in the oven; remove after the remaining water has cooled.

SHARE YOUR TIPS

If you have a unique way of solving a cooking problem, we'd like to hear from you, and we'll consider publishing your tip in one or more of our works.

Just write down your cooking tip and mail it to *Cuisine*, Tips Editor, 2200 Grand Ave., Des Moines, IA 50312, or contact us through our e-mail address shown below. Please include your name, address, and daytime phone number in case we have questions. We'll pay you $25 if we publish your tip.

E-mail: Cuisine@cuisinemagazine.com

Web address: cuisinemagazine.com

a latin grill

Skirt steak with chimichurri sauce—it's a Latin favorite and as classic as the merengue. This thin cut of beef is inexpensive, but delivers big-dollar flavor. And the simple chimichurri sauce matches perfectly with this quick grill.

If you haven't had much experience cooking "foreign" food, don't worry. This is a great meal to start with. First, it doesn't require learning new cooking techniques.

Second, it's fast, simple, and inexpensive—skirt steak is reasonably priced. But best of all, this entire Latin dish is made up of familiar things. It's just steak and French fries!

Skirt Steak: This Latin grill uses a cut of beef called skirt steak. You may not know the name but you've probably eaten it—in fajitas at Tex-Mex restaurants. Fajitas are the skirt steak's claim to fame.

Skirt steak belongs to a small group of meat cuts known as "butcher steaks." There are only one or two cuts per animal. In the old days, butchers would just take them home instead of selling the few they had.

Today, skirt steak is growing in popularity because it's so flavorful. But it can be tricky to find for two reasons. One, the demand for fajitas at restaurants cuts into the supply. And two, a skirt steak isn't very big. Each steak (there's only one per steer) weighs between 2 and 5 pounds—and that doesn't make too many fajitas.

But the flavor of skirt steak makes it worth hunting for. Your best bet is a Mexican market. This is a distinctive-looking cut—long and thin with a lot of fat, connective tissue, and a pronounced grain. You'll probably be able to spot it right away, but if you can't find it, just ask. In Spanish, it's called *arrachera* [ah-rrah-CHEH-rah].

GRILLED SKIRT STEAK

(MAKES 4–6 SERVINGS)
WORK TIME: 30 MINUTES
GRILL/REST TIME: 12–15 MINUTES
TRIM OFF FAT AND SILVERSKIN:
1   1½–2 lb. skirt steak (flank steak may be substituted, *see sidebar*)
MARINATE STEAK IN:
3   T. olive oil
3   T. fresh lime juice
2   T. brown sugar
½   t. crushed red pepper flakes
2   cloves garlic, minced
1   Recipe chili seasoning for oven-baked French fries, *Page 13*

NUTRITIONAL INFORMATION PER 5-OZ. SERVING: CALORIES 335; TOTAL FAT 18(G); CALORIES FROM FAT 51%; SODIUM 112(MG); CARB. 5(G)

The butchers at the market may want to trim and mechanically tenderize the steak (poke holes in it) for you, but politely refuse. Tenderizing will turn it into a giant minute steak.

Other Benefits: The skirt steak isn't the only thing you'll like about this Latin grill. Chimichurri, a pungent parsley and garlic sauce, is perfect with grilled meat—and fish. *Papas fritas* (fried potatoes) are as popular in Latin cuisines as they are here. But the best thing about them is that they're baked (not fried) and still deliver plenty of flavor.

SKIRT AND FLANK STEAK: TOUGH LOVE

Skirt and flank steak aren't like the elegant cuts of meat on display at pristine meat counters. They are oddly shaped, not very pretty, and can be tough to chew. So why bother with them? Because they taste great.

How tough a cut of beef is has to do with where it's located on the steer. The more activity a muscle group engages in, the tougher the tissue becomes. That's what makes the meat chewy. But well-developed muscle tissue also tastes better and "beefier" than the less-exercised muscles, like tenderloin.

Skirt Steak

Take a look at these two photos. Skirt steak is the long, thin diaphragm (breathing) muscle between the abdomen and chest cavity. See all the fat and connective tissue, and how muscle fibers run in a definite direction? That's flavorful but tough stuff.

Flank steak comes from the sides of the animal. It's a little thicker than skirt with less fat and connective tissue, but also with strong fibers.

So what do you do? The key is to grill these cuts quickly so they don't dry out and get tougher. Then slice it thinly against the grain, as on Page 9.

Flank Steak

TRIM AND MARINATE

If you've grilled meat before, then trimming and marinating should be pretty familiar to you. But skirt steak is a little different—here's the scoop.

Trimming: One of the first things you'll notice with skirt steak is all the fat. Now, usually I'll suggest that you leave some fat on meat as you trim it. A little isn't *all* bad—it adds moisture and flavor as it melts during cooking.

But since skirt steak cooks in about six minutes, any fat on it won't have a chance to melt off. So remove as much of the surface fat as you can. But go ahead and leave any fat that's embedded in pockets.

This cut has a lot of connective tissue (silverskin) that you'll want to trim off, too. The silverskin shrinks when heated and causes the meat to curl. But more importantly, it's tough and makes the meat chewy. Again, remove as much of it as you can.

Marinating: Meat is marinated for two reasons: flavoring and tenderizing. But marinating this skirt steak is just for flavor. Here's why.

Meat fibers are tenderized when they're broken down by acids in the marinade, like lime juice. But it has to marinate a long time (at least 1–2 hours) before you see results. And the meat often turns mushy, not tender.

But skirt steak only needs to marinate up to 30 minutes. And even that is flexible—15 minutes is fine if you're short on time. The way it's sliced, *right*, will determine its tenderness.

I Trim off as much fat as possible from both sides of skirt steak. Some of it is loosely attached and can be removed by hand. Otherwise, use a knife for the places where it's firmly attached.

2 To remove the tough silverskin, get underneath it with the knife tip and cut a "flap." Grip the flap, then shave the silverskin away from the meat. Trim off as much silverskin as you can.

3 Mix the marinade ingredients in a large, shallow dish, like a casserole. Lay the steak in the dish (it's okay to drape it, or cut the steak in half or thirds), and turn to coat the other side. Let steak marinate up to 30 minutes at room temperature.

BUTTERFLYING FLANK STEAK

Butterflying is a simple trimming technique I use to slice this thicker flank steak so it's thin like the skirt steak. This helps it cook quickly and evenly.

Don't worry, the procedure is simple. First, trim off any silverskin and fat. Then butterfly, following the photos below. Don't panic if you trim one side a little too thin and create a hole or two in the meat—it'll still taste fantastic.

First Cut–about ¼" deep down the center

Second Cut– to the right

Third Cut–to the left

First Cut

▲ *Lay the steak lengthwise. Make the first cut down the center, across the width, about ¹⁄₄" deep. For the second cut, slice the steak in half lengthwise to the right. Stop 1" before the end.*

▲ *Now, on the other half of the steak, make a third cut like the one you just did. When finished, the two flaps should open like cupboard doors.*

▲ *Unfold the flaps and flatten seams with a meat mallet. Marinate and grill flank steak like the skirt steak.*

GRILL, REST, AND SLICE

Now *this* is what I call fast food—once the steak is marinated, it only takes about 10 minutes from the grill to the plate. Here's what you need to know.

Grilling: While the steak is marinating, prepare the grill. The coals should be red hot when you put the steak on. That way, the outside will sear quickly without overcooking the inside, making it dry and tough.

Which reminds me: Skirt and flank steak are best if they're cooked to medium-rare, medium at the most. If they cook any longer, the meat will get drier and tougher by the minute.

Resting: You've heard me say this a lot—let the steak rest before carving it. This allows the juices to redistribute throughout the meat, making the steak more tender, juicy, and evenly colored on the inside.

Slicing: Both skirt and flank steak are made up of long, strong muscle fibers that are tough to chew. Take a look at the large photo below. Thinly slicing against the grain (¹/₄" thick) makes the fibers shorter and easier to eat. Slicing at an angle (on a bias, *see inset photo*) makes the pieces a little bit wider for a nicer presentation. **Ali**

─── *Alternative* ───

GRILLING FLANK STEAK
Grilling flank steak isn't too different from the skirt steak, but there is one small adjustment you may have to make.

The meat at the seams tends to be more rare than the rest of the steak when you remove it from the grill. But be sure to remove the steak after the allotted time, or the thinner sections will overcook. Remember, you can always put rare meat back on the grill. But well-done meat is history!

4 Preheat grill. When hot, remove steak from marinade and season with salt and pepper. Place steak on grill, cover, and cook until seared, 2–3 min.

5 Flip steak over, cover, and cook another 2–3 min. Transfer meat to a cutting board, tent with foil, and let steak rest 5–8 minutes before slicing.

SLICING STEAKS
Slicing these steaks against the grain makes them more tender. Be sure to really look at the steak before slicing to see how the grain runs. The grain on flank steak runs the long way, left to right—easy to cut against.

But on skirt steak, the grain goes up and down. Trying to slice against it would be difficult (and the slices would be *very* long).

It's easiest if you first cut the skirt steak in half or thirds *with* the grain. Then slice the portions in strips *against* the grain—with a very sharp knife.

Steak Sauces

Who says sauces have to be complicated? These steak sauces use simple ingredients *and* equipment—perfect for laid-back grilling.

Now that the grill has been dusted off and fired up, cooking suddenly gets simpler. These two steak sauces fit right into the easy going style of summer grilling.

Ingredients: You probably won't see anything unusual in the recipes for the Chimichurri and Grilled Tomato Ketchup. Both focus on ingredients you may have on hand or can easily find at the grocery store.

Equipment: Now take a look at the recipe steps—no fancy equipment is necessary. A food processor is about the only thing you'll need. (And a grill for the tomato ketchup.)

Ease: The best thing about both sauces is that they can be made a day or two ahead of time. They actually improve with age. But be sure to serve them at room temperature—the flavors are more intense that way.

A traditional sauce from Argentina

In Argentina, chimichurri is the equivalent of ketchup here. It translates loosely to "spiced parsley sauce," and that's an understatement. It's garlicky and spicy, but also fresh-tasting and addictive. It's ideal with skirt steak, but excellent on fish and chicken, too.

No two chimichurri recipes are alike, but the basic ingredients include garlic, parsley, oil, and vinegar. Use curly parsley for this—it's always available, inexpensive, and has a milder flavor than flat-leaf. And go ahead and use all of it, even the stems.

Traditionally, chimichurri is made by mincing the ingredients by hand, but a food processor makes the sauce smoother. It'll thicken as it stands, so thin the sauce out with water, lime juice, or a little oil. Or spread the thicker stuff on sandwiches!

CHIMICHURRI

(MAKES ABOUT ¾ CUP)
WORK TIME: 10 MINUTES
MINCE IN FOOD PROCESSOR:
4–5 cloves garlic
½ t. crushed red pepper flakes
ADD; PROCESS UNTIL SMOOTH:
2 bunches fresh curly parsley, including stems
½ cup fresh oregano leaves
4–6 T. light olive oil
4–6 T. white wine vinegar
4–6 T. fresh lime juice
　 Salt to taste
　 Additional oil, lime juice, or water for thinning (if needed)

1 In a food processor fitted with a steel blade, process the garlic and red pepper flakes until garlic is minced. Add the herbs and process until also minced. Scrape down the sides of the bowl and add remaining ingredients.

2 Process sauce until smooth and thick. Thin with liquid, if needed. Serve, or cover and chill.

New age ketchup

There's nothing wrong with the "red sauce" in a plastic bottle. But sometimes it's nice to have something a little more sophisticated. This tomato ketchup is simple but looks fancy. Of course, it's great on beef, but it also works well with chicken and pork.

The vegetables go right on the grill (medium-high), no oil or seasonings. Char them, but not until *totally* black. And watch the jalapeno—it chars fast.

Unlike the chimichurri, take care not to process the tomato sauce until it's completely smooth—just pulse it gently. You want to be able to see small tomato and onion chunks.

This sauce gets better with age, so it's fine to make it a day or two ahead. But wait to add the cilantro just before serving. This way it will stay bright green and won't turn black.　■

GRILLED TOMATO KETCHUP

(MAKES ABOUT 2 CUPS)
WORK TIME: 10 MINUTES
GRILL TIME: 10–15 MINUTES
GRILL UNTIL CHARRED:
4 whole Roma tomatoes
½ small red onion, peeled
1 whole jalapeno pepper
COMBINE WITH VEGETABLES IN FOOD PROCESSOR; PULSE UNTIL COARSE:
2 T. apple cider vinegar
1 T. brown sugar
2 t. prepared yellow mustard
2 t. fresh lime juice
　 Salt and black pepper
FOLD IN:
¼ cup chopped fresh cilantro leaves

1 Preheat grill. Peel and halve onion (save one half for another use). Grill vegetables until charred and soft, 10–15 min. Remove stem from pepper; quarter onion. Place all ingredients in processor; pulse until coarse.

2 Don't overprocess—sauce should be chunky, not smooth. Fold in cilantro before serving.

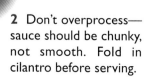

oven-baked
French Fries

Deep-fried French fries are best left to the fast food pros. Sure, deep-frying tastes great and creates crispy, golden fries, but it smells up the house. Then what do you do with all the leftover oil?

These oven-baked French fries are a home cook's dream—simple, and the kitchen smells great. But the best part is they taste as good as drive-thru fries, without the fat.

There are two keys to great oven fries. The first has to do with the type of potato—russets work well because of their high starch and low water content. The fries get crisp without turning soggy.

The second factor to good oven fries is slicing the potatoes thinly, about the width of a pencil. Be patient as you do this—if they're too big, they'll be soft and greasy.

Oven fries take some time, but you can make them ahead, then reheat, *see column, right.* **Ah**

BASIC OVEN FRIES
(MAKES 4–6 SERVINGS)
WORK TIME: 15 MINUTES
COOK TIME: 35–45 MINUTES
CUT INTO ¼" STICKS:
3–4 large russet potatoes,
    unpeeled (about 2 lbs.)
TOSS WITH:
2   T. olive oil
    Salt and black pepper*

*Any of the seasonings, see box right, can be substituted for the black pepper.

THE SLICE IS RIGHT

The key to crisp oven fries is the way they're cut—thin. This can be a little tricky with big russets like these. So here are a couple of tips.

First, slice a thin piece off one side of the potato. This creates a flat surface and keeps the potato from rolling on the cutting board.

Second, as you're slicing the planks into sticks, *see Step 3*, don't cut more than two or three planks at a time. The starch in the potato is slippery and causes the planks to slide, which is a little dangerous. But it also makes it difficult to cut the potato into even sticks.

1 Preheat oven to 475°; spray 3 or 4 baking sheets with nonstick spray. Create a flat surface on potatoes by slicing off a thin piece from one side.

2 To slice planks, turn potato on its flat side and cut ¼" thick planks. You want them as even as possible, but don't worry if they're not perfect.

3 Now, stack the planks together and cut into ¼" sticks. Toss potatoes in a large bowl with oil, salt, and pepper (or one of the seasonings, *right*).

4 Arrange potatoes in single layers on baking sheets; bake 15 min. Flip with spatula and continue baking 20–30 min. until golden. Serve right away.

REHEATING

These fries are best right out of the oven, but you can get a head start on them by cutting, partially baking, then reheating. Here are the details.

Follow the four steps above, but bake the fries 15 minutes, flip them, and bake another 15 minutes. Remove from the oven and set aside.

Then, just before serving, reheat the fries at 475° for another 10–15 minutes, or until they're heated through and crisp. The fries are best if they're made no more than 2–3 hours in advance before reheating.

VARIETY—THE SPICE OF LIFE

A big plate of basic oven fries served with plenty of salt, pepper, and ketchup is pretty darn good. But if you want something different, here are three easy and flavorful options.

Just toss the potatoes, oil, and salt with any of these seasonings, then bake them like the basic oven fries. But keep an eye on the seasoned fries while they bake—the seasonings (especially the herb and cheese) may start to burn. If that happens, reduce the heat and flip them often.

Chili Seasoning
½ t. sugar
¼ t. chili powder
¼ t. cayenne
⅛ t. paprika

Herb Seasoning
1 T. fresh thyme leaves, minced
1 T. fresh rosemary leaves, minced
1 T. fresh oregano leaves, minced

Cheese Seasoning
¼ cup finely grated Parmesan cheese

black bean BASICS

COOKING BLACK BEANS

(MAKES ABOUT 3 CUPS)
WORK TIME: 5 MINUTES
COOK TIME: 50–60 MINUTES
SORT THROUGH AND RINSE:
½   lb. dried black beans
ADD AND SIMMER:
3   cloves garlic
3   sprigs fresh thyme
2   dried bay leaves
      Cold water to cover beans

Each of these recipes starts with cooked beans. Here's what to do.

First, **sort through** the beans and discard any stones or debris. Then **rinse** them and place in a large sauce pan. **Add** the garlic, herbs, and enough cold water so the beans are covered by 1–2".

Bring to a boil over high heat. Cover, reduce heat to medium, and **simmer** until beans are tender, 40–50 minutes. Be sure *all* the water doesn't evaporate during cooking—add 1–2 cups more water if the beans get dry.

Eat a few beans to gauge how they're cooking. Try some after 30 minutes, then again every 10 minutes until done. They should be tender, *not* crunchy *or* mushy.

Before using, remove herbs, but not the garlic—it adds flavor.

Caribbean black bean salad

This salad is a loose spin-off on traditional Caribbean black beans and rice. Keep a few of these changes and tips in mind as you prepare it.

First, try using couscous [KOOS-koos] instead of rice. Couscous is a tiny pasta common to North Africa—you can buy an instant variety in most grocery stores. But for more flavor, you can *toast* the couscous first with onion and spices, then *steam* it with orange juice and chicken broth.

Second, bean salads tend to turn cloudy when tossed with vinaigrette. To prevent this, take care not to cook the beans until they break down and turn mushy. Then drain and rinse the cooked beans to remove the cloudy cooking liquid. And finally, *gently* toss the beans with vinaigrette so they don't break apart. I know it's messy, but your hands are the best tool.

Third, this salad is served with grilled sweet potatoes rather than traditional plantains (a starchy vegetable that resembles bananas and tastes like squash). Sweet potatoes taste as good and are readily available.

One last thing: Cinnamon sounds like a strange ingredient for a vinaigrette, but don't leave it out! It's a common flavor in Caribbean cuisine.

RECIPE NOTES:
(MAKES 4–6 SERVINGS)
WORK TIME: 45 MINUTES
COOK TIME: 15 MINUTES

CITRUS VINAIGRETTE
WHISK TOGETHER:
⅓   cup fresh lime juice
¼   cup orange juice
1   T. fresh ginger, peeled, grated
1   T. brown sugar
1   T. garlic, minced
1   t. lime zest, minced
¼   t. ground cinnamon
½   jalapeno, seeded, minced
SLOWLY WHISK IN:
2   T. light olive oil
       Salt to taste

Editor's Note: Half the vinaigrette will be used with the couscous; the other half with the black beans.

1 WHISK together juices, ginger, sugar, garlic, zest, cinnamon, and jalapeno in a small mixing bowl.

2 SLOWLY whisk in olive oil. Season with salt and set aside.

CARIBBEAN BEANS AND SWEET POTATOES

GENTLY COMBINE:
3 cups cooked black beans, drained, rinsed, *left*
2 T. mint leaves, chiffonade
½ Recipe Citrus Vinaigrette, *left*
   Salt to taste

TOSS TOGETHER AND GRILL:
3 sweet potatoes, peeled, sliced in ¼" rounds (1½ lb.)
2 t. olive oil
   Salt and black pepper

PLATE WITH COUSCOUS.

1 GENTLY combine the black beans, mint, vinaigrette, and salt in a large mixing bowl. Set aside.

2 TOSS the sweet potatoes with the oil, salt, and pepper in a bowl. Preheat grill to medium and cook potatoes 10–12 minutes (5–6 minutes per side) until soft.

3 PLATE by placing some couscous in the middle of a plate, then top with some beans. Now, fan a few potato slices on the side.

TOASTED COUSCOUS

BRING TO A BOIL:
½ cup orange juice
½ cup water
¼ cup low sodium chicken broth
   Pinch of salt

SAUTE IN 1 T. LIGHT OLIVE OIL:
½ cup yellow onion, diced

ADD AND TOAST; COVER, STEAM:
2 cups instant couscous
   Hot juice/broth, *above*

FLUFF COUSCOUS; TOSS WITH:
½ cup mango, peeled, diced
½ cup cucumber, seeded, diced
½ cup red bell pepper, seeded, diced
¼ cup scallions, bias cut (green and white part)
½ Recipe Citrus Vinaigrette, *left*
   Salt to taste

1 BOIL orange juice, water, broth, and salt in a small sauce pan. Set aside and keep warm.

2 SAUTE onion in a large sauce pan with 1 T. olive oil over medium heat until softened and lightly golden, about 10 minutes.

3 ADD couscous to onions and stir until toasted and lightly brown, 8–10 min. Remove from heat and pour hot juice/broth over couscous. Cover and let steam at least 10 min.

4 FLUFF couscous with a fork (like raking leaves) and transfer to a large bowl. Toss couscous with remaining ingredients and ½ of the Citrus Vinaigrette. Cover and set aside.

Brazilian black beans & rice

SOAKING BLACK BEANS

There's a lot of debate about presoaking beans to shorten the cooking time. But to me, it's not worth it. First of all, black beans tend to cook faster than other bean varieties (about 50 minutes per pound). Plus, they seem to cook more evenly and resist breaking if they're *not* presoaked.

But if the beans are taking a longer time to cook, it could just be that they're older and, therefore, drier. Just keep simmering them, adding a little water if the beans look dry.

The Caribbean isn't the only place where black beans and rice rule. Feijoada [fay-ZHWAH-duh] is Brazil's most famous regional dish: black beans and rice accompanied with fresh oranges and sauteed greens.

Traditionally, feijoada is served alongside meats, like pigs' feet and beef tongue. Don't worry, not here. Bacon gives it plenty of meaty flavor. But if you want *more*, try feijoada with some grilled smoked kielbasa. Just don't omit the Tomato-Orange Relish and sauteed collard greens—they're great companions to the smoky beans.

The feijoada is thickened by mashing some of the beans then adding them back to the pot. But if it gets too thick, thin it with a little water.

RECIPE NOTES:
(MAKES 4–6 SERVINGS)
WORK TIME: 45 MINUTES
COOK TIME: 30 MINUTES

FEIJOADA

PREPARE AND COOK:
½ lb. black beans, *see Page 14*
SAUTE:
½ lb. thick-sliced bacon, diced
SAUTE IN 1 T. BACON FAT:
1 cup white onion, diced
STIR IN:
1 t. dried leaf oregano
½ t. paprika
¼ t. cayenne
ADD:
3 cloves garlic, minced
ADD AND MASH:
1 cup cooked beans and liquid
ADD BEAN PASTE AND BACON BACK TO BEANS; SEASON WITH:
Salt and Tabasco to taste
PLATE FEIJOADA WITH:
Cooked white rice
Sauteed collard greens, *right*
Tomato-Orange Relish, *right*

1 PREPARE and cook ½ lb. black beans following the procedure on Page 14. *Do not* drain cooked beans.

2 SAUTE bacon in large saute pan over medium heat until crisp, 10–12 minutes. Remove and drain on paper towels. Pour off all but 1 T. bacon fat.

3 SAUTE diced onion in reserved bacon fat over medium-high heat until slightly softened, 5–8 minutes.

4 STIR in the oregano, paprika, and cayenne; saute until onions turn golden, about 5 minutes more.

5 ADD GARLIC and saute just until you start to smell it, 1–2 more minutes. Take care not to burn garlic.

6 ADD 1 cup cooked beans (with cooking liquid) to the onion mixture; mash until a chunky paste forms—a potato masher works great, but a fork is fine.

7 ADD BEAN paste and bacon back to beans; season with salt and Tabasco. Simmer over low heat, stirring often to avoid burning. Thin with water if needed.

8 PLATE Feijoada by first placing some cooked white rice and greens on a plate. Top with some beans and Tomato-Orange Relish, and serve.

TOMATO-ORANGE RELISH

SUPREME:
2   navel oranges

TOSS ORANGES WITH:
2   cups Roma tomatoes, diced
1   T. light olive oil
1   T. fresh lime juice
¼   cup white onion, thinly sliced
¼   cup parsley, roughly chopped
    Salt and black pepper to taste

SERVE AT ROOM TEMPERATURE.

1 SUPREME oranges by first slicing off the top and bottom of the orange so it's stable on your work surface. Then trim off the peel and pith (the white layer underneath), following the natural curve of the orange.

Over a bowl to catch juices, cut the oranges into segments by cutting down both sides of each segment, inside the membrane. Remove all segments, then squeeze the juices from the membrane into the bowl.

2 TOSS oranges with remaining relish ingredients in a large bowl. It's best to use your hands since the orange segments are fragile and may break apart if tossed with a spoon.

You can make the relish ahead—just add the oranges and parsley right before serving or they'll deteriorate. Serve relish at room temperature.

SAUTEED GREENS

PREPARE:
2   bunches collard greens
    (6–8 cups prepared)

SAUTE GREENS IN:
1   T. olive oil

ADD:
1   T. garlic, minced
2–3 T. chicken broth or water
    Salt and black pepper

1 PREPARE greens by removing tough stem. Roll up leaves into a cylinder and cut into wide ribbons.

2 SAUTE greens with olive oil in large saute pan over high heat, 1–2 minutes.

3 ADD garlic and saute greens another 1–2 minutes, tossing constantly. Add chicken broth (or water), salt, and pepper, and cook uncovered, 3–4 more minutes until tender but not mushy—they should still be bright green! Serve immediately.

black bean BASICS

USING CANNED BEANS

Canned black beans work fine in these recipes. But they aren't *exactly* the same deal—canned beans are slightly brown with a milder flavor and softer texture. They're best used for things like refried beans or the feijoada.

Be sure to rinse them well before using. The canning liquid is usually high in sodium.

SOUTHWESTERN SLAW

JULIENNE INTO ⅛" WIDE STICKS:

- ¾ cup red onion
- ¾ cup red bell pepper, seeded
- ¾ cup jicama, peeled
- ¾ cup carrot, peeled

ADD:

- ¼ cup fresh chives, cut in 3" lengths
- 3 T. fresh lime juice
- 2 T. light olive oil
  Salt and black pepper

1 JULIENNE the vegetables. One easy way to cut the carrot is to first peel off ⅛"- thick strips with a vegetable peeler, then cut them into julienne sticks. Toss all the vegetables in a bowl.

2 ADD remaining ingredients to vegetables and toss gently. Slaw can be prepared two hours ahead.

Mexican black bean wrap

In Mexico, black beans are often mashed to make refried beans. They're a far cry from refried beans out of a can—they look better and taste great.

Traditionally, refried beans are fried in lard or oil. But that step is omitted here to make a healthier dish.

RECIPE NOTES:

(MAKES 6 WRAPS)
WORK TIME: 45–50 MINUTES
COOK TIME: 30–40 MINUTES

CHIPOTLE MAYONNAISE

COMBINE:

- 1 cup prepared mayonnaise
- 2 T. chipotle pepper in adobo sauce, minced
- 1 T. fresh lime juice
- 1 T. minced fresh parsley
- 1 t. garlic, minced
- 1 t. sugar
  Salt to taste

COMBINE all ingredients in a small bowl. The mayonnaise may be made 2–3 days ahead, covered, and chilled until ready to serve.

REFRIED BLACK BEANS

SAUTE IN 2 T. OLIVE OIL:
1   cup white onion, diced

ADD AND SAUTE:
1   T. garlic, minced
1   t. dried leaf oregano
½   t. cayenne

ADD AND MASH:
3   cups cooked black beans, *Page 14*
1   cup bean cooking liquid

SEASON BEANS WITH:
2   T. fresh lime juice
    Salt to taste
    Tabasco to taste

Editor's Note: To reheat, place refried beans in sauce pan with a little water. Heat over low, stirring often to prevent scorching. Or reheat in microwave.

1 SAUTE onion in 2 T. olive oil over med. heat until softened and slightly golden, 10–15 min. Stir often to prevent burning. (Use a nonstick saute pan so the mashed beans won't stick.)

2 ADD and saute the garlic, oregano, and cayenne. Cook for another minute—just until you can smell the garlic. Do not burn.

3 ADD AND MASH 1 cup cooked beans and *some* of the cooking liquid into the onion mixture.

Continue mashing beans with small amounts of cooking liquid until all the beans and liquid are incorporated. The beans should be chunky and thick, like mashed potatoes.

Reduce heat to low and cook to evaporate moisture, 10–15 min., stirring often to prevent burning. They should now be very thick, like peanut butter, and somewhat dry. The beans will thicken as they cool.

4 SEASON beans with lime juice, salt, and Tabasco. Use immediately, or transfer to a bowl, cover, and chill. They don't need to be reheated to assemble the wraps (they'll warm when wraps are fried).

BLACK BEAN WRAPS

WARM IN 300° OVEN:
6   8" flour tortillas

ASSEMBLE WRAPS WITH:
    Refried Black Beans, *above*
1   cup Monterey Jack cheese or cheddar cheese, shredded
2   cups torn cooked chicken (I use purchased rotisserie chicken)
    Chipotle Mayonnaise, *see left*
    Southwestern Slaw, *see left*

TO FRY WRAPS, HEAT:
6   T. vegetable oil (2 T. per 2 wraps)

PLATE WRAPS, GARNISHING WITH:
4   cups romaine lettuce, cut into ribbons
    Additional mayonnaise and slaw, if desired

Editor's Note: For a healthier wrap, omit frying in Step 3.

1 WARM tortillas by wrapping in a damp kitchen towel and placing on a baking sheet. Warm in the oven 8–10 minutes until pliable. Remove; keep covered until assembling wraps.

2 ASSEMBLE wraps by spreading ½ cup beans on a tortilla. (Leave 1" around the edge so beans don't ooze out.) Top with a strip of some cheese, chicken, mayo, and slaw.

Roll the tortilla like you'd roll up a carpet—start at one side (parallel to the row of fillings), and roll up and over fillings to the end. Press to seal shut.

3 TO FRY WRAPS, heat 2 T. vegetable oil in heavy skillet over medium heat. Place wraps (two at a time) in skillet, seam side down, and fry, turning until brown and crisp on all sides.

To cut wraps on a bias, hold a sharp knife at a 45° angle to the wrap. Then, with a quick, deliberate motion, slice through the wrap.

4 PLATE wraps by placing some ribbons of sliced romaine on six serving plates. Arrange two halves of a wrap on lettuce, one leaning on the other with its cut side up. Garnish each plate with additional slaw and serve with remaining mayonnaise.

Wares

Test Kitchen Debut

We just finished our new test kitchens and they're great! Here's a quick tour to show you where we spend most of our time coming up with ideas for each issue of *Cuisine*.

Before I start, you need to know that we buy everything retail, just as you would. Why is this so important? Simple—we tell it like it is. Since there is no advertising in *Cuisine*, we don't have anybody leaning on us to use their products. Now, on with the tour.

The new test kitchens were completed the first of February. As you can see by the blueprint, there are three kitchens—each with its own refrigerator, sink, stove, and storage.

They're like traditional home kitchens, but with a few differences. Instead of cabinets above the counters, we have shelving. This way we're not constantly opening and closing doors looking for ingredients and equipment. You'll also notice that the ventilation system (hoods) are bigger than normal. Oversized is best when

there are two floors of offices above. The smell of garlic cooking can be annoying (and distracting!).

The idea behind these kitchens is to recreate a home kitchen as closely as possible. So most of the equipment we have is similar to yours. Sure, we'd like to use Sub-Zero refrigerators and Viking stoves, but many of us don't own them. Instead, we use well-built appliances (GE refrigerators and Dacor ranges) that can handle daily use.

If you want to see the kitchen in action, check out *Cuisine*cam—a camera mounted in our test kitchen that takes a picture every 30 seconds to show you what we're cooking. Go to our web site **cuisinemagazine.com**, and watch our successes and mistakes. (We make plenty of them!) Now I can really say "see you in the kitchen."

View through Galley Kitchen to Double Kitchens: The long, narrow kitchen is used for daily cooking, but it's mainly intended for preparing the food we use when we shoot our photographs.

FREEZER

STAIN
STEEL

Visit our web site **cuisinemagazine.com** and click on *Cuisinecam* to see live photos of the staff working in the test kitchen (photos are updated every 30 seconds). The camera is focused on the maple islands where we do a lot of preparing and tasting.

5

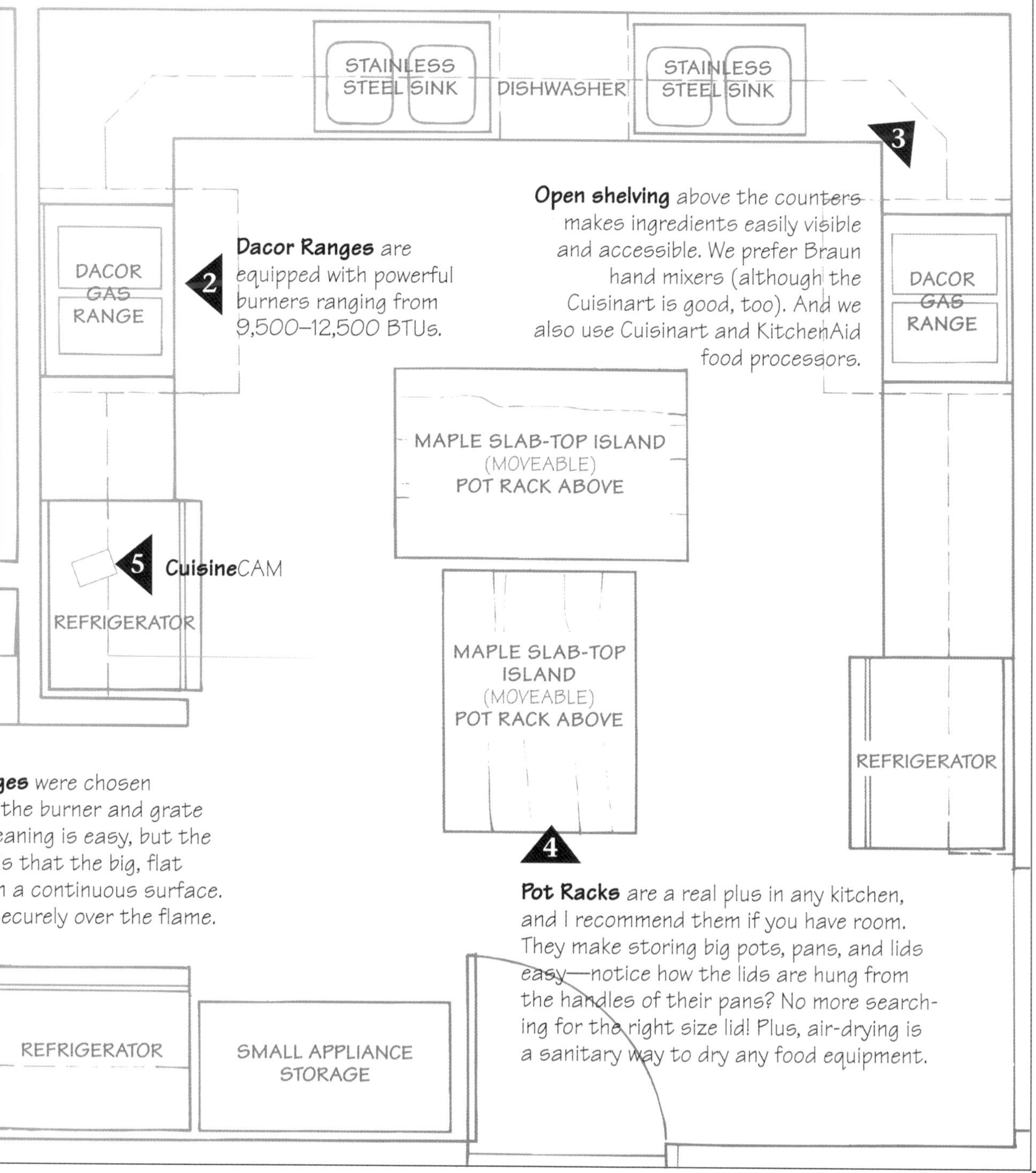

STAINLESS STEEL SINK — **DISHWASHER** — **STAINLESS STEEL SINK**

3

DACOR GAS RANGE

2 **Dacor Ranges** are equipped with powerful burners ranging from 9,500–12,500 BTUs.

Open shelving above the counters makes ingredients easily visible and accessible. We prefer Braun hand mixers (although the Cuisinart is good, too). And we also use Cuisinart and KitchenAid food processors.

DACOR GAS RANGE

MAPLE SLAB-TOP ISLAND
(MOVEABLE)
POT RACK ABOVE

5 **Cuisine**CAM

REFRIGERATOR

MAPLE SLAB-TOP ISLAND
(MOVEABLE)
POT RACK ABOVE

REFRIGERATOR

4

Dacor Ranges were chosen because of the burner and grate design—cleaning is easy, but the best thing is that the big, flat grates form a continuous surface. Pans rest securely over the flame.

Pot Racks are a real plus in any kitchen, and I recommend them if you have room. They make storing big pots, pans, and lids easy—notice how the lids are hung from the handles of their pans? No more searching for the right size lid! Plus, air-drying is a sanitary way to dry any food equipment.

DISHWASHER — **REFRIGERATOR** — **SMALL APPLIANCE STORAGE**

fresh rhubarb

Rhubarb is something you just don't notice much. In spring, the big deal is asparagus. In summer, it's peaches and plums, and the rhubarb has come and gone. Don't let that happen this year.

Varieties: There are two varieties of rhubarb you'll most likely see—hothouse and field-grown.

Hothouse rhubarb has thin, pale pink stalks and small, light green leaves. Unfortunately, it can sometimes be a little stringy.

The field-grown variety (found in gardens) is deeper red with bigger stalks and large, dark green leaves that look like red Swiss chard. It's much easier to eat than the hothouse type (not as stringy). No matter which one you use, both have that tart rhubarb flavor and can be used interchangeably.

Choosing: When choosing rhubarb, look for stalks that are firm and crisp with a vivid pink or red color, depending on variety.

If you buy rhubarb from the market, chances are the leaves will have been cut from the stalk—they're poisonous, and removing them is a safety measure so people don't eat them (like beet or turnip greens). So if someone gives you rhubarb from their garden, be sure to trim off the leaves before using it.

If the stalks have bruises on them, simply cut them away with a paring knife. Some recipes call for peeling larger stalks (they can also be stringy), but I don't like to. Most of the color is on the outside, plus the stalk gets too soft when cooked.

▲ *It's critical to remove the leaves from rhubarb stalks before using—they're poisonous. They're usually trimmed from the stalks at your grocery store.*

▲ *Remove the root end; trim rhubarb according to recipe directions. See how it's lighter colored in the center? The red color is primarily on the outside.*

Cooking: Rhubarb is normally cooked one of two ways: baked to mush in a pie or a crisp, or simmered into a sauce with *lots* of sugar for an ice cream topping.

Both treatments are fine, but I do something different—I soak the stalks in hot sugar syrup, similar to poaching. The rhubarb retains its shape and doesn't get too sweet. Be warned, the rhubarb is still pretty tart. Be sure to pair it with sweeter flavors, as in the tart, *right*.

You've got to try this redesigned rhubarb pie. The oatmeal crust and ricotta filling balance the sour rhubarb perfectly. No more gooey pies of the past—this tart puts the rhubarb on top!

POACHED RHUBARB

(FOR ONE 9" TART)
WORK TIME: 5 MINUTES
COOK TIME: 30 MINUTES
TRIM:
1¼ lb. rhubarb, cut into 4–5" pieces,
    halved lengthwise if thick
BOIL; ADD RHUBARB AND POACH:
2   cups water
1   cup sugar

1 Cut the rhubarb stalks into 4–5" sticks. If they're thick (more than 1" wide), slice stalks in half lengthwise so you have uniform-sized pieces.

2 Bring the sugar and water to a boil in a large, shallow pan, stirring occasionally to dissolve sugar. Add rhubarb, remove pan from heat, and cover.

3 Poach rhubarb in the syrup about 15 minutes, or until slightly softened. Drain carefully, allowing excess liquid to drip off stalks; cool. Discard liquid.

Rhubarb Tart

If you like rhubarb, you'll love this tart. Besides preparing rhubarb in a new way (poaching), this tart combines features of other desserts into one. The crust is similar to the topping on fruit crisp, and the filling is like a light version of cheesecake. Put them together and you've got a great match.

Rhubarb: Unlike pie and crisp, this tart puts the rhubarb on top. It's a dramatic (but simple) presentation and really shows off that red color.

I've found a great cooking method for rhubarb—briefly soaking the stalks in hot sugar syrup until they soften. (It's like poaching, but more gentle.) This method sweetens the stalks without turning them into mush.

Crust: If you're concerned about rolling out pastry dough to make this tart crust, don't be. All you need is a food processor and your hands. But take care not to overprocess it—if the butter gets too soft, the sides of the crust will shrink down during baking.

Prebaking the crust before filling helps it stay crisp. And brushing it with egg creates a protective coating against the moist ricotta filling.

Filling: Instead of a heavy cream cheese filling, this one uses lighter-tasting ricotta. Its mild flavor balances out the tart rhubarb and sweet crust.

Ricotta can be grainy, so I blend it first in a food processor. For the best texture, process it for a full minute.

Making the crust

OATMEAL-PECAN CRUST

(FOR ONE 9" TART)
WORK TIME: 10 MINUTES
PREBAKE TIME: 15–18 MINUTES
IN FOOD PROCESSOR, BLEND:
⅔ cup all-purpose flour
⅓ cup sugar
⅓ cup oats (not instant)
1 t. ground cinnamon
¼ t. salt
ADD AND PULSE:
⅓ cup pecan halves
4 T. cold unsalted butter, cubed
ADD 1 T. AT A TIME AND PULSE:
1–2 T. milk
FORM CRUST; FREEZE. BRUSH WITH:
1 egg, beaten

4 In food processor fitted with a steel blade, blend flour, sugar, oats, cinnamon, and salt. Add pecans and butter; pulse until mixture looks like cornmeal.

5 Add the milk 1 T. at a time, pulsing after each addition until dough holds together when pinched (it will still be crumbly). Take care not to overprocess.

6 Grease a 9" tart pan with removable bottom with nonstick spray. Press the dough evenly into the pan—it's easiest

if you do the sides first, then the bottom. Be sure crust isn't too thick where the bottom meets the sides.

7 Preheat oven to 400°; freeze crust 15–20 min., until firm. Brush frozen shell with beaten egg. Prebake 15–18 min., until set and lightly browned. Cool.

Filling and baking

RICOTTA-CITRUS FILLING

WORK TIME: 10 MINUTES
COOK TIME: 35–40 MINUTES
BLEND IN FOOD PROCESSOR:
1 cup whole milk ricotta
ADD AND PROCESS:
¼ cup sugar
1 egg
1 T. fresh lemon juice
1 t. orange zest, minced
½ t. vanilla
Pinch of salt
FILL PREBAKED SHELL,
STACK RHUBARB ON TOP,
AND BAKE.

8 In a food processor fitted with a steel blade, blend ricotta until *very* smooth, about one minute. Scrape sides of bowl, add remaining ingredients, and process until blended. Pour filling into the cooled shell and spread evenly. Arrange poached rhubarb on top, stacking as if you were building a campfire.

9 Place tart on a baking sheet and bake 35–40 minutes, or until filling is puffed slightly and lightly browned. Cool tart completely on a rack before serving.

WHAT'S HAPPENING IN FOOD?

PERFECT PORK ▶

Great pork is hard to beat. And tough to come by. But the pork from the **Niman Ranch Pork Company**, based in Thornton, Iowa, has cornered the market.

Hog farmer Paul Willis has joined California's fine meat purveyor, Bill Niman, to provide restaurants and gourmet stores with some of the best pork available. The animals are raised free-range (not in confinement pens) and on high-quality grains (with no antibiotics or hormones). Check out **www.nimanranch.com**, or call **(510) 808-0330** to order.

▲ SUPER STEAK KNIVES

It's about time to fire up the grill, and **LamsonSharp** delivers just what you need to cut through big T-bones and ribeyes. Each of these 10" steak knives is made of high-carbon, stainless steel. The 4$\frac{1}{2}$" blade runs through the rosewood handle (full-tang) for great balance. And it's riveted for durability. To order, call LamsonSharp at **(800) 872-6564**, or log on to their Web site, **www.lamsonsharp.com**.

◀ OLIVE OIL SOAPS

Olive oil isn't just for vinaigrettes. **Bella Cucina Artful Food** introduces a line of all-natural, organic soaps that take advantage of the moisturizing qualities of olive oil.

These aromatherapy soaps come in unique scents like Lemon Polenta, Peppermint Sage, and Rose Milk. And because they contain more oil than traditional soaps, they *really* soften your hands. Order the $6 bars by calling **(800) 580-5674**.

◀ NEW WAVE WHISKING

Whisking eggs and whipping cream has gone one step further with this stainless steel **Ball-Tipped Wire Whisk**.

Unlike traditional whisks, the wires are independent of each other with a ball at each tip. These ball-tipped wires actually increase the whisking area within the bowl—now cream whips in no time! And food won't get stuck in the wires. But be warned: whisking can be a little messy. Call Solutions at **(800) 342-9988** to order.

QUESTIONS AND ANSWERS

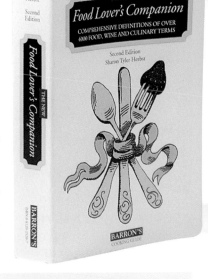

Q *I can't find the Krups La Glaciere electric ice cream maker you recommended in the Wares article in Issue 4 (July/August 1997). Can you help me?*

A Krups no longer makes that model. Girmi, however, makes a model with all the great features that the La Glaciere wowed us with.

The **Girmi Gelatiera** (#GL14) has the same 50-watt, base-mounted motor with a circular paddle. It produces almost one quart of ice cream in about half an hour. Best of all, it runs the same price as the Krups ($60) and comes with a three year warranty. We love ours. Call Euro Cuisine **(888) 343-5554** to order one or find out more.

Q *In Issue 19, there was a recipe for "to-die-for" Molten Cakes. I was wondering if I can make the batter, freeze, and then bake them?*

A Yes, you can. First, be sure to cover the batter-filled ramekins with plastic wrap (to protect them from freezer burn) and bake them within a week. If they stay there any longer than that, they may end up tasting like your freezer.

Second, thaw them for at least half an hour before putting them in the oven. After thawing, you should be able to follow the directions to the letter.

Just don't bake the cakes first and then freeze them—they'll end up overbaked when you reheat and not as molten.

Q *I love your glossary every month, but I'm looking for a more extensive encyclopedia of kitchen terms. Can you recommend one?*

A The *Food Lover's Companion*, by Sharon Tyler Herbst (Baron's Educational Series, Inc., 1995, $12.95) is excellent. It includes more than 4,200 food, drink, and culinary terms such as cooking techniques, foreign foods, ingredients, and kitchen equipment. This small, but information-packed book also includes charts on measurement equivalents, altitude adjustments for baking, and ingredient substitutions. If information is power, this book is a real power tool.

Q *What is cake flour? I can't seem to find it in my grocery store and I'd like to make the Coconut Cake in Issue 20. Is there a substitute?*

A Cake flour is low-protein flour milled from soft (low-protein) wheat. A couple of common brands are Softasilk and Swans Down. Cake flour has the least amount of gluten (protein), which gives strength and structure to baked products, like bread. So if there's less gluten in the flour, cakes and pastries turn out more tender and have a finer texture.

Most grocery stores carry cake flour. But if you can't find it, all-purpose can be used, with a few adjustments. For each cup of flour, substitute two tablespoons cornstarch for two tablespoons of the flour, then sift together. This lowers the protein and raises the starch content, approximating cake flour.

To make the 1$\frac{1}{2}$ cups cake flour for the Coconut Cake, put three tablespoons cornstarch in the bottom of a $\frac{1}{2}$ cup measure, and add all-purpose flour to fill the cup. Then sift this together with one more cup of all-purpose flour.

Q *I love your magazine! I happened to notice that you use a product called "stretch-tite." I've seen it in a catalog, but not recently. Where can I buy it?*

A Don't worry if your favorite catalog no longer carries it—go straight to the source, Polyvinyl Films in Sutton, MA. Call them at **(800) 343-6134** or check out their web site at **www.stretchtite.com** and they'll tell you where you can find it

We first talked about **stretch-tite** and **freezer-tite** in Issue 12. Now we

don't know what we'd do without it in our test kitchen! It seals well, and holds up really great—especially when pounding food like in this issue's chicken article, *see Pages 28–29.*

Q *I've been told that I shouldn't put my good knives in the dishwasher. Why not?*

A There are three good reasons to wash those expensive knives by hand. *Number 1:* Soaking those wood handles will make them warp, split, and lose their finish. *Number 2:* The caustic chemicals in dishwashing detergent (like bleach) can actually rust and pit the carbon in quality blades. *Number 3:* The force of the rinse cycle can bang your knives against other objects in the dishwasher and damage the cutting edge.

Wash your knives individually in warm water with mild detergent and then dry. *Don't* soak them in a soapy sink—what you can't see can cut you.

Q *I made the Bolognese from Issue 19. I have to admit, I thought was just too salty. Is there an error in the recipe or am I just salt-sensitive?*

A After retesting the Bolognese recipe, we found that the amount of salt given is correct. Even still, it may be that the amount is just too much for your taste. In fact, more times than not, *we* even disagree over the saltiness of a recipe during testing.

It's a matter of biology. The taste buds on your tongue detect and are sensitive to certain flavors—sweet, sour, salty, and bitter. Some people taste certain ones more acutely than others. You might just be one of those people who has a high sensitivity to salt. That could actually be a benefit—less need to worry about high blood pressure.

So, from here on out, with the exception of certain recipes, we're suggesting that people salt to taste.

Q *I dropped my chef's knife last night and broke off the tip. What's the best source to replace it?*

A First off, before you replace your knife, you might be able to get the tip repaired. If the tip isn't too far gone, both *Bladesmith's, Inc.* **(206) 623-1088** in Seattle, or *Corrado Cutlery* **(800) 416-4413** in Chicago, can repair it for you for about $10 (including shipping!). However, if the knife is beyond repair, try local cookware or department stores for a new one. Generally, they'll carry one or two brands, but you'll pay for the convenience of buying it off the shelf.

These two catalog sources are great: *Knife Merchant* **(800) 714-8226**, or *Professional Cutlery Direct (PCD)* **(800) 859-6994**. Expect to pay as much as 20% less than retail (not including shipping). Plus, the selection is much better—*PCD* has more than 10 major brands.

Q *I subscribed to a great magazine in the early 1980s called* Cuisine. *Is your magazine the same one—just with a new look? I'm confused.*

A Actually, the two magazines share nothing but their name. The original *Cuisine* magazine was published by a company out of Santa Barbara, CA, and has been out of circulation for several years. I, too, thought it was a great magazine and "cut my teeth" on it. I have all their back issues thanks to my Aunt Ginny.

The current *Cuisine* magazine is almost four years old and is published by August Home Publishing (which is 22 years old) out of Des Moines, Iowa.

GLOSSARY

Buffalo mozzarella: A type of fresh mozzarella, which is usually packaged in whey or water. Most buffalo mozzarella sold in the United States is made from a combination of water buffalo and cow's milk.

Chipotle chile: [chih-POHT-lay] A dried, smoked jalapeno pepper that has wrinkled, dark brown skin with a smoky-sweet flavor. Chipotles are often sold canned in *adobo sauce*—a dark red sauce made from ground chiles, herbs, and vinegar.

Prosciutto: [proh-SHOO-toh] An Italian "ham" that is seasoned and salt-cured (not smoked). It's then air-dried, pressed, and sold thinly sliced. The best are aged 18–24 months.

Sun-dried tomatoes: Tomatoes that have been dried—either in the sun or by artificial methods. Drying makes them chewy, sweet, and intensely flavored. They are usually sold packed in oil or dry-packed in bags.

Supreme: A technique for segmenting citrus fruit that removes its peel and pith (the white, bitter layer between the outer peel and the flesh).

Water bath (bain-marie): [bahn mah-REE] A French cooking technique in which a container of food is placed in a large, shallow pan of warm water. The warm water surrounds the food with gentle heat. The container and pan of water is then placed in the oven or on top of the stove. This technique is ideal for delicate foods like sauces and custards—it keeps them from breaking or curdling.

ABBREVIATIONS

t. = teaspoon
T., Tbsp. = tablespoon
oz. = ounce
lb. = pound
Dash = scant $1/8$ of a teaspoon
Pinch = $1/16$ of a teaspoon

the basics of
stuffed chicken breasts...

Do you have 10 minutes and a mallet? Here are two classic ways to stuff a chicken breast followed by three quick recipes to perk up the "baked chicken blahs."

There are two classic ways to stuff a chicken breast. One way is to layer and roll the breast producing a swirl inside when it's sliced. Use this when the ingredients are dry and flat like ham, dry cheeses, greens, or herbs.

The other way to stuff a breast is to form it into a pocket. You've heard of chicken cordon bleu or Kiev? The pocket method is used with these because the sides are sealed so the ingredients (butter or soft cheese) don't leak out when cooked.

Pounding: Pounding the breast correctly is critical to the final look of the dish. There are three key steps.

First is size. Each breast half should weigh 6–7 ounces. This size is easy to work with, and makes a nice finished roll or pocket.

Second is placing the breast with the smooth-side down (where the skin was), and *gently* pounding it. You want the smooth side to remain intact while the ragged side receives the impact of the mallet. And since chicken has little connective tissue, it's important to use gentle strokes when pounding—the meat can tear easily.

Finally, the shape is critical to the outcome. A 4 x 7" pounded rectangle makes a perfect roll or pocket.

POUNDING

Working with one chicken breast at a time, place each inside a sheet of plastic wrap. With the smooth side down (where the skin used to be), gently pound each breast to ¼" thick. Shape it into a 4 x 7" rectangle using the technique in Step 1 on this page. Don't pound too hard or the delicate meat will tear and create holes.

ROLLED CHICKEN BREAST

1

The breast doesn't always form a 4 x 7" rectangle—it looks more like Florida. Trim the flattened "panhandle." Add it to narrow area to make a wider shape. Gently pound edges together to join.

2

Lay the breast on a sheet of plastic wrap to prevent sticking. Spread filling evenly (I'm using a white filling just so you can see it well). Leave a ½" margin on all sides to help seal the roll.

3

Begin rolling. You can use the plastic wrap to help tuck and roll. If you want, use toothpicks to secure seam. Wrap each breast in plastic and chill with the seam down until ready to cook.

CHICKEN BREAST POCKET

1

Trim and shape the flattened chicken breast as in Step 1, *left*. Spread prepared filling about a $^1/_4$" thick on half of the breast. Leave a $^1/_2$" margin around all the edges for easy sealing.

2

Fold over the unfilled portion of the chicken breast to meet the filled side—like making a turnover. Press the bare edges together to create an initial seal. Cover pocket with plastic wrap.

3

Gently tap around the edges with the flat side of a meat mallet to seal in the filling. If the filling oozes out, the edges might not seal well. Refrigerate up to a day or until ready to cook.

...with
white bean ragoût

Roasting the tomatoes and garlic

1 Preheat oven to 425°. Place prepared tomatoes in an ovenproof saute pan. Cut the top from a garlic bulb to expose the cloves. Add bulb to the pan.

2 Drizzle tomatoes and garlic with oil and roast in oven for 30 minutes until garlic cloves are soft. Remove pan from oven and set aside to cool.

3 When cool, squeeze the garlic bulb at the base to release the cloves. Finely mince the garlic and return it to the roasted tomatoes. Set aside.

GOAT CHEESE AND SUNDRIED TOMATO ROLL

(MAKES 4 ROLLS)
WORK TIME: 1 HOUR
COOK TIME: 1 HOUR

ROAST:

1½ cups Roma tomatoes, seeded and cut into chunks
1 head garlic, top removed
¼ cup olive oil

PREPARE AS ON PAGE 28:

4 6–7 oz. chicken breast halves

STUFF BREASTS WITH:

½ cup goat cheese, crumbled
¼ cup oil-packed sundried tomatoes, diced

DUST WITH:

Seasoned flour*

BROWN CHICKEN IN:

¼ cup olive oil

BAKE AND REMOVE CHICKEN.

DEGLAZE PAN AND REDUCE BY HALF:

1 cup dry white wine

WHISK INTO WINE:

2 T. cold unsalted butter

FOR RAGOÛT, GENTLY MIX AND WARM:

Roasted Tomatoes and Garlic
2 cans (15-oz. each) small white beans, drained and rinsed
¼ cup white wine vinegar
2 T. olive oil
1 T. fresh thyme leaves
2 t. fennel seed, toasted and crushed
Salt and black pepper to taste

*Seasoned flour: blend ⅓ cup all-purpose flour with 1 tsp. salt and 1 tsp. black pepper.

NUTRITIONAL INFO. PER ROLL WITH BEANS:
CALORIES 932; TOTAL FAT 52(G); CALORIES FROM FAT 51%; SODIUM 956(MG); CARB. 51G

WHAT IS RAGOÛT?

Ragoût [ra-GOO] is a French word that means "to stimulate the appetite." Seems like a pretty wide playing field, doesn't it? But ragoûts are usually categorized as stews—flavorful foods that are cooked for a long time to develop a rich, deep taste.

Meats are often main features in ragoûts. But this white bean version is made without it. And the long cooking time has been cut down because it uses canned white beans. Another bonus: The ragoût can be made a day or two ahead (it's better with age), then reheated.

Preparing the chicken and ragoût

4 Place 2 T. crumbled goat cheese and 1 T. diced sundried tomatoes in an even layer on each prepared breast. Make sure to leave enough space around the edges as on Page 28.

5 Now tightly roll up the breast. Use the plastic wrap to help tuck and roll like a cigar. Secure at the seam with toothpicks. Wrap each breast in plastic wrap; chill, seam-side down for 30 minutes.

6 Heat oil in large, ovenproof pan over medium-high heat. Lightly dust each roll with seasoned flour. Place rolls in pan, *seam-side down*. Brown on all sides. Bake at 425° 15 min. to finish cooking.

7 While chicken cooks, drain and rinse beans, then place in bowl with roasted tomatoes and garlic. Blend the vinegar, oil, thyme, fennel seed, salt, and pepper. Drizzle over bean mixture.

8 Gently toss beans using your hands. Don't overmix or beans will break and make the ragoût cloudy. Warm beans through in a small saute pan, or reheat in the microwave.

9 Remove chicken from pan and keep warm. Over high heat, deglaze pan with wine; reduce and whisk in butter. Slice chicken on a bias, ½" thick. Place slices on 1 cup beans; top with 1 T. wine sauce.

...with
rosemary & grapes

Preparing the filling and making the pockets

1 Blue cheese is much too strong to use by itself. Mix the cream cheese with the blue cheese. Then, spread 2 tablespoons of filling over each breast. Seal as on Page 29. Wrap them in plastic wrap and then refrigerate. Chilling before cooking helps maintain their shape and minimizes the possibility of leaking while cooking.

ROSEMARY CHICKEN WITH GRAPES AND BLUE CHEESE

(MAKES 4 STUFFED POCKETS)

WORK TIME: 30 MINUTES
COOK TIME: 45 MINUTES

PREPARE AS ON PAGE 29:

4   6–7 oz. chicken breast halves

COMBINE:

1   3-oz. pkg. cream cheese, softened
2   T. blue cheese, crumbled

PREPARE (SEE BOX BELOW):

16   white pearl onions

DUST WITH:

Seasoned flour, *see Page 31*

BROWN CHICKEN IN:

¼   cup olive oil

BROWN ONIONS AND ADD:

2   T. garlic, minced

DEGLAZE WITH:

2   cups dry white wine

STIR IN:

2   T. honey

RETURN CHICKEN; ADD:

1   T. chopped fresh rosemary

BAKE; AFTER 10 MINUTES ADD:

32   seedless grapes, red or green

REMOVE CHICKEN; ADD TO SAUCE:

2   T. unsalted butter

SEASON WITH:

Salt and pepper to taste

NUTRITIONAL INFORMATION PER POCKET WITH SAUCE: CALORIES 392; TOTAL FAT 16(G); CALORIES FROM FAT 35%; SODIUM 170(MG); CARBOHYDRATES 54(G)

PEARL ONIONS

Pearl onions have a papery skin that needs to be removed. To do this, bring a pan of water to a boil. Add the pearl onions and blanch for three minutes. Remove the onions and place them in a bowl of ice water to stop the cooking process.

When they're cool enough to handle, cut a small bit of the root end away—but not too much or the onion will fall apart. Now, remove the loosened skin. It should pull right off just using your fingers.

Important: Thoroughly dry the onions before sauteing. Wet onions will splatter when they come in contact with hot oil.

Cooking the stuffed chicken pockets

2 Before cooking, preheat oven to 425°. Lightly dust each pocket with flour. The flour helps the chicken brown and helps thicken the sauce.

3 Heat oil in large, ovenproof saute pan over medium-high. Lightly brown pockets on both sides. It's okay if some filling seeps out. Remove and set aside.

4 Saute onions until lightly browned. Add garlic and saute for 30 seconds. Deglaze pan with wine while scraping bottom. Over high heat, reduce by half.

5 Stir honey into sauce and then return browned chicken to the pan. Sprinkle with rosemary. Place the pan in the oven and bake for 10 minutes.

6 After 10 minutes, add the grapes to the pan and bake for 5 minutes more. Cooking the grapes any longer will discolor the sauce.

7 Transfer chicken to a plate. Stir in butter to the sauce to thicken and add a sheen. Salt and pepper to taste. Spoon sauce over plated chicken.

...with greens & bourbon

Preparing the collard greens

1 To prepare the collard greens, first remove the thick rib from the leaves, see *Tips From the Test Kitchen, Page 5*. Tear leaves into 2" pieces, then blanch in boiling, salted water for two minutes. Strain greens and plunge into ice water to stop cooking process. Remove and pat dry with paper towels.

"GREEN" OPTIONS
Collard greens add a spicy bite to this rolled chicken breast—they stand up to the bourbon sauce and add a nice, contrasting color. But they're not the only option for a filler or base. Try other peppery greens, like mustard greens, or any variety of Swiss chard. Spinach is a little mild, but can be used if spicy greens are too strong for you.

If you use spinach, be sure to cook it briefly before rolling it in the breasts (cooking helps set the green color). I like to saute it quickly with a little olive oil—blanching makes it too soggy.

HAM AND GREENS ROLL

(MAKES 4 ROLLS)

WORK TIME: 1 HOUR
COOK TIME: 1 HOUR

PREPARE AS ON PAGE 28:
4   6–7 oz. chicken breast halves

PREPARE AS ON PAGE 34:
2   bunches collard greens
     (about 12 cups)

ROLL CHICKEN WITH:
     Blanched collard greens
½   lb. thinly sliced smoked
     ham (about eight slices)

DUST CHICKEN WITH:
     Seasoned flour, see Page 31

BROWN CHICKEN IN:
2   T. olive oil

REMOVE CHICKEN AND SAUTE:
½   cup shallots, minced
¼   cup garlic, minced

DEGLAZE WITH; REDUCE:
¼   cup bourbon

ADD AND REDUCE:
1½   cups low sodium chicken broth
1   cup heavy whipping cream

ADD CHICKEN BACK TO PAN AND BAKE;
REMOVE CHICKEN AND ADD TO PAN:
2   t. fresh thyme leaves
⅛   t. cayenne
⅛   t. ground nutmeg
     Salt to taste

SAUTE REMAINING GREENS IN:
2–3 T. olive oil

SLICE CHICKEN. SERVE WITH GREENS AND SAUCE.

NUTRITIONAL INFORMATION PER ROLL WITH SAUCE AND GREENS: CALORIES 787; TOTAL FAT 50(G); CALORIES FROM FAT 57%; SODIUM 1,541(MG); CARBOHYDRATES 23(G)

Filling, rolling, and cooking

1) Layer with greens

2) Layer with ham

3) Roll chicken breast

2 Prepare chicken breast for a roll as on Page 28. Place a single layer of greens (about ¼ cup) on each breast. Then top greens with a layer of ham (2 slices per breast). Be sure to leave a bare edge at one end to help seal the roll.

3 Heat oil in large, ovenproof saute pan over med.-high heat. Place chicken in pan seam-side down to help seal. Brown on all sides. Remove and set aside.

Roll the breast (you can secure it with a toothpick if you wish) and wrap tightly in plastic wrap. Refrigerate until ready to cook (at least 30 min.). Just before cooking, preheat oven to 425° and dust the chicken lightly with seasoned flour.

4 Add shallots to pan and saute for I minute. Add garlic; saute 30 seconds. Deglaze with bourbon, scraping bottom. Reduce until almost evaporated.

5 Add broth and cream and bring to a boil. Return chicken to pan; transfer pan to oven and bake 12 minutes. Remove chicken; cover to keep warm.

6 To finish the sauce, add thyme and spices, and reduce over med.-high until thick, like maple syrup. In another skillet, lightly saute remaining greens in oil.

7 Divide sauteed greens among 4 plates. Slice chicken into ½" slices and fan out over the greens. Drizzle chicken and greens with ¼ cup sauce.

mega mall muffins

You've seen these muffins. The big, oversized beauties sold at malls. Almost impossible to pass up. Their huge, crunchy, streusel tops are beguiling. Let's face it, the lid *is* the muffin.

You can get that lid look at home along with mega taste and tenderness. Maximum lid impact comes from toppings of streusel, coarse sugar, or a shiny glaze. And the only necessary equipment is a regular muffin pan.

The blueberry and rhubarb muffin recipes share the same procedures and techniques but have different combinations of ingredients. They each use a different fat (butter and oil) and acid (yogurt and buttermilk). I'm giving both recipes—you can decide which combination you like best. Both produce beautiful, dome-shaped muffins.

The mixing procedure consists of *folding* the wet and dry ingredients together. Don't overmix—it'll affect doming and texture. Right after mixing, fill the muffin cups and bake.

After baking, wait five minutes before unmolding muffins. Then twist the lid and lift out—if it sticks, run a knife under the rim of lid to loosen.

Cool muffins by placing upside down on a cooling rack. Otherwise, the warm muffin stem could collapse under the weight of the big top! **A**

BLUEBERRY-MAPLE MUFFINS

(MAKES 6 MEGA MUFFINS)
WORK TIME: 10 MINUTES
COOK TIME: 20–25 MINUTES

WHISK; SET ASIDE:
2 cups all-purpose flour
1 T. baking powder
½ t. salt

WHISK; SET ASIDE:
1 cup plain lowfat yogurt
¾ cup sugar
6 T. unsalted butter, melted
2 eggs, room temperature
½ t. imitation maple flavoring

COMBINE:
2 T. all-purpose flour
2 T. sugar

ADD AND TOSS:
1 cup fresh blueberries

FOLD WET INTO DRY MIX;
FOLD IN COATED BLUEBERRIES.

TOP WITH:
Choose topping from *Lid List*

NUTRITIONAL INFORMATION PER MUFFIN: CALORIES 443; TOTAL FAT 14(G); CALORIES FROM FAT 29%; SODIUM 491(MG); CARB. 70(G)

Making the muffins

1 Spray entire 12-cup muffin pan (*inside* and the surface *between* cups) with nonstick spray. A light gray nonstick pan works great. But stay away from dark pans—they overbrown.

2 Preheat oven to 375°. Whisk dry ingredients. Whisk wet ingredients. Set both aside. Rinse fruit. Now gently toss the damp fruit in the flour/sugar mixture until coated.

3 Use a rubber scraper to fold wet ingredients into dry, *just* until flour is barely visible. Don't overmix. The batter will be lumpy—that's okay. Now gently fold in the coated fruit.

4 Fill cups using an ice cream scoop. Use a heaping ½ cup batter (about 2 scoops) each. You want the batter *mounded* above the pan. Stagger muffins so tops don't bake together.

5 Put sugar and streusel toppings on muffins *before* baking. If using sugar, generously sprinkle top of muffin. For streusel, gently press chunks onto top, leaving ¼–½" border.

6 Bake 20–25 min. in center of oven. They're done when inserted toothpick comes out clean. (If glazing, brush on glaze; bake additional min.) Let sit 5 min. Remove; cool on rack.

Three muffin lids

All three of these toppings create crunchy muffin lids that work great on both muffins. You make the call!

FOR THE SUGAR TOPPING: Sprinkle coarse sugar (like bakeries use) on unbaked muffins for a simple but showy lid. Buy it at a kitchen supply or gourmet store. Or order from **King Arthur Flour** at (800) 827-6836, Item #1240 (Sparkling White Sugar). A 1 lb. package is $3.95 plus S&H.

FOR THE STREUSEL TOPPING:
COMBINE; PRESS ONTO UNBAKED MUFFINS:
½   cup brown sugar, packed
⅓   cup all-purpose flour
⅓   cup oats (not instant)
¼   cup unsalted butter, melted
Combine with fingers until crumbly.

FOR THE BAKED GLAZE:
WHISK; BRUSH ON BAKED MUFFINS:
½   cup powdered sugar, sifted
1   T. plain lowfat yogurt
¼   t. vanilla
Remove pan of fully baked muffins from oven. Immediately brush with glaze. Bake an additional minute to set the glaze.

RHUBARB-LEMON MUFFINS

(MAKES 6 MEGA MUFFINS)
WORK TIME: 10 MINUTES
COOK TIME: 20–25 MINUTES
WHISK; SET ASIDE:
2   cups all-purpose flour
1   T. baking powder
½   t. salt
½   t. ground ginger
WHISK; SET ASIDE:
1   cup sugar
½   cup buttermilk
¼   cup oil (sunflower, canola, or vegetable)
2   eggs, room temperature
1   T. lemon zest, finely minced
COMBINE:
2   T. all-purpose flour
2   T. sugar
ADD AND TOSS:
1¾ cups fresh rhubarb, ¼" dice
FOLD WET INTO DRY MIX;
FOLD IN COATED RHUBARB.
TOP WITH:
Choose topping from *Lid List*

NUTRITIONAL INFORMATION PER MUFFIN: CALORIES 433; TOTAL FAT 12(G); CALORIES FROM FAT 24%; SODIUM 483(MG); CARB. 75(G)

strata _frittata_

These aren't your typical baked egg casseroles—
Sunday brunch just moved up a notch!

You read "Egg Basics" in the last issue of _Cuisine._ Now put that knowledge to use with three baked egg dishes—a strata, a frittata, and a tortilla. The key to all of them is low, slow heat so the eggs are creamy, not tough.

The best way to describe strata is a bread pudding souffle that's not sweet. Slices of dry bread are layered with Bacon Pesto and Swiss cheese, then soaked with beaten eggs. When baked, the strata puffs like a souffle.

A frittata is an Italian omelet, but casual—it looks like a fat pancake. The eggs are mixed with the other ingredients (artichoke hearts, prosciutto, and chives), and then cooked slowly on top of the stove and finished under the broiler.

The Spanish tortilla is a thin frittata made with fewer eggs. If you've had tapas (Spanish appetizers), you may have had one—it's a common snack. Because it's thin, it's great for layering with several ingredients.

Editor's Tip: To dry bread slices, first cut rounds of French bread with a cookie cutter (be sure it fits inside the ramekins). Then line a baking sheet with a rack and toast the bread at 375° for 10–15 minutes, until dry.

BACON PESTO STRATA
(MAKES 4)
WORK TIME: 1 HOUR
COOK TIME: 40 MINUTES
BUTTER FOUR-1¼ CUP RAMEKINS;
DUST WITH:
¼   cup bread crumbs (1 T. in each)
FOR BACON PESTO—
SAUTE:
6   slices thick-cut bacon, chopped
WILT IN 1 T. BACON DRIPPINGS:
3   cups fresh spinach, stemmed
COMBINE IN FOOD PROCESSOR:
     Sauteed bacon and spinach, _above_
¼   cup fresh parsley leaves
2   T. plain yogurt
DRY TWELVE ¼"-THICK SLICES OF
FRENCH BREAD. BEAT TOGETHER:
6   eggs
¾   cup plain yogurt
¾   cup whole milk
⅛   t. cayenne pepper
ASSEMBLE STRATAS WITH:
     Dry bread slices spread with pesto
½   cup Swiss cheese, shredded
     Egg mixture
BAKE STRATAS. GARNISH WITH:
     Fresh Fruit Kabobs, _right_

NUTRITIONAL INFO. PER STRATA: CALORIES 506;
TOTAL FAT 28(G); CALORIES FROM FAT 51%;
SODIUM 1,010(MG); CARBOHYDRATES 33(G)

1 Prepare ramekins. For pesto, saute bacon; remove. Then wilt spinach in 1 T. bacon fat. Process bacon, spinach, parsley, and yogurt until paste forms.

2 Beat together eggs, yogurt, milk, and cayenne pepper in a large bowl until blended. The mixture will be about as thick as heavy cream. Set aside.

3 _Before drying bread, be sure to cut it to fit ramekins (see Editor's Tip, above). Small baguettes work well too._ Spread 1 T. pesto on one side of each slice of dry bread.

tortilla

CREATING THE KABOB

Fruit kabobs are an easy, colorful garnish for the strata (or any other egg dish). Choose your favorite seasonal fruits—just be sure they're big enough for spearing! Strawberries, kiwi, melons, and pineapple work really well.

You can use a melon baller to scoop out the melon, or simply cut them into large chunks. Cut the pineapple and kiwi into wedges, leaving the peel on (it looks nice). The strawberries can be left whole, or halved if really big. Then just slide pieces of the fruit onto a wooden skewer.

4 Place one slice bread in ramekin, *pesto side up,* and sprinkle with 1 T. cheese. Add ¹/₄ cup egg mixture to cover bread. Layer again with bread, cheese, and egg.

5 For the third layer, place bread *pesto side down* and top with ¹/₄ cup egg. Place ramekins on baking sheet; weight down bread and let soak 30 minutes.

6 Preheat oven to 375°. Remove weights and bake 30–40 minutes, until brown and puffed. Cool 5 minutes. Remove from ramekins; serve with fruit kabobs.

This frittata makes an elegant brunch or light lunch dish. Serve it with toasted bread and salad. First, remove the crusts from six slices of a good, dark bread. Toast the slices, and place one on each serving plate. Top bread with a wedge of frittata, then garnish with mixed greens that have been tossed with your favorite vinaigrette.

ARTICHOKE FRITTATA

(MAKES ONE 10" FRITTATA; SERVES 6)

WORK TIME: 15 MINUTES
COOK TIME: 20 MINUTES

SAUTE IN 2 TEASPOONS OLIVE OIL;
REMOVE AND SET ASIDE:

- 1 cup canned artichoke hearts, drained and quartered
- ½ cup thinly sliced prosciutto, torn into strips

ADD TO SAUTE PAN:

- 12 eggs, beaten

TOP WITH; BAKE AND BROIL:

- Sauteed artichokes and prosciutto
- ¼ cup Parmesan cheese, grated
- 1 T. fresh chives, chopped

SERVE FRITTATA WITH:

- 6 slices pumpernickel (or other dark bread) trimmed and toasted
- 6 cups mixed greens, lightly tossed with vinaigrette (1 cup/serving)

GARNISH WITH:

- Fresh whole chives

NUTRITIONAL INFORMATION PER ⅙ SLICE:
CALORIES 216; TOTAL FAT 14(G); CALORIES FROM FAT 59%; SODIUM 352(MG); CARBOHYDRATES 4(G)

1 Preheat oven to 425°. Heat oil in a 10" ovenproof, nonstick skillet over med. heat. Add artichokes and prosciutto; saute until prosciutto starts to curl.

2 Remove and set aside. Wipe pan clean; coat with nonstick spray. Add eggs; cook until curds form. Add artichokes and prosciutto; top with cheese and chives.

3 Place pan in oven; bake 7–8 min. (center won't be set). Remove from oven; preheat broiler. Broil 2 min., until eggs are fully set and top is lightly browned.

4 Remove from oven and run rubber spatula under frittata to loosen. Slide out onto cutting board, and slice into six wedges. Plate as shown above.

tortilla

SPANISH TORTILLA

(MAKES ONE 10" TORTILLA; SERVES 2)

WORK TIME: 20 MINUTES
COOK TIME: 15 MINUTES

COMBINE AND SET ASIDE:

- ½   cup Roma tomatoes, diced
- 1   T. basil, chiffonade
- 2   t. fresh lime juice
- 2   t. olive oil

PREPARE AND SET ASIDE:

- 4   oz. fresh buffalo mozzarella, sliced ¼" thick
- ½   avocado, peeled, thinly sliced

SAUTE IN 1 TABLESPOON OLIVE OIL:

- ¾   cup Russet potatoes, peeled, diced
- ½   cup yellow onion, diced
     Salt and black pepper to taste

ADD TO PAN AND BROIL:

- 4   eggs, beaten

LAYER WEDGES OF TORTILLA WITH:

     Sliced mozzarella and avocado

GARNISH WITH:

     Tomato mixture, *above*
     Parmesan cheese, grated

NUTRITIONAL INFORMATION PER SERVING:
CALORIES 531; TOTAL FAT 39(G); CALORIES
FROM FAT 66%; SODIUM 508(MG); CARB. 22(G)

1 In a bowl, combine tomatoes, basil, lime juice, and oil; set aside. Prepare cheese and avocado (drizzle avocado with lime juice to prevent browning).

2 Preheat broiler. Heat oil in oven-proof, nonstick skillet over med. heat. Saute potatoes and onions until lightly brown, 8–10 min. Beat eggs; add to pan.

3 Place pan in oven about 6" from broiler. Broil tortilla 2–3 minutes, until eggs are set. Rotate pan for even browning. Watch so it doesn't burn.

4 Transfer tortilla to cutting board and slice into 6 wedges. Layer 2 wedges with cheese and avocado, *see below*. Garnish with tomatoes and Parmesan.

Top a wedge of tortilla with a mozzarella slice.

Arrange avocado slices on second tortilla wedge.

Garnish third wedge with tomatoes and Parmesan.

cheese flan

A favorite traditional dessert in Spanish-speaking countries, flan is custard with a caramel syrup. Add cream cheese and it's a cross between cheesecake and custard in both taste and texture.

The caramel syrup for flan comes from sugar that's been caramelized in the bottom of the flan dish. After baking, the flan is chilled. While chilling, that hard sugar begins to break down into a syrup. When unmolded, the flan has an automatic syrup glaze.

But standard stovetop caramelizing is tricky—one minute it's not quite ready, and the next it's burned. This *baking* method offers a slower, gentler approach that gives a little more leeway. And it's done in a glass pie plate to get a true read on the color and avoid burning the sugar. Medium amber is the color to look for. If it approaches black, it'll taste burned. With caramelizing simplified, cheese flan is an easy, yet impressive dessert.

Thanks to Don and Norma Malecki and the Summit Gourmet Club of Cincinnati (our new friends from the Cuisine Cruise) for turning us on to cheese flan from San Juan.

CHEESE FLAN

(MAKES ONE 10" FLAN)
WORK TIME: 55 MINUTES
BAKE TIME: 45–50 MINUTES
CHILL TIME: TWO DAYS

FOR THE CARAMEL–
CARAMELIZE IN OVEN; COOL.
1   cup sugar

FOR THE CUSTARD FILLING–
BEAT UNTIL CREAMY:
1   package (8 oz.) cream cheese
½   cup sugar
ADD:
1   can (14 oz.) sweetened condensed milk (not evaporated)
1¼   cups whole milk
6   eggs
1   T. vanilla

NUTRITIONAL INFORMATION PER ⅟₁₀ SLICE: CALORIES 392; TOTAL FAT 16(G); CALORIES FROM FAT 35%; SODIUM 170(MG); CARBOHYDRATES 54(G)

Caramelizing

1   TO CARAMELIZE SUGAR preheat oven to 350°. Spray a 10" glass pie plate with nonstick spray. Add 1 cup sugar; shake to evenly distribute. Bake on center rack of oven. AFTER 25 MINUTES the dry sugar turns golden and edges begin to melt. Leave it alone. AFTER 35 MINUTES edges are melted, leaving an island of sugar. Watch it closely. When the sugar island is the size of a small orange (AFTER 40 MINUTES), remove from oven and swirl plate (be careful—it's hot) so caramel runs back and forth over dry sugar, leaving small clumps. Continue baking until clumps are melted (AFTER 45–50 MINUTES) and color is medium amber. Swirl plate to even the caramel. Cool on a rack 30 minutes until completely hard.

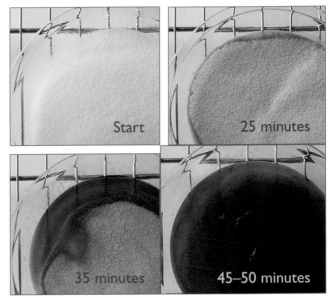

Start

25 minutes

35 minutes

45–50 minutes

Making and baking the filling

2 While caramel cools, bring cream cheese to room temperature. In a large mixing bowl, beat cream cheese and sugar on low speed. Increase speed to high, beating until creamy.

3 Add remaining ingredients and beat on low to incorporate. Increase speed to medium, scraping the bottom and sides of the bowl. Beat until completely smooth.

4 Bake the flan in a water bath, following the directions for *Safer Water Bath* on Page 5. To avoid spilling, reserve the final cup of flan liquid and add *after* placing dish in pan.

5 Bake at 350° for 45–50 min. Flan is done when top is golden, center 3" still jiggles slightly, and knife inserted near center comes out clean. Cool. Cover with plastic; chill.

48 hours later

Chill the flan for two days? Definitely—and here's why. Time allows the caramelized sugar to break down, converting it into the wonderful syrup essential for flan.

It's a perfect make-ahead dessert—just unmold and serve. If you *must* unmold sooner, make sure it's completely chilled. It'll still work, but there won't be as much syrup.

6 To unmold, slowly run a sharp knife around the flan two times, pressing knife tip to the bottom to loosen caramel, and back of knife against side of the dish for smooth flan edges.

7 Invert onto a flat serving plate. Gentle shaking may be enough to unmold flan. If not, microwave a damp towel for 30–60 seconds and lay over dish until flan loosens and unmolds.

8 Lift off dish and scrape dish bottom to loosen remaining syrup—get every drop you can. Pour over the flan. Some hard caramel will still remain in the dish—soak in hot water to clean.

GRAND *finale*

Cuisine

Introducing a dressed up version of the traditional flat flan.

This hits new heights with its impressive cheesecake stature. To achieve the look, bake in a deep souffle dish instead of a pie plate, and top with fresh strawberries and edible flowers.

Prepare the flan on Pages 42–43 with minor changes. Caramelizing the sugar takes longer—60 minutes total. (Remove from the oven and swirl after 55 minutes.)

Bake the flan for 90 min. A 2" circle in the middle will still jiggle slightly.

Tall summer flan

▲**Caramelize sugar** in a 7 x 3" souffle dish sprayed with nonstick spray, *see Page 42*. For unmolding insurance, brush melted butter on sides of dish before adding flan filling. Cover with foil; bake in a water bath 70 min. Remove foil; bake 20 min. more.

▲**Unmold chilled flan** just before serving. Run a sharp knife around the flan two times (press knife against side of the dish, with tip reaching to bottom). Invert onto a flat serving plate. Pour syrup over the top and cap it off with fresh berries and a few edible flowers.

Issue No. 22 July/August 2000
www.CuisineMagazine.com

Cuisine

an illustrated guide to creative home cooking

the best
cherry pie

Cuisine

Editor
John F. Meyer

Art Director
Cinda Shambaugh

Associate Editor
Susan Hoss

Assistant Editors
Juliana Hale
Sara Ostransky

Senior Graphic Designer
Holly Wiederin

Graphic Designer
Stephanie Hunter

Test Kitchen Director
Kim Samuelson

Contributing Photographers
Scott Little, Dean Tanner

Food Stylist
Janet Pittman

Pre-Press Image Specialist
Troy Clark

Publisher
Donald B. Peschke

CORPORATE:
Director of Finance: Mary R. Scheve • *Creative Director:* Ted Kralicek • *New Media Manager:* Gordon C. Gaippe • *Special Publications Executive Editor:* Douglas L. Hicks • *Senior Photographer:* Crayola England • *Multi Media Art Director:* Eugene Pedersen • *Technology Analyst:* Carol Schoeppler • *Web Site Product Specialist:* Adam Best • *Web Content Managers:* Terry Walker, David Briggs • *Controller:* Robin Hutchinson • *Senior Accountant:* Laura Thomas • *Accounts Payable:* Mary Schultz • *Accounts Receivable:* Margo Petrus • *Production Director:* George Chmielarz • *Electronic Publishing Director:* Douglas M. Lidster • *Network Administrator:* Cris Schwanebeck • *Production Coordinator:* Noelle M. Carroll • *Pre-Press Image Specialist:* Minniette Johnson • *H.R. Assistant:* Kirsten Koele • *Facilities Manager:* Julia Fish • *Receptionist:* Jeanne Johnson • *Administrative Assistant:* Sherri Ribbey • *Mail Room Clerk:* Lou Webber

CUSTOMER SERVICE & FULFILLMENT:
Operations Director: Bob Baker • *Customer Service Manager:* Jennie Enos • *Customer Service Representatives:* Anna Cox, Jeanette Rankin, April Revell, Deborah Rich, Tammy Truckenbrod • *Technical Representative:* Johnny Audette • *Buyer:* Linda Jones • *Administrative Assistant:* Nancy Downey • *Warehouse Supervisor:* Nancy Johnson • *Fulfillment:* Sylvia Carey, Sheryl Knox, Dan Spidle

CIRCULATION:
Subscriber Services Director: Sandy Baum • *New Business Director:* Glenda Battles • *New Business Manager:* Todd L. Bierle • *Promotion Manager:* Rick Junkins • *Billing Manager:* Rebecca Cunningham • *Renewal Manager:* Paige Rogers • *Assistant Subscription Manager:* Joy Krause • *Circulation Marketing Analyst:* Kris Schlemmer • *Associate Circulation Marketing Analyst:* Paula M. DeMatteis • *Creative Manager:* Melinda Haffner • *Senior Graphic Designers:* Robin Dowdell, Mark Hayes

Cuisine™ (ISSN 1089-6546) is published bi-monthly (Jan., Mar., May, July, Sept., Nov.) by August Home Publishing Co., 2200 Grand Ave., Des Moines, IA 50312. Cuisine© is a trademark of August Home Publishing Co. ©Copyright 2000 August Home Publishing. All rights reserved. Subscriptions: Single copy: $4.99. One year subscription (6 issues), $21.94. (Canada/Foreign add $10 per year, U.S. funds) Periodicals postage paid at Des Moines, IA and at additional mailing offices. "USPS/Perry-Judd's Heartland Division automatable poly". Postmaster: Send change of address to Cuisine, P.O. Box 37100 Boone, IA 50037-2100. Subscription questions? Call 800-311-3995, 8 a.m. to 5 p.m., Central Standard Time, weekdays. Online Subscriber Services: www.CuisineMagazine.com. Cuisine© does not accept and is not responsible for unsolicited manuscripts. PRINTED IN U.S.A.

www.CuisineMagazine.com

from the editor:

July and August are what I call "lemonade" months. Time to ease back on the daily grind and try to enjoy the sultry days of summer. So what's the lure of these lazy days? Meandering through the local farmer's markets, eating vine-ripe tomato sandwiches on white bread, slipping on baggy shorts with big T-shirts, or just walking around without socks and shoes. It's something different for each person except one thing—grilling. Just starting charcoal and burning off the grate brings on a Pavlovian reaction of sensory overload. A smoking grill a block away can cause mouths to salivate and even change a menu at the last minute.

So, to help you enjoy your summer even more, here are several grilling articles. They're all good, of course! Pork tenderloin is a natural on the grill, and the kebab sandwiches make a fun and unique presentation out of regular shish kebabs. But maybe the best one is the easiest—s'mores (back cover). Don't let this old campfire dessert fool you. Loaded with summer flavor, *semi*-low in calories (for a dessert), and made for adults, this simple dessert makes grilling an art.

Hopefully, you're noticing some good changes in *Cuisine*. I'm interested in what you think and would like to hear your opinions. There is a *new* survey on our specially created web site **http://survey.CuisineMagazine.com** (it's only for our readers). Participate by answering a few questions about some of the changes and your name will be entered (if you want) to win a KitchenAid stand mixer. Then, after completing the survey, kick off your shoes and put on some baggy shorts—it's time to do some serious grilling.

32

contents
Issue 22 JULY/august 2000

feature articles

Tips *and techniques* from our readers

Radish Leaves

Don't throw out those fresh radish leaves! Instead, try mincing them. Then they can be tossed with salad, added to vegetables as they're cooking, or sprinkled over cooked vegetables. The leaves aren't spicy-hot like the radishes themselves, but they'll add a certain peppery zest.

Pat Coate
Denton, TX

Test Kitchen Tip from Sue: Slicing angel food and pound cakes with a knife can cause uneven ripples or scrunching. So for the Grand Finale on the back cover, I used an electric knife instead. Check out the smooth results.

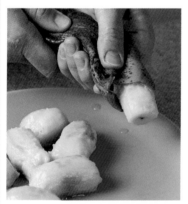

Freezing Bananas

In our house, bananas only have about a one day window when we can eat them. We just don't like them too ripe! So when they get past their peak, I toss them in the freezer, just as they are. When I've accumulated several, I make banana bread.

To "peel" a frozen banana, first let it thaw for about 15 minutes. Then cut off the blossom end and squeeze the banana to push out the flesh, one half at a time. All the brown strings will stay inside the peel.

Lori Miller
Cincinnati, OH

Test Kitchen Tip from Juli: In the summer, using a sauce on anything grilled just seems way too heavy. So for a light and flavorful finish, I put a pat of herbed or citrus butter on top after plating.

Frozen Roux

When I make stock, I use the resulting fat to make roux. Then I freeze the roux in small disks for later use. When making gravy, I just add a frozen disk or two. The roux melts slowly, so there are no lumps, and it flavors and thickens at the same time.

Cleaning Scallions

For a fast and efficient way to clean scallions, use a paper towel instead of a knife.

Wrap a paper towel around the stem of the green onion. Grip the onion and slide the towel down the stem, peeling off the top layer. Now, snap the root end off. This not only removes unwanted layers, but also the grit and dirt particles.

Michael Welch
Sacramento, CA

Here's my method: Chill stock overnight. Transfer congealed fat to a saucepan to make roux. Cool and scoop tablespoons of roux onto a parchment-lined baking sheet; freeze. Once frozen, store roux disks in a plastic freezer bag.

Jack Chandler
Poway, CA

Club Soda Pancakes

Here's a tip I use all the time. To make the lightest pancakes, I use my favorite recipe, but replace the liquid with an equal amount of club soda. It makes a noticeable difference—the pancakes are thicker, yet light and fluffy. This tip works great for waffles too.

Margaret Kucharavy
Syracuse, NY

A Little Liqueur

I like using liqueurs for special baking. But large, expensive bottles make my pantry a crowded, pricey place. And most recipes only need a few tablespoons. So I buy small bottles (like you get on airplanes) at a liquor store for $3.00 or less.

Pat Neaves
Kansas City, MO

Steam-Warming Tortillas

Corn tortillas are usually fried to soften them for rolling, but I *steam* them instead. Just add about a tablespoon of water to a heated nonstick pan. Quickly "fry" until the water has evaporated, turning once. The tortilla will be soft but not sticky.

Edie Pero
Roy, WA

Aluminum Foil "Strings"

I was preparing the boneless leg of lamb in Issue 20 when I realized I didn't have cooking string. So I *made* strings by rolling 1 x 18" aluminum foil strips. I used them just like string, but twisted the ends (instead of tying) to secure. This also works for any roast or for tying chicken legs together.

David Starkey
New York, NY

Test Kitchen Tip from Sara: Our Classic Cookies on Pages 14–17 turn out great using Edie's freezing tip (see left). We used it over and over again with excess dough from cookie testing.

Freezing Cookie Dough

Most raw cookie doughs store well in the freezer. Here's the quickest and easiest method.

Use a cookie scoop to portion balls of dough onto a baking sheet lined with parchment paper. Place the baking sheet in the freezer for about an hour, or until the dough balls are frozen. Then place the frozen balls into a resealable plastic freezer bag.

When you want fresh-baked cookies, all you have to do is bake the frozen dough balls at the usual temperature, adding a few minutes to the baking time.

Edie Pero
Roy, WA

Freezing Fresh Ginger

For easier handling of fresh ginger, I keep it in the freezer. When I need some, I cut a chunk off the frozen root, peel the skin with a vegetable peeler, and easily slice. The ginger can be frozen up to six months, wrapped in plastic.

Arlene Lawson
Granada Hills, CA

Salty Grip

Skinning a fish fillet can be slippery business. So I put salt on my fingers before grabbing ahold of the skin of the fish. The salt prevents my fingers from slipping while gripping the fish skin. Otherwise it would be impossible to hold onto! (Don't salt the fingers of your other hand—it holds the fillet knife.)

Leah Dundon
Nashville, TN

share your  with Cuisine

If you have a unique way of solving a cooking problem, we'd like to hear from you, and we'll consider publishing your tip in one or more of our works.

Just write down your cooking tip and mail it to Cuisine, Tips Editor, 2200 Grand Ave., Des Moines, IA 50312, or contact us through our e-mail address shown below. Please include your name, address, and daytime phone number in case we have questions. We'll pay you $25 if we publish your tip.

E-mail: Cuisine@CuisineMagazine.com
Web address: www.CuisineMagazine.com

greens on the grill

Tired of the same old tossed salad? This grilled salad can double as a side or even a main course. If that's not enough, it's quick and easy to boot.

Grilled salad is just the thing. It's summer's best vegetables roasted quickly on the grill and then tossed with an herb vinaigrette while still warm.

Let's face it, summer vegetables are good just by themselves, but grilling brings out their best flavors. It naturally enhances their sweetness and adds a great smoky flavor. As a final bonus, some of the black char acts just like a summer herb.

Grilled salad goes great with the Balsamic Pork Tenderloin on Page 8, but can be served alone since it's combined with pasta and cheese. Forget your droopy lettuce, this salad is hot!

Grill-ready vegetables

1 Cut vegetables for the grill in big, flat pieces. This way they'll cook evenly and will be easy to move around. You'll cut them up later into smaller pieces.

Make onion lollipops with ½"-thick onion slices. This thickness is best so they don't burn easily. ►
Tip: Secure slices with small bamboo skewers (soaked in water for 20 minutes). This keeps the rings from separating.

◄ *Cut the red peppers into planks about the size of a business card. Remove seeds and veins.*

Tip: To cut through a pepper easily, cut from the inside rather than the tough waxy exterior. Even a dull knife can cut through this soft surface.

▲ *Slice the summer squash or zucchini in half, lengthwise.*

Cut tomatoes in half, top to bottom. Scoop out all of the seeds and pulp. ►
Tip: If the watery pulp is not removed, the tomato will be too mushy to cut into pieces.

Pull out stems of the portobellas and discard. Scoop out all of the dark gills (where the stem was) with a spoon. ►
Tip: If the gills aren't removed, they can turn the salad black.

Grilling and assembling the salad

2 The cut vegetables will be grilled so they need to be well-coated with olive oil. This prevents sticking and also adds flavor. In a large bowl, toss the cut pieces with the oil, salt and pepper.

3 For orzo, bring broth and rosemary to a simmer. Add orzo and cook over medium-low heat until all the broth is absorbed, about 25 minutes. Season to taste. Cover to prevent drying out.

GRILLED SUMMER VEGETABLE SALAD
(MAKES 6 CUPS)
WORK TIME: 10 MINUTES
COOK TIME: 25 MINUTES

TOSS WITH ¼ CUP OLIVE OIL; GRILL:
1   large red onion, ½" slices
2   large (or 4 small) portobella mushrooms, stemmed, gills removed
2   summer squash or zucchini, halved lengthwise
1   red bell pepper, seeded, quartered
4   Roma tomatoes, halved, seeded
FOR THE HERBED VINAIGRETTE*—
WHISK TOGETHER:
3   T. olive oil
1   T. apple cider vinegar
½   t. chopped fresh parsley
½   t. chopped fresh thyme
½   t. chopped fresh rosemary
¼   t. kosher salt
    Pinch black pepper
FOR THE CREAMY ORZO—
SIMMER:
6   cups low-sodium chicken broth
2   t. chopped fresh rosemary
ADD:
2   cups orzo
GARNISH WITH:
¼   cup dry goat cheese, crumbled
    *Vinaigrette Option: Use 3 T. of your favorite bottled vinaigrette

NUTRITIONAL INFORMATION PER CUP:
CALORIES 379; TOTAL FAT 20(G); CALORIES FROM FAT 46%; SODIUM 330(MG); CARBOHYDRATES 40(G)

4 Vegetables take different amounts of time to cook. First, put on onions and portobellas. After three minutes, start grilling the squash and peppers. In another three minutes, add tomatoes, skin side down. All the vegetables should all be done in five more minutes. Turn the vegetables midway through grilling, except the tomatoes—you just want to char the skin.

Serving the salad

7 Whether you're using this grilled salad for a side or main course, serve it on a bed of orzo. Then, place the grilled vegetables over the top and garnish with crumbled dry goat cheese.

5 Make the vinaigrette (or use your favorite bottled dressing). Cut the grilled vegetables into bite-sized chunks and put them all together in a mixing bowl. Add the vinaigrette to the grilled vegetable mixture.

6 Now, toss the salad. Some of the vegetables are fragile and stirring with a utensil might crush them. Instead, use your hands to toss! It's okay. Your hands are the best tool you have in the kitchen.

pork tenderloin
the inside story

Pork tenderloin is often confused with pork loin. It must be the word

"loin" that causes the problem, and that's too bad. Loin is good, but

tenderloin is simply the most tender and flavorful cut of pork there is.

Try these two complete meals to discover the tenderloin's talents.

Because pork tenderloin is so tender, it's best when cooked quickly, over high heat—like a good steak. It's a natural, then, for grilling. Here are two recipes (each with their own salad) that you'll really like. Both get a brief marinade, a quick grill, and are brushed with a glaze just before serving.

No grill? Don't worry. Prepare the tenderloins in a 450° oven and roast for the same amount of time as you would grill. You can use these recipes all year long. And why not? Pork tenderloin is the leanest of all pork cuts. At 4.1 grams of fat for a three-ounce serving, it's nearly as lean as chicken breast.

pork and safe cooking

The USDA and many cookbooks still emphasize cooking pork to an internal temperature of 160°. This is to kill the trichinella parasite that used to be so prevalent in pork. It's different now!

Today's pork is not only leaner, it's safer. Safety is still important, but that temperature thinking is dated. We now know the parasite is killed at 137°. Also, in the past hogs were fed everything. Strict guidelines about what hogs can eat make trichinella infestation almost nonexistent.

Now it's okay to cook pork to a lower temperature, so it doesn't have to be white and dried out. A little pink in the pork says a lot—it's moist and flavorful. For these recipes, cook the pork to about 145–147° (medium) and then let it rest for five minutes under foil. The temperature will keep rising (from residual heat) to over 150° as it sits. It'll be pink and perfect.

BALSAMIC TENDERLOIN

(MAKES SIX 4-OZ. SERVINGS)
WORK TIME: 15 MINUTES
COOK TIME: 12–15 MINUTES
TRIM AND TIE:
2   pork tenderloins (2–3 pounds)
MARINATE IN:
¾   cup olive oil
¼   cup apple cider vinegar
2   T. chopped fresh rosemary,
     (or 2 t. dried)
1   T. kosher salt
1½   t. black pepper
3   cloves garlic, minced
GRILL PORK; BRUSH WITH:
¼   cup Balsamic Glaze, *Page 10*
SERVE WITH:
     Grilled Summer Vegetable
     Salad, *Page 7*

NUTRITIONAL INFORMATION PER 4-OZ. SERVING: CALORIES 294; TOTAL FAT 15(G); CALORIES FROM FAT 46%; SODIUM 462(MG); CARBOHYDRATES 7(G)

what is pork tenderloin?

Even restaurants get confused. Their menu says pork tenderloin, but what you get are large slices of pork loin.

The confusion is understandable (although unacceptable). Both are cuts of pork from the loin area. But think about it. If you order beef tenderloin you wouldn't expect a New York strip—they're also from a similar area but are completely different cuts. So let's clear this up. Here's what you should know about pork tenderloin.

Look at the loin chop in the photo above. The bone is the spine and the loin muscle is on top—it's the back of the hog. See how the tenderloins are smaller and *underneath* the loin? At that location, the tenderloins don't get much exercise. As a result, they're soft and tender. Advantages to this lazy muscle are less fat and calories than other cuts of pork. And because it is so lean, tender, and small, it cooks quickly.

This boneless loin roast is made up of two loins wrapped together (the dividing line is where they meet). It's a portion of the whole loin—they can be over 2' long and up to 10 pounds.

Whole tenderloins are less than a foot long and taper at one end. Each one weighs only 1–1½ pounds, enough for 2 or 3 people. They usually come vacuum-sealed (Cryovac-packed) in pairs.

working with tenderloin

There are a couple things to do to the tenderloins before heading to the grill.

First, remove what little fat is on the tenderloin. Then trim off the silverskin—it's tough, thick connective tissue that looks like packing tape.

It's not such a big deal if you don't remove all the fat (it'll melt during grilling). But be sure to remove all the silverskin—if cooked, it'll shrink and twist, turning the tenderloin into a meat corkscrew. Plus, it's *really* chewy.

1 The fat sits loosely on top of the tenderloin. Cut it off, or even pull it away with your fingers. Any fat remaining will melt during grilling.

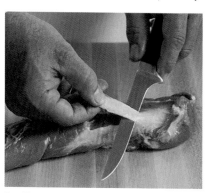

2 Slip your knife just under the silverskin. Holding one cut end of the skin tightly, run your blade under the membrane and cut it away.

getting ready to grill

Before actually grilling, you'll want to do a few things to make sure the tenderloins come out perfectly. First, tie the pork to help maintain its shape. Second, make a marinade. Then while the tenderloins marinate, prepare the balsamic glaze and let it cool.

Tying the Tenderloins: Tying is optional, but there are a couple of good reasons to do it. First, securing the narrow tail to the body of the tenderloin will keep it from getting overcooked. And second, tying the whole tenderloin maintains its round shape and helps it cook more evenly.

Marinating: Marinating does two things—it tenderizes and flavors. Vinegar tends to break the meat down and make it a little more tender, but tenderloins are already tender. The real function of this marinade is flavor. Even marinating for a short time can really enhance the flavor of meats.

Preparing the Glaze: A great way to add flavor and color to anything grilled is by using a balsamic glaze. For this glaze, use an *inexpensive* balsamic vinegar. You don't want to use fine vinegar since most of it will evaporate anyway. The reduction will make it sweet and it will taste like aged balsamic vinegar.

Be warned, though. The vinegar will simmer for a long time without getting thick. Then, all of a sudden, it's thick! So keep an eye on it—there's a small gap between done and burned.

3 To make the tenderloins consistent in size, fold over the narrow tail end of the tenderloin and tie it in place up over the body. Use only *cotton* kitchen twine (cotton won't burn or melt).

5 Chop garlic and rosemary; combine with the other marinade ingredients in a measuring cup. If using dried rosemary, grind it with a spice grinder or mortar and pestle to release oils.

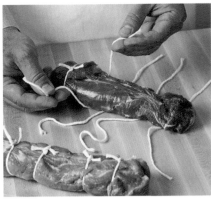

4 Continue tying the rest of the tenderloin at 1½" intervals along the entire length. Pull the string tightly around the meat and knot. You'll use about five 5" pieces of string for each tenderloin.

6 Place the tenderloins in a resealable plastic bag and pour the marinade over them. Put the bag in a pan to catch any leaks, seal it, and store upright in the refrigerator for up to an hour.

BALSAMIC GLAZE

(MAKES ¼ CUP)

COOK TIME: 15–17 MINUTES

SIMMER AND REDUCE:

1 cup balsamic vinegar

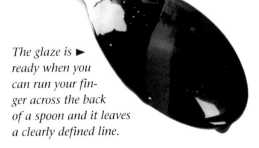

The glaze is ►
ready when you
can run your fin-
ger across the back
of a spoon and it leaves
a clearly defined line.

7 Bring balsamic vinegar to a simmer over high heat (about three minutes), then reduce heat to medium-low. Keep it simmering gently, uncovered. Reduce to ¼ cup, about 13 minutes.

8 You want the glaze to be thick enough to coat the back of a spoon. Any longer and it'll have the consistency of hot tar and taste burned. Transfer the vinegar to another container to cool.

grilling the tenderloin

Before putting the tenderloins on the grill, prepare the vegetables and orzo for the salad, *Pages 6–7*. That way, everything will be ready at once.

Grilling Time: Rely on a timer and a thermometer to help you determine doneness. Since tenderloins aren't flat, like a steak, rotate them a couple of times as they cook. Once you've turned them the last time, check the temperature with the thermometer. I think they're best cooked to medium, just a little pink. This should take 17 minutes, more or less.

Glazing: The concentrated sugars in the glaze will create a shiny, smooth coating on the meat—but look out. They'll also burn in a heartbeat if cooked too long. That's why the glaze is brushed on right when the pork is done. Then, grill it for less than a minute, just until the glaze turns a rich, deep mahogany.

Resting: Tent the tenderloins under foil and rest for about five minutes before serving. Here's why: During cooking all the juices in the meat run to the middle (away from the heat). Resting allows those juices to filter into the more done areas. If cut too soon, all the juices in the middle would burst out like a water balloon. A lot of flavor would end up on your cutting board.

Once rested, slice the tenderloins on the bias. This shows off more of that terrific glaze and tender, pink center.

9 Preheat grill to medium-high. Place the tenderloins on the grill, cover, and cook four minutes. Then rotate tenderloins, cover and cook another four minutes. Rotate a final time and cook to the doneness you want (see chart).

11 Timing is important but also check the meat's internal temperature with a thermometer to get the doneness you want. These are grilled to an internal temperature of 146°.

10 When done, brush the tenderloins all over with the balsamic glaze. Grill for one minute, rotating every 20 seconds to set the glaze. The glaze may make them stick to the grill, so this time, use a spatula to help turn them.

Is it done yet? (1-lb. tenderloin)		
DONENESS	MINUTES ON GRILL (lid closed)	INTERNAL TEMP.
Medium-rare	15	145°
Medium	17	150°
Medium-well	19	155°

▲ *Some cookbooks will tell you pork is done at 160°, but that's well-done, and well-done pork is dry pork. At 140° the meat is rare, but hot enough to kill any bacteria. At 150° it's medium and still tender. Between 150° and 160° it's still juicy, but past 160°, it's gone.*

12 Tent the tenderloins with foil and let rest for five minutes. Then, remove the strings and slice diagonally into ½"-thick slices. The angled cut gives you larger slices. And the slices will fan out nicely on the plate.

serving

13 Now is the time to show off your work. First, make a bed of orzo on the plate. Then, put some of the grilled vegetables on top, and sprinkle with crumbled dry goat cheese. Now, lean several slices of the tenderloin against the salad. A serving of pork is about 4–6 ounces. That's three or four slices each.

very asian variation

Pork tenderloin can adapt to almost any cultural taste. This Asian variation is loaded with flavor, light and refreshing—great for even the hottest summer day.

Asian Pork Tenderloin is surprising in several ways. Like good Asian food, it possesses intense flavor, but doesn't taste heavy or leave you feeling full. While the presentation can be fancy, this dish's roots have humble beginnings. The pork can be done on the backyard grill, and the salad is made with common, instant-style ramen noodles. But the most surprising thing about this dish is how simple it is. The sauce and salad ingredients can be prepared a day ahead, and the meat takes only 15 minutes to grill.

Here's what makes this dish so good. **Asian Noodle Salad** is easy and can be made ahead—just add the dressing before serving. Cutting the vegetables takes the most time since the dressing is made in a food processor.

Yakitori Sauce [yah-kee-TOH-ree] is a soy-based sauce used as a marinade, glaze, and a dip. The ingredients are simple and intensely flavored.

Gremolada is an Italian garnish made from parsley, lemon, and garlic. I put an Asian twist to it by substituting peanuts, ginger, and cilantro.

It's all in the vegetables

1 Like many Asian dishes, cutting and preparation takes more time than the actual assembling and cooking. This salad is no exception. Here's what to do.

Prepare bok choy stalks. Use the leafy part for color and the stem for flavor. Shred the leaves and dice (small) the white stems.

Remove top of the red pepper and cut in quarters. Then, cut into narrow strips. It's easiest to slice strips if you cut from the inside.

For carrot matchsticks, make slices by cutting ribbons using a peeler. Stack ribbons and cut into thin matchsticks with sharp knife.

Cut off the stem ends. Then, slice the individual pea pods in half lengthwise. Cut through each pod to expose the peas.

ASIAN NOODLE SALAD
(MAKES 4 CUPS)
WORK TIME: 25 MINUTES
COOK TIME: 3 MINUTES
CUT:
1	cup bok choy, shredded & diced
¾	cup snow peas, halved
½	cup red peppers, cut in strips
½	cup carrots, cut in matchsticks
½	cup bean sprouts (*optional*)
¼	cup scallions, sliced
¼	cup fresh cilantro, leaves only

COOK IN BOILING WATER, COOL:
1	3-oz. package ramen noodles

FOR THE HOT AND SWEET DRESSING—
COMBINE IN FOOD PROCESSOR:
¼	cup sugar
¼	cup orange juice
¼	cup ketchup
¼	cup apple cider vinegar
2	T. chili garlic paste or sauce
2	T. smooth peanut butter
1	T. toasted sesame oil
2	cloves garlic
1½	t. dry mustard
1	t. soy sauce
¼	t. kosher salt
¼	cup fresh cilantro, leaves only

Slice scallions into rounds, using the whole onion. The white part has an "oniony" flavor and the green part tastes more like chives.

Cilantro not only tastes great but also looks nice. Remove the stems so you use only the good-looking whole leaves.

Making the salad

2 If you make this salad ahead of time, keep the vegetables, noodles, and dressing separate until you're ready to serve. This salad tastes great chilled or at room temperature. It goes perfectly with the Asian Pork Tenderloin, but can be served by itself or with other entrees.

3 Break noodles in half into boiling water. Cook for 3 minutes. Drain and rinse in cold water to stop cooking. Most ramen noodles have a broth packet included—pitch it.

4 Dressing can be mixed by hand or with a food processor. Blend all ingredients except cilantro until smooth. Now, add cilantro and *pulse* so dressing doesn't turn muddy.

5 Combine noodles, vegetables, and dressing. Toss by hand to prevent crushing. Serve right away (within an hour) or it'll get mushy and all the colors will start to bleed.

Yakitori Sauce

Yakitori is a Japanese term meaning pieces of grilled marinated chicken. The flavor is so classic that I'm using a similar marinade made from common ingredients that any grocery store will carry—soy sauce, sugar, and sherry.

The yakitori marinade works hard in this recipe, getting used in three ways. First, half is used in its simplest form to marinate the pork. Then, plum preserves are added to the other half and reduced to make a syrup. The contrast of the sweet and salty is what Asian cooking is all about—you know, the yin-yang thing. Some of this syrup is used to glaze the pork and the rest is used as a dipping sauce.

Reduction: Yakitori sauce is made using a simple technique called reduction. As liquid cooks, it evaporates. This intensifies the flavor and thickens the consistency without adding any fat.

ASIAN PORK TENDERLOIN
(MAKES SIX 4-OZ. SERVINGS)
WORK TIME: 15 MINUTES
COOK TIME: 30 MINUTES
MARINATE TIME: 60 MINUTES
TRIM, TIE, GRILL (PAGES 8–11):
2   pork tenderloins (2–3 pounds)

FOR THE YAKITORI MARINADE—
SIMMER, REDUCE, THEN COOL:
2   cups dry sherry
1   cup soy sauce
6   T. sugar
2   T. fresh ginger, coarse chop
3   cloves garlic, coarse chop
3   scallions, coarse chop

FOR THE GRILLING SAUCE—
ADD TO ½ OF YAKITORI MARINADE:
1   cup plum preserves (or jam)

SERVE WITH:
   Asian Noodle Salad
GARNISH WITH:
   Gremolada
   Yakitori Sauce

FOR THE GREMOLADA—
CHOP BY HAND AND COMBINE:
1   T. lemon zest (about 1 lemon)
¼   cup dry roasted peanuts
¼   cup fresh cilantro leaves
2   T. fresh ginger, peeled, grated

Making Asian pork

6 Bring yakitori ingredients to a simmer over high heat. Reduce heat to medium-low and simmer for 10 minutes, reducing slightly. Strain and cool.

7 Marinate tied pork tenderloins in a resealable plastic bag with half of the *cooled* Yakitori sauce. Seal the bag and marinate in refrigerator for one hour.

Serving

10 Asian dishes are presented simply. First plate the colorful salad (you can put it into a cup of bibb or other soft lettuce). Add the sliced glazed pork, then top both with gremolada. Garnish the dipping sauce with tiny slices of scallions.

8 Mix other half of yakitori sauce with plum preserves. Bring to simmer to dissolve preserves. Reduce to pancake syrup consistency (about 20 minutes).

9 Grill the marinated tenderloins as on Page 11. Brush on Yakitori Plum Sauce during final rotation. When done, let the meat rest 5 minutes and slice.

three classic cookies

Of course, you already have recipes for the three most popular cookies—chocolate chip, oatmeal-raisin, and peanut butter. So why try these? Because they're moist, chewy, and loaded with the good things that give them their names.

Good cookie philosophy is simple—cookies should be soft and chewy (*never* overbaked), with crisp edges. There should be plenty of the ingredients they're named for—chocolate chips, raisins, and so on. And all cookies should be eaten warm. Here's how to hit cookie nirvana.

Cookie Texture: The texture of any cookie is largely determined by the type of fat used—should it be butter or shortening? Butter gives great flavor, but tends to produce flat cookies that spread. Shortening provides structure, but adds nothing to the taste. Two of these classics use both—oatmeal-raisin uses *all* butter because the oatmeal keeps the dough from spreading.

Never overbake cookies—it makes them dry and hard. I suggest underbaking most cookie recipes. Once out of the oven, let the residual heat from the baking sheet finish them.

Eat the Cookies Warm: Just-baked warm cookies taste best. So bake only what you'll eat, then refrigerate the remaining dough—it will only get better. Just as marinating enhances the flavor of meats and vegetables, sugar does the same for cookie dough. During refrigeration, the sugar dissolves and deepens the flavor.

THE COOKIE SCOOP

Why use a cookie scoop? It's definitely a quick and easy way to turn out cookies. But there's more to it than that. The dough packs into the scoop, producing thick, uniform cookies. Since they're all the same size, they bake at the same rate. And the tall mound gives a height boost, reducing spreading.

Look for cookie scoops at department and kitchen stores, or even your local restaurant supply house (they call them "dishers"). I use a #40 in these recipes. The number stands for scoops per gallon and should be imprinted on the scoop. A #40 scoop measures 2 T. of dough and is 1 3/4" in diameter.

chocolate chip

1 Preheat oven to 350°. Whisk dry ingredients; set aside. Combine wet ingredients with a hand mixer on low. To cream, increase speed to high and beat until fluffy and the color lightens.

2 *Stir* the flour mixture into the creamed mixture until no flour is visible. (Overmixing develops the gluten, making a tough cookie.) Now stir in the semisweet and milk chocolate chips.

3 Use a cookie scoop (2 T. per scoop) to measure and drop dough 2" apart onto an ungreased baking sheet. Bake on center rack of oven 12–14 minutes, until *lightly* browned and edges are set.

4 Remove from oven; leave cookies on baking sheet for 2 minutes to firm up. Transfer to a wire rack to cool. If you're reusing the warm baking sheet, reduce the baking time slightly.

MORSELS OF TRUTH

Chip Shape: You may have heard the rumor about wax being added to chocolate chips to help them hold their shape during baking. I called several manufacturers and they assured me that it was just that— a rumor. No wax is added.

Then why do the morsels hold their shape when baked in a cookie? Because they're left undisturbed in the dough during baking and cooling. When chips are baked by themselves they will hold their shape, unless stirred or touched while still warm.

Chip Choices: Milk chocolate chips alone make cookies too sweet. But using a small amount alongside semisweet chips makes the perfect bitter and sweet combination.

So what's the best brand of chocolate chips to use? I really like Ghirardelli and Guittard. They have rich flavor and are moist and creamy. But you decide. Do a side-by-side taste test. If you don't like eating the chips, don't bake with them.

oatmeal-raisin

1 Preheat oven to 350°. Whisk dry ingredients; set aside. Combine wet ingredients with a hand mixer on low. To cream, increase speed to high and beat until fluffy and the color lightens.

2 *Stir* the flour mixture into the creamed mixture until no flour is visible. (Overmixing develops the gluten, making a tough cookie.) Now add the oats and raisins; stir to incorporate.

3 Fill cookie scoop with dough. (Use a #40 scoop—it measures 2 T. dough.) Press against side of bowl, pulling up to level dough. Drop 2" apart onto baking sheet sprayed with nonstick spray.

4 Bake 11–13 min. (on center rack), until golden, but still moist beneath cracks on top. Remove from oven; let cookies sit on baking sheet for 2 min. before removing to a wire rack to cool.

OATMEAL-RAISIN COOKIES

(MAKES 3 DOZEN COOKIES)
WORK TIME: 15 MINUTES
BAKE TIME: 11–13 MINUTES

WHISK TOGETHER; SET ASIDE:

2   cups all-purpose flour
1   t. baking soda
1   t. baking powder
1   t. kosher salt

CREAM "WET" INGREDIENTS:

1   cup unsalted butter, softened
1   cup sugar
1   cup dark brown sugar, packed
2   eggs
2   t. vanilla

STIR FLOUR MIXTURE INTO CREAMED. THEN STIR IN:

3   cups oats (not instant)
1½ cups raisins

FORM COOKIES AND BAKE.

NUTRITIONAL INFORMATION PER COOKIE: CALORIES 164; TOTAL FAT 6(G); CALORIES FROM FAT 32%; SODIUM 122(MG); CARB. 26(G)

DARK BROWN SUGAR

Does the dark brown sugar called for in these recipes really make a difference? Absolutely.

Dark brown sugar has a stronger molasses taste than golden brown sugar, giving it deeper flavor. It provides noticeable depth (both in flavor and color) to all of the cookie recipes. So don't substitute.

VARIATION

Try using dried cherries or dried cranberries in place of the raisins (Ocean Spray markets dried cranberries as "Craisins"). Be sure to use only *real*, dried cherries or cranberries. You don't want the ones with added juice concentrates—they taste fake and overpower the cookies.

Substitute 1 cup chopped dried cherries or dried cranberries for 1½ cups raisins.

peanut butter

PEANUT BUTTER COOKIES
(MAKES 3 DOZEN COOKIES)
WORK TIME: 15 MINUTES
COOK TIME: 11–13 MINUTES

WHISK TOGETHER; SET ASIDE:
3   cups all-purpose flour
2   t. baking soda
1   t. kosher salt

CREAM "WET" INGREDIENTS:
1¼   cup chunky peanut butter
1¼   cup dark brown sugar, packed
¾   cup sugar
¾   cup vegetable shortening
¼   cup unsalted butter, softened
2   eggs
1   t. vanilla

STIR FLOUR MIXTURE INTO CREAMED MIXTURE. FORM COOKIES; BAKE.

NUTRITIONAL INFORMATION PER COOKIE: CALORIES 189; TOTAL FAT 10(G); CALORIES FROM FAT 48%; SODIUM 185(MG); CARB. 22(G)

1 Preheat oven to 350°. Whisk dry ingredients; set aside. With hand mixer on low, combine wet ingredients. Increase to high; cream until fluffy. *Stir dry mixture into creamed mixture.*

2 Drop dough 2" apart onto ungreased baking sheet using a 2 T. cookie scoop. For moist cookies, bake "as is"—don't flatten. For crisp cookies, press a fork onto the top, making criss-cross marks.

3 Bake 11–13 minutes (on center rack of oven), until edges are set. Tops should only be *slightly* browned. Let cookies sit on baking sheet 2 minutes to set up. Transfer to wire rack to cool.

COOKIE ADDITIONS
For a variation, replace traditional fork marks with lines of chocolate or jelly. You can also roll the dough in chopped peanuts for more crunch.

Chocolate/Jelly Drizzle: Place ½ cup semisweet chocolate chips or jelly into a resealable plastic bag. Press out air, seal, and place bag in hot water for five minutes. Massage bag to smooth out the lumps.

Arrange cookies on rack over paper towels. Twist top of bag; snip off a tiny corner. Gently squeeze bag, moving back and forth over cookies.

Double Peanuts: Double the peanut power by rolling the scooped balls of dough in ½ cup finely chopped honey roasted peanuts. Press gently so the peanuts stick to the dough. Bake and cool as directed.

weeknight
chicken salads

For nights when you don't feel like cooking, these chicken salads step up to the dinner plate.

Admit it—there are nights when you just don't feel like making dinner. But before dialing for pizza, think of these chicken salads as a healthy, great-tasting alternative.

The best part is most of the cooking has been done for you: The chicken is from a rotisserie bird you pick up at the store on your way home from work. Making the salads is a breeze.

Another bonus is these salads look as good as they taste. The basic chicken salad, *below*, is dressed up from the typical sandwich. The pesto salad can take on a deli pasta salad any day. And the presentation of the cobb salad is so nice no one will want to eat it (but not for long).

the weeknight key

A purchased rotisserie chicken is a great cooking trick. One chicken yields about a pound of meat—perfect for four people. Plus, it's really convenient.

You can use leftover grilled or roasted chicken too. The grilling or roasting adds another flavor dimension to the salads.

▲ *For each salad, pull the chicken meat off the bones in large pieces, discarding fat and skin; cut into chunks. Be sure to remove all bits of bone and cartilage from the meat.*

weeknight Basic chicken salad

BASIC CHICKEN SALAD

(MAKES ABOUT 4 CUPS)

WORK TIME: 30 MINUTES

COMBINE:

4	cups rotisserie chicken meat, chopped into large chunks (about 1 pound)
1	cup celery, diced
¼	cup reduced-fat mayonnaise
¼	cup plain low-fat yogurt
¼	cup chopped fresh parsley
¼	cup scallions, chopped (white and green parts)
2	T. fresh lemon juice
	Salt and black pepper to taste

SERVE CHICKEN SALAD IN:

Cucumber Wraps, *see right*
or Egg Roll Baskets, *see right*

VARIATION–

ADD TO ABOVE INGREDIENTS:

½	cup dried tart cherries
½	cup cashews or pistachios, coarsely chopped
1	T. minced fresh tarragon

NUTRITIONAL INFORMATION PER 1 CUP BASIC CHICKEN SALAD:
CALORIES 321; TOTAL FAT 14(G); CALORIES FROM FAT 39%; SODIUM 380(MG); CARBOHYDRATES 6(G)

1 Combine chunks of chicken with all ingredients (including the items for the salad variation, if using). Chill until ready to serve. May be made one day ahead.

This chicken salad is all about "less is more." The ingredients are simple, but the really big deal is that it's made with light mayonnaise and plain yogurt—low in calories *and* tastes good! And if you want to take the basic salad one step further, you can make an easy variation just by adding dried tart cherries, nuts, and fresh tarragon.

Plain chicken salad can be pretty ho-hum. So here are a couple solutions: Present it in a cucumber wrap or egg roll basket—they're simple to make and look terrific. For easy slicing, use cucumbers that are no more than 2" wide. And be sure to buy *egg roll* wrappers, not wonton skins (they're too small). Look for them in the produce section.

Cucumber wraps

▲ *Use a Y-peeler to slice thin strips of cucumber for the wraps. The strips should be 1½–2" wide. Once you get down to the seeds, turn the cucumber over and slice on the other side.*

▲ *On a serving plate, press two cucumber strips around sides of a lightly oiled 3" ring mold; they will overlap. Lightly pack 1 cup chicken salad inside ring; carefully lift off mold. Serve right away.*

Egg roll baskets

▲ *Preheat oven to 350°. Oil four ¾-cup custard cups with nonstick spray. Drape a 6" square egg roll wrapper over each cup, shaping into a basket. Brush outside of wrappers with vegetable oil.*

▲ *Bake baskets until golden and crisp, 15–18 min. Cool completely before removing (they will become more crisp as they cool). May be prepared a day in advance; store in airtight containers.*

weeknight Pesto chicken salad

PESTO CHICKEN SALAD

(MAKES ABOUT 5 CUPS)
COOK TIME: 12–15 MINUTES
WORK TIME: 45 MINUTES
FOR PESTO—

MINCE IN FOOD PROCESSOR:
½   cup fresh basil leaves, packed
¼   cup fresh parsley
¼   cup fresh thyme leaves

ADD AND BLEND:
3   T. white wine vinegar
1   T. fresh lemon juice
¼   cup Parmesan cheese, grated

DRIZZLE IN:
¼   cup olive oil
     Salt and black pepper to taste

1 Mince herbs in food processor. Scrape bowl and add vinegar, lemon juice, and cheese; blend. With machine running, drizzle in oil. Season with salt and pepper. Pesto will be thin.

DRIZZLE WITH 2 T. OLIVE OIL;
ROAST:
½   lb. asparagus, trimmed
     Salt and black pepper to taste

TOSS WITH:
¼   lb. cooked gemelli* or fusilli pasta (about 1 cup dry)
4   cups rotisserie chicken meat, cut into large chunks (about 1 pound)
1   cup grape or cherry tomatoes, halved (about ½ pint)
1   cup yellow teardrop tomatoes, halved (about ½ pint)

GARNISH SALAD WITH:
¼   cup pine nuts, toasted

Gemelli are pasta twists 1–2" long. (Fusilli, or corkscrews, work fine too.) The shape is perfect for trapping the pesto. Cook as directed on the box.

2 Preheat oven to 425°. Trim ends from asparagus and place in a single layer on baking sheet. Drizzle with oil and season with salt and pepper. Roast 12–15 min., until lightly browned. Cool.

3 Cook pasta but don't rinse (the starch makes the pesto cling better). Cut asparagus into 2" pieces, then toss with pesto, pasta, chicken, and tomatoes. Garnish with toasted pine nuts.

weeknight Platter
chicken salad

Cobb salad is almost more popular now than it was in the 1930s. This revived version combines old traditions with new ideas.

I'll be up front with you: This is *not* the original recipe for cobb salad created by Robert Cobb of the Brown Derby restaurant in Hollywood, California. But the spirit behind it is the same—rows of ingredients arranged on greens. Here's where the changes take place.

Vinaigrette: The traditional cobb is tossed with a simple oil and vinegar dressing. But for this vinaigrette, grill tomatoes and shallots (use a disposable foil pan right on the grill), then blend in the food processor. And even though it tastes great on its own, adding a little mayonnaise will give it more body. For the nicest presentation, serve the vinaigrette on the side instead of tossing it with the rest of the salad.

Croutons: There were no croutons on the first cobb salad. But why not? The crunchy, chewy texture is a great contrast to the vegetables. And here, the bread is grilled, adding flavor.

Presentation: The way cobb salad is presented is what makes it so cool—all the components lined up in rows, then tossed at the table. This new cobb salad isn't too far away from that concept.

The thing that is different is the chicken and vegetables are in large pieces. In the old cobb, they were diced fairly small, making every bite taste the same. But with larger pieces, the taste experience is different each time.

REVIVED COBB SALAD
(SERVES 6–8)
WORK TIME: 1 HOUR
COOK TIME: 30 MINUTES

FOR THE VINAIGRETTE—
TOSS IN 2 T. OLIVE OIL; GRILL:
5   whole Roma tomatoes
5   shallots, peeled
1   rosemary sprig
PULSE IN FOOD PROCESSOR:
   Grilled vegetables and their accumulated pan juices
2   T. balsamic vinegar
2   T. brown sugar
1   T. fresh thyme leaves
1   T. fresh lemon juice
   Salt, black pepper, and Tabasco to taste
STIR IN (OPTIONAL):
¼   cup mayonnaise

FOR THE CROUTONS—
BRUSH WITH 3–4 T. OLIVE OIL; GRILL:
½   lb. crusty Italian bread, sliced

FOR THE SALAD—
PREPARE AND ASSEMBLE:
½   lb. bacon, diced and sauteed
10–12 cups escarole or romaine lettuce, chopped (about 2 heads)
4   cups cooked rotisserie chicken meat, cut into chunks (about 1 lb.)
3   cups grape or cherry tomatoes, halved (about 1½ pts.)
1   cup (4 oz.) blue cheese, crumbled
2   ripe avocados, peeled, halved and thinly sliced

NUTRITIONAL INFORMATION PER ⅛ SALAD WITH ¼ CUP VINAIGRETTE (NO MAYO):
CALORIES 532; TOTAL FAT 32(G); CALORIES FROM FAT 54%; SODIUM 716(MG); CARBOHYDRATES 30(G)

1 Preheat grill to medium-high. Toss the tomatoes, shallots, and rosemary with oil. Grill until soft, 15 min. Pulse vegetables and pan juices with all vinaigrette ingredients. Stir in mayonnaise, if desired.

4 This is
a really big salad—get out the
largest platter you've got. To assemble, first,
create a bed with the chopped greens. Then
arrange chicken chunks in a wide row diagonally down the center of the platter.

5 Now arrange the
tomato halves down both sides of
the chicken. Then sprinkle the crumbled blue
cheese next to the tomatoes. Keep the rows
compact so all the ingredients fit.

6 Slice the
avocado just before serving to
keep it from turning brown; fan out the slices
next to the cheese. Sprinkle the cooked
bacon around the avocado. Serve the salad
with vinaigrette and croutons on the side.

2 As tomatoes grill, brush bread
slices with olive oil. Grill bread on
both sides until toasted, 2–3 minutes
per side. Remove from grill and cool.
Cut into 1" cubes. Set croutons aside.

3 Prepare the salad ingredients before
assembling (except avocado), then chill.
Slice the lettuce into wide ribbons and
refrigerate it in resealable plastic bags
lined with damp paper towels.

kebabs in hand

What do you get when you take a grilling stand-by like shish kebabs and turn it into a sandwich? More fun and flavor than regular kebabs.

Kebabs aren't your typical sandwich filler. But they make a great, casual meal that's ideal for entertaining. Most of the components can be made ahead, grilling is quick, and presentation is simple—everyone makes their own sandwich!

The sandwiches come together in four main steps: making and grilling the kebabs, tossing a salad, mixing a sauce, and grilling the bread.

one

Making kebabs: These kebabs are made with meat and vegetables. Here's how to get the best flavor, and make sure everything cooks evenly.

Marinating the meat—Meat is marinated for two reasons: to tenderize and enhance flavor. But the primary purpose behind marinating the meat here is flavor.

Each of the kebabs uses meat that's tender to start with, so there's no need to marinate for long periods of time. 15–30 minutes is all that's needed to infuse the meat with a little flavor.

After mixing, reserve $1/4$ cup of the marinades to brush on the kebabs as they grill. *Don't* use the meat marinade for basting—it may have bacteria in it from the raw meat.

Preparing the vegetables—While the meat is marinating, prepare the vegetables. Each recipe indicates how they should be cut—the important thing to remember is that they should be slightly larger than the chunks of meat. They'll be done when the meat is cooked through.

Assembly—There are three things to consider before assembling the kebabs: the type of skewer to use, whether or not to double skewer, and the spacing of the meat and vegetables.

There are two types of skewers you can use: metal and bamboo. Both will work—choose what's most convenient for you. Just be sure the skewers are at least 12" long so they hold enough meat and vegetables for each sandwich.

If using bamboo, soak them in cold water for 30 minutes before assembling the kebabs. This helps keep them from burning and disintegrating on the grill.

There are several kinds of metal skewers on the market—I prefer those that have a flat blade, not round or square. This helps keep the meat and vegetables from spinning around the skewer when turning them on the grill.

Double skewering, *see box below*, is a technique that also keeps meat and vegetables from spinning around. Plus, the kebab is sturdier and easy to handle. If you have enough skewers, do it.

Spacing the meat and vegetables slightly apart allows them to cook faster and more evenly. Take a look at the kebabs in the photo, *right*. See how the turkey and vegetables aren't touching on the far right kebab? This is so the turkey cooks through without overcooking the vegetables. Since beef is cooked to medium or medium-rare, the meat and vegetables are close together.

Grilling Techniques—Grilling kebabs is as simple as grilling steak. But there are a few things to remember.

First, make sure the grill is hot. The smaller pieces of meat and vegetables will cook faster (and won't dry out) if the gas is cranked up fairly high.

Second, brush the the grill grate with vegetable oil before putting the kebabs on. There's not much fat in the meats or oil in the marinades, and the kebabs may stick. Also, when turning them, first get underneath the kebabs with a spatula, then turn with tongs.

Finally, baste the kebabs with some of the reserved marinade during grilling—it will help keep the vegetables from scorching.

two

The Salad: It might seem odd to put salad on a sandwich. But it adds flavor and crunch to the kebabs—like lettuce and tomato on a burger.

The nice thing about these salads is they can be made a couple of hours ahead then chilled. Actually, they taste *better* if made in advance. But don't make them too far ahead—the vegetables will get mushy and break down.

three

The Sauce: I'm not talking ketchup and mustard here. The sauces for these kebabs are a little more exotic. But that doesn't mean they're difficult. They're all made with ingredients you probably have already, like mayonnaise and yogurt. And each one can be mixed up ahead, just like the salads. The Cajun Kebab (Page 30) doesn't even have a sauce—the broccoli slaw makes its own.

four

Serving: Here's where things get really fun. Take a look at the photo on Page 24 and the one to the right. Serving the kebab in bread or a tortilla is not only cool, but practical—food won't fly off the skewer like it tends to do when you use a fork to remove it.

Now, I can't take all the credit for this idea. According to Steven Raichlen in his cookbook *The Barbecue! Bible* (1998, Workman Press), Central Asian cooks have been wrapping pita bread around kebabs for a while. The difference is they eat the bread separately.

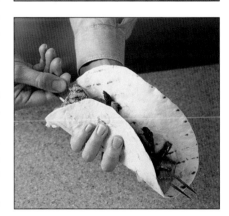

But with these kebab sandwiches, everything stays inside the bread—no plates, no forks. Top it off with salad and sauce and you've got dinner sitting right in the palm of your hand.

Double Skewering Tip
It can be hard to hold two bamboo skewers while threading meat and vegetables. I found that an inexpensive block of florist foam (or block of styrofoam) helps hold the skewers in place. Just stick the blunt ends of the skewers into the foam and start threading. Look for florist foam in craft and discount stores.

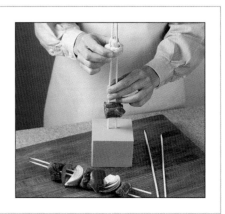

kebabs in hand:
greek style

Greek food is all about summer—just think about all the Greek vegetables available, like zucchini, eggplant, tomatoes, and cucumbers. This sandwich takes advantage of them all.

But it's not just vegetables. There's beef, too—top sirloin. Top sirloin can vary in tenderness depending on the section of the muscle it's cut from. If you can, buy it cut from an area close to the short loin. It'll be more tender.

Of course, you've got other choices when it comes to cuts of beef—sirloin and tenderloin also work fine for kebabs. But the bottom line is tenderness. Anything chewy will be too difficult to eat (and remember, you're going to eat these sandwiches with your hands). Whatever you do, don't buy precut stew meat. It's tough and should be braised in liquid for long periods of time. Grilling turns it into rubber bands.

Pita bread (or pocket bread) is a natural for this sandwich. It's a Middle Eastern flat bread that forms a pocket when you cut it in half. But for this sandwich, the pita doesn't need to be halved—use a whole one for each kebab. And grill just until they're soft.

RECIPE NOTES: (MAKES 6 SANDWICHES)
WORK TIME: 1 HOUR
COOK TIME: 6–8 MINUTES

one

GREEK KEBABS
COMBINE; RESERVE ¼ CUP:
⅓	cup olive oil
3	T. fresh lemon juice
3	T. red wine vinegar
1	T. minced fresh rosemary
2	t. sugar
1	t. garlic, minced
½	t. black pepper
	Salt to taste

ADD TO REMAINING MARINADE:
1	lb. top sirloin, trimmed of fat and cut into 1½" cubes

PREPARE:
1	zucchini, cut into half-moons
½	eggplant, cut into wedges

ADD TO VEGETABLES:
2	T. olive oil
	Salt and black pepper to taste

COMBINE the first eight ingredients in a resealable plastic bag. Pour off and reserve ¼ cup for basting.

ADD the beef cubes to the remaining marinade in the plastic bag; mix to coat. Marinate meat at least 30 minutes before assembling kebabs.

PREPARE zucchini by halving it lengthwise, then cutting into half-moons 1"-thick. Cut the eggplant lengthwise into quarters and slice it into 1"-thick wedges. Place vegetables in another resealable plastic bag.

ADD the olive oil, salt, and black pepper to the bag; toss to coat. Set aside until ready to assemble the kebabs.

Assembly: Thread a cube of beef onto a soaked bamboo (or metal) skewer, see *Assembly, Pages 24–25.* Then add a piece of zucchini and a wedge of eggplant, threading closely together. Alternate meat with vegetables, ending with meat. Use 3–4 cubes of meat per skewer.

Grilling: Preheat grill to high; brush grill grate with vegetable oil. Place kebabs on grill and brush with some of the ¼ cup reserved marinade. Close lid and cook 3–4 minutes. Carefully turn skewers with tongs, and brush with more marinade.

Cover and continue cooking until meat is medium-rare to medium, another 3–4 minutes. Vegetables should be cooked but not mushy.

two

TOMATO-CUCUMBER SALAD

COMBINE:

1½ cups grape or cherry tomatoes, halved
1½ cups cucumber, seeded, diced
½ cup red onion, slivered
2 T. red wine vinegar
2 T. minced fresh parsley
Salt and black pepper to taste

COMBINE all the salad ingredients in a medium bowl. Chill until ready to serve. Bring to room temperature before serving.

To sliver an onion, cut it in half from stem to root. Cut side down, make thin slices following the curve of the onion. After slivering half of it, rotate onion and sliver the other half.

three

GOAT CHEESE SAUCE

MINCE IN FOOD PROCESSOR:
1 clove garlic, peeled

ADD AND BLEND:
½ cup (3½ oz.) soft goat cheese
¼ cup plain low-fat yogurt
1 T. minced fresh oregano
1 T. fresh lemon juice
Pinch of cayenne
Salt to taste

MINCE the garlic in a food processor fitted with steel blade. Scrape down the sides of the bowl.

ADD remaining ingredients and process until smooth. Chill sauce until ready to serve. *Note:* This sauce can be made a day in advance, but the garlic flavor will intensify. Tone it down with a little more yogurt.

four

Brush both sides of six 6" pita breads with olive oil. Place the oiled pitas on the grill during the last two minutes of grilling. You just want to warm them until soft and pliable. Take care that they don't get too crisp.

To serve, hold a pita in one hand and a kebab in the other. Place the kebab inside the bread, wrapping the pita firmly around it. Carefully pull out the skewer, leaving the meat and vegetables inside the pita.

Top sandwich with some of the Tomato-Cucumber Salad and a dollop of Goat Cheese Sauce. Serve right away.

kebabs in hand:
asian style

These kebabs are similar to yakitori [yah-kee-TOH-ree], Japanese grilled chicken. The key to their great flavor is the marinade—it's sweet, salty, and glazes the meat nicely during grilling.

But that's where the similarities end. These kebabs are made with turkey tenderloin instead of chicken. Tenderloins are all white meat (they're a muscle group located in the breast), but quick grilling helps keep the meat moist.

Surprisingly, asparagus and scallions make great kebab vegetables. But they can be a little tricky to thread on the skewers—if possible, use thin bamboo or flat metal skewers (not a square blade) to avoid splitting the vegetables.

Using flour tortillas for an Asian sandwich isn't as big of a stretch as you might think. If you've eaten Peking duck at a Chinese restaurant, you've had Mandarin pancakes—the Chinese equivalent to tortillas.

RECIPE NOTES:
(MAKES 6 SANDWICHES)
WORK TIME: 1 HOUR
COOK TIME: 15 MINUTES

EDITOR'S NOTE:
Scallions may be substituted for the aspara-gus, if desired. Cut the root end from the scallions, then trim into 2" pieces using the white and light green part only.

one

ASIAN KEBABS
FOR MEAT MARINADE, COMBINE, REDUCE, AND RESERVE ¼ CUP:
- ½ cup soy sauce
- ½ cup dry sherry
- 3 T. brown sugar
- 2 T. scallions, chopped
- ½ t. toasted sesame oil
- 2 cloves garlic, smashed
- ½" piece of fresh ginger, smashed

REMOVE TENDON; MARINATE:
- 1 lb. turkey tenderloin, cut into 1½" cubes

PREPARE:
- ½ lb. white mushrooms, cleaned and halved
- ½ lb. asparagus, trimmed into 2" pieces, OR
- 12 scallions, *see below*

ADD TO VEGETABLES:
- 2 T. olive oil
- Salt and black pepper to taste

COMBINE the marinade ingredients in a small saucepan and bring to a simmer. Reduce to ¾ cup, about 10 minutes; cool slightly (do not strain). Reserve ¼ cup and pour the rest into a resealable plastic bag.

REMOVE tendons from the turkey by cutting underneath them with a knife tip. Trim as much as you can, but it's okay if a little is left on. Cut into 1½" cubes; add to the plastic bag and marinate 15–30 minutes.

PREPARE the mushrooms and aspara-gus; place vegetables into another resealable plastic bag.

ADD the olive oil and seasonings to the plastic bag, tossing to coat veg-etables with oil. Set aside until ready to assemble kebabs.

Assembly: Thread a piece of turkey onto two soaked bamboo (or metal) skewers, *see Double Skewering, Page 25.* Then add two pieces of aspara-gus and a mushroom. Space the turkey and vegetables slightly apart so the turkey cooks quickly. Con-tinue threading, alternating meat and vegetables, ending with turkey.

Grilling: Preheat grill to high; brush grate with vegetable oil. Place kebabs on grill and brush with some of the ¼ cup reserved marinade.

Cover the grill and cook kebabs 4–5 minutes. Carefully loosen with a spatula, then turn with tongs; brush kebabs with additional marinade.

Cover the grill and continue grilling kebabs until turkey is thoroughly cooked and asparagus is cooked but not mushy, 3–4 more minutes.

two

CUCUMBER-CARROT SALAD

COMBINE:

1¼ cups cucumber, halved lengthwise, seeded, thinly sliced into half-moons
½ cup shredded or julienned carrot
3 T. seasoned rice vinegar
1 t. sugar
¼ t. crushed red pepper flakes
A few drops toasted sesame oil
Salt to taste

COMBINE all the salad ingredients in a medium bowl. Chill until ready to serve. Bring to room temperature before serving.

To julienne, first peel and trim the ends from a carrot (larger ones are easier to work with). Cut the carrot in half crosswise.

Using a Y-peeler, shave off long strips. Stack strips on top of each other, then slice lengthwise into thin pieces.

four

Brush both sides of six 8" flour tortillas with olive oil. Grill tortillas on both sides (about one minute per side) until warmed through and pliable. Don't overcook or they'll be too crisp.

To serve, spread some of the Sherry Mayonnaise on one side of the tortilla.

With a tortilla in one hand and a kebab in the other, place the kebab inside the tortilla, wrapping it firmly around the kebab. Carefully remove the skewer.

To finish the sandwich, top with some of the Cucumber-Carrot Salad.

three

SHERRY MAYONNAISE

COMBINE:

1 cup mayonnaise
1 T. sugar
1 T. fresh lemon juice
1 T. dry sherry
1 clove garlic, minced
Salt and cayenne to taste

COMBINE all ingredients in a small bowl. Chill until ready to serve.

Note: The mayonnaise can be made 2–3 days ahead and chilled until ready to serve. If the garlic becomes too strong, add a little more mayonnaise.

kebabs in hand:
cajun style

New Orleans is the place for oyster po' boys—submarine sandwiches of fried oysters, lettuce, tomatoes, and tartar sauce. According to local legend, a husband presented his wife with one after a wild night in the French Quarter (which is why it's also called "the peacemaker"). This kebab sandwich doesn't have a history that colorful, but it tastes just as good. Here are some things to keep in mind as you make them.

Be sure to purchase shrimp labeled 16–20, meaning there are 16–20 shrimp in a pound. That's a perfect size for the sandwiches—smaller shrimp are susceptible to overcooking, and larger ones are too difficult to eat in a sandwich.

It's important that the shrimp marinates for just 15 minutes. Any longer and the lemon juice in the marinade will start to "cook" the shrimp, making them tough. And take care not to overcook when you grill the kebabs. Two or three minutes per side is all you need.

Don't bother buying a fancy French bread for these. In fact, the soft-crust types work best because they don't get too crunchy when toasted on the grill.

Unlike the other kebab sandwiches, this one doesn't have a sauce—the broccoli slaw makes its own. Pile the slaw in the bread *first* so the sauce soaks in!

RECIPE NOTES: (MAKES 6 SANDWICHES)
WORK TIME: 1 HOUR
COOK TIME: 5–8 MINUTES

one

CAJUN KEBABS

COMBINE; RESERVE ¼ CUP:
⅓	cup olive oil
3	T. honey
3	T. fresh lemon juice
3	T. Cajun seasoning
2	T. minced fresh parsley
2	T. Worcestershire sauce
2	t. lemon zest, minced
	Salt and crushed red pepper flakes to taste

PEEL AND DEVEIN; MARINATE:
1	lb. large shrimp (16–20 count)

COMBINE:
1	yellow bell pepper, cut into large chunks
12	cherry tomatoes
2	T. olive oil
	Salt and black pepper to taste

COMBINE first nine ingredients in resealable plastic bag. Pour off and reserve ¼ cup.

PEEL shrimp by first removing the legs. Then peel away the shell and gently pull off the tail section.

DEVEIN the shrimp by cutting a small slit down the back with a paring knife. Remove the vein; rinse the shrimp.

Add the shrimp to the marinade in the plastic bag and toss to coat. Chill shrimp 15 minutes.

COMBINE vegetables, oil, salt, and pepper in another resealable plastic bag; toss to coat. Set aside.

Assembly: Thread one shrimp onto a soaked bamboo (or metal) skewer, *see Assembly, Pages 24–25.* To keep shrimp from curling during grilling, thread down the center of the body from head to tail. Add a bell pepper chunk and tomato. Alternate shrimp with vegetables, ending with shrimp.

Grilling: Preheat grill to high; brush grate with vegetable oil. Place kebabs on grill and brush with some of the ¼ cup reserved marinade. Cover and cook kebabs 2–3 minutes.

Carefully turn kebabs (use a spatula to turn them if they stick), then brush with additional marinade. Cover and continue grilling until shrimp are cooked through but not rubbery, another 2–3 minutes.

two & three

BROCCOLI SLAW

COMBINE:
½	cup mayonnaise
½	cup red bell pepper, diced
½	cup scallions, sliced
¼	cup minced fresh parsley
2	T. honey
2	T. fresh lemon juice
	Salt, black pepper, and Tabasco to taste

ADD AND TOSS:
3	cups broccoli slaw mix

COMBINE the mayonnaise, red bell pepper, scallions, parsley, honey, lemon juice, and seasonings in a large mixing bowl.

ADD the broccoli slaw and toss to coat. Chill until ready to serve. Serve slaw cold.

four

GRILLED FRENCH BREAD

SLICE:
6	slices French bread, cut diagonally 2" thick

COMBINE; BRUSH ON BREAD:
6	T. unsalted butter, melted
1	t. garlic, minced

SLICE the French bread diagonally 2" thick. Then slice each piece in half, but not all the way through! You want to create a hinge (like what's on a hot dog bun) so the fillings stay in the bread.

COMBINE the melted butter and garlic; brush on both sides of bread slices. Grill bread until toasted and warmed through, about one minute per side.

To serve, first place some of the slaw inside the grilled bread (the slaw "juice" acts as the sauce). Holding the bread in one hand and a kebab in the other, place the kebab on the slaw and carefully pull out the skewer, leaving the shrimp and vegetables behind.

butterflied chicken

Split, butterflied, flattened, or even spatchcocked. Call it what you want—this is the best way to prepare a chicken for roasting. Then, grill it over indirect heat to make it as juicy as it is flavorful.

The problem with grilled or roasted chicken is inconsistency. Seems the white meat turns to flavorless sawdust before all the dark meat is completely cooked (rare around the joints).

To solve the problem, it's best to flatten and then skewer the chicken (this is known as butterflying or spatchcocking). Butterflying works for big or small fowl, but really gets the best results when gently roasted over indirect heat on an outdoor grill. You end up with a tender, moist chicken that's done all the way through. The best part about the combination of butterflying and indirect cooking is that it requires minimum preparation and only a little attention while grilling.

The secret to this method is getting the chicken to a uniform thickness. That's where flattening comes in. It's not hard. All you need is a good pair of kitchen shears and a knife.

Butterflying: First, remove the backbone. This allows the chicken to be split. To make the cavity easy to spread open with your hands, make a small cut on the *inside* of the breast bone. Now the chicken should be pretty flat, but you'll want to skewer it to keep it that way.

Indirect Grilling: Once the chicken is skewered and seasoned, roast it on a grill using indirect heat. This means that the chicken is not over the heat source, but rather off to the side. It's a gentle heat which makes this almost foolproof. You can leave the chicken on 20–30 minutes longer than directed and it's still great.

Side Dish: Be sure to try the grilled vegetables on Page 35. They're very fresh-tasting and cook right along with the chicken (they get *direct* heat). Not only does this meal taste good, but you might not even have to step inside your kitchen to get this dinner ready.

BUTTERFLIED CHICKEN

(MAKES 8 PIECES)
WORK TIME: 20 MINUTES
COOK TIME: 20 MINUTES/POUND
COMBINE FOR SPICE MIXTURE:
1   T. chili powder
1   T. paprika
2   t. black pepper
2   t. kosher salt
1   t. cayenne
BUTTERFLY:
1   4–5 lb. roasting chicken
BRUSH WITH OLIVE OIL; SPRINKLE WITH SPICE MIXTURE. GRILL CHICKEN THEN BASTE WITH:
1   T. cilantro leaves, snipped
    Juice of 1 lime

NUTRITIONAL INFORMATION PER ⅛ CHICKEN: CALORIES 298; TOTAL FAT 18(G); CALORIES FROM FAT 57%; SODIUM 679(MG); CARB. 2(G)

Preparing the chicken for grilling

spice mixture

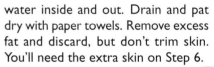

excess fat   giblet packet

1 Combine spices in a small bowl and set aside. Remove giblet packet from inside chicken. Discard, or freeze for future stocks. Rinse chicken with cold water inside and out. Drain and pat dry with paper towels. Remove excess fat and discard, but don't trim skin. You'll need the extra skin on Step 6.

2 With the bird breast side down, remove the backbone with kitchen shears or a sharp knife. Cut along one side of backbone, then the other. Discard, or freeze for future stocks.

3 Next, cut out the wishbone. It's shaped like a "Y" and located on either side of the bird's shoulders. You may be able to remove it with your fingers or with a small knife.

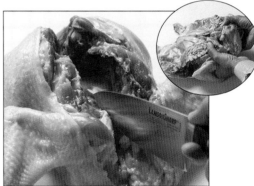

4 Now, make a small cut in the breast-bone. To flatten the chicken even more, grasp the chicken (*see inset*). With firm pressure, bend the breast backwards to spread the cut even more.

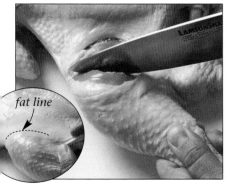

fat line

5 Locate the yellow fat line on the leg. Cut on that fat line to score the joint. This helps ensure that the joint area will cook along with the rest of the bird. Repeat with the other leg.

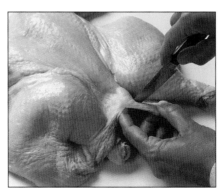

6 Turn both legs inward, towards the center (knock-kneed). See the extra skin below the legs? Make a 1" slit through the skin on each side. Insert leg ends through the slits to secure.

7 Now, remove the wing tips—they don't really have a lot of meat and tend to burn. Locate the joint and cut through it with kitchen shears. Now, twist the wings under the breast.

skewering and seasoning

Skewering a butterflied chicken isn't necessary, but you may want to do it for structure and maneuverability.

Skewering: With the backbone removed and breastbone cracked, there isn't much structure left in the chicken. Using skewers keeps the legs and wings in a rigid position for grilling.

Skewering also helps to move the chicken around on the grill. To cook the bird evenly, it's best to rotate it every 15 minutes. You can do this by picking it up by the skewers rather than running the risk of tearing the skin or meat with a spatula or metal tongs.

Seasoning: I just wanted to touch on this briefly because everyone is so different when it comes to salt and other spices. The recipe calls for about three tablespoons of spice mixture. While this is what I recommend, you don't have to use it all—especially if you're salt or heat sensitive. The amount of rub used is up to you.

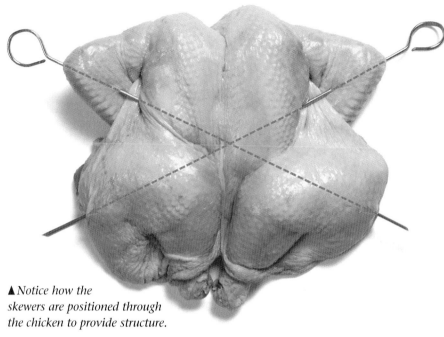

▲ *Notice how the skewers are positioned through the chicken to provide structure.*

WHICH SKEWER?
The length of the skewer is more important than what it's made from. I used both wooden and metal skewers with the same results.

The real problems came up when I used different sizes. If they're too short, they have a hard time going through a whole chicken or there will be nothing to to grab for turning while cooking. Also, the smaller wooden skewers just aren't strong enough (too thin) to penetrate the meat without breaking.

Look for skewers that are about 12" long. My local grocery store carries metal ones for 50¢ each and also wooden ones in packages of 100 for about $2.50.

8 Before you begin skewering, take a look at the example above. Start the skewer tip through the two bones that now make up the end of the wing. Push and weave it through the breast meat.

9 The skewers should go through the breast easily since its bone is broken. Now, continue pushing it right along the thighbone. If necessary, pull the skewer out and start over again.

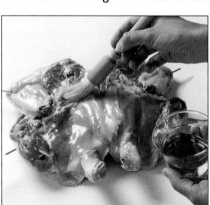

10 Place the chicken breast side down and brush with olive oil. This will give the spices something to stick to. Now, sprinkle the chicken with *half* of the spice mixture, covering every part.

11 Turn the chicken over and brush with olive oil. Sprinkle with the spice mixture. This is the "presentation side" because it doesn't come in contact with the grill—no sticking or tearing.

grilling and carving

You would think that grilling is the hard part. Actually, you just did the toughest part—the preparation. Grilling over indirect heat requires very little attention. The chicken only has to be *rotated* every 15 minutes. The skin will be crisp and dark and the meat moist.

Don't forget to baste the chicken with cilantro-lime juice during the final 15 minutes of grilling. The refreshing mixture makes the skin glisten and complements the chili powder.

Carving is pretty simple. As tender as the meat is, the breastbone and ribs pull right out of the finished chicken just using your fingers. This makes it easy to carve. I give each person pieces of dark and white meat so no one ever feels slighted.

12 Preheat both sides of a gas grill to high. When ready to grill, reduce one side to medium-high and completely turn off the other. The chicken is placed breast side up on the side with no heat. Rotate the chicken every 15 minutes until it registers 165° (roughly 20 minutes per pound). During the last 15 minutes, baste the chicken with the cilantro-lime juice. Remove from grill and tent with foil for 10 minutes, or until cool enough to carve.

Carving

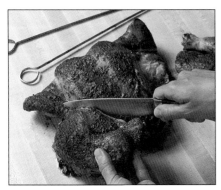

13 To carve, place the chicken on a cutting board, breast side up. Remove the leg quarters first. Locate the thigh joint next to the breast and cut completely through.

14 Next, cut between the drumstick and thigh. If you turn the leg over, you should see where you made the cut on Step 5. Use your knife to cut between the joints.

GRILLED VEGETABLES
(SERVES 4)
WORK TIME: 10 MINUTES
COOK TIME: 15 MINUTES
COOK IN ALL-METAL SAUTE PAN:

2	ears of corn, husked and cut into 2" pieces
4	new potatoes, cut into ½" slices
2	cups sugar snap peas
¼	cup olive oil
	Salt and pepper to taste

GRILL FOR 15 MINUTES ON MEDIUM–HIGH DIRECT HEAT.

15 Turn the chicken over. In the middle is the breast bone—remove it using your fingers. Now, pull off the rib bones on each side of the breast. This should be easy since the meat is so tender.

16 With the chicken skin side up, cut the breast in half, top to bottom. You'll have two breast halves with wings, and the other two halves will be boneless. You now have eight pieces!

Michigan cherry orchards in July.

Shaking the cherry trees.

Flushing with cold w

seeing red

If you've had cherry pie, you've had a taste of Michigan. Here's a look into the soul of the pie.

Michigan knows cherries—75% of the country's total tart cherry crop is grown there, with most coming from northern Michigan. Lake Michigan has a lot to do with that. The soil is sandy and rich in clay, which provides good drainage for the trees. Plus, the lake buffers the orchards from cold air in the winter, and keeps them cool in the summer.

Harvesting: So what do you do when four million cherry trees ripen at once? Move fast—harvesting happens during three frantic and furious weeks in July. Here's how it works.

Shaking: Once ripe, cherries are shaken out of the trees using special tractors. First, the tractor wraps a tarp around the trunk, under the branches, like an inverted umbrella. Then it "grabs" the tree trunk and shakes the tree for 5–8 seconds. The cherries fall into the tarp and are funneled into a portable water tank located on the back of the tractor.

Cooling: The fruit must be cooled quickly after shaking to help preserve it until processing. The tank on the tractor starts the cooling, but once it's full (it holds 1000 pounds of fruit) the tank is removed, then flushed with more cold water. The fruit must be processed within 24 hours of shaking, or it'll spoil.

Processing: Prior to processing, most cherries are sorted according to size and condition, then pitted. After that, there are several ways they could go. Freezing, drying, and canning into pie filling or jam are the most common treatments. But the most interesting technique is in making maraschino cherries.

The Cherry on Top: So how *do* they make that garnish for your banana split? First, unpitted cherries soak in swimming pool-sized pits filled with a bleaching solution. They'll sit there for up to a year until most of the color has been leached out—in the end they'll be a beige-pink color and have a soft texture. Then, the fruit is pitted and soaked again, this time in dye, sugar syrup, and flavoring. By the time they're canned, the maraschinos are vibrant red and have firmed up.

Tart cherries aren't usually used for maraschinos. Napoleons and Queen Annes work better because they're lighter in color and have a more neutral flavor.

CHERRY CHOICES

Cherries fall into two categories: tart and sweet. There are several varieties in each, but here are the common ones.

◄ Montmorency [mah-meh-RAHN-see] is the most widely grown tart cherry, making up most of Michigan's crop. They're bright red, small, and quite tart. And *the best* for pies.

But it's tough to find fresh tart cherries unless you live in northern Michigan—they don't ship well. But lucky for us, frozen cherries work just fine in pies (and other dishes). Page 42 lists some mail-order sources if your store doesn't carry them. It's expensive, but the pie is worth it.

◄ Napoleon and Queen Annes are sweet cherries that are slightly tart. Their lighter red color with gold streaks makes them perfect for maraschino cherries, *see article, left.* But they're also used to make jams and jellies.

◄ For eating, Bings are the most popular sweet cherry. The fruit should be firm (but not hard) and free of blemishes. Store in the refrigerator in plastic bags.

TART CHERRY PIE

(Makes One 9" Lattice-Top Pie)

Work Time: 35–45 Minutes

Cook Time: 1 Hour

For the Dough—

Combine:

2½ cups all-purpose flour

3 T. sugar

¼ t. kosher salt

Cut In:

¾ cup cold unsalted butter, cubed

½ cup cold vegetable shortening

Stir In:

10–12 T. ice water

For the Filling—

Thaw:

6 cups frozen cherries (2 lbs.) (reserve 1 cup cherry juice)

Add (If Needed):

Apple-cherry juice concentrate, thawed, (to make 1 cup juice)

1⅓ cup sugar

3 T. instant tapioca, ground

1 T. fresh lemon juice

¼ t. almond extract

Pinch of salt

Before Baking, Top Lattice

With:

¼ cup half & half

3 T. cinnamon sugar

the best cherry pie

This is a great cherry pie—that's a bold statement, but true. And even though the lattice top is what catches your eye, what will *really* hook you is the inside. Believe it or not, this cherry filling uses frozen tart cherries, not fresh and not canned. As it turns out, frozen cherries are as good as (maybe even better than) fresh.

Frozen food doesn't always get the credit it deserves. But there are good reasons for using frozen cherries. First of all, they're pitted. And if you've ever had to pit pounds of cherries, you'll appreciate that. But be careful—you *still* may find a few stray pits in frozen cherries.

Second, frozen cherries are available in regions where it's hard to find fresh. Plus, the convenience of frozen means you can make cherry pie all year, not just during the summer.

But not all frozen cherries are alike—the juice content varies. If they're too juicy, the filling is runny. Not enough, it's gluey. That's why the cherries are thawed first.

One cup of juice is all you need for this recipe. To see how much you have, strain the thawed cherries and measure the juice. Discard anything over one cup. But if there's not enough, add *undiluted* apple-cherry juice concentrate to make one cup.

a promising pie crust

Making pie crust scares people. But keep these things in mind and you'll be fine.

First, be sure the butter and shortening are cold. And use *ice* water, not just cold water from the tap. Keeping things cold ensures that the fats won't melt as easily during mixing and rolling. It's those chunks of butter that melt away during baking, creating the flaky crust people love.

Second, resist the urge to knead the dough. Overworking is the main reason pie crust gets tough—the protein in flour (gluten) overdevelops. Handle the dough gently, and add just enough water to keep it from crumbling.

1 Combine dry ingredients in a large bowl. With pastry blender, cut in fats until the size of peanuts, *see inset*. Using a fork, stir in water 3–4 T. at a time. It shouldn't be sticky.

2 Cover dough with plastic wrap and chill at least 30 minutes before rolling out (may be made one day ahead). On lightly floured surface, roll half the dough into a 12" circle about ⅛" thick.

lessons in lattice

The lattice for this pie is woven first, then transferred. Why? It keeps the strips (and your hands) free of the juicy cherry filling. Here's how to do it.

First, trace the pie plate on a piece of parchment. This will help you position the strips evenly as you weave. Then place the parchment on the *back* of a baking sheet (this will make it easier to transfer the lattice to the pie).

Now roll the remaining dough like the first. But this time, try shaping it into a square so the strips are even.

Don't worry if it's not perfect—short strips can go on the sides. A pastry wheel is great for cutting the strips, but a paring knife works too. You should have 24, but a few less or more is okay.

As you weave, try to position the strips close together so the lattice is easier to transfer. But don't be concerned if the strips aren't the same width, or evenly spaced. It won't be noticeable once the lattice is on the pie. And chill the lattice for half an hour before transferring—it'll be a lot easier to handle.

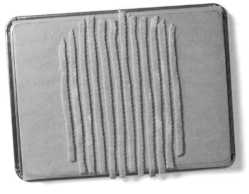

5 Place the traced parchment on the back of a baking sheet. Lay half of the strips (12) vertically across the circle. Use any shorter strips on the sides.

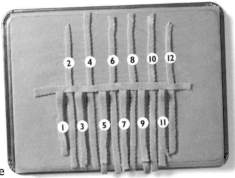

6 To weave, fold back the "odd" strips (1, 3, 5, etc.) halfway to the center of the circle. Lay a strip horizontally across the middle; then fold up the odd strips.

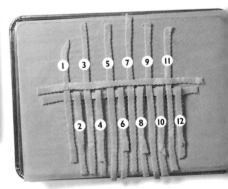

7 Now fold back the "even" strips (2, 4, 6, etc.) and place another strip horizontally across. Continue weaving until half the strips (about 6) are used.

3 Transfer circle to 9" glass pie plate—first fold it into quarters, then unfold it in the plate. Without stretching, adjust circle so it reaches the edges. Chill dough while weaving the lattice.

4 For the lattice top, roll the remaining pie dough into a 12" square about ⅛" thick. Don't panic if your square is uneven—mine is. Use a pastry or pizza wheel to trim edges, if necessary; cut ½" wide strips. The shorter pieces can be placed at the sides.

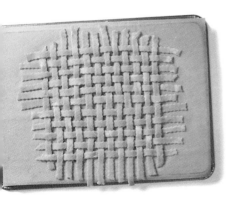

8 Once you've woven to the end, turn the pan around and weave the other half with the remaining strips. Chill. Don't freeze or the strips will break.

the proof is in the pudding—tapioca

Most fruit pies are thickened with cornstarch or flour. But here, you're going to use tapioca—it doesn't taste heavy or starchy, and you use much less of it than other thickeners.

Tapioca comes from cassava, a tuber native to South America. The most common form is "minute" or instant—the same thing used to make tapioca pudding. It's great for pie fillings because it thickens quickly. Plus, it's inexpensive and easy to find.

To prevent tiny lumps from forming in the filling, the tapioca is ground first, then combined with the remaining ingredients. Use a coffee grinder (or mortar and pestle), and process until it looks like "powdery" sugar.

I like to blend the tapioca and sugar together before adding it to the cherries and juice. Otherwise, the tapioca may clump after it's mixed with liquid. If this happens, just break up the lumps between your fingers.

This filling is *really* juicy—don't worry, it's not a mistake. Just be sure to bake the pie on a parchment-lined baking sheet to catch any overflow.

9 Preheat oven to 425°. Combine thawed cherries (and juice), sugar, tapioca, lemon juice, almond extract, and salt. Fill the chilled pie shell.

11 Remove bottom sheet, then carefully place lattice over filled pie shell. Remove top sheet; adjust lattice strips. It's okay if they're not perfectly even.

10 To transfer lattice to pie, place a second piece of parchment on top of chilled lattice. Lifting bottom sheet, drape lattice over your forearm.

12 Leaving 1" overhang, trim dough from sides using kitchen shears. Press lattice and bottom crust together, turn edge under, and crimp, *see inset.*

13 Lightly brush the lattice with half & half (it's okay if it drips into the filling); sprinkle with cinnamon sugar. Bake pie on a baking sheet (to catch overflow) in lower third of oven for 30 min. Reduce heat to 350° and bake 20–30 more min., until filling is thickened and bubbly, and crust is browned. Cool.

▲ *Here are two kinds of pastry blenders you're most likely to see. The one to the left has thin wires and the one on the right has flat blades. Both work equally well.*

What is basil chiffonade, as called for in the lasagna recipe in Issue 19?
Jim Tucker
Bettendorf, IA

Chiffonade means to cut into strips or shreds. To chiffonade basil, make a stack of basil leaves and roll them up like a cigar. Then thinly slice across the cigar into thin strips.

TURKEY JELL-O

What is that clear Jell-O like substance that forms around my turkey bones in the refrigerator? Should I throw it out?

Sarah Cresap
Patuxent River, MD

The stuff that looks like clear Jell-O is gelatin (or collagen), a protein found in animal meat and bones. When cooked, it dissolves into a liquid (as broth or pan drippings). And cooled, it solidifies and looks like Jell-O.

Don't throw it out—reheat and strain it! It will be a good, strong broth you can use as a base for gravy, soup, sauce, or in any recipe that calls for poultry broth.

This protein-rich broth will have an especially intense flavor. It adds a lot of extra body to your sauce, or whatever else you are cooking. Any fat from the meat will raise to the top of the chilled collagen—skim it off. The broth will be flavorful yet low in fat.

PASTRY BLENDER POINTERS

How is a pastry blender used? My butter sticks to it in one solid mass and doesn't work itself into the flour.
Karen Nelson
Warasta, NY

Here are a few hints to help you get started. First, make sure your butter is very cold. This way it will be less sticky to work with. Second, cut the cold butter into smaller pieces. If you start with a big chunk of butter, you'll end up with just that. Finally, before blending, toss the butter pieces with your flour mixture to coat them. This helps to keep them from sticking to each other and to the pastry blender.

With a rocking motion, keep the blades of the pastry blender in contact with the mixture as much as you can. Keep rocking the blades over the butter to cut it up. You may notice that the flour and butter will climb up the sides of the bowl. Gently shake the bowl every so often to keep the mixture at the bottom where you're blending.

Each recipe will usually give you an idea of what consistency to reach, such as small peas or coarse bread crumbs. Work longer for finer textures.

TOO SALTY FOR ME!

I liked your lasagna recipe in Issue 19, but the Bolognese Sauce was way too salty.

Alan Leban
Milpitas, CA

Even after retesting the recipe, we thought it was fine. Then, we realized many cooks might be using table salt rather than the kosher salt used in our kitchens.

We tried it with table salt and you were right! It was far too salty. The recipe should have specified

TOTAL NUTMEG

How far can I grate my whole nutmeg? Is the whole thing safe to use?
Leo Frazier
Tigard, OR

While there is a difference in appearance between the inside and the outside of the nutmeg, the flavor is the same. All of the nutmeg is usable.

kosher salt or salt to taste. Here's the problem with using table salt.

Because kosher salt has a coarse texture, less of the surface area of the grain comes in direct contact with the tongue, so it doesn't seem as salty. We like to use kosher salt in our recipes because it has a cleaner flavor than table salt, which tends to have a bitter, chemical taste.

In the future, we will specify kosher salt in our recipes. If you choose to use table salt, just use half the amount called for.

ALTITUDE ADJUSTMENT

Living at 4200 feet above sea level, I have difficulty with cake recipes. What's going on? Is there something I can do?

Karen Head
Salt Lake City, UT

This can be a confusing subject, but this is *generally* what happens. At high altitudes, the air pressure is lower, causing coarse or over-risen cakes. Briefly, here's why.

Coarse Texture: Liquids boil at a lower temperature at higher altitudes. Because of that, the liquid evaporates too soon. This concentrates the fats and sugar, creating a coarse texture.

Over-rising: Cakes tend to fall or overflow the pan at high altitudes because they're rising faster than they're baking. There's no structure to support the rising batter.

Try these things to help solve the problems. First, fill the pans just half-full to prevent them from overflowing. Next, *increase* the oven temperature 15–25° and *reduce* the baking time by 20%. The higher temperature allows the cake to bake at the same rate it rises. And the shorter baking time means less liquid evaporates.

If you *still* have problems, try one of the adjustments in the chart below—the ranges given are simply guidelines. For more help, try Colorado State University's Cooperative Extension at **(970) 491-6198** or **www.colostate.edu.**

Adjustment	3,000 ft.	5,000 ft.	7,000 ft.
Reduce baking powder for each teaspoon	$1/8$ tsp.	$1/8$–$1/4$ tsp.	$1/4$ tsp.
Reduce sugar for each cup	0–1 T.	0–2 T.	1–3 T.
Increase liquid for each cup (includes butter and eggs)	1–2 T.	2–4 T.	3–4 T.

Over-rising: *reduce baking powder*
Coarse texture: *adjust sugar and liquid*

STOCK TIP

I often need chicken broth for cooking but don't always have the time to make my own stock. Is there a store brand you can recommend?

Marna Miraz
Shelburne, VT

We've run a bunch of blind taste tests over the years to determine the best store-bought broth. The result keeps coming up the same—Manischewitz.

The staff has tested bouillons, concentrates, and canned broth comparing color, aroma, flavor, "chicken-ness," and overall appeal. Manischewitz has a natural chicken flavor that is the next best thing to homemade. It even has a lower sodium percentage than the others we tried. Look for it in your grocery store, or call for the nearest purveyor: **(201) 333-3700** or **www. manischewitz.com**

What is Demerara Sugar?
Karen Duke
St. Paul, MN

Demerara is raw sugar—it's brown with a coarse texture. It's not available in the U.S., so substitute turbinado sugar ("Sugar in the Raw").

STICK WITH STONES

What is a pizza stone? I'm not even sure how to clean one.

Dalit Livni-Rav
Dallas, TX

Pizza and bread stones (they're the same things) are rounds or square slabs of porous ceramic. They absorb moisture from the dough as it bakes, sort of like a sponge absorbs water. This is what gives bread and pizza that light, crispy crust.

Here are some hints for caring for baking stones. First, before ever baking on it, the stone must be seasoned. Put it in a 500° oven for an hour, then turn off the oven and let it sit overnight to cool. Now, it's ready to use and you can just leave it in the oven all the time. The stone actually makes your oven more efficient—it moderates the heat, helping maintain a constant temperature as the oven heats and cools.

As for cleaning, just use hot water and a nylon scrubber—metal scrubbers can leave marks. *But don't use soap!* The stone will absorb that, too, affecting the taste of foods. Any stains that develop on the stones are just from oils in the dough. It's natural and nothing to worry about.

Any residual crumbs left on the stone after baking should be brushed off to prevent smoking.

◄ *Stones come in various shapes and sizes. The round stone has been seasoned and has absorbed oils.*

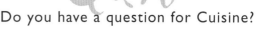

Do you have a question for Cuisine?

If you have question about a cooking term, procedure, or technique, we'd like to hear from you. We'll consider publishing your question in one or more of our works.

Just write down your question and mail it to Cuisine, Q&A Editor, 2200 Grand Ave., Des Moines, IA 50312, or contact us through our e-mail address shown below. Please include your name, address, and daytime phone number in case we have questions.

E-mail: Cuisine@CuisineMagazine.com
Web address: www.CuisineMagazine.com

what's happening in food?

*Ordering Information: Classic French stock reductions by More Than Gourmet. Call **(800) 860-9385** for a source near you.*

Talk about fast food— these stock reductions make sauces a snap.

The classic demi-glace from **More Than Gourmet** has been featured here before. I'm a big fan—it tastes great and eliminates the impractical simmering required to make classic demi-glace.

But there's more where that came from. Roasted Chicken Stock and Demi-Glace, Roasted Vegetable Stock and Demi-Glace, even rendered Duck Fat (great for frying potatoes) are just a few of the choices. For more information on these products, log on to **www.morethangourmet.com**

resources

Frozen Tart Cherries

*Friske Orchards
(231) 588-6185
10 lbs. (minimum order) costs $75.00 which includes shipping (FedEx overnight).*

*Orchard's View
(800) 286-7209
$4.25/20 oz. bag plus shipping charges (2nd Day Air).*

*Peterson Farms, Inc.
(231) 861-7101
$4.50/20 oz. bag plus shipping charges (FedEx).*

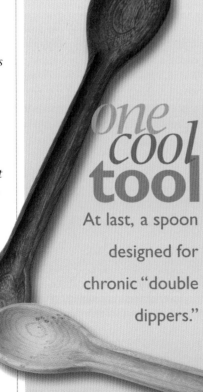

*Tasting spoons from The Spoonman, $9.95 plus shipping. Call **(830) 995-3986**, or order online at thespoonman. com*

one cool tool

At last, a spoon designed for chronic "double dippers."

We use a lot of plastic spoons in the test kitchen for tasting food. But with a big staff, double dipping is unacceptable.

Here's a solution. These wooden tasting spoons, carved by Jim and Karen Kuhlmann of Comfort, TX, are made for double dippers like me. The large and small bowls are connected by a handle that has a trough carved down the middle. To taste, scoop soup or broth into the large bowl, tip the spoon back so the liquid runs down the trough, then sip it from the small bowl.

Wooden spoons are perfect for tasting because they don't conduct heat—and the liquid actually cools off a little as it travels down the handle.

books for cooks

Here are the summer's topselling cookbooks on barnesandnoble.com

1. **Julia and Jacques Cooking at Home**, Child, Pepin, and Nussbaum, *Alfred A. Knopf*, $40. Techniques and banter from our favorite chefs.

2. **The Cake Mix Doctor,** Anne Byrn, *Workman*, $14.95. Make amazing desserts from box cake mixes.

3. **The French Laundry Cookbook** Keller, Heller, and Jones, *Artisan*, $50. A coffee table cookbook from one of California's top restaurants.

4. **Top Secret Restaurant Recipes** Todd Wilbur, *Penguin*, $12.95. Theme restaurant dishes and food lore.

recipe index

Food Sleuth question for our next issue: If you were to have one final meal, what would it be? E-mail us your response at: Cuisine@ CuisineMag-azine.com Or write to us at: Cuisine, 2200 Grand Avenue, Des Moines, IA 50312.

foodsleuth

48 lbs.
Amount of pork the average American consumes each year [1]

7,000
Number of cherries on the average cherry tree [2]

80
Average number of hot dogs each American consumes in a year [1]

16.9 billion lbs.
Total amount of beef Americans consume each year [1]

Banana cream
Filling inside the first Hostess Twinkie [1]

250
Number of cherries in the average cherry pie [2]

Under 25
The age that 63% of Americans purchase their first grill [4]

50%
Number of Americans who drink tea—80% of which is iced [1]

Horseradish
First item processed by H.J. Heinz Company [3]

60%
Of Americans who own grills, percentage of those who own a gas grill [4]

3
Average number of hamburgers each American eats per week [1]

Steak
The most popular grilled item [4]

Sources:
[1] John F. Mariani, *Encyclopedia of American Food & Drink*, Lebhar/Friedman Books
[2] Cherry Marketing Institute, Inc.
[3] H.J. Heinz Company
[4] Weber-Stephans Product Company

food events

National Cherry Festival
Traverse City, Michigan
July 1–8
Over 500,000 people descend on the northern shores of Lake Michigan for the annual weeklong harvest celebration. Call **(231) 947-4230** or e-mail **info@cherryfestival.org** for more information.

Gilroy Garlic Festival
Gilroy, California
July 28–30
No vampires here at the 21st annual weekend tribute to the stinking rose. Enjoy garlic in every way imaginable—even ice cream. For more information call **(408) 842-1625** or e-mail **clove@gilroygarlic festival.com**

Iowa State Fair
Des Moines, Iowa
August 11–20
THE state fair, biggest and best of them all. Incredible food—most of it served on a stick. For information call **(800) 545-FAIR**.

Cheesecake dipped in chocolate is just one of the hundreds of foods on a stick at the Iowa State Fair.

GRAND *finale*

You probably had s'mores as a kid—now have one as an adult. Go ahead, pick it up and eat it with your hands. It tastes better that way. Remember?

Grilled dessert sandwiches for four

CAKE POCKETS:

4   1"-thick slices angel food cake from a loaf, split (*see Page 31*)

4   sections bittersweet chocolate (1 oz. each)

FRUIT KEBABS:

1   banana, peeled, cut into four chunks

1   T. fresh lemon juice

2   ¾"-thick rings fresh pineapple, cored, each cut into quarters

½   cup cinnamon sugar

FRUIT SALAD:

2   kiwis, peeled and diced

8   strawberries, rinsed, hulled, and sliced

▲Tuck one-1 oz. section of chocolate inside each split cake slice; set aside. Drizzle banana with lemon juice; dredge banana and pineapple in cinnamon sugar. Divide fruits on four skewers. Place cake and kebabs on oiled grill; cover. Grill over med. heat, 2–3 min.

▲Turn cake and kebabs, cover, and grill 2–3 more minutes, until chocolate is melted. Remove from grill, place kebab inside cake, and pull out the skewer. Top each sandwich with some of the kiwi and strawberry fruit salad. Serve immediately—with napkins!

Issue No. 23 Sept/Oct 2000
www.CuisineMagazine.com

Cuisine

an illustrated guide to creative home cooking

Weeknight

pasta

3 hot classics ready in 30 minutes

Seared Scallops

appetizer and salad

phyllo-fast

Apple Strudel

Pork Braise

with spaetzle

Editor
John F. Meyer

Art Director
Cinda Shambaugh

Associate Editor
Susan Hoss

Assistant Editors
Juliana Hale
Sara Ostransky
Matt Bereza

Senior Graphic Designer
Holly Wiederin

Graphic Designer
Stephanie Hunter

Test Kitchen Director
Kim Samuelson

Contributing Photographers
Scott Little, Dean Tanner

Contributing Food Stylist
Janet Pittman

Pre-Press Image Specialist
Troy Clark

Publisher
Donald B. Peschke

CORPORATE:
Director of Finance: Mary R. Scheve • *Creative Director:* Ted Kralicek • *New Media Manager:* Gordon C. Gaippe • *Special Publications Executive Editor:* Douglas L. Hicks • *Senior Photographer:* Crayola England • *Multi Media Art Director:* Eugene Pedersen • *Technology Analyst:* Carol Schoeppler • *Web Site Product Specialist:* Adam Best • *Web Content Managers:* Terry Walker, David Briggs • *Controller:* Robin Hutchinson • *Senior Accountant:* Laura Thomas • *Accounts Payable:* Mary Schultz • *Accounts Receivable:* Margo Petrus • *Production Director:* George Chmielarz • *Electronic Publishing Director:* Douglas M. Lidster • *Network Administrator:* Cris Schwanebeck • *Production Coordinator:* Noelle M. Carroll • *Pre-Press Image Specialist:* Minniette Johnson • *H.R. Assistant:* Kirsten Koele • *Facilities Manager:* Julia Fish • *Receptionist:* Jeanne Johnson • *Administrative Assistant:* Sherri Ribbey • *Mail Room Clerk:* Lou Webber

CUSTOMER SERVICE & FULFILLMENT:
Operations Director: Bob Baker • *Customer Service Manager:* Jennie Enos • *Customer Service Representatives:* Anna Cox, Jeanette Rankin, April Revell, Deborah Rich, Tammy Truckenbrod • *Technical Representative:* Johnny Audette • *Buyer:* Linda Jones • *Administrative Assistant:* Nancy Downey • *Warehouse Supervisor:* Nancy Johnson • *Fulfillment:* Sylvia Carey, Sheryl Knox, Dan Spidle

CIRCULATION:
Subscriber Services Director: Sandy Baum • *New Business Manager:* Todd L. Bierle • *Promotion Manager:* Rick Junkins • *Billing and Collections Manager:* Rebecca Cunningham • *Renewal Manager:* Paige Rogers • *Assistant Subscription Manager:* Joy Krause • *Circulation Marketing Analyst:* Kris Schlemmer • *Associate Circulation Marketing Analyst:* Paula M. DeMatteis • *Senior Graphic Designers:* Robin Dowdell, Mark Hayes

www.CuisineMagazine.com

from the editor:

There's no time like fall. While most of us consider it a short transitional season, no other time of the year works harder on *all* our senses. You know the story—the green foliage bursts into blooms of gold and red. Leaves fall and crack under our feet, or rustle in the increasingly strong northern winds. Goose bumps signal the coming of winter—time to dig out those favorite, oversized sweaters.

But other than Thanksgiving, nothing does a number on our senses of taste and smell like the foods of fall. It's all about robust stews, hearty soups, baking breads, and of course, the beguiling aroma of baking apples with brown sugar and cinnamon. Maybe our senses are just heightened a bit as temperatures drop and windows close, concentrating all those great smells. But my guess is that the pleasing aromas trigger a lot of good memories—funny how that works.

So, make the seasonal transition with some of our favorite recipes. There's a great stew made with pork and served with tiny German dumplings called spaetzle (spaetzle is cropping up in all the trendy restaurants now and it's not hard to make). Then, try baking your own homemade pretzels. Crisp on the outside and soft and warm on the inside—these are real memory triggers. Dip them in your favorite mustard for the perfect tailgating appetizer or party snack. And finally, what could be better than hot apple strudel with gingered whipped cream? It's worth the effort just for the smell.

Enjoy fall, all your senses will thank you.

John

36

contents

feature articles

in every issue

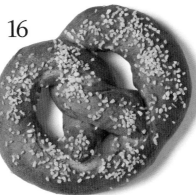

Tips

and techniques from our readers

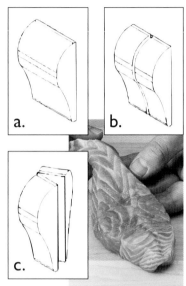

a.

b.

c.

Prepping Iron
To season cast iron, rub the inside of a clean skillet with a coat of vegetable oil. Then place in a 350° oven for one hour. Cast iron should be seasoned when first purchased, and then after each time the pan has been scrubbed clean.

Cleaning Cast Iron

Cooking in a cast iron skillet is great, but the cleanup afterward can be long and tedious. So to easily remove burnt-on food, add one or two drops of dish soap and enough water to cover the bottom of the skillet. Bring to a boil for 5 minutes; cool. After cooling, wash the pan—it'll be much easier to clean.

Paula Coomes
Ravensdale, WA

Salmon Engineering

I like grilling salmon steaks but don't like those horseshoe-shaped cuts. The little legs flop around and I don't care for the bone that goes through the middle of the steak (or its fishy taste). So, I use the fillet to make a steak. All you do is skin it and then make one simple cut.

To make 1"-thick steaks, lay a 2"-wide fillet skin side down, *see Figure a.* Use a sharp knife and slide the blade between the skin and flesh. Now, with the blade angled towards the cutting board, cut away the skin.

Now cut the sections in half, but not all the way through (leave about $1/8$"), *see Figure b.* Then fold the halves back on themselves, forming the shape of a traditional steak, *see Figure c.* Pin halves together with toothpicks so the steak doesn't unfold while grilling.

Matt Mehalic
Ellicott City, MD

An A for Effort
Our Salmon Engineer, Matt Mehalic, went all-out to illustrate his salmon tip. He emailed an animated drawing of the salmon being cut. The illustrations, above right, are still shots from his animated version.

Tomato Math

Here's a way to ripen green tomatoes that you'll have to pull off the vine before the first frost. Place green tomatoes in a paper bag along with an apple. The apple produces ethylene gas which helps speed up ripening.

Edith Samuelson
Hayward, MN

Aromatic Grilling

At the end of the growing season, I cut and dry the last of my herbs and their woody stems. Then I tie the stems and herbs with dental floss into separate, tight bundles. To impart more flavor into grilled foods, I soak a bundle in water for 30 minutes, then put it right on the coals.

Margaret Elliott
St. Louis, MO

Double-Duty Huller

I found another use for my strawberry huller—use it to pull out pin bones left in a fish fillet. Just run your hand over the fillet to locate any bones. When you feel one, grasp it with the huller and gently pull it out.

Lise Savarese
Salem, SC

Cutting Squash Safely

I can't wait to bake my first squash of the fall season. But cutting into a rock-hard squash can be difficult and even dangerous. So I use the microwave to soften it just enough to make cutting easier and safer.

First, pierce the squash all over with a paring knife, going about 1" deep. Then microwave the squash on high power for three minutes (any longer and it will start to cook). Remove the squash with a kitchen towel (it's hot!) and cut it in half.

Pat Jones
Bismarck, ND

Charcoal in the Wind

Grilling when it's windy can be a challenge, especially if breezes blow out the flame. To prevent that, put a briquet in each section of a cardboard egg carton. Close the carton, place it on top of more briquets in the grill, and light. The carton burns away, leaving behind hot coals.

John-Anthony Langdale
Temecula, CA

Soda Bottle Funnel

Make wide-mouth funnels to use in the kitchen by first piercing a 2-liter plastic soda bottle about 4" from the top (probably where the label begins). Then, use a pair of scissors to cut around the bottle.

Danya Diab
Amherst, NY

Pineapple Pieces

Here's a simple way to cut fresh pineapple into bite-sized pieces.

First, twist off the leafy top (if the fruit is ripe, it will come off easily) and cut the pineapple lengthwise into quarters; halve each quarter lengthwise.

With wedges flat side down, trim off the thin strip of core at the top of each wedge. Then cut between the skin and fruit (like skinning a fish), and slice each strip of pineapple into pieces.

H. McKnight
Los Angeles, CA

Test Kitchen Tip from Matt
It's hard work cleaning a pan that has caramelized or burnt-on sugar on the bottom. To make it easier, just boil water in the pan—the cemented sugar will dissolve and loosen.

Olive Oil Bottle

Since sunlight can cause oil to go rancid quickly, I transfer my cooking oils (olive, vegetable, canola, etc.) to dark-colored, empty wine bottles. Funnel oil into clean bottles, then use wine or soda stoppers to seal out air.

The dark color helps protect oils from light. Plus, the different bottle shapes look great, and they're easy to store and use.

Robin DeMay
Kansas City, MO

share your Tips with Cuisine

If you have a unique way of solving a cooking problem, we'd like to hear from you, and we'll consider publishing your tip in one or more of our works.

Just write down your cooking tip and mail it to Cuisine, Tips Editor, 2200 Grand Ave., Des Moines, IA 50312, or contact us through our email address shown below. Please include your name, address, and daytime phone number in case we have questions. We'll pay you $25 if we publish your tip.

Email: Cuisine@CuisineMagazine.com
Web address: www.CuisineMagazine.com

scallops

If you thought shrimp were easy to work with, you'll love scallops—they're available year-round, come ready to cook, and can be prepared in minutes.

Scallops are unlike any other shellfish. They're sweet and rich with a nutty flavor. If you're on the fence when it comes to seafood, scallops just might win you over.

For some reason, though, most people only eat scallops when they go out to a restaurant. But scallops have a place in your kitchen. They're practically preparation free (don't need shelling or deveining) and cook in a matter of minutes.

The cool thing about scallops is that they adapt well to most seafood recipes—especially shrimp. Use them interchangeably and cook for the same amount of time.

Here are two recipes that are quick and easy—an appetizer and a salad. The appetizer is a variation on shrimp scampi, but it has a vodka sauce and is served on sauteed cucumbers.

Spinach and bacon are two classic ingredients that go great with scallops, and are the basis for the salad. Fall is the perfect time to make the accompanying relish with fresh corn, tomatoes, peppers, and onions. It tastes as good as it looks.

Cooking this delicate shellfish is easy—they're seared. Searing cooks the scallops quickly, plus it enhances their flavor by developing a golden brown crust on the outside.

Sea Scallop

Bay Scallop

All about scallops

Do you remember the Shell Oil signs? Those were scallops. But in most markets you won't find scallops in their shells. Ever wonder why?

The reason is that the shells don't close tightly leaving the meat inside susceptible to quick deterioration once out of the water. Besides, all you really eat is a muscle (called the abductor). The rest of the scallop contaminates quickly and is discarded before infecting the edible portion.

What you'll most likely find in stores are already-shucked scallops (abductor muscle). They can be sold in several forms—wet, dry, or frozen.

Wet is the most common. They are chemically treated to plump them up and can be easily recognized by the milky liquid they sit in. My favorite are *dry* (untreated) scallops. They're pink or cream and have little or no liquid (clear, if any). Finally, there are *IQF* (individually quick frozen) scal-

Calico Scallop

lops. They're usually fresher than "fresh" scallops since they're often frozen right on the boat just after harvesting.

There are over 400 species of scallops in the world. In the United States, we usually only see three types.

Sea Scallops: The largest of these three are sea scallops (the shells can be as big as salad plates). They range in color from cream to peach, and are available nationwide year-round.

Bay Scallops: These slightly pink or pale orange, cork-shaped scallops are delicious. Unfortunately, their season and fishing area are limited to winter in the northeast.

Calico Scallops: Tiny calico scallops are widely available. They may be labeled bay scallops, but their smaller size and lower price give them away. Calicos are steam-shucked so they're partially cooked when purchased.

Storing, cleaning, and cooking

▲ *Scallops have a very short shelf life, and will stay fresher longer if stored in a very cold environment. Keep them in an ice-filled container in your refrigerator.*

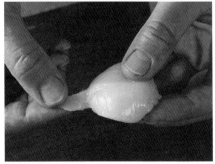

▲ *Scallops come virtually clean and ready to cook, but a tendon or "foot" may be attached—remove it. The tendon is edible, but very chewy when cooked.*

▲ *The scallop on the right is undercooked and translucent in the middle. On the left it's cooked correctly, opaque in the center. Overcooked, they're opaque but tough.*

scallop appetizer

This variation of shrimp scampi uses scallops and a unique searing technique to create a thick, flavorful sauce.

A typical scampi dish is a combination of butter, garlic, wine, and lemon juice. Tastes great, but the sauce can separate. This recipe is different. Don't worry, it still has butter and garlic. The difference is how the scallops are seared.

Searing: In this "scampi" recipe, the scallops are floured before searing. There are a couple of reasons for doing this. First, the flour absorbs moisture from the scallop so that it sears into a beautiful golden brown crust.

Second, the flour thickens and holds the sauce together. Even though the scallops are only *lightly* dusted, it's just enough to help bind the ingredients together so they don't separate. It also helps the sauce cling to the scallops once they're cooked.

Sauce: One convenient thing about scampi is that the sauce is made right in the pan. It begins with the brown crusty stuff (fond) left from searing the scallops. To loosen all this flavor from

the bottom of the pan, add a liquid (vodka) and scrape. This is called deglazing. *But a word of caution: Be sure to add the vodka off heat to prevent the alcohol from igniting.* Then reduce the heat and return the pan to the burner. If it does ignite, don't panic. The alcohol will eventually burn off, or you can put out the flame by covering the pan with a lid. Just watch out for your eyebrows!

Garnishing: There are two simple garnishes that tie this dish together: sour cream with dill, and sauteed cucumbers. The cold sour cream and crisp cucumbers create a nice contrast to the richness of the scallops.

SCALLOP "SCAMPI"

(MAKES 6 SERVINGS)
WORK TIME: 15 MINUTES
COOK TIME: 8–10 MINUTES

SAUTE IN 1 T. UNSALTED BUTTER:

1   cucumber, peeled, seeded, sliced
1   t. lemon zest, minced
   Salt and pepper to taste

FLOUR AND SAUTE IN 2 T. OLIVE OIL:

12 sea scallops, patted dry

ADD AND SAUTE:

2   t. garlic, minced

COMBINE; ADD TO PAN:

¾   cup vegetable broth
¼   cup vodka
1   T. fresh lemon juice

RETURN SCALLOPS TO PAN; SWIRL IN:

2   T. cold unsalted butter
   Salt and pepper to taste

FOR GARNISH, COMBINE:

½   cup sour cream
1   T. chopped fresh dill
1   T. half & half

NUTRITIONAL INFORMATION PER SERVING:
CALORIES 237; TOTAL FAT 15(G); CALORIES
FROM FAT 57%; SODIUM 256(MG); CARB. 12(G)

1 Peel the cucumber and slice in half lengthwise. Scoop out seeds with a spoon and discard. Slice cucumber on bias into ¼"-wide half moons.

2 Saute cucumbers with lemon zest in 1 T. butter just until heated through, about 2 minutes. Season to taste; divide between six small serving dishes.

3 Dredge scallops in ¼ cup flour and saute in olive oil over medium-high heat, 1½–2 minutes per side; remove. Add garlic and saute until aromatic.

4 Remove pan from heat. Deglaze with broth, vodka, and lemon juice. Return pan to medium heat and simmer until liquid has reduced by half.

5 Add the scallops back to the pan and simmer for 1 minute to thicken the sauce. Swirl in cold butter to melt. Season with salt and pepper.

6 To serve, place two scallops on top of cucumbers; pour 1–2 T. sauce over each serving. Garnish with sour cream and additional dill sprigs, if desired.

scallop salad

Put a twist on an old favorite—add seared scallops and a warm tomato-corn relish to a traditional spinach salad. You'll end up with dinner that's as colorful as fall itself.

There are some classic combinations that just go together—peanut butter and jelly, salmon and dill, Rogers and Astaire. Scallops have classic partners too: bacon and spinach. With a few other ingredients, these are the basis for the scallop salad. Here, seared scallops are served on a bed of spinach and a hot bacon relish made with corn and tomatoes.

Searing: The keys to a good sear are a hot pan and not moving the scallops around. First, get the pan hot so the scallops sizzle when they touch it. You can't sear unless it sizzles.

Second, leave the scallops put— don't keep moving them around. You want the scallops to end up with a deep brown crust accented by white cracks fanning out along the surface. If you move the scallops around, you won't get that good-looking crust.

Relish: The tomato-corn relish is loaded with both color and flavor, but there is a little more to it than just good looks. It also serves as the dressing.

Like traditional spinach salad, warm bacon drippings are used to make the dressing. And for even more flavor, the liquid that's released as the vegetables saute is also added to the relish.

Crouton: All salads need croutons and these homemade ones work great. They're buttered (perfect with scallops) and their size and shape makes them as interesting as they are good.

SCALLOP-SPINACH SALAD

(MAKES 4 SERVINGS)

WORK TIME: 15 MINUTES
COOK TIME: 25 MINUTES

FOR CROUTON GARNISH, TOAST:

4   slices white bread, crusts
    removed
1   T. unsalted butter, melted

FOR THE SALAD, SAUTE:

4   slices thick-cut bacon,
    chopped

SEAR IN 1 T. BACON DRIPPINGS; REMOVE:

12 sea scallops, patted dry
    Salt and pepper to taste

SAUTE IN 1 T. BACON DRIPPINGS:

1   cup fresh corn kernels
½   cup red onion, thinly sliced
½   cup red bell pepper, diced
    Salt and pepper to taste

ADD AND SIMMER:

½   cup cherry tomatoes, halved
¼   cup apple cider vinegar
2   T. brown sugar

ADD SCALLOPS BACK TO PAN AND STIR IN:

2   T. chopped fresh parsley
    Salt and pepper to taste

SERVE OVER:

6   cups fresh spinach leaves

NUTRITIONAL INFORMATION PER SERVING:
CALORIES 324; TOTAL FAT 15(G); CALORIES
FROM FAT 40%; SODIUM 649(MG); CARB. 35(G)

1 Preheat oven to 350°. Trim off bread crusts and cut diagonally into triangles. Brush both sides with melted butter. Bake 15 minutes on baking sheet.

2 Saute bacon in skillet until crisp; remove. Pour off drippings, reserving 2 T. Over high heat, sear scallops in 1 T. drippings, 1½–2 minutes per side.

3 Remove scallops from pan; reduce heat to medium. For relish, add remaining drippings to pan. Saute corn, onion, and pepper until tender, about 2 min.

4 Add cherry tomatoes to the mixture along with cider vinegar and brown sugar. Simmer relish just until warmed through, about 2 minutes.

5 Stir in parsley, salt, and pepper. Add bacon and seared scallops back to the pan. Toss and simmer to reheat scallops, about 1 minute.

6 Divide spinach between four bowls or plates. Spoon hot pan juices and vegetable relish over fresh spinach, allowing the spinach to wilt slightly.

7 Top each salad serving with three seared scallops. Garnish with two toasted croutons placed on top of the salad. Serve immediately.

simple sides

Eating fresh vegetables is healthy but boring. Loading them with calorie-heavy cheese sauce tastes great but it's counterproductive. So here are three light, refreshing recipes that show you just how good fresh vegetables can taste—without cheese sauce.

For too long, cauliflower, broccoli, and green beans have been prepared one way—steamed until they're overcooked, water-logged, and flavorless (that's the reason for the cheese sauce). But they deserve better treatment because they really *do* have flavor. It all comes out in the cooking method—roasting.

Roasting may not be a traditional way to prepare these vegetables. But it does things for them that steaming can't. First, roasting caramelizes the vegetables, enhancing their natural flavor. And since there's no water involved, the texture stays firm, slightly crisp.

The key to roasting is making sure the vegetables aren't crowded on the baking sheets, or they'll steam, not caramelize. And watch the time—overroasting is as bad as oversteaming.

cauliflower

I was not a big fan of cauliflower—until I roasted it. Roasting makes it different: flavorful and firm, not soft and bland like you're used to.

Look for cauliflower that has a creamy-white, compact head (called "curd") with few or no black spots. The leaves at the base are the best indicator of freshness and should be crisp and green. If the head is pale yellow and the leaves are limp, don't buy it. It's old and the sweet, mild flavor has started to turn bitter.

To prepare cauliflower, trim off any dark patches with a paring knife. Then use the knife to separate the head into florets—it's neater than breaking it apart by hand. Be sure to wash and dry the florets thoroughly before roasting. Bugs tend to hide inside the head.

broccoli

Surprisingly, broccoli is great roasted. At first, I thought the green color would fade, but it's fine—just as long as it's not overroasted.

When buying broccoli, look for stalks that aren't dried out or slimy. And the blue-green buds should be tightly packed—if they come off easily, or are yellow or wilted, don't buy it.

Trim the florets from the stalk as shown on Page 14. Try to leave as long a stem as possible—it looks nicer on the plate. Cut really large florets in half or quarters. It's important that the florets are about the same size so they cook evenly. If you *really* like broccoli, you can roast the stalks too. Just peel off the tough skin with a vegetable peeler until no strings remain, slice into coins, and then roast with the florets.

green beans

There's no reason to resign green beans to casseroles anymore. Fresh beans are the way to go, and roasting makes them even better.

When you purchase green beans, don't just grab handfuls and stuff them into a bag. Take time to hand-select the beans—it takes longer, but you'll pick more flavorful and tender beans that way. Green beans should be firm, crisp, and evenly colored. Avoid those with brown spots, bruises, or bulging seeds inside (the bean is overripe and starchy). Snap a bean in half: It's fresh if moisture forms at the break.

Green beans don't need much preparation before cooking—just snap off the stem end. You can remove the curvy tip, too, but I leave it on. It makes a humble bean look elegant.

cauliflower

ROASTED CAULIFLOWER WITH MUSTARD BUTTER

(MAKES ABOUT 6 CUPS)
WORK TIME: 10 MINUTES
COOK TIME: 20 MINUTES

TOSS IN 2 T. OLIVE OIL; ROAST:

1   large head cauliflower (about 3 lbs.), trimmed into florets
1   lb. unpeeled red potatoes, halved, then cut into thirds
Salt and pepper to taste

FOR THE MUSTARD BUTTER—
COMBINE; TOSS WITH HOT,
ROASTED CAULIFLOWER:

4   T. unsalted butter, softened
2   T. whole grain mustard
2   t. prepared horseradish
1   t. honey

STIR IN:

¼   cup chopped fresh parsley

NUTRITIONAL INFORMATION PER CUP:
CALORIES 225; TOTAL FAT 13(G);
CALORIES FROM FAT 52%; SODIUM
205(MG); CARB. 24(G)

1 Preheat oven to 450°. Remove leaves from the base of the cauliflower; cut florets from stalk, halving larger ones. Toss florets and red potatoes with olive oil, salt, and pepper.

2 Place vegetables in single layers on two baking sheets. Roast in lower half of oven 10 minutes; stir, then rotate pans. Roast 8–10 more minutes, until tip of a knife can pierce vegetables easily.

3 While the vegetables are roasting, combine the butter, mustard, horseradish, and honey in a large mixing bowl. Add the roasted vegetables and parsley; toss to coat. Serve immediately.

Serving Suggestion: This is a great side dish for roast beef, roast pork, or turkey—try it at your next Thanksgiving dinner. The vegetables can be roasted while the turkey rests.

broccoli

ROASTED BROCCOLI WITH GINGER-SESAME DRESSING

(MAKES ABOUT 6 CUPS)
WORK TIME: 15 MINUTES
COOK TIME: 15–18 MINUTES

TOSS WITH 2 T. OLIVE OIL; ROAST:

2–3 stalks (about 2 lbs.) broccoli, cut in florets (1 lb. florets)
1   T. sesame seeds
    Salt and pepper to taste

FOR THE VINAIGRETTE—
WHISK TOGETHER:

2   T. low sodium soy sauce
2   T. seasoned rice vinegar
2   T. fresh orange juice
1   t. fresh ginger, peeled, grated
½   t. crushed red pepper flakes
⅛   t. toasted sesame oil

DRIZZLE IN:

¼   cup salad oil (like canola)

NUTRITIONAL INFORMATION PER CUP:
CALORIES 165; TOTAL FAT 15(G); CALORIES FROM FAT 82%; SODIUM 401(MG); CARB. 7(G)

Serving Suggestion: This broccoli is a great partner to simple roast chicken or mild fish, like red snapper and halibut. Serve the meal with steamed white rice for an Asian touch.

1 Preheat oven to 450°. To trim broccoli, hold stalk upside down and make angled cuts at the base of each floret, near the stem. Cut large florets in half. Peel stems and cut into coins, if desired.

2 Toss broccoli with oil, sesame seeds, salt, and pepper. Place on two baking sheets in single layers; roast 10 minutes. Stir, then roast 5–8 minutes more, or until stems can be pierced with a knife.

3 While broccoli roasts, whisk soy sauce, vinegar, orange juice, ginger, red pepper flakes, and sesame oil in a mixing bowl; drizzle in salad oil. Toss roasted broccoli in vinaigrette to coat.

green beans

ROASTED GREEN BEANS WITH GREEK DRESSING

(MAKES ABOUT 6 CUPS)
WORK TIME: 15 MINUTES
COOK TIME: 10 MINUTES

DRIZZLE WITH 2 T. OLIVE OIL;
ROAST:

1   lb. green beans, trimmed
½   cup walnuts, coarsely chopped
     Salt and pepper to taste

FOR THE VINAIGRETTE—
WHISK TOGETHER:

¼   cup red wine vinegar
1   T. fresh lemon juice
2   t. sugar
2   t. chopped fresh oregano (or ½ t. dried)
1   t. garlic, minced
     Salt and pepper to taste

DRIZZLE IN:

¼   cup olive oil

ADD:

½   cup red onion, thinly sliced

TOSS BEANS IN DRESSING. BEFORE SERVING, GARNISH WITH:

2–3 T. feta cheese, crumbled

NUTRITIONAL INFORMATION PER CUP:
CALORIES 229; TOTAL FAT 21(G);
CALORIES FROM FAT 83%; SODIUM 360(MG); CARB. 11(G)

1 Preheat oven to 450°. Snap off tips of beans at the stem end; place beans and nuts in single layers on two baking sheets. Drizzle with olive oil; sprinkle with salt and pepper. Toss to coat.

2 Roast beans in lower half of oven 5 minutes; stir and roast 5 more minutes. In a large bowl, whisk vinegar, lemon juice, sugar, oregano, garlic, salt, and pepper. Drizzle in oil; add sliced onion.

3 Toss roasted beans and walnuts in dressing, then transfer to a large serving platter or individual plates. Garnish beans with crumbled feta; serve warm or at room temperature.

Serving Suggestion: The distinctive flavor of lamb is great with these green beans—the tangy dressing and cheese balance lamb's richness. Grilled steak or salmon also works well.

soft pretzels

BASIC SOFT PRETZELS
(MAKES 16 PRETZELS)
WORK TIME: 50 MINUTES
RISING TIME: 45 MINUTES
COOK TIME: 20 MINUTES

WHISK TOGETHER AND PROOF:
2   cups warm tap water (115°)
1   t. molasses
1   packet active dry yeast (2¼ t.)

STIR IN; KNEAD, RISE, AND SHAPE:
2   T. rye flour
1   T. kosher salt
4–5 cups all-purpose flour

BRING TO BOIL; ADD PRETZELS:
10 cups water
3   T. baking soda

BRUSH PRETZELS WITH:
    Milk

SPRINKLE WITH; BAKE:
    Coarse salt, *see page 19*

NUTRITIONAL INFORMATION PER PRETZEL:
CALORIES 121; TOTAL FAT 0(G); CALORIES
FROM FAT 3%; SODIUM 2,538(MG);
CARBOHYDRATES 25(G)

They get you every time. You walk into a mall and smell fresh pretzels baking. There's no resisting that aroma. Now, fill your kitchen with the same temptation.

In Europe, pretzels were considered a mark of a baker's skill. Even today, you can see a pretzel sign hanging over a bakery. So what makes a good pretzel? In my opinion, it has to be crisp on the outside, soft and chewy on the inside, plenty of flavor, and above all—hot!

Now, you can have all of that great aroma and taste in your home, and it's not that hard. In fact, this can be a family event by having everyone twist, shape, and flavor their own pretzels.

There are all kinds of secrets about pretzel-making. Interesting things like how to shape them, and how to get that outside so brown and crispy (mall pretzels can't do this, but you can). And finally, how to get all that flavor out of just flour, water, and yeast. It's ordinary bread dough with a definite twist!

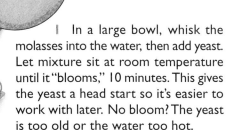

1 In a large bowl, whisk the molasses into the water, then add yeast. Let mixture sit at room temperature until it "blooms," 10 minutes. This gives the yeast a head start so it's easier to work with later. No bloom? The yeast is too old or the water too hot.

2 Add rye flour, salt, and as much all-purpose flour to the yeast mixture as you can mix in with a spoon, about 4–5 cups. (You can do the mixing with a stand mixer, too.)

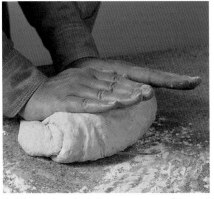

HAS IT DOUBLED?

▲ *Here's a test to see if the dough has risen enough. Give the dough a poke with your finger. If you leave a hole in the dough, it's ready. If the dough bounces back, it needs to rise a while longer.*

3 Turn the dough out onto a floured surface and knead by folding dough in half and pushing it together with heels of your hands. Knead until smooth, adding flour as needed, 10–15 minutes.

4 Lightly grease a large bowl with vegetable oil and place the dough in the bowl, turning once to coat. Cover with plastic wrap and let rise in a warm place until doubled, about 35 minutes.

The pretzel dough

Making a good pretzel starts with a process that's like making bread dough.

Proofing Yeast: To proof yeast means that you first dissolve it in warm water, then let it "bloom" (it will start to bubble and grow). You want to make sure the yeast blooms for two reasons. The first is to make sure that it is still alive (it can die if it gets too cold, hot, or old). The second is that if the yeast blooms first in the warm water, it'll save rising time later on.

Rye: Most pretzels rely on the buddy system for flavor. In other words, they have to come with toppings or dips for their taste. But the pretzels you're about

to make taste great on their own. The secret is rye. Rye flour is ground from the whole rye grain and it gives pretzels flecks of color as well as a great hearty, earthy flavor. The interesting thing is that you'll never know rye is in there. In fact, many good pizza restaurants put a little rye in their dough for flavor.

Kneading: When flour and water are combined, long strands of protein (gluten) form. These strands start out all jumbled, like a pile of hay. But as you knead, the gluten strands connect and begin to line up. The hay-like gluten will change from being a disorganized strands to smooth elastic sheets.

Rising: As yeast grows, it releases carbon dioxide bubbles into those smooth sheets of gluten. Rising happens as the gluten traps the carbon dioxide—like inflating a balloon.

Rising creates the texture of bread. If you look closely at a piece of bread, you'll notice it's made up of tiny holes and thin walls. The walls were formed by the gluten and the holes were created by the carbon dioxide.

And finally, have you ever tried to shape a dough that kept springing back in place? Dough needs time to double to handle well. Rising stretches the dough, making it relaxed and pliable.

Pretzel secrets

Change common bread dough into pretzels with a few of these secrets.

Boiling: Pretzels are boiled for the same reasons bagels are. Boiling does a couple of things. First, it sets the pretzel's shape. Second, it gives pretzels their distinctive chewy texture.

Bread doughs are acidic and acidic foods don't brown well. Put a little baking soda in the boiling water—this will balance the acid and help brown the pretzels.

Steaming: Professional bakeries use steam-injected ovens for light bread with crisp crust. Steam keeps the surface of the dough soft, so the pretzels will rise higher before the crust sets. Then the surface of the dough dries, making the crust crispy.

Pretzels are best hot, but here's how to enjoy them later. Let them cool completely, then freeze in a resealable plastic bag. Reheat at 350° for 10 minutes on a baking sheet. They'll be as good as freshly baked.

What you want to avoid is storing them at room temperature—they'll dry out. And don't wrap them airtight in plastic. The salt on top will draw out moisture, leaving soggy little bumps.

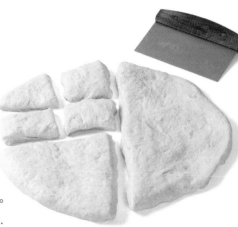

5 Punch down the dough and divide in half. A bench knife is good for this. Divide each half again for a total of 4 equal sections. Then cut each section into 4 equal pieces. You will now have a total of 16 pieces of dough.

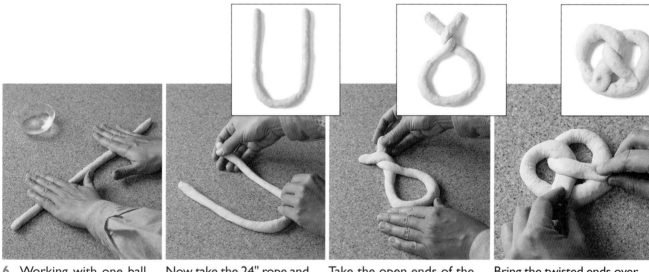

6 Working with one ball at a time (keep the rest covered), roll it into a 24" length. Use water to keep your work surface tacky.

Now take the 24" rope and shape it into a horseshoe or a letter "U."

Take the open ends of the horseshoe and twist them together just once.

Bring the twisted ends over the loop of the horseshoe and press firmly to seal them. Repeat with remaining portions of dough.

7 Place the formed pretzels on two baking sheets (8 per sheet) greased with non-stick cooking spray. Space them so they have room to rise. Cover and rise 15 minutes, or until slightly "poofy." While pretzels rise, preheat oven to 450°. And put a roasting pan in the oven for ice (it will create the steam).

8 In a 12" pan at least 3" deep, bring 10 cups water to a boil; stir in 3 T. baking soda. Add three pretzels to the pan and boil until they puff slightly and rise to the top, about 30 seconds.

9 Flip pretzels and boil 30 seconds more. Using a flat slotted spatula or skimmer, transfer pretzels back to baking sheets greased with nonstick spray. Repeat with remaining pretzels.

10 Brush pretzels with milk and sprinkle lightly with coarse salt (or choose a topping from the right). The milk is like glue for the topping and makes the pretzel look glossy when baked.

11 Bake pretzels, one sheet at a time, on the middle rack of the oven. (The pan for the ice should be on the rack underneath it.) Just before baking, dump ice cubes into roasting pan for steam.

12 Bake pretzels 20 minutes, or until golden brown. Remove from baking sheet; cool slightly on a rack. Add more ice to the steam pan and bake second batch. Pretzels taste best when warm.

PRETZEL SALT

True pretzel salt is more compressed than other salt. This is what makes it so white, pellet-like, and the reason it dissolves more slowly than other salts.

You probably won't find it at the store. I got a pound for $2.50 from King Arthur Flour: **(800) 827-6836**, or order at www.kingarthurflour.com

You can also use kosher salt or coarse sea salt. But go easy—it will have a stronger taste than pretzel salt.

---

toppings

Salt is the most traditional topping for pretzels. But bucking tradition keeps life interesting. Here are a few non-traditional suggestions:

Grated cheese:
Drier cheeses like Parmesan, Cheddar, and Swiss are good as pretzel toppings.

Mustard: Whole grain or Dijon mustard spread onto pretzels gives them a flavorful, surprisingly mild mustard flavor after baking. You can even add salt, cheese, or other toppings over the mustard layer.

Seeds: How about sesame seeds, poppy seeds, or caraway seeds? Or try a mixture of sesame seeds and poppy seeds.

cheddar
& ale soup

Soup is to autumn what salad is to spring—a clear sign of changing seasons. Cheddar soup is a great way to warm up to the cold nights.

The key to a good Cheddar & ale soup is compromise and balance. The powerful flavors of both the cheese and the beer need to meet in the middle of the road. Here's what I mean.

The Beer: The best way to choose a beer for this soup is by color. Mass produced, light-colored lagers are too mild to stand up to the Cheddar. *True* dark ales are strong, bitter, and could overwhelm the soup. Use a beer that falls in between in both color and flavor.

The Cheese: Sharp, orange-colored Cheddar cheese gives this soup its distinctive flavor and color. Mild Cheddars are too bland (all you'll taste is beer) while extra-sharp is too tangy. White (or Vermont) Cheddar has great flavor, but doesn't add any color. Store brands of sharp Cheddar (like Kraft) work best for this soup. They melt well, are usually less expensive, and taste fine.

Cheese soup secret

Okay, you've picked out the perfect beer and cheese. But there's another hurdle to overcome. Adding the cheese to hot soup can be tricky—it may turn grainy and stringy if not done correctly.

To prevent this problem, you want to follow two rules. The first is to use a roux [ROO]. Roux is a mixture of fat and flour that's slowly cooked, then used to thicken soups and sauces. The starch in flour stabilizes the cheese, preventing it from turning grainy.

The other rule to follow is to always add the cheese to the soup toward the end of cooking. Aged hard cheeses (like sharp Cheddar) don't react well to heat and should be added late in the cooking process. It's also important to use grated cheese so it doesn't require much heat to melt. And once you've added the cheese, stir the soup constantly and vigorously—this prevents stringing.

CHEDDAR & ALE SOUP *(8 CUPS)*

WORK TIME: 30 MINUTES
COOK TIME: 30 MINUTES

BRING TO BOIL:
3 cups low-sodium chicken broth
1 cup dark beer
½ cup yellow onion, minced
½ cup celery, minced
½ cup carrot, peeled, grated
2 T. Worcestershire sauce
1 t. Tabasco
1 t. paprika
1 t. dry mustard

IN A SMALL SAUCEPAN, MELT:
6 T. unsalted butter

ADD AND COOK:
½ cup all-purpose flour

WHISK IN:
2 cups skim milk, warmed

STIR INTO BOILING SOUP AND SIMMER:
   Roux-thickened milk, *above*
1 lb. sharp Cheddar cheese, grated
   Salt and pepper to taste

FOR THE GARNISH—
SAUTE:
2 cups precooked smoked kielbasa
   or Polish sausage, diced
2 cups sauerkraut, drained

OFF HEAT, ADD:
¼ cup chopped fresh parsley

1 In a large stock pot, combine liquids, vegetables, and seasonings. Simmer over medium-high heat 10 min. to extract vegetables' flavors. Don't cook them until they turn mushy—it's nice having some texture in a cheese soup.

2 Make roux in a saucepan by melting butter over medium-low heat, then stirring in flour. Cook 2 minutes, stirring constantly, then whisk in warm milk. Stir and gently simmer another minute to eliminate any "floury" flavor.

4 Bring the soup to a simmer, then turn off the heat and add the cheese all at once. Again, whisk vigorously until the soup is creamy and smooth like the photo, *right*. To serve, ladle into bowls and top with sausage garnish.

SAUSAGE GARNISH

Saute sausage in a dry skillet over medium-high heat until brown. Add sauerkraut; cook until juices evaporate, 4–5 minutes. Remove from heat, cover, and keep warm. Stir in parsley just before serving.

3 Increase heat under stock and bring to a boil. Add roux-thickened milk to the stock and *whisk vigorously* to prevent lumping and scorching. The stock will still be dark, but will continue to get lighter when the cheese is added.

German cabbage soup

If it weren't for coleslaw, cabbage would have no life at all. So before you turn your back on cabbage soup, give this a try. It may just change your mind.

In Germany, cabbage is practically a national treasure. From holiday meals to liqueurs, it seems to appear everywhere. But in America, the virtues of cabbage remain undiscovered—except for the ubiquitous coleslaw offered at every hot dog and fried chicken joint. This soup is a step toward cabbage dignity. And don't let its vegetarian quality fool you—it packs plenty of great flavor.

Cabbage is at its best in the fall, right after autumn's first frost. Not many vegetables can survive those harsh temperatures, let alone get *better*. But cabbage is high in starch, and with the dip in temperature, these starches are converted into sugars making cabbage sweet and mild.

There are several types of cabbage available in grocery stores: green, red, Savoy, Napa, and bok choy. While the curly leaves of Savoy cabbage are pretty, the common green variety is best for this German Cabbage Soup. It's sturdy and holds up well during simmering.

Roux-thickened skim milk is added for body. That way, the soup is not as heavy as one made with a cream-based broth (but just as flavorful).

German Cabbage Soup

(Makes 10 Cups)

Work Time: 30 Minutes

Cook Time: 45 Minutes

Saute in 2 T. Unsalted Butter:

1 cup yellow onion, diced

½ t. caraway seeds

Add; Cover and Cook:

2 T. unsalted butter

8 cups green cabbage (one small head), cored and chopped

Deglaze with:

½ cup dry sherry

¼ cup fresh lemon juice

Add; Boil, then Simmer:

5½ cups vegetable broth (three 14.5-oz. cans)

2 cups red potatoes, diced

¼ cup carrot, peeled, grated

½ t. black pepper
    Salt to taste

For the Roux, Combine:

6 T. unsalted butter, melted

½ cup all-purpose flour

Whisk into Roux; Add to Soup:

2 cups skim milk, warmed

Combine; Garnish Soup with:

½ cup sour cream

¼ cup prepared horseradish

1 T. chopped fresh chives

⅛ t. kosher salt

⅛ t. cayenne

Nutritional Information per Cup: Calories 221; Total Fat 13(g); Calories from Fat 49%; Sodium 706(mg); Carb. 22(g)

WORKING WITH CABBAGE
The first step in working with cabbage is removing the core (it is bitter and tough). For a whole head, peel off the outer leaves, then cut the head in half. Now cut down both sides of the v-shaped core; remove.

To chop the cabbage, place half a head, cut-side down, on a cutting board and slice it lengthwise into ribbons. Then gather the ribbons and cut into cubes; rinse. (It's easier and more thorough to rinse *chopped* cabbage rather than a whole head.)

1 Melt 2 T. butter in a large stock pot over medium heat. Add onion and caraway; saute until onions are soft, about 5 minutes. Add 2 T. butter and cabbage. Cover and cook 10–15 minutes, until cabbage is *slightly* brown.

2 Increase heat to medium-high and deglaze the pot with sherry and lemon juice. Add vegetable broth, potatoes, carrot, pepper, and salt. Bring soup to a boil, reduce heat to medium, and simmer for 15 minutes.

3 Meanwhile, for roux-thickened milk, melt 6 T. butter in a small saucepan over medium heat. Whisk in flour; cook, stirring, for about 2 minutes. Gradually add warm milk to the roux; cook 3 minutes, whisking constantly.

4 Increase heat under the soup to medium-high and bring to a simmer. Then stir the milk mixture into soup— it should begin to thicken immediately. Cover and remove soup from heat. If it seems thick, add a little more milk.

5 To make the garnish, combine sour cream, horseradish, chives, salt, and cayenne in a small mixing bowl. Before serving, garnish soup with a dollop of the sour cream-horseradish mixture and additional chives, if desired.

harvest braise

Autumn brings two wonders of the season—foliage and comfort food. Celebrate fall with this flavorful pork stew served over warm buttered spaetzle.

There's something familiar about a one-pot stew that makes it so comforting. It's simple, inexpensive, and bursting with the flavors and smells of harvest.

Now, do you call it a braise or a stew? Technically, a stew has smaller pieces of meat and more liquid than a braise. With that out of the way, you can use the terms interchangeably (kind of like saying broth instead of stock).

Our harvest braise features pork, earthy shiitake mushrooms, and warm buttered spaetzle. This little German dumpling is a classic side dish for pork.

The whole dish is served with a simple yet colorful tomato relish—but it's not just for looks. Acids are typically added to many sauces to balance the rich flavors. This tomato relish does the same thing and it also adds color.

HARVEST BRAISE

(MAKES 10 CUPS)
WORK TIME: 30 MINUTES
COOK TIME: 60 MINUTES

BROWN IN 2 T. OIL:
3 lbs. boneless, country-style pork ribs, trimmed

REMOVE MEAT; DEGLAZE WITH:
½ cup dry red wine

ADD MEAT AND SIMMER:
1 can (14.5 oz.) beef broth

IN SEPARATE PAN, SAUTE IN 1 T. OIL:
2 cups yellow onion, diced
5 minced fresh sage leaves, or 1 t. dried
2 clove garlic, minced

SPRINKLE WITH:
3 T. all-purpose flour

SAUTE IN 2 T. OIL:
8 oz. button mushrooms, stem-on, halved
8 oz. shiitake mushrooms, stems removed

ADD TO MEAT AND SIMMER:
1 can (14.5 oz.) diced tomatoes with juice

STIR IN AND SIMMER:
2 cups white pearl onions, blanched and peeled
  Onion/flour mixture
  Sauteed mushrooms
  Salt and pepper to taste

SERVE WITH:
  Tomato Relish, *see Page 27*
  Spaetzle, *see Page 28*

NUTRITIONAL INFORMATION PER CUP (BRAISE ONLY): CALORIES 502; TOTAL FAT 41(G); CALORIES FROM FAT 74%; SODIUM 258(MG); CARBOHYDRATES 10(G)

Pork for braising

Country-style ribs are an inexpensive cut from the pork shoulder, a hard-working muscle that's full of connective tissue. Meats with a lot of this type of tissue taste best when braised for several reasons. The long cooking time not only breaks down the tough fibers, but also produces a rich gravy (a result of this tissue melting). Roasting can't do this as effectively.

Take a look at the photo to the right and you'll see where country-style ribs come from. At the top is a pork shoulder (also known as a Boston butt). This cut makes up half of the usable meat from the pig's shoulder. The other half is called the picnic ham.

Next, blade steaks are cut from the pork shoulder. If you can't find country-style ribs, buy blade steaks and remove the bone.

Finally, strips (about 1" wide) are cut from the blade steak. They're called country-style ribs, but aren't ribs at all. The name "country" was adapted from a high-quality sausage (country sausage) that was once made strictly from pork

Pork shoulder

Blade steaks

Bones and excess fat removed

Trimmed, boneless, country-style ribs

shoulder. The term "rib" refers to the thin strip it's cut into.

Country-style ribs will have a tough, white web-looking substance that should be cut out. Some of this is called elastin, the strongest of the connective tissues. Be sure to remove the elastin because it won't break down during braising—it only turns harder.

Trimming the ribs

Whether you use country-style ribs (above) or blade steaks (right), you'll treat them the same way. First trim away the fat and elastin. Now,

cut the meat into 1"-wide finger-length pieces. The recipe calls for 3 pounds of meat—after trimming, you'll end up with about 2½ pounds of useable meat.

Before cooking

Like most dishes, efficient cutting and preparation can speed up kitchen time. Here are three steps you'll want to complete before cooking: preparing the sage, mushrooms, and the pearl onions.

Sage is a strong-flavored herb, so a little goes a long way. Finely mince the leaves and discard the stems.

Clean both types of mushrooms and slice the buttons in half. Leave the shiitakes whole, but remove and discard the woody stems.

Cut an "x" in the stem end of the pearl onions; blanch in boiling water for 3 minutes. Rinse in cold water, then cut off the stem end and remove the papery skin.

Foundations of a braise

A classic braise technique begins by browning meat for both color and flavor, then cooking it in liquid for a long period of time. This breaks down (melts) the tough connective tissue while infusing the meat with flavor from the braising liquid. The foundations for any braise are caramelization, deglazing, and simmering.

Caramelization: A braise always begins by first sauteing meat to a deep brown color (caramelization). This does two things: colors both the pork and the resulting sauce. It also leaves dark brown pieces in the bottom of the saute pan called *fond* (this is the French name for pan drippings).

Caramelization is the process where the carbohydrates in meat turn to sugar when heated. And just like real sugar, the meat will eventually brown and caramelize. You may have heard of this process of caramelization being referred to as the Maillard Reaction.

For good caramelization, I like to brown in batches. But be careful! The fond can burn and release a bitter flavor into the braise.

1 Season meat and brown in batches over high heat (1 T. oil per batch). Use a large saute pan because this is what you'll braise in. Brown (caramelize) on all sides; remove meat from pan. On the bottom of the pan will be the *fond*.

2 Reduce heat to medium and add the wine to the pan. Scrape fond off the bottom with a wooden spoon or heat-resistant spatula (called deglazing). Let wine reduce until nearly dry, about 5 minutes. Return meat to pan.

3 Pour beef broth halfway up the meat, about 1³/₄ cup. Cover and bring to a simmer over very low heat for 30 minutes. A braise should be covered with a tight-fitting lid to keep the steam in. Open only when necessary.

4 In a separate pan, saute onion, sage, and garlic over medium heat. Cook until the onions begin to become translucent (about 8 minutes, but don't let them brown). This is called sweating, which releases the onion's flavor.

Deglazing: Fond is valuable for flavor and color, but it has to get off the bottom of the pan to do any good. Deglazing gets the fond into the braise.

Any liquid can be used to deglaze, but I prefer wine. It provides some acidity to cut the richness of meat, as well as adds a deep flavor to the sauce.

To deglaze, add wine to the fond and begin scraping with a wooden spoon or heat-resistant spatula. The loosened fond incorporates into the wine and becomes the primary flavoring agent of the braising broth.

Simmering: Simmering is when bubbles slowly come to the surface of the pan. To braise correctly, cover the meat halfway with beef broth, then bring to a simmer. This is different from boiling because simmering is much more gentle to the meat. The meat not covered by liquid is steamed by evaporating broth.

What's really important in simmering is the broth level—it may become too low. If this happens, add more liquid to bring it halfway up the meat. This maintains the steam and simmer.

FRESH TOMATO RELISH
(MAKES 2 CUPS)
WORK TIME: 15 MINUTES
COMBINE:

3	red tomatoes, diced
1	yellow tomato, diced
3	T. red wine vinegar
1	T. olive oil
	Salt and pepper to taste

GARNISH WITH:

4	scallions, bias-cut

▲ *For scallions, first remove root end. Trim ragged green end and rinse thoroughly. Cut diagonally using both white and green parts.*

5 Remove the onions from the heat and sprinkle with flour; blend thoroughly. This mixture will be used to thicken the braise. Remove the onion mixture from the pan and place in a covered bowl to keep from drying out.

6 In the same pan you used for onions, saute mushrooms over medium-high heat until golden brown. Don't overcook the mushrooms—you still want them to be a little plump. If you're going to make spaetzle, mix the dough now.

7 After braising the pork for 30 minutes, add diced tomatoes along with their juice; simmer, covered, 15 minutes more. At this point, put the water or chicken broth on for cooking the spaetzle, and bring to a boil.

8 After 15 minutes, add pearl onions, onion/flour mixture, mushrooms, salt, and pepper to the braise. Incorporate the vegetables and continue simmering another 15–20 minutes. This is when the flour will thicken the sauce.

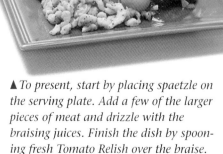

▲ *To present, start by placing spaetzle on the serving plate. Add a few of the larger pieces of meat and drizzle with the braising juices. Finish the dish by spooning fresh Tomato Relish over the braise. Garnish with bias-cut scallions.*

Spaetzle [SHPET-sluh] is a simple German dumpling—it only has five ingredients. This spaetzle is made by pushing dough through a flat cheese grater over boiling water. It gets a little messy but when it's done, you get a hearty little noodle.

Mixing: When making spaetzle dough, it's important to mix the eggs and flour first. Milk is added later because it has a higher water content than egg. If mixed with straight flour, it could turn gluey.

Resting: Spaetzle dough must rest 30 minutes before cooking. Resting is important because the dough is mixed quite hard and has developed gluten. Resting relaxes the gluten and produces a less chewy and stretchy dumpling.

Drying: Once the spaetzle is cooked, it must dry for about 10 minutes so it will brown when sauteed. If you put wet spaetzle into a saute pan, the butter will slide off rather than flavor the dumplings. So give it time to dry. Spaetzle can even be made hours before serving—it reheats well.

spaetzle

This warm, buttery dumpling is at the heart of German cooking. It's a perfect side dish for holding the rich gravy of the Harvest Braise.

SPAETZLE
(MAKES 6 CUPS)
WORK TIME: 45 MINUTES
COOK TIME: 5 MINUTES

WHISK TOGETHER:
6   eggs, beaten
3   cups all-purpose flour

ADD, THEN REST 30 MINUTES:
1   cup 2% milk
1   T. minced parsley leaves
1   t. kosher salt

COOK SPAETZLE IN; DRY:
2   quarts boiling salted water
    or chicken stock

SAUTE IN:
2   T. unsalted butter

SEASON WITH:
    Salt and pepper to taste

NUTRITIONAL INFORMATION PER CUP: CALORIES 343; TOTAL FAT 9(G); CALORIES FROM FAT 23%; SODIUM 617(MG); CARB. 50(G)

Making spaetzle

1 Whisk together flour and eggs in a mixing bowl. Stir in the milk, parsley, and salt. It is important to let the mixture rest for 30 minutes to relax the gluten. At this point, the mixture will look like heavy pancake batter.

2 Bring salted water or stock to a boil. Place 1 cup of batter on a cheese grater, grating side down. Using a rubber spatula, firmly push the batter

through the holes using a back-and-forth motion. Repeat with one more cup, then cook spaetzle 2–3 minutes, or until they float to the top.

3 Using a skimmer or slotted spoon, transfer spaetzle to a colander; rinse in cold water. Lay spaetzle on a greased baking sheet to dry. (They'll stick to your hand when ready to saute.) Repeat process with remaining batter.

4 Spaetzle can be held up to a day before sauteing. To brown, melt 1 T. butter in nonstick skillet over high heat. Add half the spaetzle; stir until golden brown. Season with salt and pepper; serve. Repeat with second batch.

SPAETZLE MAKERS

I had the best luck using a simple cheese grater for spaetzle. But if you're a gadget nut or received a spaetzle maker for your wedding here's the scoop on performance.

Sliding Box: Spaetzle dough is put in the box and moved over a cheese grater-looking surface. This produced nearly uniform spaetzle, but the box also created the most waste. There was too much dough left in the chamber and on the grater making it difficult to clean.

Round Disk: This produced better-looking spaetzle and not too much waste, but there was a problem. The disk is set over a pan of boiling water while the mixture is pushed through with a bowl scraper. Before the spaetzle hit the water, they began cooking from the steam. This clogged up the holes and made cleaning a pain.

Cutting Board: Spaetzle dough put on a wet cutting board and scraped into boiling water made long, noodley spaetzle. An off-set spatula or knife kept in hot water prevented sticking. The cutting board and spatula were easiest to clean and it made little waste.

Food Mill: If all else fails, put the dough in a food mill and grind out spaetzle into a pan of boiling water. There is some waste, but the mill is very quick and easy to use. It makes short, fat spaetzle.

The center of these three dishes is pasta. Here are tips for making perfect noodles every time.

The Pot: When cooking pasta, think big in terms of the pot. It should be able to hold 4–5 quarts of water per pound of pasta without the risk of boiling over. That way, the pasta can move freely in the water, speeding up the cooking time and preventing sticking. A lid is helpful for boiling the water quickly, but not critical.

The Water: Salting the water is a step that often gets overlooked. But don't forget it—it's essential for the best pasta flavor. Italians say the water should taste like the sea, but that's pretty salty for me. Two tablespoons kosher salt (or three teaspoons table salt) for four quarts of water is good.

Whatever you do, don't add oil to the cooking water! All it does is coat the pasta, keeping the sauce from clinging to it.

Cooking: We're always told to cook pasta until it's *al dente* [al-DEN-teh], but what does that mean? In Italian, it means "to the tooth," not crunchy or mushy. Use the time on the pasta package as a guideline, then taste the pasta each minute during the last five minutes of cooking. It's done when it's no longer crunchy.

Rinsing: As soon as the pasta is cooked, drain but *do not* rinse it. Rinsing removes the starch which helps the sauce stick to the pasta. And excess water from rinsing dilutes the flavor of the sauce.

Tossing: Immediately toss the pasta with the sauce or else the strands will stick. And remember this Italian saying: The sauce can wait for the pasta, but the pasta can *never* wait for the sauce.

The most difficult thing about these classic Italian pasta dishes is pronouncing their names. They are a breeze to make—dinner in 30 minutes or less. In fact, you probably have some of the ingredients in your pantry right now. So what are you waiting for?

penne *all' arrabbiata*

Arrabbiata [ahr-rah-bee-AH-ta] means "angry" in Italian, and this pasta dish is spicy. Traditionally, the spiciness comes from Italian peppers (*peperoncini*), but here it comes from crushed red pepper flakes. Don't let that scare you. The heat is pleasant, not overwhelming.

This sauce is different because it's made with sauteed salami instead of pancetta (an Italian bacon). Besides being easy to find, salami adds a unique flavor to the sauce. For this dish, buy Genoa salami, a pork and beef sausage seasoned with white peppercorns. You can usually find it sold in bulk at the deli counter of grocery stores—buy a 6-oz. chunk, and be sure to remove any rind from the outside before cubing. Avoid using presliced sandwich salami. It's thin and can burn quickly.

Penne [PEH-neh] is a short, hollow pasta, with or without ridges. The hollow center is perfect for trapping sauce inside, but if you can't find it, fusilli (corkscrew) works also.

PENNE ALL' ARRABBIATA
(MAKES 6 CUPS)
WORK TIME: 15 MINUTES
COOK TIME: 30 MINUTES
COOK:
1   pound dry penne
SAUTE IN 2 T. OLIVE OIL:
1   cup red onion, thinly sliced
2   t. garlic, minced
6   oz. Genoa salami, cubed
½   t. crushed red pepper flakes
ADD AND REDUCE:
3   cups (two 14.5-oz. cans)
    canned diced tomatoes with juice
1   T. tomato paste
1   T. brown sugar, packed
1   T. balsamic vinegar
    Salt and pepper to taste
TOSS WITH PASTA:
⅓   cup torn fresh basil leaves
¼   cup Parmesan cheese, grated

NUTRITIONAL INFORMATION PER CUP:
CALORIES 466; TOTAL FAT 17(G); CALORIES FROM FAT 33%; SODIUM 1,051(MG); CARBOHYDRATES 60(G)

1 Bring water to a boil for the pasta. Meanwhile, heat the oil in a large saute pan over medium-high heat. Add the onion and saute until soft and beginning to color, about 5 minutes. Add the garlic, salami, and red pepper flakes; saute until salami caramelizes, 5–7 minutes.

2 Add tomatoes, tomato paste, brown sugar, and vinegar. Reduce heat and simmer until slightly thickened, 10–15 minutes. Season to taste with salt and pepper. Once the water comes to a boil, add penne and cook until al dente (see package for times).

3 Drain the pasta, reserving ¼ cup liquid to thin the sauce, if necessary. Transfer sauce to a large, shallow bowl. Add the drained pasta, torn basil, and Parmesan to the sauce (tearing the basil won't discolor it like cutting does); toss to coat. Serve pasta immediately.

spaghetti *alla carbonara*

Bacon and eggs—they're not just for breakfast anymore.
This traditional pasta dish puts morning food on your dinner table.

WEEKNIGHT PASTA

1 To make bread crumb topping, pulse bread cubes in a food processor until coarse. Toast crumbs with olive oil in a small saute pan over medium heat, stirring constantly to prevent burning. When golden and crisp, transfer crumbs to a bowl and toss with parsley, lemon zest, and salt. Set aside.

Italians really have fun with food, all the way down to naming the dishes. Carbonara [kahr-boh-NAH-rah] means charcoal, and legend says that the dish, made with eggs, pancetta, cream, and Parmesan, was created by coal miners.

But this recipe isn't *exactly* what the miners came up with. Here, bacon is used instead of traditional pancetta. Bacon is readily available, less expensive, and adds a smoky flavor that pancetta doesn't have. I use thick-sliced bacon because of its meaty texture, but regular bacon works fine too (use about eight slices). The bread crumb topping isn't traditional either, but it adds great contrast in both texture and flavor.

Technically, the eggs in this sauce are not fully cooked. Now, I don't have a problem with that since the odds of eating an egg that has salmonella bacteria is less than 1%. But if you're at all leery about it, don't worry—there's a simple way to avoid any problem.

Try using pasteurized eggs (like Egg Beaters) in place of the whole eggs. Pasteurized eggs are heated just below the "scrambling point," killing any salmonella that may be present. It works great and the difference in flavor is hard to detect. The Egg Beaters tend to clump a little (looking like bits of scrambled egg), but that's minor. Here, use ³/₄ cup of Egg Beaters for the three eggs.

SPAGHETTI ALLA CARBONARA
(MAKES 6 CUPS)

WORK TIME: 30 MINUTES
COOK TIME: 30 MINUTES

FOR THE BREAD CRUMB TOPPING—

PULSE IN FOOD PROCESSOR:
2   slices (½" thick) crusty Italian bread, cubed (2 cups crumbs)

TOAST CRUMBS IN:
2   T. olive oil

TOSS CRUMBS WITH:
2   T. chopped fresh parsley
2   t. lemon zest, minced
    Salt to taste

FOR THE CARBONARA—

COOK:
1   lb. dry spaghetti

SAUTE:
½   lb. (5 slices) thick-sliced bacon, diced

DRAIN FAT; ADD AND REDUCE:
¼   cup dry white wine
1   T. fresh lemon juice

WHISK TOGETHER:
3   eggs
⅓   cup Parmesan cheese, grated
3   T. heavy cream
½   t. black pepper
    Salt to taste

TOSS PASTA AND BACON IN EGG MIXTURE.
GARNISH WITH BREAD CRUMBS.

NUTRITIONAL INFORMATION PER CUP: CALORIES 654; TOTAL FAT 32(G); CALORIES FROM FAT 44%; SODIUM 930(MG); CARB. 61(G)

2 For the pasta, bring a large pot of salted water to a boil over high heat. Meanwhile, saute the bacon in a large saute pan until cooked through but not crisp, about 8 minutes. Drain fat; add wine and lemon juice to the bacon in the pan. Reduce until nearly evaporated, another 4–5 minutes. Set aside.

3 Add the dry spaghetti to the boiling water and stir often, forcing the strands down into the water. Cook until al dente (refer to the package for cooking times). While pasta is cooking, whisk together the eggs, Parmesan, heavy cream, pepper, and salt in a large, shallow bowl.

4 Add the bacon pieces and reduced wine mixture to the eggs. Once the pasta is cooked, reserve $1/4$ cup pasta water (to thin sauce if needed), then drain but do not rinse. Shake pasta to remove excess water and immediately add it to the egg mixture. Quickly toss to coat—tongs work great here.

▲ *To plate, twist some pasta around the tongs in the mixing bowl, then mound in the center of a plate. Top with more pasta, and twist again to achieve height.*

▲ *Garnish the pasta generously with some of the bread crumb mixture and serve immediately.*

linguini *alla puttanesca*

There's no elegant way to say this—
Puttanesca comes from the Italian
word for harlot. And believe me,
you'll be enticed by the aroma and
flavor of this pasta sauce.

WEEKNIGHT PASTA

This puttanesca sauce [poot-tah-NEHS-skah] has big flavors in it, namely from anchovies, olives, and capers. But those strong flavors balance out perfectly.

If you don't like anchovies, you may be tempted to omit them. Don't! There aren't that many, and the flavor isn't the same without them. I recommend using anchovy paste, not fillets—it's convenient and can be stored in the refrigerator indefinitely. Find tubes of paste in the same aisle as canned tuna.

Olives and capers are the other flavor keys to this dish. Kalamatas are Greek olives with a salty, fruity flavor; capers are sun-dried, pickled flower buds (they look like green peppercorns). Both are common in grocery stores—look for them with the condiments.

LINGUINI ALLA PUTTANESCA

(MAKES 6 CUPS)
WORK TIME: 15 MINUTES
COOK TIME: 30 MINUTES
COOK:
1 lb. dry linguini
SAUTE IN 2 T. OLIVE OIL:
1 T. garlic, minced
1 t. anchovy paste
¼ t. crushed red pepper flakes
ADD AND SIMMER:
3 cups (two 14.5-oz. cans) canned diced tomatoes with juice
2 T. oil-packed sun-dried tomatoes, minced
1 T. brown sugar
2 t. balsamic vinegar
ADD:
¼ cup kalamata olives, pitted and slivered
3 T. chopped fresh oregano (or 1½ t. dried)
3 T. chopped fresh parsley
2 T. brined capers, drained Salt to taste
OPTIONAL—
TOP EACH SERVING WITH:
3–4 T. oil-packed albacore tuna, drained, in large chunks

NUTRITIONAL INFORMATION PER CUP: CALORIES 401; TOTAL FAT 8(G); CALORIES FROM FAT 18%; SODIUM 672(MG); CARB. 69(G)

1 For the pasta, bring a large pot of salted water to a boil over high heat. Meanwhile, heat a large saute pan over medium heat. Add the olive oil, garlic, anchovy paste, and red pepper flakes. Stir, cooking for 30 seconds—it will smell strong because of the anchovies.

2 Add the tomatoes, sun-dried toma-toes, brown sugar, and vinegar; stir to combine. Simmer sauce until slightly reduced, 10–15 minutes. While sauce simmers, prepare olives and herbs; pour capers into a small dish—it's easier to measure them that way.

3 Meanwhile, add linguini to the boil-ing water; stir often to force the strands to the bottom of the pot and prevent them from sticking. Cook pasta until al dente (refer to package for times). Before draining, remove ¼ cup cook-ing liquid to thin the sauce if needed.

4 Finish the sauce with the olives, herbs, capers, and salt, plus some pasta water if it seems thick. Transfer the sauce to a large, shallow bowl and top with the drained pasta. Toss until pasta is evenly coated with sauce.

TUNA TOPPING

Here's a solution for that can of oil-packed tuna you bought by mistake—put chunks of it on top of the pasta before serving. Italian cooks often add canned tuna to pastas, and it works great here. White albacore tuna has the mildest flavor so use it if you can. Water-packed tuna is fine, but tuna packed in olive or vegetable oil is more flavorful.

Optional: Top pasta with chunks of canned tuna. Serve Puttanesca warm or at room temperature.

apple strudel

The best thing about this apple strudel is you don't have to make pastry dough—it's made with purchased phyllo dough. But what separates phyllo from other types of pastry dough is what's between the layers for flavor.

Cuisine doesn't take many shortcuts—teaching cooking techniques is what we're about. But there are some cooking shortcuts worth taking, like using phyllo [FEE-loh] dough for this strudel.

For traditional strudel, delicate pastry dough is hand-stretched until it's thin enough to read a newspaper through. But that's a skill better left to pros. Phyllo dough is a good substitute.

Phyllo is a layered pastry dough that means "leaves" in Greek. Like strudel dough, it's paper-thin and creates a flaky crust. But it can be a little quirky to work with—phyllo must stay moist or it'll dry out and shatter, yet not so moist that the edges stick together.

Don't let that scare you—it's still easy to work with. And with fall here, it's almost mandatory to make a dessert out of all the good apples available. But it's easy to get stuck in the apple pie comfort zone—strudel is an impressive classic that breaks out of the rut.

In this strudel, I layer cinnamon, sugar, walnuts, and bread crumbs between the phyllo. This serves two purposes. Of course the cinnamon and sugar provide flavor, but it's the crumbs and nuts that create space between the layers for height and flakiness.

Apple strudel is good. And learning to work with phyllo is even better. No prior experience is necessary! All you need are a few handling basics and you'll be on your way.

APPLE STRUDEL (SERVES 6)

WORK TIME: 45 MINUTES   BAKE TIME: ABOUT 35 MINUTES

THAW:
1   package phyllo dough

FOR THE FILLING—
WHISK TOGETHER:
¼   cup sugar
1   T. apple juice concentrate
1   T. lemon juice
1   t. lemon zest, finely chopped
½   t. ground cinnamon
¼   t. kosher salt
⅛   t. ground nutmeg
ADD:
⅓   cup raisins
PEEL, CORE, AND CUT INTO ½–¾" PIECES:
3–4 Gala apples (2½–3 cups)

FOR LAYERING BETWEEN PHYLLO—
TOAST:
½   T. unsalted butter
½   cup fresh bread crumbs (1 slice)
REMOVE FROM HEAT AND TOSS WITH:
⅓   cup sugar
⅓   cup chopped walnuts
1   t. ground cinnamon

FOR BRUSHING THE PHYLLO—
MELT:
4   T. unsalted butter

NUTRITIONAL INFORMATION PER SERVING:
CALORIES 302; TOTAL FAT 14(G);
CALORIES FROM FAT 40%; SODIUM 182(MG);
CARBOHYDRATES 45(G)

Strudel filling

The best apples for strudel are varieties that keep their texture and flavor after baking—Gala, Jonagold, and Golden Delicious are my choices for this apple strudel. Baking just enhances their flavor and they won't get mushy. Braeburns and Fuji are great for eating, but didn't fare as well after baking.

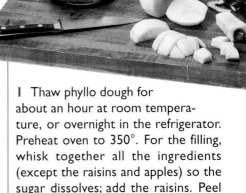

Streamlined strudel-making

Strudel-making doesn't require a lot of special equipment. Here's a list of what you'll need for streamlined success.

Phyllo Dough: Phyllo can be found in your grocer's freezer section—it comes rolled up in a long box of about 20 sheets. When brushed with butter, layered, and baked the sheets become a flaky, delicate pastry. Brands such as Athens, Apollo, and Pepperidge Farms are good and vary only slightly in size.

Parchment Paper: Parchment paper is the primary tool for rolling the fragile strudel into a log. It comes in sheets or rolls about 12–15" wide. Check the width of the phyllo before buying paper—it should be at least as wide as the phyllo dough. Reynolds has just come out with a line of parchment so it should be showing up soon at your grocer, *see One Cool Tool, Page 42*. If you

have a hard time finding it at the grocery store, check a kitchen supply store, or order it from King Arthur Flour, *see Resources, Page 43*.

If you don't have parchment paper, wide foil is a distant second choice. It can work in a pinch, but it's stiffer and not as helpful in the rolling process.

Cookie Sheet: Like most baked goods, the strudel must be baked on a flat surface—I like to use a cookie sheet (the kind with only one raised side) so I can slide the unbaked, rolled strudel from the counter to the cookie sheet. If all you have is a baking sheet with raised edges, flip it over and use the back.

Pastry Brush: A flat, wide pastry brush is good for "painting" melted butter on the phyllo. A wide brush head applies butter smoothly and quickly, minimizing tears or drying out.

1 Thaw phyllo dough for about an hour at room temperature, or overnight in the refrigerator. Preheat oven to 350°. For the filling, whisk together all the ingredients (except the raisins and apples) so the sugar dissolves; add the raisins. Peel and cube the apples, then toss in the raisin mixture (the lemon juice in it will prevent the apples from browning). Set aside, tossing occasionally.

2 Prepare the ingredients for between the layers of phyllo. First, pulse bread in a food processor until fine. Then melt butter in a skillet and add bread crumbs. Toast over medium-low heat until brown, stirring so crumbs don't stick. Remove from heat and cool. Toss with sugar, walnuts, and cinnamon.

"Phool" proof phyllo

Here are a few tips to make your first encounter with phyllo dough a success.

Thawing Phyllo: It's crucial that the phyllo sheets are *completely* thawed before using, otherwise they'll crack as you unroll them. Thawing doesn't take long—only 1–2 hours at room temperature. You can also thaw it overnight by keeping it in the refrigerator.

Always thaw phyllo wrapped in plastic wrap. Phyllo dough dries out *fast*, so it's important that it comes in contact with air as little as possible.

Pliable Phyllo: Once the phyllo is thawed, remove it from the packaging and carefully unroll it onto a sheet of parchment. You'll end up with a large rectangular stack of phyllo.

Like I said before, phyllo must be kept moist (but not soggy) so that you can work with it easily. To keep it pliable, use indirect moisture by placing another piece of parchment on top of the phyllo. Cover this with a dry towel and then a damp towel, *see right*.

Layering Phyllo: Peel off sheets of phyllo one at a time and start layering. The key is to be gentle. Use both hands to layer each sheet. Small wrinkles and cracks are common. To prevent weak spots and further tearing, butter any cracks carefully, and try not to position tears on top of each other. Because the phyllo dries out so easily, once you start layering the phyllo, don't stop until the strudel is completely filled and rolled.

▶ *To keep phyllo pliable, stack the following directly on top of each other: Begin with parchment paper, then the stack of phyllo, another parchment sheet, a dry towel, and top it off with a damp towel (wet it, then wring it out).*

wet towel
dry towel
parchment
phyllo
parchment

◀ *Each sheet of phyllo is so thin you can see through it—much like tissue paper.*

Preparing and assembling the phyllo

3 Roll back parchment and towels. Begin at corner to separate sheets. As you lift, run a hand between layers to gently separate and peel off top sheet. Place on parchment; roll towels back.

4 With one hand lightly anchoring the dough, begin at top third of sheet and gently brush (away from you) a *thin* coat of melted butter onto phyllo. Continue coating to cover entire sheet.

5 Sprinkle three heaping tablespoons of the bread crumb mixture over the buttered phyllo. Bread crumbs help absorb moisture given off by the baking apples, helping keep the dough crisp.

6 Place another phyllo sheet directly on top of prepared sheet; repeat steps 4 and 5. Continue repeating until there are 4 complete layers. It's okay if a few nuts poke through while brushing.

7 Pick up handfuls of apple filling and let the juice drain through your fingers. Form a 3"-wide "apple mound" on one end of the layered phyllo. Be sure to leave a 2" margin on the one side and both ends.

Rolling the strudel

8a This step is important. You're going to roll in one continuous movement. You might want to use your fingers to stuff and tuck, but don't. Begin by lifting parchment up then forward.

8b Continue rolling the paper forward without stopping. It may seem like the phyllo can't enclose the filling without tucking and tightening—but it can. Just keep moving forward.

8c Once the filling is fully enclosed, you can gather the paper up for better control. Don't worry if the strudel is loose or lopsided, it'll be fine. Just leave it alone or it could crack.

8d Complete the roll to the end of the phyllo sheets—they need to be under the strudel. Go ahead and replace any apples that may have tumbled out. The filling will stay in place during baking.

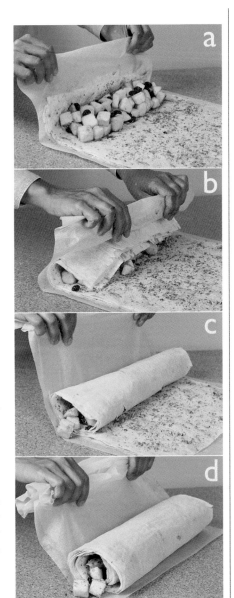

9 To transfer, hold cookie sheet even with counter and gently pull the roll onto the pan; tear off excess parchment paper. Brush outside of the roll with melted butter—there will be just enough left from the layering. Bake about 35 minutes, or until golden.

10 Cool strudel on the cookie sheet 10 minutes. Use an electric or serrated knife for slicing the strudel so you don't crush the layers. Trim off ends first, then slice at an angle into 1½"-wide slices. Sprinkle with powdered sugar; serve with whipped cream.

FLAVORED CREAMS

In Vienna, strudel is traditionally served *mit schlag* (with whipped cream). Heavy cream whips best when *everything* is cold—that especially means the fat in the cream. The fat molecules are what give the cream structure when whipped. If the cream is whipped too long, it begins to create heat and guess what? It can melt—the whipped foam collapses. So, be sure to chill your cream, bowls, and beaters. The *schlag* will stay stiff.

APPLE CREAM
1   cup heavy cream
2   T. brown sugar
1   T. apple juice concentrate
½   t. lemon zest, minced

CARAMEL CREAM
1   cup heavy cream
2   T. caramel syrup
½   t. vanilla

SOUR CREAM
1   cup heavy cream
¼   cup sour cream
1   T. powdered sugar

CINNAMON-RUM CREAM
1   cup heavy cream
2   T. brown sugar
2   t. rum
½   t. vanilla
¼   t. ground cinnamon

LEMON-GINGER CREAM
1   cup heavy cream
2   T. powdered sugar
1   T. lemon juice
½   t. lemon zest, minced
¼   t. ground ginger

Q&A
questions & answers from our readers

PARSLEY

Is there any difference between curly parsley and flat-leafed or Italian parsley?

Kerrie White
East Falmouth, MA

The obvious difference between curly and flat-leaf parsley is their appearance. Both have the same spicy-sweet flavor, but flat-leaf parsley is milder. You can use them interchangeably.

Curly parsley is more common in the US and Great Britain while flat-leaf is more common in Europe. Flat-leaf holds up better when growing and cooking than the curly variety, but curly parsley keeps longer once picked.

There are many classic French and Italian preparations that are based on parsley. So don't treat it just as a garnish—use it as a main herb or even salad greens.

What's a mirepoix?
Herman Frazier
Lady Lake, FL

Mirepoix [mihr-PWAH] is a diced combination of vegetables used to flavor stocks, sauces, and soups. It's usually made up of equal parts celery, onion, and carrot.

SCALDED MILK

Some recipes call for scalded milk. What's the purpose of it and how do I do it?

Jenny Pulsipher
Provo, UT

Before milk was pasteurized, it was scalded to kill any bacteria that may have been present. But today, obviously, that's not necessary. Some recipes still call for scalded milk since it can enhance the flavor (like steeping vanilla beans) or shorten cooking time (like making custards).

To scald milk, heat it in a heavy pan (to prevent scorching) just until bubbles start to form around the edge of the pan.

CLARI-TEA

Why does my iced tea become cloudy? It doesn't taste any different, but doesn't look as nice.

Sarah Severns
Montpelier, VT

One of the main culprits in cloudy tea is temperature shock. If tea changes temperature suddenly, it may get cloudy. So when you brew iced tea, give it a chance to cool down before icing or chilling it.

According to Lipton and The Republic of Tea, some types of black teas are more likely to cloud—Assam and its many blends (like British or Irish Breakfast) tend to be cloudiers.

However, black teas from China and Ceylon brew more clearly.

Sometimes tea will get cloudy if it's kept too long in the refrigerator. This is from the natural oils that separate from the tea over time.

Another thing that can cause clouding is excess calcium in the water. Avoid this problem by using filtered water for brewing.

If your tea still turns cloudy, try brewing your iced tea in cold water. Cold-brewed tea won't be as dark or as strong so use extra tea or brew it longer.

GETTING A REACTION

What is nonreactive cookware? How do I know what I have?

John Reising
Warren, MI

Nonreactive cookware simply means foods don't *react* to the material they're cooked or stored in. It's impossible to see, but some cookware is porous and can chemically react with highly acidic or alkaline foods (they develop an off-taste or change colors). Aluminum and cast iron are the most problematic pans.

However, there are some materials that are so hard, that acidic and alkaline foods can't react. Glass, stainless steel, and enameled cookware are good examples of common nonreactive materials.

Some foods that react:

(acidic)	(alkaline)
rhubarb	corn
tomatoes	dried beans
wine	eggs
vinegar	hard water
lemon juice	baking soda

Reactive metals:
aluminum
cast iron
carbon steel
unlined copper (poisonous!)

Nonreactive materials:
glass
ceramic
stainless steel
enameled iron
anodized aluminum
nonstick surfaces

AGAINST THE GRAIN

Why do recipes instruct you to cut meat against the grain?

Bruce Haley
Madisonville, KY

Meat is made up of long strings of muscle fiber. When you look at a piece of meat, you can see the fibers laid out together, running in one direction. These fibers are strong—after all, they've been moving entire body parts around.

By cutting meat against the grain, you cut each fiber into a shorter length. These shorter fibers are easier to chew and the meat will feel tender (like rice). If you cut the meat with the grain, you haven't cut the fibers at all. You'll have to use your teeth to break up those long muscle strands. It will be like eating strands of licorice.

Before slicing meat, determine the direction the muscle fibers run and cut across them.

▲ *Notice how short the grain is on these slices. This makes it tender.*

▲ *The long strands of grain on these slices make the meat chewy.*

WILD OATS

What are the differences between quick, old-fashioned, and Irish oats? Can I use them all in baking?

Sylvia Sims
Portland, ME

Old-fashioned oats (rolled) and quick oats (minute) are the most common kinds you'll find in grocery stores. They both start out as roasted, hulled oat grain, and then are processed to cook faster. Then the oat grain is steamed and flattened, so it's partially cooked and thinner. At this point, they are called old-fashioned oats.

Quick oats actually come from old fashioned oats—they are just rolled thinner, then cut into small pieces. This makes them cook quickly.

Irish (or Scottish) oats are roasted, hulled oat grains sliced in small pieces, but they're not precooked like the other two. Precooking takes much of the oils and flavor out of oatmeal.

So here's my opinion; if you want to bake with oatmeal, use old-fashioned or quick oats (use them interchangeably). If you want to eat a bowl of oatmeal, do yourself a favor and eat Irish oats—there's no comparison.

CLARIFY SOMETHING

What is clarified butter used for and how do you make it?

Mark Doton
Monterey, CA

Butter adds a rich flavor to sauces or sauteed dishes. The problem is it burns. It's the milk solids that burn first. If they're removed, what's left is a clear yellow oil (clarified butter) that won't burn as quickly as regular butter.

The key to clarifying butter is to go slow and low. Slowly melt unsalted butter over low heat. As it melts, the butter separates into three layers: a foam of milk solids floating on top, clarified butter in the middle, and more milk solids on the bottom.

Using a ladle, skim the foam from the top and discard. Next, carefully ladle off the clarified butter without stirring up the milk solids on the bottom—discard those too.

The clarified butter can be used right away, refrigerated, or even frozen. Use it for sauteing as you would a good oil.

Q&A

Do you have a question for Cuisine?

If you have question about a cooking term, procedure, or technique, we'd like to hear from you. We'll consider publishing your question in one or more of our works.

Just write down your question and mail it to Cuisine, Q&A Editor, 2200 Grand Ave., Des Moines, IA 50312, or contact us through our email address shown below. Please include your name, address, and daytime phone number in case we have questions.

Email: Cuisine@CuisineMagazine.com
Web address: www.CuisineMagazine.com

▲ *Quick*
▲ *Old-fashioned*
▲ *Irish oats*

whif
what's happening in food?

Ordering Information: Fruit preserves and toppings from Rocky Top Farms. Call (800) 862-9303, or visit www.rockytopfarms.com to send for a catalog, or place an order.

Rocky Top Farms' fruit preserves and butters are all about quality—from start to finish.

Tom Cooper of Rocky Top Farms in Ellsworth, MI is committed to quality and it shows. For one thing, he and his family grow most of the fruit that goes into their preserves and fruit butters on their 300-acre farm. Plus, it's all made in small batches in a 40-gallon copper kettle right in the main barn—with no preser- vatives. And his dedication to his products doesn't stop there. Even the gift boxes are constructed on- site from Michigan white cedar.

Naturally, Michigan cherries are featured in Rocky Top Farms' preserves and butters (there's even Dijon Cherry Mustard). But you won't go wrong with any of the other great-tasting preserves, sauces, honey, toppings, and vinegars. Select an assortment for a great holiday gift—it's not too early! Call the Farm for a catalog.

food sleuth

40,060 lbs.
Weight of the world's largest cheese, Belle of Wisconsin, an aged Cheddar made in 1988. [2]

350 lbs.
Weight of the world's largest pumpkin pie, made every year at The Pumpkin Show in Circleville, Ohio. [3]

Quiche
One of the few items not offered at Oktoberfest in Cincinnati, Ohio. [1]

Sources:
[1]Greater Cincinnati Chamber of Commerce
[2]Wisconsin Milk Marketing Board
[3]Circleville Pumpkin Show

Reynolds parchment is now available in grocery stores. Get your free parchment recipe booklet by calling (800) 433-2244.

one cool tool

Easy-to-find parchment from Reynolds makes baking better.

Parchment paper is *the* wonder tool in professional bakeries and kitchens. And lining baking sheets and cake pans isn't all it's good for. Parchment can be folded into "envelopes" for steaming fish and vegetables *en papillote*. Or rolled into cones to make disposable pas- try bags. But where it really comes in handy is during clean-up—messes stay on the paper, not stuck to the pans.

Up until now, home cooks often had to mail-order their parchment paper supply. But this fall, grocery stores will begin carrying professional- quality parchment made by Reynolds (yes, the foil people). Look for it in the same aisle as foil—you won't want to be without it during the holiday baking season.

recipe index

Salads & Soups

Provençe on a barge!

Chalon-sur-Saone
Mâcon
Lyon
Vienne
Tournon
Viviers
FRANCE
Avignon
Arles
Nice

Does taking a beautiful barge through the heart of the culinary world interest you? It's another *Cuisine* Cruise, and I can't wait.

We leave October 20, 2001 and sail up the Rhone River aboard the brand new French river ship, *MS Rhone Princess*, hitting culinary hot spots like Vienne, Lyon, and Mâcon. While exact details aren't ironed out yet, we're lining up trips to olive groves, city markets, chocolate factories, vineyards, and several cooking classes with local chefs. For more information, you can contact Lew or Judy at **The Travel Center** by email at **trvlcats@aol.com**, or at **(800) 383-4444**. This ship isn't big (60 cabins) so make your reservations early!

resources

National Pork Producers Council
(515) 223-2600
www.nppc.org
for consumer facts and nutritional information

King Arthur Flour Company
(800) 827-6836
www.kingarthurflour.com
Parchment paper: item #5223, 15" x 33' roll, $8.95 + shipping & handling

Athens Foods
(216) 676-8500
distribution information and recipes for their complete line of pastry dough and phyllo products

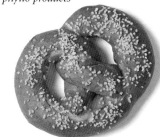

Photo: Paula Norton

Bratwurst and sauerkraut by the shovelful at Cincinnati's Oktoberfest. Got a bun?

food events

Warrens Cranberry Festival
Warrens, Wisconsin
September 22–24
Here at the "Cranberry Capital of Wisconsin" you'll celebrate 140 years of cranberry cultivation and culture. Events range from needlework to recipe contests. For more information, call **(608) 378-4878**, or visit **www.cranberryexpo.com**

The famous cranberries of Warrens, Wisconsin star in their own festival this September.

Oktoberfest USA
From coast-to-coast, towns and cities are rolling out their best food and drink for the premier festivals of autumn. Here are the top five:
Milwaukee, Wisconsin
Sept. 9–10, 16–17, 23–24
(414) 462-9147
Helen, Georgia
Sept. 14–16, 21–23, 28–Oct. 4
(800) 858-8027
Cincinnati, Ohio
Sept. 16–17 **(513) 579-3191**
Fredericksburg, Texas
Oct. 6–8 **(830) 997-4810**
San Diego, California
Oct. 7–8, 14–15
(619) 442-6637

Photo: Paula Norton

Celebrate the season at Oktoberfest, marching to a town near you.

The Pumpkin Show
Circleville, Ohio
October 18–21
You're bound to find the great pumpkin at this historic festival. This free show features parades, seasonal contests, and plenty of specialty foods. Call **(740) 474-7000**, or visit **www.pumpkinshow.com**

grand *finale*

You've probably heard of the southern favorite "grits and shrimp."

Here's a spin off appetizer using baked grits molded in shells

and served with "scampi-style" scallops.

Grits shells with scallop "scampi"

GRITS SHELLS
(6 SHELLS)

IN LARGE SAUCEPAN, BOIL:
3   cups water
¼   t. kosher salt

REDUCE HEAT; WHISK IN:
¾   cups stone-ground
       yellow grits (*not* instant)

*COOK GRITS, COVERED, UNTIL
VERY STIFF, ABOUT 12 MINUTES.*

OFF HEAT, WHISK IN:
2   T. unsalted butter
1   T. heavy cream
       Salt and pepper to taste

*SPRAY SCALLOP SHELLS WITH
NONSTICK SPRAY; DUST EACH
SHELL WITH:*
½   t. fine bread crumbs

▲ Prepare grits according to the recipe, *left*. Spray natural or ovenproof ceramic scallop shells with nonstick spray. Dust with fine bread crumbs. Spoon ½ cup grits into each shell and level with a rubber spatula. Chill grits until cold so they unmold easily.

▲ Preheat oven to broil with a rack in the *middle*. Unmold shells onto a nonstick baking sheet; broil until tops brown and shells are heated through.

Make Scallop Scampi, *Pages 8–9*. Serve two scallops and sauce with each shell; garnish with dill and lemon twist.

Issue No. 24 Nov/Dec 2000
www.CuisineMagazine.com

Cuisine

an illustrated guide to creative home cooking

seafood chowder

make-ahead chowder for an easy holiday meal

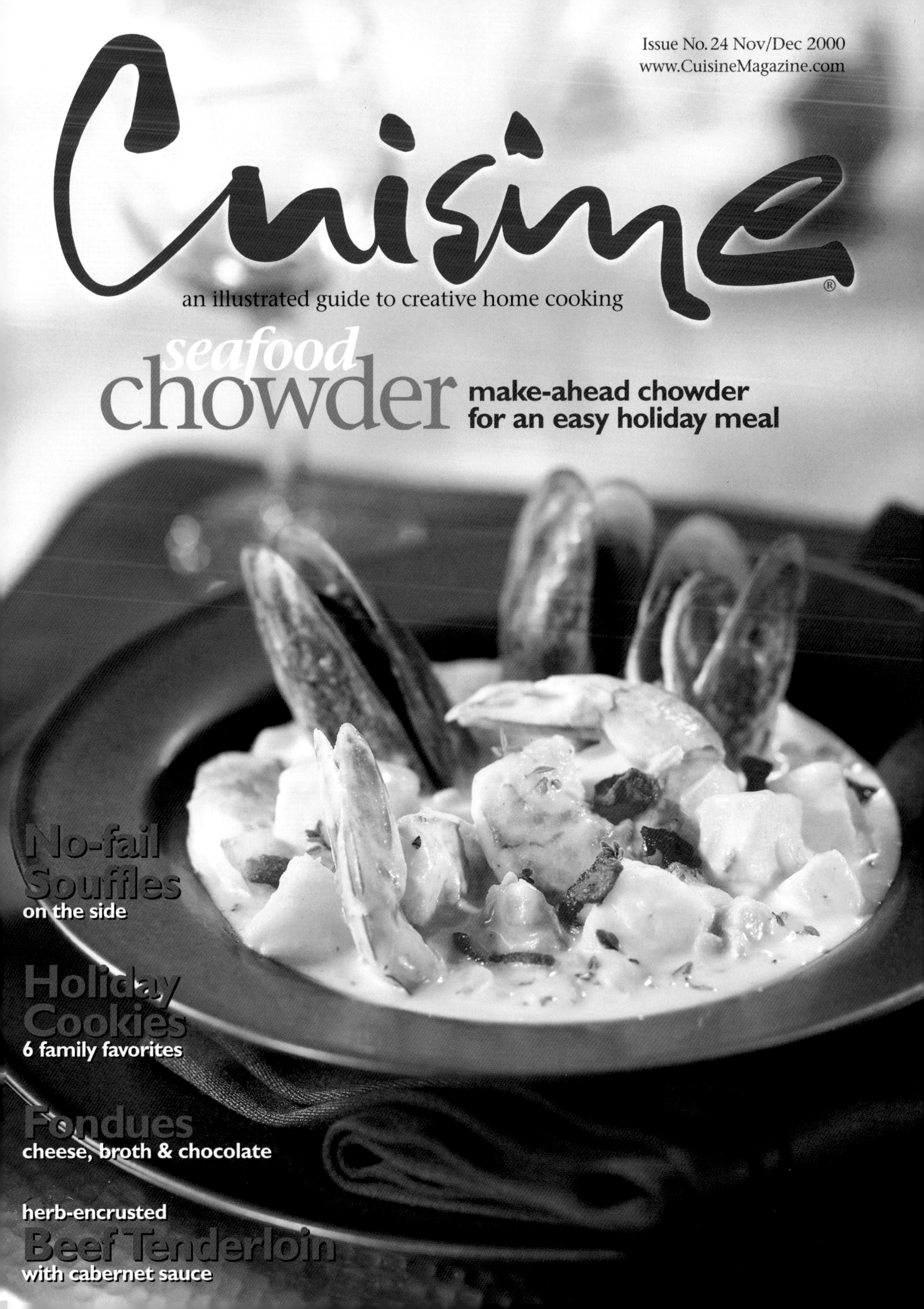

No-fail Souffles
on the side

Holiday Cookies
6 family favorites

Fondues
cheese, broth & chocolate

herb-encrusted
Beef Tenderloin
with cabernet sauce

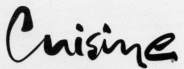

Editor
John F. Meyer

Art Director
Cinda Shambaugh

Associate Editor
Susan Hoss

Assistant Editors
Matt Bereza
Juliana Hale
Sara Ostransky

Senior Graphic Designer
Holly Wiederin

Graphic Designer
Stephanie Hunter

Test Kitchen Director
Kim Samuelson

Contributing Photographers
Scott Little, Dean Tanner

Contributing Food Stylist
Janet Pittman

Pre-Press Image Specialist
Troy Clark

Publisher
Donald B. Peschke

CORPORATE:
Director of Finance: Mary R. Scheve • *Creative Director:* Ted Kralicek • *New Media Manager:* Gordon C. Gaippe • *Special Publications Executive Editor:* Douglas L. Hicks • *Senior Photographer:* Crayola England • *Multi Media Art Director:* Eugene Pedersen • *Technology Analyst:* Carol Schoeppler • *Web Site Product Specialist:* Adam Best • *Web Content Managers:* Terry Walker, David Briggs • *Controller:* Robin Hutchinson • *Senior Accountant:* Laura Thomas • *Accounts Payable:* Mary Schultz • *Accounts Receivable:* Margo Petrus • *Production Director:* George Chmielarz • *Electronic Publishing Director:* Douglas M. Lidster • *Network Administrator:* Cris Schwanebeck • *Production Coordinator:* Noelle M. Carroll • *Pre-Press Image Specialist:* Minniette Johnson • *H.R. Assistant:* Kirsten Koele • *Facilities Manager:* Julia Fish • *Receptionist:* Jeanne Johnson • *Administrative Assistant:* Sherri Ribbey • *Mail Room Clerk:* Lou Webber

CUSTOMER SERVICE & FULFILLMENT:
Operations Director: Bob Baker • *Customer Service Manager:* Jennie Enos • *Customer Service Representatives:* Anna Cox, Jeanette Rankin, April Revell, Deborah Rich, Tammy Truckenbrod • *Technical Representative:* Johnny Audette • *Buyer:* Linda Jones • *Administrative Assistant:* Nancy Downey • *Warehouse Supervisor:* Nancy Johnson • *Fulfillment:* Sylvia Carey, Sheryl Knox, Dan Spidle

CIRCULATION:
Subscriber Services Director: Sandy Baum • *New Business Manager:* Todd L. Bierle • *Promotion Manager:* Rick Junkins • *Billing and Collections Manager:* Rebecca Cunningham • *Renewal Manager:* Paige Rogers • *Assistant Subscription Manager:* Joy Krause • *Circulation Marketing Analyst:* Kris Schlemmer • *Associate Circulation Marketing Analyst:* Paula M. DeMatteis • *Senior Graphic Designers:* Robin Dowdell, Mark Hayes

Cuisine® (ISSN 1089-6546) is published bi-monthly (Jan., Mar., May, July, Sept., Nov.) by August Home Publishing Co., 2200 Grand Ave., Des Moines, IA 50312. **Cuisine**® is a trademark of August Home Publishing Co. ©Copyright 2000 August Home Publishing. All rights reserved. Subscriptions: Single copy: $4.99. One year subscription (6 issues), $21.94. (Canada/Foreign add $10 per year, U.S. funds.) Periodicals postage paid at Des Moines, IA and at additional mailing offices. "USPS/Perry-Judd's Heartland Division automatable poly". Postmaster: Send change of address to **Cuisine**, P.O. Box 37100 Boone, IA 50037-2100. Subscription questions? Call 800-311-3995, 8 a.m. to 5 p.m., Central Standard Time, weekdays. Online Subscriber Services: www.CuisineMagazine.com. **Cuisine**® does not accept and is not responsible for unsolicited manuscripts. PRINTED IN U.S.A.

www.CuisineMagazine.com

from the editor:

The holidays seem to bring out the "cook" in all of us. Throughout the year, we struggle to find recipes that are quick and somewhat balanced—then, during the holidays, we throw that line of thinking right out the window. Thanksgiving cooking that lasts for days. Carbohydrate overloading. Elaborate dinner parties with foods and recipes we've never tried. What are we thinking?

Not to worry. In this issue, there are plenty of festive recipes you can make without breaking the time bank *or* pushing the patience meter. The Herb-encrusted Beef Tenderloin with potato rings is a perfect example. It fell right into our "easy-elegant" holiday criteria with a dynamite make-ahead sauce and a restaurant-chic look. You probably know by now that all of our recipes are tested and tasted over and over. Most of the time, just a bite is taken. With each test of the tenderloin, there was nothing left on the plates, and I even overheard the comment "I bet you'd pay $30 for this at a restaurant". I knew we had a winner.

If you're more into the "casual-elegance" thing, take a look at the Seafood Chowder on Page 24. Chowders have long been an American holiday tradition, but it's the way this creamy white soup is made that's so appealing for the hectic holidays. The chowder base can be made ahead. It can be dressed up or down by the kind of seafood you use. And best of all, you'll never overcook the seafood.

Finally, you have to try the Panna Cotta on Page 36. Even though it's embarrassingly simple to make, this creamy dessert is loaded with good flavor and an elegant look—it has holiday written all over it.

Have a nice holiday. I hope *Cuisine* can make it a little easier.

John

6   8

contents
Issue 24 NOV/dec 2000

feature articles

in every issue

Tips

and techniques from our readers

Keeping Bugs at Bay

It's good to keep dry staples on hand, but they attract bugs—especially on the lower pantry shelves. I don't want pesticides near the food, so instead I put bay leaves on the shelves. I replace them with fresh leaves every six months or so.

Mary Helen Haskell
Normal, IL

Shake It

Empty spice bottles are a great help around the kitchen. I remove the stickers and label them with a marker. Then I fill them with ingredients I use regularly, like c*ornmeal* to shake in bread pans, *flour* for rolling pins, or my home-made *dry rub* mixes for meat. They're also great for both regular and powdered *sugar*.

I also fill old Worcestershire sauce bottles with *olive oil* to sprinkle on salads or to lightly coat frying pans for sauteing.

Saundra Hollenbeck
Lafayette, TN

No Weep Whipped Cream

In Issue #20, someone asked how to keep whipped cream from getting weepy. After I whip mine, I put it in a strainer (over a bowl). Any liquid drips out.

Josephine Stoy
Nashua, NH

Steaming Hot Tortillas

Tortillas are easier to roll or fold if you steam them first. Put a few tortillas on a clean, slightly damp kitchen towel and wrap it up well. Microwave for about 30 to 35 seconds. They'll come out hot and ready to use.

Chad Adelman
Winter Park, FL

Low-Tech Spin Dry

To dry washed greens, put them in a plastic grocery bag lined with several layers of paper toweling. Then close the bag and spin it around in a loop a few times, like a lasso. The greens are dry and ready to dress.

Nicole Camire
Burlington, VT

Basic Basil Care

Basil wilts so quickly, but it perks up if I set it in cool water for about 30 minutes. Then I blot the leaves dry and store them at room temperature in a Ziploc bag—if basil is stored in the refrigerator, it turns black.

Betty Delacroix
Charlotte, NC

Garlic Butter in a Squeeze

A friend showed me a quick way to make garlic butter. She took butter from the refrigerator and a couple of cloves of garlic, then put both of them into a garlic press. With just a squeeze, it made perfectly manageable, soft garlic butter in seconds.

Debra Lucas
Pelham, AL

Cupcake Menorah

I'm 11 years old and love to bake. Last Hanukkah, I made our menorah out of cupcakes. It was a decoration pretty enough to eat.

Chelsea Rohrbach
Thousand Oaks, CA

Grind it Clean

To clean an electric coffee grinder, just add a small amount of rice and turn it on until the grinder no longer has any odor. It works great for removing both coffee odors and pungent smells from grinding spices.

Lee Zoloto
Scottsdale, AZ

Test Kitchen Tip from Matt: This tip is an old favorite, but it's come in handy this issue. To crush peppercorns without a mortar and pestle, put them in a coffee filter. Hold the filter closed with one hand and smash the peppercorns with a mallet.

Reviving Vanilla Beans

I went to use a vanilla bean recently only to find that it had totally dried out. I knew I wouldn't be able to split the bean or use its seeds. I took a chance and soaked it in filtered water for 8 hours. It worked just great! I ended up with a completely hydrated (and now usable) vanilla bean.

Laura Ciampa
Atlanta, GA

Kid-size Tarts

When you have extra pie dough from making pie, roll and cut the dough into small shapes. Put a teaspoon of jam in the middle then fold the dough over, like ravioli. Top them with cinnamon sugar and bake until golden brown. They're really fun to make.

Cady Chambers, age 11
Roy, WA

Editor's Note: Thanks, Cady. You might try topping your tarts with the glazes on Pages 15 or 17.

Self-Cleaning Pizza Stone

If there is burnt buildup on your pizza stone, leave it in your oven the next time you run the cleaning cycle. Anything stuck to the stone turns into light gray ash. Just the oils are left behind. Like seasoned cast iron, the stone is almost nonstick.

Shawn Kearns
Corona, CA

share your *Tips* with Cuisine

If you have a unique way of solving a cooking problem, we'd like to hear from you, and we'll consider publishing your tip in one or more of our works.

Just write down your cooking tip and mail it to Cuisine, Tips Editor, 2200 Grand Ave., Des Moines, IA 50312, or contact us through our email address shown below. Please include your name, address, and daytime phone number in case we have questions. We'll pay you $25 if we publish your tip.

Email: Cuisine@CuisineMagazine.com
Web address: www.CuisineMagazine.com

herb-encrusted
beef tenderloin
with cabernet sauce

Beef tenderloin is for very special occasions. But roll it in fresh herbs and serve it with a sauce laced with pomegranate seeds, and you have an all-out celebration.

Some events demand that you pull out all the stops and bring out the very best. Beef tenderloin is the best of the best, and this presentation really shows it off. But here's the real secret—this showy dish is easy to prepare.

The herb crust plays a big part in this dish. It not only provides a spicy flavor to this low-fat cut of beef, it also keeps the meat juicy by holding in moisture.

The hardest part of this dish may be the shopping. Problem is, tenderloin is not a stock item in some stores—although Sam's Club carries them. Order at least a week ahead from a regular grocer, then have the butcher trim it up. He *should not* charge you for this, and should give you all the extra meat. It will leave you with plenty of cuts for shish kebabs and filets for grilling.

ENCRUSTED BEEF TENDERLOIN

(MAKES SIX 4-OZ. SERVINGS)
WORK TIME: 15 MINUTES
COOK TIME: 40 MINUTES
FOR THE TENDERLOIN—
CLEAN AND TRIM:
2   lb. beef tenderloin, center cut
COAT WITH:
2   T. Dijon mustard
GRIND IN FOOD PROCESSOR:
½   cup bread crumbs
1   cup fresh parsley leaves
2   T. black peppercorns, crushed
4   cloves garlic
2   t. lemon zest (1 lemon)
2   t. fresh thyme leaves
2   t. fresh rosemary leaves
1   t. kosher salt
FOR THE ACCOMPANIMENTS—
PREPARE AND SERVE TENDERLOIN WITH:
6   roasted red potatoes
4   cups mesclun mix salad greens
6   French bread rounds, toasted
1½ cups Cabernet Sauce

NUTRITIONAL INFORMATION PER SLICE:
CALORIES 350; TOTAL FAT 17(G); CALORIES
FROM FAT 43%; SODIUM 751(MG);
CARBOHYDRATES 5(G)

Tenderloin preparation

Stop here for a warning! Unfortunately, some markets will package "whole beef tenderloin" already cut up without the center section (the best part). Make sure you get the whole thing and not two butt ends packaged together.

Buying: An average beef tenderloin weighs about seven pounds and is roughly two feet long. It should be in one piece. Now, I won't say this about other cuts of beef, but grade is not that important with tenderloin since it's such a tender piece of meat. USDA Choice and Select grades are both good.

Trimming: You want the butcher to do most of the work. First, he'll remove the hard, white exterior fat and chain muscle. Then, ask him to cut off the butt and tip ends—the center section is what you want, *see Photo below*.

That leaves just the silverskin—a tough, thin membrane under the fat layer. If you're lucky, he'll remove this or you'll have to do it yourself as I'm doing in Step 1. It has to be removed because heat won't melt it. Silverskin shrinks and twists as it cooks.

Herb Crust: Beef tenderloin may be fork-tender, but it doesn't have much flavor on its own. Here's where the herb crust comes in. It's loaded with pepper, garlic, and lemon zest, like gremolada with a temper. But don't worry about it turning brown during roasting—the moist, fresh herbs and salt will keep the crust a pleasing shade of green.

Once you've made the herb crust, you'll need to apply it to the tenderloin. Here's a neat trick: First, spread the herb mixture evenly onto a piece of parchment or waxed paper. Then, roll the meat over the mixture, patting it tightly with the paper. There's no mess or waste, and it comes out smooth.

1 Preheat oven to 450°. To trim off the silverskin, cut a flap under one end. Hold end of membrane taut as you slide knife underneath it to cut it away.

2 Coat the tenderloin with Dijon mustard using a pastry brush. Don't forget the ends. This mustard layer will help the herb crust stick to the roast.

3 Peppercorns won't break up in food processor so crush them before processing (see peppercorn tip, Page 5). Then process crust until finely chopped.

4 Spread the herb mixture in a layer on a sheet of parchment or waxed paper. Lay the tenderloin on the herbs and roll to coat. Pat extra on the ends.

---

*The **butt** end is sometimes passed off as whole tenderloin. The butt and **tip** have tender meat that can be grilled or stir-fried.*

*The **center** of the tenderloin is where chateaubriand and filet mignon come from. This is the part to use. It is uniform in size and will cook evenly.*

*The **chain** runs the length of the tenderloin. It is more fatty, but still has usable meat that can be cut up and sauteed.*

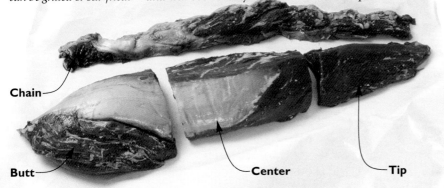

Chain

Butt

Center

Tip

Making the sauce

Unlike most meats, roasted tenderloin leaves little drippings to make a sauce. The reason is simple—there's no fat. But this Cabernet Sauce doesn't need drippings for flavor—that's why you can make this sauce a day ahead. Cabernet Sauce is based on a classic brown sauce. Chunks of ham and mushrooms take the place of drippings, creating a rich base. Tomato paste provides some body and a mahogany color. It may seem odd to put vinegar (an acid) in a sauce, but adding just a *little* bit cuts the oiliness and accentuates the sauce's flavor.

CABERNET SAUCE

(MAKES 1½ CUPS)
WORK TIME: 10 MINUTES
COOK TIME: 15 MINUTES
SAUTE IN 2 T. OLIVE OIL:

4 cups mushrooms, sliced (8 oz.)
1½ cups white onion, minced
1 cup honey roast ham, minced
4 cloves garlic, minced
ADD:
2 T. tomato paste
DEGLAZE WITH:
⅔ cup cabernet sauvignon
ADD:
2 T. unsalted butter
SPRINKLE WITH:
2 T. all-purpose flour
ADD AND SIMMER:
2 cups beef broth (14-oz. can)
1 sprig fresh thyme
STRAIN AND ADD:
1 t. balsamic vinegar
Salt and pepper to taste
SPRINKLE EACH PLATE WITH:
Pomegranate seeds

POMEGRANATE SEEDS

Pomegranate seeds can be a doubled-edged sword. While they contain an unusual, but addictive, sweet-tart flavor, they also can stain your cutting board, clothes, and hands. To extract the seeds from their hive with minimum mess, slice the pomegranate in half and put it in a large bowl of cool water. Under water, work the seeds out of the pomegranate with your fingers. The seeds will sink to the bottom and the pulp will float to the top.

5 Heat oil in saute pan to medium. Saute mushrooms, onion, ham, and garlic until brown and crust forms in pan. Add tomato paste; cook until mahogany color.

6 The crust on the pan is where the best flavor is. Deglaze pan with cabernet, scraping the bottom to remove the crust and work it into the sauce.

7 Simmer until wine is nearly evaporated. Add butter; sprinkle in flour. Cook 2 minutes to eliminate starchy taste. Add thyme sprig and broth; whisk smooth.

8 Return to simmer to thicken sauce slightly. Strain and discard solids. Add vinegar and season to taste with salt and pepper. Reheat when ready to serve.

The perfect roast

The sauce is ready and the tenderloin is crusted. How should you cook it?

Roasting: Tenderloin isn't going to be good if it's overcooked. Since it has little fat, there's nothing to melt and keep it moist. No room for error here. High heat is the way to go. The meat cooks quickly on the outside, leaving the center tender and juicy. For even cooking, be sure to put a rack under the meat to let the heat circulate.

Doneness: Don't think for a moment I'm going to tell you how to cook this past medium. Medium rare is perfect—130°, medium is okay—135°.

Be sure to let the meat rest after roasting. While resting, meat cooks just a little further—this is called residual heat. Moisture in the center now starts to spread out towards the cooked edges.

Garnish: The potato ring and crouton are finishing touches that add that dramatic restaurant look. The crouton gives the tenderloin a little deserving pedestal to stand up on. And wait till you taste it when it's soaked up the sauce—unbelievable! The potato ring can be made ahead and reheated while meat is resting. It's simple, but elegant. Think of it as an edible bud vase.

9 Slice potatoes so bottoms are flat and tops are angled; core holes. Coat with olive oil and season with salt and pepper. Roast for 20 minutes at 450°.

10 Cut rounds of French bread to fit slices of tenderloin. Brush with oil and toast in oven for 10 minutes at 450°. You can do this even a day ahead.

11 Coat roasting rack with nonstick spray to keep herb crust from sticking. Place meat on the rack in a shallow roasting pan. Roast for 40 minutes.

12 The meat is medium-rare when it reaches 130°. Let rest 10–15 minutes under aluminum foil tent. Now is the time to reheat sauce and potatoes.

Going for the restaurant look

Place a small bunch of mesclun greens into the hole of the potato to make a bouquet. Put one on each plate. Serve with a little vinaigrette if you like.

Slice tenderloin into six portions, each about an inch thick. Use a really sharp knife so the crust doesn't fall off. Put crouton on plate next to potato ring.

Top crouton with a slice of tenderloin. Pour a little sauce on meat and plate. *Don't* over do it and cover up meat. Sprinkle with pomegranate seeds.

souffles on the side

There's no reason to fear souffles. These new generation side dishes have character, flavor, *and* structure.

Souffles carry a reputation for being a little temperamental—they fall easily. Any time you work with delicate egg whites, the result can be unpredictable. But these side souffles are more stable than regular souffles for several reasons. They have plenty of body in them (spinach or potato) that adds support. Added to this are more flour and egg yolk. Finally, they are twice-baked, giving them a second chance to rise.

So what is a souffle? It is a light, airy dish that can be either savory or sweet. It usually starts with an egg yolk-based sauce that is lightened with stiffly beaten egg whites. When this mixture is baked, the egg whites expand causing the souffle to rise, giving them their classic inflated brown crowns.

These sturdy side souffles can be made the day ahead and refrigerated. Oh sure, they'll fall a little, but not like a regular souffle would.

Hopefully, this will give you the confidence to try making souffles. These two classic combinations are definitely worth trying.

Souffle basics

Four things are needed for stable yet light souffles: the right baking dishes, a stable white sauce, properly beaten egg whites, and a hot oven.

Baking Dishes: Baking souffles in the right dishes will make a difference in how they rise. Ceramic souffle dishes (ramekins) are best because they pull heat up through the porous bottom.

Flip a ramekin over—see how the bottom isn't glazed? The extra heat that goes through the bottom expands the whites, pushing the souffle up and creating the characteristic domed top. The dish's straight sides also help in rising.

White Sauce: Traditional souffles start with a white sauce stabilized with flour and egg yolks. Because these souffles can be made a day ahead, they need even more stability. This sauce has *more* flour and yolks to help keep the souffles from *totally* deflating after baking.

The only trick to making the sauce is tempering, or adding yolks to hot liquid. If it's not done right, the yolks could scramble. The most important thing is to slowly add the yolks to the hot white sauce, whisking constantly. Do this and you won't have a problem.

Egg Whites: Beaten egg whites give souffles height, puffiness, and golden brown color. They're also what scare people away from souffle-making. Don't worry! Here are a few guidelines.

First, be sure the whites are at room temperature before beating. Warm egg whites expand more than cold whites and you'll get more volume from them. Second, be sure there's no fat (yolk) in the whites—they'll never whip. If yolk gets into the whites, dip it out with a piece of egg shell or bread. Finally, the beaters and bowl must be dry before they touch the whites. Water also prevents whites from whipping.

Beat them on high speed until they firm up and start to come away from the sides of the bowl, 1–2 minutes. Do not overbeat! Overbeaten whites look lumpy and have liquid pooling at the bottom of the bowl. Souffles made with overbeaten whites will not rise well.

Temperature: You need a hot oven so the souffles rise right away. The high temperature also forms a protective skin on top which helps keep the souffle moist inside. But in the end, it's this skin that blooms into a brown crown.

Spinach Souffle
(Makes 6 Souffles)
Work Time: 30 Minutes
Cook Time: 45 Minutes

Separate and Set Aside:
5   eggs

Melt 3 T. Unsalted Butter, then Add:
3   T. all-purpose flour

Gradually Stir In:
1   cup whole milk

Temper In, then Season with:
     Reserved egg yolks
1   t. kosher salt
½   t. cayenne
¼   t. ground nutmeg

Saute in 1 Teaspoon Unsalted Butter:
1   cup yellow onion, finely diced

Add:
1   cup cooked spinach, fresh or frozen (10-oz. package), drained
½   cup Swiss or Gruyere cheese, grated

Beat and Fold In:
     Reserved egg whites

Before Twice-Baking, Heat:
1   cup heavy cream
½   cup Swiss or Gruyere cheese, grated

Garnish Souffles with:
1   T. chopped fresh parsley

Nutritional Information per Souffle:
Calories 395; Total Fat 33(g); Calories from Fat 74%; Sodium 576(mg); Carbohydrates 11(g)

1 Separate eggs so whites can come to room temperature; whisk together yolks. Spray six 4 oz. ramekins with nonstick spray; place on a baking sheet.

2 For white sauce, melt butter in sauce pan over medium heat. Whisk in flour. Cook 2 minutes, then gradually whisk in milk. Cook and stir 3 minutes longer.

3 Turn off heat and temper yolks into the sauce, adding them gradually and whisking constantly. Add seasonings; cover sauce and set aside.

Souffle method

The two main elements of souffles are ready to go—the white sauce and beaten egg whites. Here's how to combine, then bake them for maximum height.

Folding: The purpose of folding is to mix something dense (white sauce) with something light (beaten egg whites)—without losing the air from the whites.

First pour half the whites onto the sauce. Then, with a gentle, scooping motion, bring the sauce up from the bottom, over the whites. Rotate the pan and fold a few more times. Add the second half of whites and fold just until whites are incorporated. Don't overmix—the whites will deflate.

First Bake: It's crucial to fill the ramekins and bake the souffles right away. Air bubbles in the whites will start to pop immediately and the souffles won't rise.

Here are a couple of souffle baking tips. First, use a baking sheet to put all the souffles on. They can go in and out of the oven at the same time—safely. Second, bake them on the middle rack of the oven. If the rack is too high, the tops will burn before the inside is baked.

4 Preheat oven to 400°. In a small skillet over medium heat, saute onion in butter until soft and set aside. Press excess water from spinach. Add onion, spinach, and cheese to sauce.

5 Beat room temperature egg whites with an electric mixer at high speed. Peaks will start forming after 1–2 minutes. Firm peaks will hold their shape like shaving cream. Do not overbeat!

6 Add half the whites to the sauce, folding to incorporate and lighten the batter. Gently fold in second half of whites, but don't overmix—it deflates them and the souffles will sink, not rise.

7 Fill each ramekin to the top—it'll give the souffles height. Place baking sheet on middle rack of oven and bake 20–25 minutes. Souffles will jiggle when touched, yet feel firm on top when done.

Reheating: the twice-bake

Twice-baking does a couple of things. First, it gives the souffles a chance to rise another time, even the day after they're baked. Second, baking them with a sauce creates a little more character that most souffles lack.

Heat the cream and cheese on the stove 2 minutes before pouring it on the souffles. This way, the souffles won't burn before the sauce thickens and browns.

Cool souffles 10 minutes. Loosen with a knife and transfer to a casserole dish; chill if desired. To twice-bake, preheat oven to 425°. Simmer cream and cheese 2 minutes then pour over souffles. Bake 10–15 minutes. Garnish with parsley.

potato bacon souffles on the side

POTATO BACON SOUFFLE

(MAKES 6 SOUFFLES)

WORK TIME: 30 MINUTES
COOK TIME: 45 MINUTES

SEPARATE AND SET ASIDE:
5   eggs

MELT 3 T. UNSALTED BUTTER; ADD:
3   T. all-purpose flour

GRADUALLY STIR IN:
1   cup whole milk

TEMPER IN, THEN SEASON WITH:
     Reserved egg yolks
1   t. kosher salt
½   t. cayenne
¼   t. ground nutmeg

BAKE, PEEL, THEN CRUMBLE:
1   7-oz. russet potato
     (about 1 cup)

SAUTE UNTIL CRISP; DRAIN:
1   cup thick-sliced bacon,
     chopped (10 slices)

ADD TO WHITE SAUCE:
     Crumbled potato
     Sauteed bacon
½   cup Cheddar cheese, grated
3   T. chopped fresh chives

BEAT AND FOLD IN:
     Reserved egg whites

BEFORE TWICE-BAKING, HEAT:
1   cup heavy cream
½   cup Cheddar cheese, grated

GARNISH WITH:
1   T. chopped fresh chives

These potato souffles make a great side dish for holiday turkey, ham, or encrusted tenderloin. But if you've had enough of holiday feasting, serve them as a light meal with salad and bread.

1 Separate eggs and make white sauce as on Page 11. Bake the potato in a 450° oven 45 minutes; peel. When cool, crumble into dime-size chunks. Reduce oven temperature to 400°.

2 Saute and drain bacon; add bacon, potato, cheese, and chive to the white sauce. Beat and fold in the egg whites. With sprayed ramekins on a baking sheet, fill with mixture. Bake 20–25 min.

3 Cool and unmold souffles; chill if desired. To twice-bake, preheat oven to 425°; arrange souffles in casserole dish. Heat cream and cheese; pour over souffles. Bake 10–15 min. Garnish with chives.

cranberry pumpkin

three quick breads

Studded with fruit and nuts, these quick breads make great holiday gifts—if you can part with them.

What is quick bread, anyway? Some familiar quick breads are biscuits, corn bread, muffins, and these loaf breads. What they all have in common is that they use baking soda or powder to rise instead of yeast. This chemical leavening is instant, so there's no rising time, like with yeast— hence the term *quick* bread.

Here's how it works. When baking soda comes in contact with an acidic ingredient (like buttermilk or fruit puree) it reacts, releasing carbon dioxide. The bubbles get trapped in the batter and make it rise.

Mixing: Quick breads mix quickly using the *dump* method. Wet ingredients are dumped into the dry ones and barely folded in. The batter will be lumpy, but don't overbeat or the loaf will be tough and full of holes.

Keep two things in mind when mixing. First, mix the dry

ingredients well. This disperses the baking soda so the loaf can rise evenly. Second, beat the eggs, oil, and sugar until the color lightens. Then add the other wet ingredients. This works air into the batter, so the carbon dioxide can expand and raise the loaf.

Pans: These recipes are made for $8^{1}/_{2}$ x $4^{1}/_{2}$" pans, but pans can be deceiving in volume. Fill *your* pan no more than $^{2}/_{3}$ full so it won't overflow. And use glass or light-colored metal pans. Ones with dark finishes can burn the bread where it touches the sides.

CRANBERRY PUMPKIN BREAD

(MAKES ONE 8½ x 4½" LOAF)
WORK TIME: 15 MINUTES
COOK TIME: 65–70 MINUTES

TOSS TOGETHER AND SET ASIDE:
½ cup frozen cranberries, halved
1 T. sugar
1 T. all-purpose flour

COMBINE DRY INGREDIENTS:
2 cups all-purpose flour
1 t. kosher salt
½ t. baking soda

WHISK TOGETHER:
1 cup sugar
½ cup vegetable oil
2 eggs

ADD TO WET MIXTURE:
1 cup canned pumpkin puree
¼ cup buttermilk
½ t. vanilla extract

FOLD WET INTO DRY MIXTURE; ADD:
½ cup pecans, chopped
Reserved cranberry mixture

WHISK TOGETHER FOR THE GLAZE:
½ cup powdered sugar
1 T. cream cheese
1 T. orange juice
½ t. orange zest, minced
Pinch of salt

NUTRITIONAL INFORMATION PER ½₁₂ LOAF: CALORIES 306; TOTAL FAT 14(G); CALORIES FROM FAT 41%; SODIUM 279(MG); CARBOHYDRATES 42(G)

1 Preheat oven to 325°; grease loaf pan. Cut frozen cranberries in half—a food processor works okay, but cut by hand for uniform pieces. Toss cranberries with sugar and flour and set aside.

2 Combine dry ingredients and set aside. In a separate bowl, whisk together sugar, oil, and eggs. Add pumpkin, buttermilk, and vanilla, then fold into the dry ingredients just until combined.

3 Gently fold the pecans and cranberry mixture into batter. Fill the prepared pan with batter so that it comes up no more than ⅔ full. Bake 65–70 minutes. Test for doneness with a skewer.

4 To prevent crumbling, let bread cool 10 minutes before removing from pan. Meanwhile, whisk glaze ingredients together. Put loaf on rack and glaze; cool completely before slicing.

Preparation is the key
I'm preparing the cranberries before even starting the batter. That's because once the batter is mixed, it starts rising, so it needs to get right into the oven. You can't stop to chop at this point.

Baking: Once the batter is mixed, put the bread straight into the oven—don't let it sit out! That's because the baking soda starts to react to the liquid acid (the buttermilk) immediately and releases carbon dioxide. In other words, it starts to rise.

The rise continues in the oven and the bread sets as it bakes. If the batter sits out in the cold it will just release the carbon dioxide and then go flat, and there won't be any way to fix it.

Testing: The bread may look done when it's nicely browned, but don't count on it. Usually the section along that characteristic crack on top takes the longest to bake completely. To test, insert a skewer into the crack. It should come out clean.

Cooling: This will be hard, but you really have to let the bread cool completely before you cut it. If it's cut while it's warm, it will crumble. Cooling develops a fine, cake-like texture.

Glazing: When I was young, I went to my friend's house where his mother would saute slices of quick bread in butter—it was great but too decadent, now.

So glaze them for an extra kick. It not only adds flavor but they look like a photograph out of a fancy food catalog.

The glaze dries out easily, so make it at the last minute. Then apply it after the breads have been removed from the pans.

CHOCOLATE CHIP BANANA BREAD

(Makes One 8½ x 4½" Loaf)
WORK TIME: 15 MINUTES
COOK TIME: 60–65 MINUTES

COMBINE DRY INGREDIENTS:

2   cups all-purpose flour
1   t. kosher salt
½   t. baking soda

WHISK TOGETHER:

½   cup sugar
½   cup vegetable oil
2   eggs

ADD TO WET MIXTURE:

1   cup ripe banana, mashed
¼   cup buttermilk
½   t. vanilla extract

FOLD WET INTO DRY MIXTURE; ADD:

½   cup semisweet chocolate chips
½   cup walnuts, chopped

WHISK TOGETHER FOR THE GLAZE:

½   cup powdered sugar
1   T. cream cheese
1   T. water
½   t. instant espresso powder
     Pinch of salt

NUTRITIONAL INFORMATION PER ¹⁄₁₂ LOAF: CALORIES 307; TOTAL FAT 16(G); CALORIES FROM FAT 45%; SODIUM 279(MG); CARBOHYDRATES 39(G)

*Freezing bananas
Those darkly freckled bananas are just right for banana bread, but that stage passes quickly. Put them in the freezer with their peel on. When you're ready to use them, thaw and peel.*

chocolate chip banana

1 Preheat oven to 325°; coat a loaf pan with nonstick spray. In large bowl, combine the flour, salt, and baking soda with a whisk, then set aside.

*Coffee Glaze
You don't have instant espresso powder? Just use 1 tablespoon of strong brewed coffee in place of the water and espresso powder.*

2 Mash the bananas with a fork or a pastry blender. Now, in a separate bowl, whisk together oil, sugar, and eggs to incorporate air. Blend bananas, buttermilk, and vanilla into the egg mixture.

3 Fold wet ingredients into dry ingredients just until combined. Gently fold in chocolate chips and walnuts. Pour batter into prepared loaf pan and bake 60–65 minutes; test with skewer.

4 While still in the pan, let bread cool for 10 minutes. Meanwhile, whisk glaze ingredients together; remove bread from pan and glaze. Cool completely before slicing—about three hours.

apple ginger

APPLE GINGER BREAD

(MAKES ONE 8½ x 4½" LOAF)

WORK TIME: 15 MINUTES
COOK TIME: 55–60 MINUTES

COMBINE DRY INGREDIENTS:
2¼ cups all-purpose flour
1 t. kosher salt
½ t. baking soda

WHISK TOGETHER:
½ cup sugar
½ cup vegetable oil
2 eggs

ADD TO WET MIXTURE:
⅔ cup applesauce
¼ cup buttermilk
2 T. fresh ginger, grated

FOLD WET INTO DRY MIXTURE; ADD:
½ cup golden raisins
½ cup pecans, chopped

WHISK TOGETHER FOR THE GLAZE:
½ cup powdered sugar
1 T. cream cheese
1 T. lemon juice
½ t. lemon zest, minced
   Pinch of salt

*NUTRITIONAL INFORMATION PER ¹⁄₁₂
LOAF:* CALORIES 313; TOTAL FAT 15(G);
CALORIES FROM FAT 43%; SODIUM
295(MG); CARBOHYDRATES 39(G)

*About ginger
Fresh ginger is
sold by the
piece called a
finger. Look for
firm pieces
with tight
skin—they are
the freshest.
Wrinkled gin-
ger fingers are
old, slightly
green, and can
taste a little
moldy.*

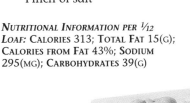

To grate ginger, ▶
*peel off the skin
with a knife or a
peeler. You can use a ginger grater if you have one,
but I use the smallest holes of a cheese grater. I find
that the strings stay on one side of the grater and the
pulp comes out the other side.*

1 Preheat oven to 325°. Coat a loaf pan with nonstick spray. In a large bowl, combine the flour, salt, and baking soda with a whisk. Using a whisk disperses the baking soda evenly.

2 In a separate bowl, whisk sugar, oil, and eggs vigorously until color lightens. Now add applesauce, buttermilk, and ginger; fold into dry mixture. Gently fold in raisins and pecans.

3 *Immediately* pour batter into pan and bake 55–60 minutes; test with skewer. Wait 10 minutes before removing bread from pan. Glaze then cool bread completely on rack (up to 3 hours).

Rules of rice

Rice is at the heart of fried rice. To fry it perfectly, it's a good idea to follow these two main rules.

The Right Rice: All rices are categorized by size: long, medium, or short grain. And the size determines what it'll be like after cooking—fluffy or sticky.

Whether rice is fluffy or sticky has to do with two starches. They are in all rice varieties, but in varying degrees. Long grain (basmati) has more starch that makes rice fluffy; short grain rice (sushi) is higher in "sticky" starch. As a result, long grain rice tends to separate easily, making it ideal for fried rice (but don't overcook or it'll be too mushy). On the flip side, fried rice will be a gluey mess if it's made with short grain rice.

Medium grain rice is between long and short in size and starch level—and some work for fried rice, some don't. Common white, converted, even Minute Rice are fine. But arborio rice (used for risotto) is not. It's too sticky.

Cold Rice: The temperature of the rice is also key—it must be cold before frying (preferably made the day before and chilled). Chilling coagulates starches, helping keep the grains separate. And cold won't stick to the pan as much when stir-fried. Just be sure to break up clumps before frying.

But you *can* use freshly cooked rice in a pinch. Spread it on a baking sheet then chill, uncovered, at least an hour before you fry it.

▲*Break up clumps of cooked rice before frying. Wet your hands a little first to keep it from sticking.*

chinese fried rice

Got leftovers? Forget about casseroles.
Make fried rice and turn them into dinner—fast.

Fried rice relies on leftovers. If you've got them (and who doesn't this time of year?), dinner is just half an hour away.

Traditionally, there's no set recipe for fried rice. The whole idea is to use what's on hand. But if you've never made it before, follow the recipe once to get a feel for it. Then go ahead and substitute, just be sure to keep amounts in control—too much stuff in the pan makes it hard to stir-fry properly.

But there is one thing in Chinese fried rice you'll *want* to include: an egg omelet. It's quick and simple to make—be sure the pan is fairly hot so the eggs set quickly (but not smoking or they'll get too brown). And keep an eye on the cooking time. Less than a minute is all it takes, or else the eggs will be rubbery.

You don't need a wok to make fried rice, just a large skillet. But make sure it's big—it's easier to stir the ingredients, plus the increased surface area ensures that they fry rather than steam. Also, a nonstick skillet is highly recommended. The rice tends to stick in standard skillets, even if it's ice cold (you may need to add more oil during frying if you use a standard skillet).

High heat is key for stir-frying and it's especially critical with fried rice—a lot of ingredients are already cooked and just need to be warmed up. Lower temperatures will make precooked meats dry and tough. But watch out. High heat burns things quickly, especially ginger and garlic. Stir and toss constantly to prevent scorching and keep the rice from sticking to the pan.

CHINESE FRIED RICE

(MAKES 5 CUPS)
WORK TIME: 20 MINUTES
COOK TIME: 10 MINUTES
COOK IN 2 TEASPOONS VEGETABLE OIL;
REMOVE FROM PAN:

2   eggs, lightly beaten
     Pinch salt

STIR-FRY IN 1 T. VEGETABLE OIL:

½   cup yellow onion, diced
2   T. fresh ginger, peeled and grated
1   T. garlic, minced (about 3 cloves)
2   t. jalapeno pepper, seeded and minced (about ½ pepper)

ADD:

2   cups shiitake mushrooms, stemmed and sliced (4 oz.)
1½   cups roast pork, beef, ham, or chicken, cubed (about 8 oz.)
1   cup red bell pepper, julienned

COMBINE; ADD AND REDUCE:

3   T. fresh lime juice
2   T. dry sherry or dry white wine
2   T. low sodium soy sauce
1   T. brown sugar, packed
1   t. chili garlic paste
     A few drops toasted sesame oil
     Salt to taste

STIR IN:

2   cups cooked, cold white rice
     Reserved egg omelet, torn

GARNISH WITH:

¼   cup scallions, bias-cut (about 4)
¼   cup coarsely chopped fresh cilantro leaves

NUTRITIONAL INFORMATION PER CUP:
CALORIES 320; TOTAL FAT 11(G); CALORIES FROM FAT 22%; SODIUM 483(MG); CARBOHYDRATES 34(G)

Before you start cooking...

◄ *Lightly beat eggs and salt in a small bowl.*

Prepare onion, ginger, garlic, and jalapeno (wear rubber gloves to mince it). ►

◄ *Remove stems from the mushrooms and slice thickly. Cut the red pepper into thin julienne strips.*

Chop leftover ► *roast meat into chunks—bigger pieces give good texture to the fried rice.*

Combine ingredients for the seasoning liquid in a small bowl or cup. ►

▲ *Cut scallions on a bias and remove leaves from cilantro. Chill until you're ready to garnish the rice.*

1   Heat 2 t. oil in a 14" nonstick skillet over medium-high heat. Add eggs and swirl to coat skillet. Cook until just set, about 45 seconds (the top will be a little runny). Try not to brown the eggs too much. Loosen with a rubber spatula and transfer to a plate; cool.

2   Increase heat to high; add 1 T. oil to skillet and stir-fry the onion, ginger, garlic, and jalapeno until slightly softened, about 2 minutes. Add the roast meat, mushrooms, and red pepper; stir-fry until vegetables soften and meat is heated through, about 5 minutes.

3   Pour in the seasoning liquid and stir to coat. Simmer until it has nearly evaporated, about 2 minutes. Stir in rice and warm through. Break the omelet into pieces with your fingers and add it to the rice. Transfer to a serving platter; garnish with scallions and cilantro.

cajun fried rice

A Chinese cooking technique plus Cajun ingredients equals a quick dinner that sizzles.

There's nothing Chinese to this Cajun fried rice except stir-frying. The same rules apply—use a big skillet (nonstick if possible), high heat, and stir constantly. But keep a few things in mind.

This Cajun fried rice doesn't use leftovers like the Chinese recipe. It starts with uncooked chicken, sausage, and shrimp. Because of that, they're stir-fried first, removed from the pan, and added back at the end. This way, the vegetables aren't as likely to turn mushy while the meats cook through. Just be sure the chicken is cut into fairly small cubes (about 1") so it cooks quickly.

Cajun food usually includes two things: spices and the "trinity" (onion, green pepper, and celery). And they're all in this fried rice too. The spice mix is pretty simple, but you can use a prepared Cajun seasoning mix if you have one. And when preparing the trinity, the vegetables should be bite-sized but not *too* small. Bigger pieces won't overcook and lose their color and texture as fast.

Tomatoes are another typical Cajun ingredient, but can be a problem in fried rice—their high water content tends to turn the rice gluey. But drier varieties, like Romas, work well. Choose ones that are red yet firm, but not underripe. They won't have good flavor. Canned tomatoes may be convenient but they're way too wet for fried rice.

CAJUN FRIED RICE (MAKES 5 CUPS)

WORK TIME: 20 MINUTES
COOK TIME: 10 MINUTES

TOSS TOGETHER; STIR-FRY IN 1 T. VEGETABLE OIL:
- 1 cup chicken breast, cubed (4 oz., about one half breast)
- 1 cup kielbasa or andouille sausage, bias-cut (4 oz.)
- 1 t. paprika
- 1 t. kosher salt
- ½ t. cayenne
- ½ t. dried thyme leaves

ADD AND STIR-FRY; REMOVE ALL MEATS:
- 8 oz. large shrimp (21–30 count), peeled and deveined

STIR-FRY IN 1 T. VEGETABLE OIL:
- ½ cup yellow onion, diced
- ½ cup green bell pepper, diced
- ½ cup celery, diced
- 1 T. garlic, minced (about 3 cloves)

COMBINE; ADD AND REDUCE:
- 2 T. low sodium chicken broth
- 2 T. dry sherry or dry white wine
- 2 T. fresh lemon juice
      Several dashes Tabasco sauce

ADD:
- ½ cup Roma tomatoes, diced (about 2)
      Reserved meat and shrimp
      Salt to taste

STIR IN:
- 2 cups cooked, cold white rice
- ¼ cup scallions, bias-cut (about 4)

GARNISH WITH:
- ¼ cup chopped fresh parsley

NUTRITIONAL INFORMATION PER CUP:
CALORIES 316; TOTAL FAT 13(G); CALORIES FROM FAT 38%; SODIUM 936(MG); CARBOHYDRATES 28(G)

Before you start cooking...

◄ Toss the chicken and sausage with seasonings.

Peel shrimp ► and remove the vein with a paring knife.

Prepare onions, pepper, celery, garlic, and tomatoes. ►

◄ Combine the ingredients for the seasoning liquid.

Prepare the scallions and parsley for garnish. Chill until ready to use. ►

1 Toss chicken and sausage with seasonings; heat 1 T. oil in a 14" nonstick skillet over high heat. Add meats and stir-fry 5 minutes. Add shrimp and cook until just pink, about 2 more minutes. Remove meats and shrimp; set aside.

2 Add 1 T. oil to skillet and stir-fry onion, green pepper, celery, and garlic until soft, about 3 minutes (take care not to overcook or the pepper and celery will turn an ugly army green). Stir constantly to prevent scorching.

3 Pour in seasoning liquid, stir to coat, and simmer until liquid is nearly evaporated, about 2 minutes. Add the diced tomatoes, reserved meat and shrimp (plus any accumulated juices), and salt to taste; stir to combine.

4 Stir in rice and scallions; continue to stir-fry until rice is warmed through, about 2 more minutes (watch the time or the shrimp will overcook). Transfer fried rice to a serving platter, garnish with parsley, and serve.

turkey fried rice

Cozy up to this "north woods" fried rice. Wild rice, pecans, and cranberries put turkey leftovers on the front burner.

This unusual fried rice is a welcome change from the typical leftover turkey recipes. But what makes it really unique is that it uses two types of rice: white and wild. The nutty flavor and chewy texture of wild rice can overwhelm the dish if it's used on its own. But when wild rice and plain white rice are mixed, the flavor and texture mellow out.

Wild rice is actually an aquatic grass seed native to Canada and the Great Lakes. Harvesting is labor-intensive, making it more expensive than white rice. But you don't need much—it doubles in volume when cooked.

The quality of wild rice varies, so if you can, inspect the grains before buying. They should be almost black and shiny-looking. Grains that are cracked and dull don't taste bad, but they cook unevenly and don't look as nice.

Wild rice is cooked differently than white rice (follow package instructions). First, it takes almost an hour. Cook just until *some* of the grains start to split open and curl. If most or all the grains are split, the rice is overcooked, starchy, and has lost a lot of flavor. If none are split, it'll be chewy and raw-tasting. The best way to determine doneness is to taste the rice often during cooking.

Second, wild rice probably won't absorb all its cooking liquid like white rice does. If there happens to be some water left in the pan after cooking, just drain it off. If you cooked the wild rice until the water evaporated, it would most likely be too mushy.

TURKEY FRIED RICE

(MAKES 5 CUPS)
WORK TIME: 20 MINUTES
COOK TIME: 10 MINUTES

SAUTE; REMOVE FROM SKILLET:
¼   cup thick-sliced bacon, diced (about 2 slices)

STIR-FRY IN 1 T. BACON DRIPPINGS:
½   cup yellow onion, diced
½   cup carrot, diced
½   cup celery, diced
1   T. garlic, minced (about 3 cloves)

COMBINE; ADD AND REDUCE:
¼   cup apple cider
2   T. apple cider vinegar or fresh lemon juice
    Salt and pepper to taste
1½ cups roast turkey, cubed or shredded (about 8 oz.)

STIR IN:
1   cup cooked, cold white rice
1   cup cooked wild rice
½   cup dried cranberries
½   cup pecans or walnuts, coarsely chopped and toasted
1   T. chopped fresh thyme leaves

GARNISH WITH:
    Chopped fresh thyme or parsley

NUTRITIONAL INFORMATION PER CUP: CALORIES 340; TOTAL FAT 15(G); CALORIES FROM FAT 39%; SODIUM 280(MG); CARB. 34(G)

Before you start cooking...

▲Dice bacon (kitchen shears work well for this). Cook wild rice, if needed—½ cup dry makes 1 cup cooked.

◄Prepare the onion, carrot, celery, and garlic.

▲Cube or shred roast turkey. Leftover roast chicken, pork, or beef are also good in this fried rice.

▲For even toasting, chop nuts first, then toast.

◄Combine the ingredients for the seasoning liquid. If you don't have apple cider, use chicken broth instead.

Chopped ► thyme is in the fried rice and used as a garnish. Parsley or sage can be substituted if you'd like.

1 In a 14" nonstick skillet, saute bacon over medium-high heat until crisp; remove. Pour off all but 1 T. drippings. Increase heat to high and stir-fry vegetables and garlic until soft, 3 minutes.

2 Add the seasoning liquid and roast turkey; stir to combine. Simmer, stirring frequently, until nearly all liquid has reduced, about 2 minutes. The mixture should not be completely dry.

3 Stir in the white and wild rice, cranberries, pecans, and thyme; stir-fry until heated through, about 2 minutes. Transfer to a serving platter and garnish with additional thyme or parsley.

seafood
chowder

The best holiday gift—time. Here's a classy dinner that can be served in minutes.

All it takes is a little do-ahead preparation and your favorite seafood.

So what is this miracle meal that comes just in time for the holidays? It's a great-looking, delicious chowder made with super-fresh seafood.

What makes this chowder unique is the way it's made. First make the chowder base a day ahead using clam broth from fresh clams. Then, just ten minutes before serving, reheat the base, and add potatoes and seafood. This cooking method is good for

two reasons. First, it minimizes any last-minute cooking. And second, the seafood won't overcook because it's added at the end, keeping it firm and flavorful. Next to an oil spill, overcooking is seafood's worst enemy. Have you ever noticed in some chowders that the potatoes and clams start to taste the same? They've been together too long. Adding the seafood at the end preserves their individual, delicate flavors.

SEAFOOD CHOWDER

(MAKES EIGHT 8-OZ. SERVINGS)
WORK TIME: 45 MINUTES
COOK TIME: 30 MINUTES
FOR THE CLAM BROTH—
COMBINE, SIMMER, AND STRAIN:
5 lb. clams in shells, scrubbed
3 cups cold water
FOR THE CHOWDER BASE—
COOK UNTIL CRISP; STRAIN:
1 lb. thick-sliced bacon, chopped
SWEAT IN ⅓ CUP BACON DRIPPINGS:
1½ cups yellow onion, diced
ADD:
½ t. black peppercorns, cracked
STIR IN:
⅓ cup all-purpose flour
WHISK IN; SIMMER:
5 cups reserved clam broth
1 cup heavy cream
¼ cup reserved cooked bacon
TO FINISH THE CHOWDER, PREPARE:
24 green-lipped mussels
24 extra large (16–20 count) shrimp
1 lb. fish, cut into 1" chunks
4 cups Yukon gold potatoes, peeled,
   cubed, and cooked
GARNISH WITH:
   Fresh thyme and remaining
   cooked bacon

*NUTRITIONAL INFORMATION PER 8-OZ.: CALORIES
1,060; TOTAL FAT 52(G); CALORIES FROM FAT
47%; SODIUM 659(MG); CARBOHYDRATES 37(G)*

CAN'T FIND CLAMS?

If you can't find fresh clams or
don't have time to make clam
broth, bottled clam juice is fine.

COMBINE; ADD IN STEP 8:
3 8-oz. bottles clam juice
2 cups water
1 10½-oz. can minced
   clams, drained

Clam quest

Broth is the foundation of a chowder.
Yes, you can get decent broth using bottled clam juice, *see box below*. But for
you seafood aficionados, making broth
with fresh clams is the way to go.

When buying clams, you'll come
across two kinds: hard or soft-shell.
Both make fine chowder as long as they
smell fresh, like the sea.

Hard-shell clams (littlenecks, cher-
rystone, and chowder) should be alive
when purchased. Shells should not be
broken, but can be slightly open. If so,
set them in ice water or tap to see if
they close. If they don't close, discard.

Fresh clam broth

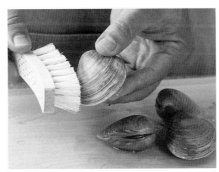

1 Scrub the clams with a stiff brush to
remove grit, then place them in a stockpot with cold water. Cover with a lid
and bring to a boil over high heat.
Reduce heat and simmer 6–8 minutes.

3 Remove the clam meat with a fork
or by hand, then cool. Place the meat
in a resealable plastic bag and refrigerate until you're ready to make the
chowder. Discard the shells.

Soft shells look a little different—
they have a neck (called a siphon) that
hangs out of the shell. If the neck
moves when touched, the clam is alive.
That protruding neck also lets a lot of
sand inside the clam, making it important to strain the broth as in Step 4.

Liquor: When clams cook, they
open and release their natural briny
juices, called liquor. The five cups
of broth the recipe calls for is
a combination of the
clam's steaming water
(3 cups) plus the clam's
liquor (2 cups).

Store live clams on ice. ▶

2 All the clams should have opened
after steaming, but discard any that
aren't (they're probably not the best
to eat). Search for any unopened clams
with tongs—the shells are very hot!

4 Strain the broth through a strainer
lined with a paper coffee filter (the
clams may've released a little sand
during simmering). Cool broth, then
chill until you make the chowder base.

The base starts here

A good chowder base is simple, yet full of character. If you put too much "stuff" in the base, you'll just mask a lot of the fresh seafood's natural flavors. The bottom line—less is more in this chowder base.

Flavoring: Chowder is traditionally flavored with salt pork or bacon. I prefer smoked bacon because it's easy to find, keeps the chowder lighter in color, and you can sprinkle the bits over the finished soup. Smoked bacon also has a hint of the outdoors—like a seafood cookout on the beach.

Once the fat has been rendered and the bacon is cooked, "sweat" the onions in the bacon drippings. Sweating is different from sauteing because the onions are covered and cooked over low heat until they soften, but not brown. This is done so you preserve the light color of the base.

As the onions sweat, add crushed peppercorns. Crushing (instead of grinding) makes recognizable pieces in the finished chowder—otherwise it looks dirty. And cooking the crushed peppercorns helps release lively, flavorful oils into the base.

Thickener: Traditionally, potatoes and their starch were used to only *slightly* thicken chowder. Today it seems like people prefer chowders a little thicker. This could be done with potatoes, but this recipe uses roux for a smoother result.

Not only does the bacon add flavor, but it also provides the fat necessary for making the roux (made of equal parts fat and flour). And by using this method, the roux can be made in the same pan the chowder base is cooked in. Just make sure that you constantly stir the roux to prevent it from scorching, and cook it long enough to eliminate the starchy taste from the flour.

Dairy: Can't milk be used in this chowder? Well, no. Give yourself a treat and use cream. Besides tasting pretty darn good, cream reduces and thickens better than milk lower in fat. Without going into a lot of detail, when you heat cream, it goes through a chemical reaction—proteins and fat join to inhibit curdling and thicken quickly. So, for the best results, use cream for taste and success.

5 Spray a stockpot with nonstick spray (to keep bacon from overbrowning, darkening the base). Cook bacon over medium heat until crisp, stirring occasionally. Strain; reserve bacon *and* fat.

6 Add ⅓ cup drippings back to stockpot. Reduce heat to medium-low and add onion. Cover and sweat about 5 minutes, stirring occasionally to prevent browning. Add cracked peppercorns.

7 Continue sweating the onions until they're translucent, about 5 minutes. Stir in flour and cook 2–3 minutes to remove all the starchy taste. Be sure to stir constantly to prevent scorching.

8 Now whisk in clam broth, 1 cup at a time, stirring constantly to prevent lumps. Add cream and ¼ cup bacon pieces (reserve the rest for garnish). Simmer base 10 minutes; cool and chill.

Seafood savvy

Properly storing and preparing seafood is critical to its final taste and texture. Clams and mussels are purchased live and must stay alive until you're ready to clean and cook. Other seafood is delicate, needing very cold storage out of water.

Clams

You cooked and picked the clam meat after you made the broth. And like the broth, the meat can be stored in the refrigerator or freezer until you're ready to make the chowder.

If you used small clams in the broth, add the meat whole to the chowder. But meat from larger clams (chowders or cherrystones) should be chopped a bit.

Mussels

If you can, buy green-lipped mussels which are usually farm-raised in New Zealand and Australia. They're colorful shells hold high-quality, plump, and flavorful meat.

Selecting: Mussels should smell like the sea and have moist shells and meat. Each should have a beard attached (threads coming out of the shell). No beard? Throw it out. It tells you the mussel's suffocated and isn't good.

Storage: Store mussels on ice. If they're in a bag, poke holes in it. Mussels are alive and need to breathe.

▲ *Pull off the beards and discard. The mussels should close after debearding. If they don't, try the following methods to see if they're alive.*

▲ *Submerge mussel in cold water 1–2 minutes; remove. They should close, but if not, tap with a knife. If they still don't close, don't use them.*

Shrimp

Selecting: Since this is an entree, buy extra large shrimp. Raw shrimp should feel firm, not soft or slimy. Avoid any that are peeled, sitting in water, or smell like ammonia.

Storage: Store shrimp directly on ice, but don't peel them—their shells protect the flesh from becoming "burned" when stored directly on ice.

▲ *Peel the shrimp and remove the legs. Leave the tail segment on—this makes for easy grabbing when eating the chowder. It also looks nicer.*

▲ *To devein, run a knife down the curved back to expose the large vein. Remove it, then rinse the shrimp under cold water.*

Chowder fish

Chowder fish should be firm in texture, low in fat, and light in color. You've got a lot of choices, but here's what to look for.

Selecting: Haddock, cod, halibut, and sea bass are all good fish to use in chowder. Fattier fish, like salmon or mackerel, have strong oils that can mask the delicate flavors of other seafood. When buying fish, ask to smell it—good fresh fish will smell almost like watermelon (weird but true). Also, touch the fish. It should be firm and not slimy.

Storage: Wrap fish in plastic and store on ice. This wrap prevents the flesh from burning and drying out.

Finishing the chowder

Okay. You've made the chowder base and all the seafood is cleaned and cut. The beauty of this chowder is that most of the work is done. All you have to do now is determine how many servings you'll need—just follow the portion chart, below right.

Once you've decided on portions, heat up the appropriate amount of base. It's best to use a large, shallow saute pan like the one I'm using in Step 9. Heat is distributed more evenly (unlike a deep sauce pan) so the seafood cooks at the same rate. The larger surface area also causes the chowder base to slightly evaporate, making it thicker.

Bring the chowder base to a simmer and add the cooked potatoes. The potatoes are more dense than the seafood and need extra time to heat through. They'll also give off starch while simmering, helping thicken the chowder.

When the chowder is at a full simmer, add all the seafood. This is when the chowder gets its big-time flavor—as the seafood cooks, each give off their own distinctive taste. The amount of liquid will also increase as the fresh mussels release their liquor. Stir often and watch for the key signs of when the chowder is ready. It should only take about five minutes.

Doneness: Here are several ways to tell when the chowder is ready.

Mussels: Mussels are the key to determining when all the seafood is done. They'll open when cooked. When this happens, the other seafood is ready.

Mussels should be tightly closed before cooking and opened after cooking—if not, don't eat them.

Fish: Properly cooked fish will stay together, yet small cracks will appear in the flesh. It should be firm, but still pliable. Translucence should be gone.

Shrimp: Shrimp turn from brown and white to pink as they cook. They should become firm, but never hard.

9 In a saute pan over low heat, reheat the portion of chowder base needed, *see Chart, right.* Add cooked potatoes and bring to a simmer, stirring occasionally, for about 10 minutes.

10 Add the prepared seafood and bring chowder back to a simmer; cook five minutes longer. Stir occasionally so all seafood cooks evenly.

▲ *Divide seafood and potatoes among serving bowls, then ladle the chowder base over everything. Garnish each serving with fresh thyme and remaining bacon pieces.*

CHOWDER PORTIONS

This chowder is made to your specifications. Use the chart below to find out how much chowder base, seafood, and potatoes will go into your chowder.

TWO

Use 2 cups chowder base, 6 shrimp, 6 mussels, 1 cup cooked potatoes, 4 oz. fish, and 1/2 cup chopped clams

FOUR

Use 4 cups chowder base, 12 shrimp, 12 mussels, 2 cups cooked potatoes, 8 oz. fish, and 1 cup chopped clams

SIX

Use 6 cups chowder base, 18 shrimp, 18 mussels, 3 cups cooked potatoes, 12 oz. fish, and 1 1/2 cups chopped clams

fondue basics

Dust off that old wedding present—fondue is back and hotter than ever!

No wonder fondue is back in style—it's casual, entertaining, and do-ahead. But for total success, you first need to know about the pot, heat sources, and set up.

The Pot: You have two choices of fondue pots, metal and ceramic. A pot made of thin metal (like that wedding gift) works fine for broth or oil fondue, but is murder on cheese and chocolate.

The pot gets too hot and burns them. Cheese and chocolate fondue are better in ceramic pots, *see Page 30 and the Back Cover*. But don't use them for broth or oil fondue. The high heat needed to properly cook in them will break the pot.

So do you *really* need both? If fondue is an occasional sport, multiple pots are impractical. In that case, try an electric pot, *see Page 32*. It's good for all types of fondue—the temperature is so easy to regulate. But if you *do* want a metal pot, buy one made of heavy-duty metal. They heat well (and stay hot) for fondues that need it, but are gentle on delicate ones like cheese.

Heat It: Metal and ceramic pots are heated by a live-flame source, typically fueled with denatured alcohol (see burner instructions provided with the pot). The alcohol emits a hot flame, but it burns off quickly and is messy to use. Cans of fuel gel (Sterno) are easier to deal with and burn longer, but the flame isn't as hot. So what do you use?

For cheese, use Sterno (watch carefully so it doesn't scorch), and for broth and oil, use alcohol. Both can be found at hardware stores. (Chocolate fondue uses *very* gentle heat—a tea candle!)

Set Up: Fondue needs a different set up than other parties. To protect the table, place the pot on a stable surface, like a cutting board. Position it so guests can reach without leaning or straining. If your pot is electric, be sure the plug easily reaches an outlet—use extension cords if needed, and tape them down to prevent tripping.

cheese fondue

Cheese fondue was made for winter Sundays—warm, casual, and easy-going. Call a friend and start dipping.

The beauty of this fondue is in its simplicity—choosing the cheese and pot are the hardest things you'll do. Here's some information that can help.

The Cheese: Traditional cheese fondue uses three Swiss cheeses: Emmental [EM-en-tahl] and Gruyere [groo-YEHR] are the bulk, and Appenzell [A-pent-zell] is added for tang. This recipe *almost* sticks to tradition—Appenzell can be hard to find, so I left it out. Kirsch [KEERSH], a cherry liqueur is also traditional, but brandy tastes just as good.

This fondue is almost all cheese, so buy the best you can. Cheese stores and specialty food shops are a good bet for variety and quality—shop there first. Many grocery stores also carry good-quality cheeses that work fine. Check the deli section first; use mass-produced cheeses (the *ungrated* kinds) in a pinch.

The Pot: A shallow, flameproof, ceramic pot like the one below is best for cheese fondue. It absorbs heat but diffuses it better than metal—important when dealing with something that scorches easily, cheese. This pot is equipped with a diffuser, a metal plate between the heat source and the pot. It spreads the flame out so the heat is less intense on the bottom—a good feature to look for.

SWISS CHEESE FONDUE
(MAKES ABOUT 2½ CUPS; SERVES 6–8)
WORK TIME: 10 MINUTES
COOK TIME: 10 MINUTES

TOSS TOGETHER:
2 cups shredded Gruyere cheese (8 oz.)
2 cups shredded Swiss or Emmental cheese (8 oz.)
1 T. cornstarch

SIMMER; REMOVE GARLIC, ADD CHEESE:
1 cup dry white wine (like sauvignon blanc)
1 T. fresh lemon juice, strained
1 clove garlic, crushed

ADD:
1 T. brandy or Cognac, (optional)
Freshly ground white pepper and nutmeg to taste

1 Toss cheeses and cornstarch together in a mixing bowl. In a large, heavy saucepan, bring wine, lemon juice, and garlic to a simmer over medium heat—bubbles should *just* break the surface. Remove garlic and discard.

Cheese chat

Cheese can be fussy—sometimes it melts perfectly smooth, and other times it curdles or turns stringy. What's going on? And how can you avoid it?

Cheese is high in protein which makes it susceptible to curdling, especially if it gets too hot (similar to egg yolks). As cheese melts, the proteins loosen and stretch out—at a certain point, the fondue is perfect. But if the proteins overheat, they rejoin, this time tightening into grainy curds.

To reduce the chance of curdling, remember three things: First, use freshly grated cheese so it melts faster with less heat. Second, add a starch, like cornstarch, to "block" the proteins from each other and prevent rejoining. And third, the wine mixture should barely simmer as the cheese is added (a few bubbles will break the surface). If it boils, the cheese is apt to curdle. But the wine *must* be at a simmer or else the cheese won't melt properly.

Stringiness is common with some cheeses, like Swiss and mozzarella. They contain a compound that links protein into strings—fine for cheese on pizza, but not fondue. Luckily, it's easier to fix than curdling. Acids, like lemon juice, help keep the compound from "stringing" proteins. So if the fondue is stringy, stir in a little more lemon juice.

Dippity do-dah

This fondue is really a sophisticated cheese sauce. So what goes with cheese sauce can be dipped in fondue. Here are some suggestions to get you going.

Bread is a natural choice. Artisan breads have great texture and flavor and are readily available. Don't limit yourself to "white" varieties—pumpernickel, whole grain, and rye are good too. Crackers and bread sticks can also be included for a crunchy texture.

Be sure to include blanched vegetables or boiled potatoes with the fondue, *see Page 33 for cooking instructions and times*. And don't forget that apples and pears taste great with cheese, too. If you want to include something for meat-lovers, cooked smoked sausage and other cooked meats like cubed chicken breast, roast beef, ham, or shrimp can also be dipped.

▲ *Allow 1 cup bite-size bread cubes per person. There should be crust on each cube so it won't fall apart in the cheese.*

▲ *Use a variety of blanched and raw vegetables for color and texture. Plan on serving about 1/4 lb. (about 2 cups) prepared vegetables for each person.*

▲ *Tart apples (Granny Smith) and firm pears (Bosc) are good dippers—figure one fruit per person. Slice just before serving; dip in lemon water to prevent browning.*

2 Add handfuls (about 1 cup) of cheese to the simmering wine, stirring with a wooden spoon. Make sure the cheese has nearly melted before adding more. Increase heat slightly if cheese doesn't seem to want to melt, but don't boil.

3 Add brandy, pepper, and nutmeg to melted cheese. Transfer to fondue pot over medium flame (it can bubble gently, but don't boil). To eat, spear dippers on forks and swirl in the fondue (stir to the bottom to prevent separating).

4 By the end of the party, a crust of browned cheese will have formed on the bottom of the pot. This is the good stuff! Pry it off while it's warm and eat it with your guests as an end to meal—if you're willing to share.

fondue
with broth

This fondue uses broth to gently cook meats and vegetables.
When you're finished, clean up is simple—drink the broth!

There are two options for dinner party fondue: cook meat and vegetables in hot oil or boiling broth. Both taste good, but broth gets my vote for a few reasons. First, because there's no oil, the house won't smell greasy. And there isn't anything to dump out when you're done—drink the broth (it becomes *really* flavorful after fondueing). Finally, even I have to admit that cooking in broth is lighter-tasting and healthier.

Broth fondue originated in Asia—the Chinese call it "fire pot." The technique is simple, but the right fondue pot will make it easier for you and your guests.

The Pots: My favorite pot for broth fondue is electric. No, it's not as romantic as a pot heated by real fire, and tends to be a bit clunky. But I can control the heat just by adjusting a dial (no messy fuel). Plus, it can hit temperatures (150–400°) that are nearly impossible to reach or maintain with fuel-generated heat. The nonstick surface makes cleaning a breeze (especially if you use the pot for a cheese fondue). The red electric pot below sells for about $40.

But if it's looks you're after, try LeCreuset's enameled cast iron fondue pot, *see Resources, Page 42.* Heat the broth on the stove right in the pot, then transfer it to the stand. The pot retains heat well and the broth stays fairly hot with a fuel burner or Sterno. But it isn't cheap ($75–$90).

▲ *West Bend*   ▲ *LeCreuset*

Stock options

Fondue vegetables—skinny dippin'

Homemade chicken or beef stock will make the best broth for this fondue. But with the holidays, who's got the time to make it? For convenience sake, canned broth is fine and just as flavorful as homemade—after "doctoring" it up with a bouquet garni and blanched vegetables.

Bouquet Garni: The simplest way to add flavor to canned broth is to simmer it with a bouquet garni [boo-KAY gahr-NEE], a bundle of herbs. It usually includes bay leaves, parsley, and thyme, but this one also has garlic and peppercorns. Tie everything in a coffee filter with kitchen string, then tie the bundle to the pan handle for easy retrieval.

Blanching: Another way to boost the broth's flavor is to blanch some of the fondue vegetables in it, like broccoli, cauliflower, carrots, and asparagus. See the photos, *above right*, for blanching instructions.

Besides flavoring the broth, blanching makes the vegetables less crunchy and helps set their color. But don't overcook them or they'll be mushy and ugly! Refer to the chart below for times.

SEASONED BROTH
(MAKES ABOUT 6 CUPS)
WORK TIME: 10 MINUTES
COMBINE IN A LARGE SAUCE PAN:
5   cups low sodium chicken broth
2   cups (14-oz. can) beef broth
FOR THE BOUQUET GARNI—
TIE IN A COFFEE FILTER; ADD TO BROTH AND SIMMER:
2   cloves crushed garlic
1   thyme sprig
1   bay leaf
1   t. whole peppercorns (may use all black or a mixture)

Okay, so maybe vegetables aren't your favorite food group. But it's important to include them with fondue—they add flavor to the broth during fondueing, and look great arranged on a big platter and set on the table.

A lot of vegetables should be blanched before fondueing, but not all of them need to be. There are some that taste best if they're just lightly cooked right in the fondue, like mushrooms, bell peppers, zucchini, and scallions. Potatoes, on the other hand, must be cooked separately in salted water, *see sidebar below*. If boiled in the broth, they'll end up turning it cloudy.

It's hard to say exactly how many vegetables you'll need for a fondue party. A good rule of thumb is to estimate half a pound of trimmed vegetables per person—at least three pounds for six people. That might seem like vegetable overload, but it gives you a chance to use small amounts of several types of vegetables. Then your guests will have a lot to choose from. Plus, they'll make the broth taste great.

You can prepare all the vegetables and assemble the platters ahead of time. Keep them chilled until you're ready to fondue.

▲*Blanching: Bring broth and bouquet garni to a boil. Add individual vegetables and blanch (see chart for cooking times).*

▲*Shocking: Using a strainer, transfer vegetables to ice water. Drain thoroughly and chill until you assemble the platters.*

To cook potatoes for fondue, cut one pound unpeeled, red potatoes into large chunks. Place in a large sauce pan with 1 T. kosher salt, cover with cold water, and bring to a boil. Reduce heat and simmer until tender, 7–8 minutes. Drain and cool.

PREPARING RAW VEGETABLES

Vegetable:	Preparation:
3 cups shiitake or button mushrooms (6 oz.)	stems removed, caps left whole
2 cups red bell pepper (1 whole)	seeded, cut into large chunks
2 cups zucchini (2 small)	halved lengthwise, sliced into ¹/₂"-thick half-moons
1 cup scallions (about 10)	cut into 2" lengths, (white and light green parts only)

BLANCHING VEGETABLES

Vegetable/Preparation:	Blanching Time:
2 cups broccoli florets (1 stalk)	2 min.
1 cup cauliflower florets (¹/₄ head)	2 min.
2 cups carrots, peeled, bias-cut into 1"-thick chunks (about 4)	2 min.
1 cup asparagus spears, halved (¹/₄ lb.)	1 min.

Meat methods

If you'd like to fondue other meats, choose them carefully. Lamb, shrimp, and kielbasa work, but their flavors will transfer to the broth. To avoid this, use two fondue pots and make two batches of broth—one for chicken and beef, the other for strongly flavored items.

Almost any type of meat can be used in fondue, but some are better than others. Here are a few things to keep in mind when choosing and preparing them.

The most important thing to consider when choosing fondue meat is the tenderness of the cut. You want one that's naturally tender, like beef and pork tenderloin or chicken breast. Another advantage to these tender cuts is that they're fairly lean and won't make the fondue broth greasy. Trim any excess fat and silverskin before slicing to make the meat even more lean and tender.

Fondue is a quick-cooking method and the meat should

be sliced as thinly as possible— about $\frac{1}{8}$" thick. This is easiest if you freeze it for an hour before slicing (trim fat and silverskin before freezing). The meat should not be rock-hard, but ice crystals will just start to form through it. And use a *very* sharp knife.

When slicing, be sure to cut the meat against the grain. Look at the meat and see which direction the fibers run (the grain). Slicing against the grain makes the fibers short and easy to chew. Longer fibers are tougher.

▼ *Arrange meat separately from the vegetables to avoid contamination. Garnish the platter with sprigs of fresh herbs.*

Like the vegetables, it can be tricky figuring out how much meat to buy. Plan on 6–8 oz. untrimmed meat per person, or 5–7 oz. trimmed meat.

PREPARE:

12 oz. boneless, skinless chicken breast, partially frozen, thinly sliced

12 oz. beef tenderloin, trimmed, partially frozen, thinly sliced

▲ *Thinly slice partially frozen meat. But make sure it's not too solid or the slices may get too thin and won't stay on the fondue fork.*

Sauce sense

Sauces are a traditional fondue condiment. And you'll want to make all three of these. They're easy to make, use everyday ingredients, and taste great together, all mixed up on your plate!

The sauces will taste better if they're made up to two days ahead and chilled. Bring them to room temperature before serving.

HORSERADISH AIOLI
(MAKES ABOUT 1 CUP)
WORK TIME: 5 MINUTES
COMBINE:

1 cup mayonnaise (may use reduced calorie)
2 T. prepared horseradish
2 t. fresh lemon juice
1 t. garlic, minced
Salt and cayenne to taste

CITRUS STEAK SAUCE
(MAKES ABOUT 1 CUP)
WORK TIME: 5 MINUTES
COMBINE:

1 cup A-1 Steak Sauce
2 T. brown sugar
1 T. ketchup
2 t. garlic, minced
2 t. Worcestershire sauce
2 t. fresh orange juice
2 t. fresh lemon juice

HOT MAPLE MUSTARD
(MAKES ABOUT $\frac{1}{2}$ CUP)
WORK TIME: 5 MINUTES
COMBINE TO MAKE A PASTE:

6 T. dry mustard
$\frac{1}{4}$ cup pure maple syrup
STIR IN:
2 T. apple cider vinegar
1 T. prepared yellow mustard
1 T. whole grain mustard

Do you fondue?

Now that the preparations are done, you can start on the fun stuff! Here are a few pointers so you can fondue with confidence.

1. Setting Up: Just before you're ready to start fondueing, bring the broth to a boil on the stove, transfer it to the pot, and place it on the table over the appropriate heat source. Set out the vegetables, meats, and sauces.

Now thread a vegetable, then a couple slices of meat onto a fondue fork. Spear a vegetable on the end so the meat won't fall off, otherwise you might end up fishing for it. Fondueing works best if there are only three or four things on your fork at a time. If there are too many, the items at the top of the fork won't be submerged in the broth.

2. Cooking: Place your fork in the broth, sit back, and cook—about two minutes for beef, three for chicken. (Assemble another fork while you wait.) Times will vary, but you'll get the hang of it after one or two tries. Try to keep the number of forks in the pot at one time to three or four so the broth doesn't cool down.

3. Dipping—and Eating!: This step is easy. Remove the fork from the pot and slide the meat and vegetables onto your plate (eating the food right off the fork is considered improper—and the fork is hot!). Then use a table fork to dip them in sauces and eat. This may seem like a lot of work for a little food, but it's fun and everything cooks so quickly, no one will even think twice.

4. Soup: This final step is the coolest one: End the fondue by pouring the remaining broth over orzo pasta and serve it as a soup.

Cook the orzo at the same time you prepare the vegetables and meat, then chill. Before serving the soup, stir sherry into the broth and place some orzo in tea cups or small bowls. Ladle the broth (and stray "dippers" from the pot) over the pasta and serve.

Cook According to Package Directions:
1   cup orzo or other small soup pasta
Drain and Toss with:
1   T. vegetable oil
Before Serving, Stir into Broth:
2   T. dry sherry (optional)

panna cotta

This can't be true! A festive dessert that takes just a few simple ingredients and actually *needs* to be made ahead. Panna cotta was made for the holidays.

Panna cotta [PAHN-nah KOH-tah] is Italian for "cooked cream." It's light and custard-like with an unusual color for a dessert—pure white. Combine this dramatic white against the deep color of a fruit puree (this one uses cranberries), and you have the perfect dessert that screams "holiday."

Gelatin: This may be the first time you've worked with gelatin. But don't confuse it with Jell-O! Gelatin is a taste-less, colorless thickening agent used in cold soups and molded desserts. Most grocery stores carry it, probably under the brand name Knox.

To work best, gelatin first has to soak in cold liquid to soften and swell. Then, it's added to a hot (not boiling) liquid to dissolve into a smooth mixture. But be careful when making panna cotta. *Do not boil the cream.* This not only destroys the thickening ability of the gelatin, but also causes ultrapasteurized heavy cream to form a gummy residue.

PANNA COTTA

(MAKES SIX 5-OZ. SERVINGS)
WORK TIME: 15 MINUTES
CHILL TIME: OVERNIGHT OR 24 HOURS
SPRINKLE OVER 2 T. COLD WATER:
2   t. unflavored gelatin
WARM; ADD GELATIN MIXTURE:
3   cups heavy cream
⅔   cup sugar
1½ t. vanilla extract
     Pinch of salt
WHISK INTO:
¾   cup sour cream

NUTRITIONAL INFORMATION PER SERVING:
CALORIES 564; TOTAL FAT 50(G); CALORIES
FROM FAT 78%; SODIUM 85(MG);
CARBOHYDRATES 27(G)

Making panna cotta

1 Sprinkle the gelatin over cold water (you won't use the whole packet) and set aside. This is called blooming and softens the gelatin so it dissolves better. In 5–10 minutes, it'll set up into a soft, pliable disc. Meanwhile, go on to Step 2.

2 In a large saucepan over medium heat, warm cream, sugar, vanilla, and salt. Stir occasionally, just until it starts to steam, 5–7 minutes (do not boil). Turn off heat and stir in bloomed gelatin until dissolved and dispersed.

3 Cool the cream mixture in the pan 5 minutes; place the sour cream in a large bowl with a pour spout. Slowly add 1 cup of warm cream into the sour cream; whisk until smooth. Now whisk in the remaining warm cream.

4 Place small, ungreased custard cups or ramekins on a baking sheet—this helps make handling and storage easier. Pour 2/3 cup panna cotta mixture into each cup. Cover with plastic wrap and refrigerate overnight or 24 hours.

5 To unmold, run a sharp knife around a chilled panna cotta, then dip cup in boiling water 5 seconds. Run the knife around edge again and invert onto a serving plate. To loosen, hold cup tightly against the plate and shake gently.

6 When it pulls away from the sides, remove the cup (if it won't release, repeat Step 5). Smooth imperfections with your finger or a sharp knife. Garnish with 1–2 T. Cranberry Wine Sauce and reserved berries. Serve cold.

Besides the amazing color contrast, this tart sauce tastes great against the milky flavor of panna cotta. Use dry red wine, like merlot or cabernet sauvignon.

Make the sauce a day ahead so it has time to thicken. The pectin in the cranberries, as well as the high amount of sugar needed to compensate for their tartness, will help it set up.

CRANBERRY WINE SAUCE
(MAKES ABOUT 3/4 CUP)
WORK TIME: 20 MINUTES
COOK TIME: 12–15 MINUTES
DISSOLVE:
1   cup sugar
1   cup dry red wine
ADD:
1½ cups fresh cranberries
REMOVE 1/2 CUP BERRIES AND SET ASIDE FOR GARNISH. SIMMER, STRAIN, AND ADD:
2   t. fresh lemon juice

In a nonreactive saucepan over medium-high heat, dissolve sugar in wine; add berries. When they start to pop, remove 1/2 cup cranberries with a slotted spoon. Spread on a plate and reserve.

Reduce heat to medium; simmer remaining cranberries in the wine 10 minutes. Strain sauce through fine-mesh strainer, pressing on solids to release juice; discard pulp. Add lemon juice to sauce; strain again to remove additional seeds, if necessary. Chill.

family favorite
holiday cookies

Holiday cookies—we've all got our favorites that define the season. They're simple, *slightly* old-fashioned (in a good way), and required at Christmas. But only during Christmas. They just don't taste the same any other time of year.

What makes these recipes special? They're family favorites from *Cuisine* readers. And you'll want them in your kitchen this season too—they're great.

The recipes are simple but it'll help to know some things before getting started. First, plan ahead—most of the doughs chill before baking. Second, a small scoop (1 T.) is helpful for making evenly shaped cookies. Third, sparkling white sugar can be purchased from King Arthur Flour, *see Page 42*. And don't forget the packaging labels, *see Page 42*. Cookies make perfect gifts.

This collection of classic holiday cookies is straight from real test kitchens—yours!

TOM'S THUMBPRINTS
(MAKES 2½ DOZEN)

CREAM FOR 2 MINUTES:
1   cup unsalted butter
½   cup sugar
½   t. almond extract

STIR IN:
2   cups all-purpose flour
½   t. kosher salt

CHILL 1 HOUR. FILL
INDENTATIONS WITH:
¼   cup seedless
     raspberry jam

Mix dough; preheat oven to 350°. Shape dough in 1 T. balls; place on ungreased baking sheets. Make a small indentation in the center of each ball with your thumb; bake 5 minutes. Remove from oven and fill each indentation with ¼ teaspoon jam; bake 5–7 more minutes. Cool for 2 minutes; transfer to a rack.

MOTHER O'S SUGAR COOKIES
(MAKES 3½ DOZEN)

CREAM:
1   cup sugar
½   cup vegetable shortening
½   cup vegetable oil
1   egg
1   t. vanilla extract

WHISK; BEAT INTO CREAMED MIXTURE:
2   cups all-purpose flour
½   t. baking soda
½   t. kosher salt
¼   t. cream of tartar

CHILL DOUGH 3 HOURS OR OVERNIGHT.
½   cup sparkling *or* granulated sugar

Mix dough; preheat oven to 350°. Shape dough in 1 T. balls; roll in sugar. Place on ungreased baking sheets; bake 12–14 minutes. Cool 2 min.; transfer to a rack.

ALICE'S CHOCOLATE FUDGE SNAPS
(MAKES 3 DOZEN)

MELT AND COOL:
4   oz. unsweetened
     chocolate
4   oz. semisweet chocolate

IN LARGE BOWL, MELT:
½   cup unsalted butter

ADD AND BEAT UNTIL FLUFFY, 2 MIN.:
1½   cups sugar
2   eggs
2   t. espresso powder
2   t. vanilla extract

COMBINE CHOCOLATE AND BUTTER
MIXTURES. WHISK, THEN STIR INTO
CHOCOLATE-BUTTER MIXTURE:
1½   cups all-purpose flour
1   t. baking soda
1   t. baking powder
¾   t. kosher salt

CHILL DOUGH 1–2 HOURS. ROLL IN:
½   cup sparkling *or* granulated sugar

Mix dough; preheat oven to 350°. Shape dough in 1 T. balls; roll in sugar. Place on ungreased baking sheets; bake 7–9 minutes. Cool 2 minutes; transfer to a rack.

CINDY'S SHORTBREAD STICKS

(MAKES 5½ DOZEN)

MIX TOGETHER:

1¼ cups all-purpose flour
½   cup unsalted butter, softened
½   cup pecans, toasted and ground
⅓   cup powdered sugar
½   t. kosher salt

ROLL; CHILL 3 HOURS OR OVERNIGHT.

FOR THE CARAMEL ICING—

BOIL UNTIL SUGAR DISSOLVES:

½   cup dark brown sugar
¼   cup unsalted butter

STIR IN:

2   T. heavy cream
¼   cup powdered sugar, sifted

DIP ICED STICKS IN:

    Toasted, ground pecans

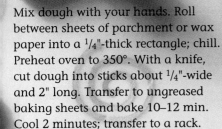

Mix dough with your hands. Roll between sheets of parchment or wax paper into a ¼-thick rectangle; chill. Preheat oven to 350°. With a knife, cut dough into sticks about ¼-wide and 2" long. Transfer to ungreased baking sheets and bake 10–12 min. Cool 2 minutes; transfer to a rack.

    To make the icing, boil brown sugar and butter for 1 minute in small saucepan. Stir in the cream, then the powdered sugar. Dip one end of each cookie in warm icing, then roll the end in additional toasted, ground pecans. Allow cookies to dry before storing.

THOMAS FAMILY COCONUT DROPS

(MAKES 3 DOZEN)

MIX TOGETHER:

3   egg whites
¼   t. kosher salt

BEAT IN:

1   cup powdered sugar
3   T. all-purpose flour
1½ t. vanilla extract

FOLD IN:

4   cups sweetened coconut
2   T. unsalted butter, melted

Mix dough; preheat oven to 350°. Form dough into 1 T. balls (a cookie scoop really helps to pack the coconut). Bake on greased baking sheets 12–15 minutes. Cool 2 minutes; transfer to a rack.

JESSIE F'S DATE PINWHEELS

(MAKES 6 DOZEN)

FOR THE COOKIE DOUGH—

CREAM:

½   cup unsalted butter, softened
½   cup sugar
½   cup light brown sugar

ADD:

1   egg
½   t. vanilla extract

WHISK; ADD TO CREAMED MIXTURE:

2   cups all-purpose flour
½   t. baking soda
½   t. kosher salt

FOR THE DATE FILLING—

BOIL UNTIL A PASTE CONSISTENCY:

1   lb. date pieces, chopped
½   cup sugar
½   cup water

STIR IN, THEN COOL:

1   t. lime zest, minced

Mix dough; divide in half. Roll each half between parchment or wax paper into ⅛"-thick square. Spread each with half of the date filling and roll up jelly roll fashion. Cover in parchment and chill at least 1 hour. Preheat oven to 350°. Slice dough into ¼"-thick rounds; bake on parchment-lined baking sheets 10–12 minutes, until lightly brown. Cool 2 minutes; transfer to a rack.

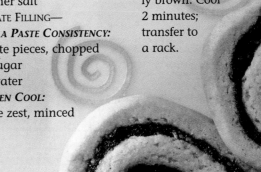

Q&A
questions & answers from our readers

UNDER PRESSURE

Champagne bottles all have this curious indentation on the bottom of the bottle. What is that?

Curtis Knight
Mt. Shasta, CA

The indentation is called a punt. It's there because champagne bubbles create about 120 pounds of pressure per square inch. That's a lot of pressure. Early champagne makers learned quickly that they had to wire a cork onto the bottles. It secured the top, but the champagne would then explode through the bottom.

Solution—the arch. Structures with an arch for support can withstand more pressure than flat

surfaces. With that arched base, champagne became safe to bottle.

Punts are sometimes found on wine bottles, but this is mostly a marketing scheme. A punt is believed to elevate its status in the wine world. Also, with a punt added, wine bottles grew taller, appearing to hold more liquid.

FLOUR POWER

When buying flour, I see a lot of bags claiming to be "unbleached." What does that mean?

Mack Mullins
Atlanta, GA

After milling, all flour is yellowish in color, like semolina. The flour must then be treated in order for it to turn white.

This treatment happens one of two ways: by exposing the flour to chlorine dioxide gas (this is "bleached" flour). Or by exposing it to air (unbleached flour). Both produce the same results and the flours can be used interchangeably. The big difference is time—bleaching makes flour usable in minutes. It takes weeks before unbleached flour can be used. At that point, it's a money issue. Bleached flour is easier and cheaper to produce.

KEY LIME... ANYTIME

I want to make an authentic Key lime pie but I can't find fresh Key limes. Should I mail-order them?

Mary McCall
Watson Station, OH

*To order Floribbean Organic Key Lime Juice, call **King Arthur Flour** at (800) 827-6836, or online at www. KingArthurFlour.com, item #1089.*

There's no need to mail-order Key limes. Excellent Key lime juices like *Nellie and Joe's* and *Key West Key Lime Juice* are readily available in grocery stores around the country. Both are pure Key lime juice and an excellent authentic substitution for Key limes. And an added bonus—both offer authentic Key lime pie recipes right on the bottle.

The reason you can't find Key limes is that they just don't transport or sit on grocery store shelves well. By the time the fruit is picked, packed, and shipped, the end result is usually disappointing—hard limes with little juice.

Mail-ordering is an expensive option—about $35/dozen. Stick with the bottled version, or even organic juice from Floribbean (but to me, it's not as good *Nellie and Joe's*).

WHERE'S THE PORK?

The Harvest Braise from Issue #23 looks wonderful, but I don't eat pork. I'd like to make the braise using a substitution for it. Any ideas?

Bettina Fitzpatrick
Buffalo, NY

Cuts of beef like chuck, brisket, and round can all stand in for the pork. And lamb labeled "for stewing" (leg or shoulder meat) would also work. Cook as you would the pork. They all have a lot of connective tissue (like pork ribs), making them good for braising.

That's because braising is a cooking method where meats are slowly simmered in liquid. This melts the tissues, tenderizes the meat, and creates a rich sauce.

KEEPING PASTRY COOL

Why must everything be kept cold when making pastry dough?

Patricia McLaurin
Pawleys Island, SC

Pastry is a rich dough, but also light, airy, and flaky. To get this result, butter in the pastry dough melts leaving spaces between the layers—this is the flakiness. While making dough, everything must be kept cold to prevent premature melting. If the butter melts during mixing, the pastry will be flat and crumbly.

TEMPER, TEMPER...

I've seen the term "temper" in many recipes. What does this mean?

Scott Sanders
Washington, DC

Tempering is a method used to mix hot liquids (like milk) into something cool (like egg yolks). This helps prevent the heat of the milk from scrambling the yolks.

To temper egg yolks, take a small amount of the hot milk and slowly drip it into the yolks while stirring. The eggs rise in temperature while the milk cools. Now it's safe to slowly mix the warm yolks into the hot milk.

▲ *Slowly add the hot milk to the egg yolks. It is important to stir constantly to avoid scrambling.*

▲ *Once yolks and a small amount of hot milk are combined, pour it into the pan while whisking.*

JIGGLY JELL-O

I've tried putting fresh pineapple in Jell-O but it never sets up. Why is this?

Warren Rice
Fort Worth, TX

Pineapple and other fruits like papaya and kiwi contain an enzyme known as papain. This breaks down meat proteins and is often used as a tenderizer. Jell-O is made from collagen, an animal protein. The papain enzyme tears down collagen, interfering with gelling. Cook the fruit first to kill the enzyme, or use canned fruit.

MEASURING PANS

How do I measure a baking pan? Mine all have smaller bottoms and wider tops.

Penny Meier
Bloomington, MN

Baking pans and sheets are always measured from the top, right side up. Most pans are smaller on the bottom and taper out at the top, giving two different dimensions.

Some pans have an inscription on the bottom with the true dimensions, but if not, you'll have to measure. Take a ruler and measure the length and width of the pan from inside edge to inside edge. Do not include the lip of the pan or handles in this measurement. The rule can also be applied to measure casseroles or round cake pans.

I have a recipe calling for Dutch-process cocoa. Where can I find it?

Monica Young
Rochester, NY

Find Dutch-process cocoa in the baking aisle of most grocery stores. It's treated to mellow the acidity of chocolate. Dutch-process cocoa also mixes with liquids better than regular cocoa—it makes great hot chocolate!

STATEMENT OF OWNERSHIP, MANAGEMENT, AND CIRCULATION (REQUIRED BY 39 USC 3685)

Publication title: Cuisine. 2) Publication number: 1089-6546. 3) Filing date: September 15, 2000. 4) Issue frequency: bimonthly. 5) Number of issues published annually: six. 6) Annual subscription price: $21.94. 7) Complete mailing address of known office of publication: 2200 Grand Avenue, Des Moines, (Polk County), Iowa 50312-5306. 8) Complete mailing address of headquarters or general business office of publisher: 2200 Grand Avenue, Des Moines, Iowa 50312. 9) Full names and complete mailing address of publisher, editor, and managing editor: Donald B. Peschke, 2200 Grand Avenue, Des Moines, Iowa 50312; Editor: John F. Meyer, 2200 Grand Avenue, Des Moines, Iowa 50312. 10) Owner: August Home Publishing Company, 2200 Grand Avenue, Des Moines, Iowa 50312; Donald B. Peschke, 2200 Grand Avenue, Des Moines, Iowa 50312. 11) Known bondholders, mortgagees, and other security holders owning or holding 1 percent or more of total amount of bonds, mortgages, or other securities: none. 12) Does not apply. 13) Publication title: Cuisine. 14) Issue date for circulation data below: July/August 2000. 15) Extent and nature of circulation:

	Average No. Copies Each Issue During Preceding 12 Months	Actual No. Copies of Single Issue Published Nearest to Filing Date
A. Total number copies (net press run)	146,415	127,293
B. Paid and/or requested circulation		
1. Paid/requested outside-county mail subscription stated on Form 3541	110,182	95,742
2. Paid in-county subscriptions	0	0
3. Sales through dealers and carriers, street vendors, counter sales and other non-USPS paid distribution	10,431	12,810
4. Other classes mailed through the USPS	0	0
C. Total paid and/or requested circulation	120,613	108,552
D. Free distribution by mail		
1. Outside-county as stated on Form 3541	157	161
2. In-county as stated on Form 3541	0	0
3. Other classes mailed through the USPS	0	0
E. Free distribution outside the mail	0	0
F. Total free distribution	157	161
G. Total distribution	120,770	108,713
H. Copies not distributed	25,645	18,580
I. Total	146,415	127,293
J. Percentage paid and/or requested circulation	99.87%	99.85%

16. This statement of ownership will be printed in the Nov/Dec 2000 issue of this publication.
17. I certify that the statements made by me above are correct and complete. (signed) John F. Meyer, Editor

whif
what's happening in food?

"Bake and take" quick breads right in these paper loaf pans—holiday gift giving just got easier!

Cuisine's quick breads on Pages 14–17 bake up perfectly in these loaf pans, and make great gifts. The lightweight, greaseproof pans withstand ovens up to 450° and bake like regular loaf pans.

Sur La Table sells the pans in three sizes, all sets of 12: *6 x 2½", item #19112, $6; 8 x 2½", item #19113, $9; 11 x 4", item #20175, $12.* To order, call them at *(800) 243-0852*, or log on to *www.surlatable.com*

And while you're at it, be sure to include a gift subscription to *Cuisine* with a loaf of quick bread! Call *(800) 311-3995*, or sign up at *www.CuisineMagazine.com*

packaging the goods

Even simple foods become thoughtful gifts when packaged beautifully. Here are a couple of suggestions for packing your kitchen gifts.

Wrap items in clear plastic boxes or bags so they're visible—show them off! Then tie them with holiday ribbon and add a label, *see below left.* And don't forget to include the recipe or any baking instructions. Be sure to give the gifts soon after packaging. The boxes and bags won't keep things fresh for very long.

Ordering Information: This dot-com company makes Internet ordering easy, but they also accept fax and mail orders.

one cool tool

Elevate your creations to gourmet status with customized labels!

Your salsa, pickles, and jam taste every bit as good as a gourmet shop's. Well, now they can *look* just as good with your own customized packaging labels. **myownlabels.com** (that's the company name) has custom-designed, professional-quality labels for your kitchen creations. Log on to their web site, or call *(888) 412-5636* to request a catalog (no phone orders). Then choose the style, color, and lettering of your labels. Each sheet of 8–24 labels is $7, additional sheets of the same label are $5. Shipping is just $3 per order, and it only takes about a week for delivery. But order early anyway—you'll love seeing your name in print!

resources

Sparkling White Sugar
King Arthur Flour
(800) 827-6836
www.KingArthurFlour.com
Item #1240, 1 lb., $3.95 + shipping & handling

Le Creuset Fondue Pot
Chef's Catalog
(800) 338-3232
www.chefscatalog.com
$74.99 + shipping & handling

recipe index

food events

International Chili Cookoff
Terlingua, Texas
November 2–4

For an authentic bowl of red, this chili cookoff is the place to be. The judging happens Saturday at high noon, but the fun starts on Friday with beans, black-eyed peas, brisket, and margaritas. Bring your dancing boots—there are live bands galore. Call **(903) 874-5601** or visit **www.abowlofred.org**

Florida Seafood Festival
Apalachicola, Florida
November 3–5

Seafood lovers unite at this Florida Panhandle festival. There are loads of fresh seafood to eat, a parade, live music, oyster eating and shucking contests, and much more. Check it out, even if you don't like seafood! Visit **www.floridaseafoodfestival.com** or call **(888) 653-8011**.

Some oyster-eating champs will eat up to 300 bivalves in 15 minutes. And keep them down!

foodsleuth

91%
Percentage of Americans that eat turkey at Thanksgiving[1]

440
Number of cranberries in a pound[4]

45 million
Number of turkeys eaten on Thanksgiving in the United States[2]

6 lbs.
Amount of weight an average American gains between Thanksgiving and the New Year[5]

22 million
Number of turkeys eaten at Christmas in the United States[3]

5 weeks
Time it takes an average American to lose the holiday weight gain[6]

Sources:
[1,2,3]National Turkey Federation; [4]Ocean Spray; [5,6]American Dietetic Association

Provençe on a barge!

Our cruise through Provençe is going to be a blast. No wonder it's filling up fast—there isn't anything like it. We're lining up tours with olive oil makers, vineyards, snail farms, chocolate makers, markets, and vineyards (oops, did I already mention wine?).

We leave October 20, 2001 and sail up the Rhône River aboard the brand new French river ship, *MS Rhône Princess*, hitting culinary hot spots like Vienne, Lyon, and Mâcon.

For information, contact Lew or Judy at **The Travel Center** by calling **(800) 383-4444**, or emailing them at **trvlcats@aol.com**

The ship has just 60 cabins so hurry and make reservations.

Chalon-sur-Saone
Mâcon
Lyon
Vienne
Tournon
Viviers
FRANCE
Avignon
Arles
Nice

Indio International Tamale Festival
Indio, California
December 2–3

Tamales rule the weekend on the streets of Old Town Indio, near Palm Springs. Sixty vendors sell every kind of traditional and gourmet tamale possible— 250,000 in two days! And if that wasn't enough, there's a carnival, tamale judging, cooking demos, and fun for kids. Call **(760) 342-6532**, or visit **www.tamalefestival.org**

photo: Alan Haberle

It's a celebration of food, heritage, and fun in Southern California.

grand *finale: dessert fondue*

Chocolate fondue is the best of everything. It's sweet, easy, and sophisticated. And don't limit this dessert to the holidays. Chocolate fondue is good any time of the year, for any occasion. What's not to like— it's chocolate!

Chocolate fondue for six

▲ Chocolate fondue is best when the flavors and textures of the dippers balance each other. Fresh fruit has texture and tartness (toss bananas and apples with lemon juice to prevent browning). Cake is soft, graham crackers are crunchy. Dried fruit is sweet and chewy; salty pretzels taste great with chocolate. For extra flavor and texture, dip chocolate-covered dippers in chopped nuts or toasted coconut.

Dipping Suggestions:

• *Pretzel sticks*

• *Dried fruit: dates, pineapple, apricots*

• *Cubes of angel food and pound cake*

• *Graham cracker quarters spread with marshmallow creme or peanut butter*

• *Fresh fruit: apples, bananas, orange slices, pineapple, strawberries*

The best chocolate fondue pot is ceramic, heated by the gentle flame of a tea candle. I bought this one at a kitchen shop for about $20.

▲ For chocolate fondue, heat $3/4$ cup heavy cream in small sauce pan over medium-high heat. When steam rises and bubbles form at the edge, pour cream over 1 cup good-quality semisweet chocolate chips; let stand 3 minutes. Stir in 2 T. brandy and 1 T. espresso powder; transfer to fondue pot.

Cuisine INDEX
VOLUME 4 ISSUES 19-24